EXPLAINING SUICIDE

EXPLAINING SUICIDE

PATTERNS, MOTIVATIONS, AND WHAT NOTES REVEAL

CHERYL L. MEYER
Wright State University
School of Professional Psychology
Dayton, OH, United States

TARONISH H. IRANI
SUNY Buffalo State
The Counseling Center, Weigel Health Center
Buffalo, NY, United States

KATHERINE A. HERMES
Central Connecticut State University
Department of History
New Britain, CT, United States

BETTY YUNG[†]

[†] Deceased.

ACADEMIC PRESS

An imprint of Elsevier
elsevier.com

Academic Press is an imprint of Elsevier
125 London Wall, London EC2Y 5AS, United Kingdom
525 B Street, Suite 1800, San Diego, CA 92101-4495, United States
50 Hampshire Street, 5th Floor, Cambridge, MA 02139, United States
The Boulevard, Langford Lane, Kidlington, Oxford OX5 1GB, United Kingdom

Notices
Knowledge and best practice in this field are constantly changing. As new research
and experience broaden our understanding, changes in research methods, professional
practices, or medical treatment may become necessary.

Practitioners and researchers must always rely on their own experience and knowledge
in evaluating and using any information, methods, compounds, or experiments described
herein. In using such information or methods they should be mindful of their own
safety and the safety of others, including parties for whom they have a professional
responsibility.

To the fullest extent of the law, neither the Publisher nor the authors, contributors, or
editors, assume any liability for any injury and/or damage to persons or property as a
matter of products liability, negligence or otherwise, or from any use or operation of any
methods, products, instructions, or ideas contained in the material herein.

British Library Cataloguing-in-Publication Data
A catalogue record for this book is available from the British Library

Library of Congress Cataloging-in-Publication Data
A catalog record for this book is available from the Library of Congress

ISBN: 978-0-12-809289-7

For Information on all Academic Press publications
visit our website at https://www.elsevier.com

Working together
to grow libraries in
developing countries

www.elsevier.com • www.bookaid.org

Publisher: Nikki Levy
Acquisition Editor: Nikki Levy
Editorial Project Manager: Barbara Makinster
Production Project Manager: Caroline Johnson
Designer: Matt Limbert

Typeset by MPS Limited, Chennai, India

Dedication

For Dr. Betty Yung

This is really Betty's book. She loved this project and wanted to take what we learned from the mountain of data we were given and turn it into a book to help others. Although she wrote some of the book proposal, and her words appear throughout a few chapters, she died before writing began in earnest. However, her passion for this project energized us all, even when she was not here with us.

And for all those who have lost loved ones to suicide whose stories remain untold.

Contents

3. Suicide Motivated by Interpersonal Relationships

4. Escape as a Motivation for Suicide

5. Grief and Failure

6. The Complexity of Suicide Motivation

7. Severe Mental Illness

8. The Intersection of Suicide and Legal Issues

9. Protective Factors and Resilience

10. Conclusions and Implications

Preface

Suicide deaths have increased astronomically since 1999. A 2016 report from the Centers for Disease Control and Prevention examining trends in suicide between 1999 and 2014 found that suicide deaths had increased for everyone in the United States, except African-American men. They increased across age groups and ethnic groups. Most startling to researchers was the increase in suicide among middle-aged white women, a group not usually considered at high risk.

It is difficult to make sense of suicide. Researchers have documented risk factors and theorized about motivations. They have developed increasingly complex taxonomies and typologies for clinicians and organizations that focus on intervention and prevention. When reviewing the literature on suicide, we found that there were some areas of agreement about risk factors, but little agreement about motivation. We were presented with a set of files of over 1200 people whose deaths were designated as suicides by the county coroner. Among those files were suicide notes, and it became our desire to learn what these case files and notes could tell us about what motivated people to kill themselves.

This book describes the findings of our research comparing suicide note writers to the larger group of people who had committed suicide within the same time frame but who had not left suicide notes. A mixed-methods approach involving both qualitative and quantitative data allowed us to delineate categories through data-driven analyses and determine which motivations were substantiated by research. We developed a unique model explaining motivations for suicide using level of chaos in an individual's life and intent to die as anchors. This book is organized around these motivations and how identification of both risk and resilience factors can lead to more successful prevention and intervention.

Understanding motivation is an essential element of both intervention and prevention. As it turned out, though, once we had analyzed our data, we realized motivation did not tell the whole story. A demographic story existed as well. Overwhelmingly, the people who kill themselves in the United States today are white men. This was true of our sample and is true nationally. It's also true of European countries and nations in Oceania where the population is predominantly white. We wanted to understand not only what circumstances might have motivated people to kill themselves, but also what other factors—historical, environmental or cultural—might have contributed. We also wanted to know what could be done to simplify identifying people at risk and getting the right help for them. The white men who make up the largest number of suicides are often not attempters, but prevention efforts are largely aimed at those who attempt suicide. We wanted to envision a national agenda for suicide prevention that could bring all who are at risk under a protective umbrella.

Additionally, this book includes a chapter unlike any other publication on the intersection of legal issues and suicide. Through this research a clearer picture of individuals completing suicide can be obtained, thus enhancing identification, understanding, prevention, and intervention.

Our examination of suicide ranges in time from historical material beginning around 1600 to the present day. Laws and taboos concerning suicide as well as medical and therapeutic treatments and the theories underlying current understanding of motivation were reviewed. A total of 1280 cases were analyzed for motivation, mental illness, and other patterns or trends that emerged. We also wanted to turn the question of suicide on its head and examine what we might do to create communities focused on living. Knowing the precipitating events, patterns and motivations can enhance the prevention efforts of anyone who comes into contact with a person who is potentially suicidal. We discuss blue zones, which are areas of longevity, and what those who took their lives said they needed (social support and a reason for living). We then propose a national agenda and some innovative changes that can be made to suicide prevention, as well as a simpler typology for determining whether someone needs an intervention.

This book is organized around these motivations and how identification of them can lead to more successful prevention and intervention. It consists of 10 chapters. Chapter 1, The History and Theories of Suicide, and Chapter 2, Findings, examine the history and theories of suicide and present our overall findings, including characteristics of the notes, circumstances of the suicide and a comparison of suicide note writers and people who committed suicide but did not leave notes. In Chapter 3, Suicide Motivated by Interpersonal Relationships, we provide an in-depth look at suicides motivated by relationship issues, while in Chapter 4, Escape as a Motivation for Suicide, we discuss escape from pain as a motivation for suicide. In Chapter 5, Grief and Failure, we examine less frequent motivations for suicide. In Chapter 6, The Complexity of Suicide Motivation, we present a model for understanding suicide and summarize our findings as they represent multiple and complex motivations. In Chapter 7, Severe Mental Illness, and Chapter 8, The Intersection of Suicide and Legal Issues, we discuss the role of severe mental illness and legal involvement of individuals who committed suicide. Chapter 9, Protective Factors and Resilience, and Chapter 10, Conclusions and Implications, discuss resilience and risk factors with implications for both professionals and family members.

No other volume in the field has taken our exact approach. Many volumes discuss motivation theories, and histories of suicide exist as well. Also, some sociological studies of suicide take place into account. However, this book is unique in that we used a psychological, historical, and social science lens to understand our cases and the broader questions about suicide.

The audience for this book includes students and professionals who work with, or will work with, individuals whose lives could be or have been influenced by suicide. These include psychologists, sociologists, social workers, clergy, law enforcement, policy makers, lawyers, corrections personnel, educators, nurses, and medical professionals. It is also pertinent for other disciplines to understand these patterns. This book could serve as a main text in any course with a focus on suicide. Another audience for this book is individuals whose family and friends have been touched by suicide. We have tried to present our research in keeping with scholarly criteria of objectivity and precision, while making the prose readable and informative. Our insights may help bring both understanding and solace.

Cheryl L. Meyer, JD, PhD
Taronish Irani, PsyD
Katherine A. Hermes, JD, PhD
Betty Yung[†], PhD

[†] Deceased.

Acknowledgments

We would like to thank the Montgomery County Coroner's office, specifically Ken Betz, Dr. Lee Lehman, and Sheri May, for providing not only the data, but also the impetus for this research. We also express our heartfelt gratitude to Dr. Jeffery Allen at the Wright State University School of Professional Psychology for connecting us with the Montgomery County Coroners when they contacted him with this research opportunity.

Wright State University provided generous support for this project including a professional development leave. The School of Professional Psychology support staff have been available and attentive to our needs. We are especially grateful to Heather Ruch who stepped in at the last minute to help us reformat our references to APA style.

Numerous graduate students contributed to the project. Wright State University doctoral candidates contributed to the coding of data and conceptualization of this project. These included Stephanie Gemmer, Tarryn Moor, Dustin Hamilton, Kolina Delgado, Jessica Heschel, Tasha Phillips, Ashley Murray, Brianna Grover, Nicole Linen, Katherine Sunder, Ting Ooi, and Emily Kiourtsis; Alexa Ralicki helped compile references. Chelsea Farrell and Katie Kukiolcznyski, graduate research assistants in the History Department at Central Connecticut State University, helped prepare the manuscript by checking the citations and accuracy of the quotations from the notes.

The library staffs at both WSU and CCSU make so much of our work possible. Specifically, we want to acknowledge Brian Olesko of Wright State University who conducted last-minute literature searches, created an enormous file of references and helped us frame our research questions.

We would like to personally thank the following:

Cheryl Meyer: Most importantly, I want to thank my family who give me what I need to do this difficult work. Deb, whom I continually recruited to help over the past 4 years, spent countless hours listening to me and helping conceptualize the material, read drafts, edited, and coded data, as well as anything else I needed done, including continual problem solving. Her help and moral support have been the one constant throughout this project and the fuel that has kept me going. I thank my children for allowing me time and space to work on this and for being who they are. I watch with amazement as they go out into the world and navigate the difficult parts with strength and courage. Margaret Fischer, my neighbor extraordinaire, kindly read an initial chapter and told me it was boring and that I needed to include more vignettes. I think it made all the difference. Finally, I am grateful to Betty Yung for inviting me to be her partner in crime on so many projects. I miss her both professionally and personally.

Taronish Irani: I am extremely thankful to my parents Dr. Homi F. Irani, and Mrs. Homai H. Irani for their love, sacrifice, patience, prayers, and unconditional support. I am honored to have you as my parents. Dad and Mom, your endless confidence in my abilities has helped me during the most difficult times. You have been my inspiration and motivation for continuing to improve my knowledge and move my career forward. I also appreciate my immediate and extended family and my close friends for their moral support and prayers. I have deep gratitude to all the people who have supported me to complete this work, directly or indirectly.

Katherine Hermes: A very special thanks is extended to Alexandra Maravel who read and proofread the entire manuscript and gave me invaluable commentary. I would like to thank Joe Hermes, Karen Ritzenhoff, Karen Blanken, and Marie Morgan for their friendship and encouragement. The CCSU Women, Gender and Sexuality Studies Program, Jacqueline Cobbina-Boivin and the Ruthe Boyea Women's Center, and colleagues in sociology, Jessica Greenebaum, and in psychological sciences, Joanne DiPlacido, Carolyn Fallahi, and Jason Sikorski, have educated me over the years on many aspects of gender and psychology. Audrey Riggins, the history department secretary, listened to stories about suicide, discussed the cases, and kept my calendar as clear as possible so the book could be finished. Professors Dann J. Broyld, Heather Munro Prescott, Robert Wolff, and Heather Rodriguez of Central Connecticut State University offered helpful advice on historical and sociological issues relating to class, gender, and race and recommended historical sources. Finally, I am adding a special remembrance for Marlene Braun, Bev Schultz, and Yan Fang, beloved friends who have passed away and who taught me much about how precious life is.

Introduction

Killing oneself has been taboo in western culture since the days of the Roman Empire. The reasons for committing suicide seem timeless; the prohibitions against it, time and place specific. We look at a particular time and place, counties in southwestern Ohio from 2000 to 2009, against the backdrop of modern American history, to try to understand the motivations, means and responses that shape suicide today. In particular, we seek to understand the ways in which those who killed themselves communicated at the time of their deaths their intentions, feelings, and thoughts. If society's healthcare providers, social workers and mental health professionals can understand what leads to suicide, it may be possible to intervene and prevent the loss of life. These findings may also help those who have lost someone to suicide understand what happened. Suicide deaths are often described as the worst deaths, the hardest for those left behind to recover from, the hardest to forget. Recognizing what occurs in suicides, from the planning to the aftermath, can be critical.

Since Emile Durkheim wrote his famous study, *On Suicide*, in 1897, psychologists, psychiatrists, sociologists, and other behavioral scientists, as well as biological scientists, have tried to unravel the mysteries of the suicidal mind by understanding motivation. Many theories have been offered after each study, but no recent, major, comprehensive typology, especially one that compares note writers and non-note writers, since Professor of Thanatology at the University of California-Los Angeles, Edwin Schneidman, who founded the Los Angeles Suicide Prevention Center, pioneered the study of suicide notes in the 1940s. The work of David Lester of the Psychology Program at the Richard Stockton College of New Jersey, with Janet Haines and Christopher L. Williams of the School of Psychology at the University of Tasmania, Australia, and Mark Davis and Valerie Callanan of the Criminal Justice Research Center at Kent State University in Ohio, has been especially influential to our research. These scholars have led the way in examining suicide from nearly every standpoint. Thomas Joiner of the Psychology Department at Florida State University has also posited a theory about suicide. These theories are discussed in Chapter 1, The History and Theories of Suicide, in more depth, but they have all contributed much to our knowledge about suicide. What also has emerged, though, is an increasingly complicated list of reasons that people commit suicide and an almost unwieldy number of risk factors to consider. After considering our findings and those of other scholars, we offer a simplified typology that we think will allow a better and no less deep understanding of motivations and how people communicate them.

This book presents findings from an original study of coroners' reports from Ohio, but this book is not merely about this research. No single study can provide definitive information about suicide. We have tried to write a book about suicide that is comprehensive and cuts across state and national boundaries. Our focus is suicide in western cultures, especially in the United States (US) and the English-speaking world, supplemented by European and Oceanic studies. Across time and place elements of suicide resonate, and since the Enlightenment, when literacy and the scientific method spread through the western world, people have struggled to understand and prevent suicide on the one hand, and to communicate their reasons for killing themselves on the other. Some of these communications were in the form of notes, others in the symbolism of their acts. We utilize history, theory, psychological autopsy, and interdisciplinary social science perspectives to shape our discussion and argument.

The population in our study is largely comprised of white male adults, with some women and ethnic minorities. All of the victims died in or near Montgomery County, or surrounding counties, in Ohio. Of the 1280 suicide victims, only 37 were under the age of 18. Only 106 were non-white, but there were racial differences that are discussed in later chapters. Historically and in the present day, African Americans kill themselves at a much lower rate than European Americans, and that will be discussed both in the sections on history and theory and in other chapters. In our sample, we know for certain that 42, or 3.28%, were veterans, and that 56, or 4.38%, were not, but of the 1182 people remaining, we cannot be sure. Kang and Bullman (2008) found that among the veteran population between 2001 and 2005 the overall risk for suicide was 1.15%, and higher if a diagnosed mental disorder existed.

We also cannot be sure of how many were gay, lesbian, or bisexual (GLB). Haas et al. (2011) suggest that among GLB individuals, the suicide rate is not higher than that of the general population in the United States. Only two in our sample were identified as gay and none as transgender. For veterans, GLBT persons, and Native Americans, we need to look to national data and statistics from other studies, and to subgroup populations within those broader demographics, as risk tends to change based on age, specific traumatic experiences, mental disorders, and substance abuse.

The victims in our sample also ranged greatly in economic and social class. Some lived in houses valued in the hundreds of thousands, while others rented apartments and paid rents in the hundreds of dollars. Many of them lived in Dayton, while others lived in rural counties surrounding the city, stretching as far north as Columbus. The counties in which they lived and died include Montgomery (the largest in our sample), Preble, Brown, Miami, Champaign, Greene, Warren, Clinton, Hardin, Scioto, Ross, Washington,

Adams, Shelby, Pickaway, Fayette, Logan, Clark, Gallia, Meigs, Athens, Clermont, Franklin, Butler, Auglaize, Darke, Madison, Logan, and Highland. The greater Columbus and Cincinnati metropolitan areas were not included in the sample. Other than Dayton, the areas we studied are largely comprised of small towns and farms, increasingly suburbanized but with a "country" aspect. Recent highway additions in the latter part of the 20th century have connected cities that were once considered distant from one another.

The "heartland," as this area is often called, experienced a great deal of change in the 1990s and early 2000s. Dayton and nearby Springfield were "rustbelt" cities that had once had industry, but were left with declining manufacturing as the 20th century came to a close. In the year 2000, Dayton's population was 166,179, less than it had been in 1990 by 15,865 people (Census, 2000). Dayton had "fifty-five well organized neighborhoods, some of which had been severely challenged by poverty, unemployment, foreclosures, and homelessness" as the economic downturn of 2001 progressed (Ferguson, 2009, p. 89). Like many cities, Dayton was attempting to revitalize its schools and rebuild communities with private, nonprofit development funds (Ferguson, 2009).

Montgomery County had just over half a million people in 2000. Moreover, it grew little in the next decade (Montgomery County, 2010). Demographic changes were also dramatic in that decade. Since 2000, the percent of married couple families had decreased 15%, and families with a female head of household increased 11%. Between 2003 and 2010, the infant mortality rate increased 10%. The number of people with disabilities in the county was higher than that of Ohio and the nation as a whole. Both violent crime and property crime were higher in the county than in Ohio or the United States (Montgomery County Health, 2014).

According to the Montgomery County Community Health Assessment (2014), suicide was the eighth leading cause of death in men, and chronic liver disease was the tenth. Suicide was the ninth leading cause of death among whites, but was not in the top ten causes for blacks. The suicide rate was also higher, at 16.4%, than the Ohio or national average of 12.3%. Accidents were the third largest cause of death in men and the ninth in women. The rate for women taken to the hospital for a suicide attempt was nearly twice that of men, but the death rate for suicide among men was four times higher than for women (Daniulaityte, Carlson, & Siegal, 2007). Our research will explore these numbers in more detail.

Women in the region at the turn of the 21st century lived in a state with one of the lowest political participation rates in the nation (43rd). In a study of feminism in the Dayton area conducted during the early 2000s, researchers found that women participated very little in cultural or civic organizations for women, and that few resources were available to address problems of health, employment, and violence. Black women were especially estranged from such organizations (Runyan & Wenning,

2004). Violence against women, as in many communities, could turn deadly. Nearly 15% of women who sought help from a women's advocacy center in Dayton reported that their partners tried to kill them and 13.5% said the police did little to help them (Anderson et al., 2003). The issue of interpersonal violence and its connection to suicide is discussed further in Chapter 3, Suicide Motivated by Interpersonal Relationships.

Substance abuse is frequently cited as a contributing factor to suicide, often in conjunction with another event such as trauma or in combination with mental illness. In many of the cities in the late 1990s and early 2000s crack and methamphetamine were the drugs of choice. Both men and women use drugs. While more men than women use drugs, some studies suggest that among crack users, women may be heavier users. In Dayton, a small study of 18 women found that the majority of them had high unemployment, and a lack of stability in work, housing and relationships (Daniulaityte, Carlson, & Siegal, 2007). Dayton was a city especially hard hit by all of these in the period we are studying. Throughout this book we will examine the use of intoxicating substances at the time of the suicide.

The particular circumstances of Ohio's geography, economy, politics, and culture may have had an impact on the individuals in our study and on their decisions to take their own lives, but we do not think Ohio was so distinctive from other places that the results from our study have only regional bearing. All of the evidence from other studies in the United States, Canada, the United Kingdom, and Oceania shows that our findings are largely complementary and corroborative. Even the economic downturn in 2000 and the recession of 2008 were experienced throughout western economies. The rise of the privatization of once-public services, from education to prisons, and austerity measures in government spending, have affected every nation whose data we consulted. Our histories and contemporary culture are intertwined and, when it comes to suicide, we share circumstances, ways of thought, causal factors, and risks.

This book is divided into several chapters that proceed from a broad picture of suicide to the specifics of our study, to reflections on how to take steps to prevent suicide in the future. At the present time, suicide is at epidemic proportions in the United States. Patterns of death are changing, and some of the truisms about suicide are being challenged as the numbers rise dramatically. In 2014, 42,773 people died from suicide compared with 29,199 in 1999. According to the Centers for Disease Control and Prevention's (CDC) latest US data released in 2016, the rate of suicides across all age groups except the elderly is at its highest level in nearly 30 years. The rate rose by 2% a year starting in 2006, double the annual rise in the earlier period of the study. In its previous major report on suicide, released in 2013, the CDC observed a steep increase in suicide among 35- to 64-year-olds. Since 2010, however, suicides have risen by 7% for the entire population (Curtin, Warner, & Hedegaard, 2016).

The National Surveys of Drug Use and Health and the US Mortality Files from the National Vital Statistics System (Han et al., 2016) also issued a joint report of pooled data in which they found that 3.2% of US adults who attempted suicide during a 1-year period died by suicide. It includes both people who died on their first attempt during a 12-month period, as well as those who died on a subsequent attempt in the same year period. One out of every 31 adults in the United States who attempted suicide in the past 12 months died by their own hand. When adjusted for age, gender, race/ethnicity, education, marital status, region (i.e., Northeast, Midwest, South, and West), and time period (study year), the report revealed a surprising link between suicide and education: the highest suicide rate (16%) was among those 45 years and older who had less than a high school education. The rates were much lower for others in the same age group who had completed high school (1.9%) or college (1.8%). The rate across all age groups decreased with education, from 9.6% for adults who had not completed high school to 1.4% for college graduates (Han et al., 2016).

The research we conducted is sometimes described as psychological autopsy. We have examined life histories, adverse life events, mental health and psychological stability, and cognitive processes all to the extent they were documented by the medical examiner or in the notes left by the victims. Some studies have suggested that the only way to understand suicide victims is to look at those who attempt suicide but survive, while other studies have shown marked differences between "attempters" and "completers." Suicide attempters and completers can demonstrate very similar depressive symptoms, but as one study showed, suicide completers were significantly more likely to use alcohol or drugs prior to their suicidal act and were more likely to leave a suicide note (Rivlin, Fazel, Marzano, & Hawton, 2010). In Chapter 9, Protective Factors and Resilience, we discuss that literature in greater depth. While we acknowledge the problem of being unable to interview directly the victims of suicide, and thus we are unable to know their deepest thoughts, we have used the notes and the information we do have to create a collective picture of the victims that shows their motivations and mental states, or the ways of thinking that shaped their decision making.

We obtained our information, as have other such studies, from a government source, the office of the county medical examiner. Since the 1960s researchers have pointed out and discussed the biases in such sources. Suicides are undoubtedly undercounted by coroners and medical examiners for a variety of reasons, including mistaking accidents and homicides as suicide. Changes in personnel or inconsistency in reporting information, even within the same jurisdiction, may also be at fault (Whitt, 2006). We discuss our methods more thoroughly in Chapter 2, Findings, but we have tried to avoid common pitfalls. Our large sample size, our use of comparative historical and contemporary data and corroboration of statistical findings, as well as our qualitative assessment of notes, will not prevent errors entirely, but it will help us correct for biases in the data from any given year.

Chapter 1, The History and Theories of Suicide, examines the history and theories of suicide. Historically, the suicides that occur in America today are consistent with those that occurred in the past. Some of the same types of motivations and situational patterns exist now as existed hundreds of years ago. Nevertheless, some motivations and methods we no longer see, and some are new. What also has changed is the societal reaction to suicide. Once a criminal act that also met with condemnation by the Christian churches, today most health professionals and many religious leaders view suicide as a mental health issue. The public, however, has held onto ideas from the past and in some places it is still unacceptable to discuss the suicide of a family member lest it reflect badly on those who remain. Silence and shame persist. At the same time, some states have enacted laws that allow for assisted suicide as mercy, and cases like the death of Brittany Maynard, a right-to-die advocate discussed in Chapter 9, Protective Factors and Resilience, have generated sympathy for some suicides. Theories about who commits suicide and why are explained to establish the current state of the field of suicidology.

Chapter 2, Findings, examines the deaths that occurred from 2000 to 2009 in Montgomery County, Ohio and its environs, using information provided by the coroner. Among the information provided was a cache of suicide notes. In this chapter we explain our methodology and we examine our findings, exploring the similarities and differences between note writers and non-note writers. Our findings are compared with those of other previous studies.

Several of our chapters focus on the major motivating factors. We used not only those motivating factors that we found, but also those identified by other researchers. Chapter 3, Suicide Motivated by Interpersonal Relationships, analyzes relationship problems and interpersonal violence, a category of suicide motivation that has existed in perpetuity. In Chapter 4, Escape as a Motivation for Suicide, we discuss the desire to escape from pain, which represents the largest motivating factor in our sample; in Chapter 5, Grief and Failure, other motivations such as grief and failure are discussed; in Chapter 6, The Complexity of Suicide Motivation, we summarize our findings, as they represent multiple and complex motivations. We discuss the patterns that have emerged from our findings and explain some of the differences and similarities between the motivation groups. In Chapter 7, Severe Mental Illness, we discuss the role of severe mental illness in suicide.

Several of our chapters go beyond a discussion of motivation to analyze structural issues. Chapter 8, The Intersection of Suicide and Legal Issues, examines the increasing encroachment of legal issues into suicidal motivation. In the past, people often had fewer interactions with the legal system, but when they did have them, it was for the ordinary aspects of life, a probated estate, a small nuisance suit, or debt case. Nowadays, people with co-occurring severe mental health disorders and substance abuse problems, who are also likely candidates for suicide, have unprecedented rates of involvement with law enforcement and the legal system. One study found that 88% had contact with the legal system and 44% were arrested at least once (Clark, Ricketts, & McHugo, 1999). The United States especially is a country in which mass incarceration has become a severe problem. Quite simply, people are being arrested and punished at unprecedented rates. The incarceration problem may apply most to the United States, and not necessarily to other countries, but many western countries still incarcerate minority populations at higher rates than the white population (Travis, Western, & Redburn, 2014). Moreover, the mortgage crisis and recession that began in 2007 resulted in high unemployment rates and forced millions into bankruptcy or foreclosure. We discuss the role legal entanglements play in motivating suicide in Chapter 5, Grief and Failure and Chapter 8, The Intersection of Suicide and Legal Issues.

Chapter 9, Protective Factors and Resilience, is a reflection on creating a culture of well-being. In some societies, longevity is a valued and attainable state. A study of "blue zones" has isolated some of the personal characteristics and societal qualities that make it possible for people to live past one hundred years of age (Buettner, 2015). While the Blue Zone study was not concerned with suicide, we propose that purposefully creating blue zone–like communities may help prevent suicide. We also look at other geographical information that, when combined with our knowledge of motivations, means and communications, can help us develop responses and methods of prevention on both the large and small scale. Finally, we look at suicide as part of death, with all its stages and emotions, and what that may tell us about intervention and prevention.

In Chapter 10, Conclusions and Implications, we review the results of our study with the results of other cited studies and discuss what can be done in the future for prevention and intervention. We explore the use of suicide prevention policies and programs in other places to see how they have had an impact on suicide rates, and discuss what a "national agenda" for suicide intervention and prevention might look like.

Despite our efforts to write a comprehensive book, some issues we could not and did not cover. Our study looks primarily at individual suicide motivated by situational factors. Some causal and contributing factors we were unable to examine. We do not look at biological or ideological causes of suicide. Research is ongoing into the question of whether suicide is ever biologically ordained, whether through heredity or genetic mutations (Sarchiapone & D'Aulerio, 2014). These studies seem promising. As early as the 17th century, long before the idea of the human genome took hold, scholars posited that suicide might run in families. But if a biological "predestination" exists, our evidence cannot support or refute it.

We also did not examine those who commit suicide for ideological reasons. Suicide bombers, self-immolators, and the like are outside the scope of our study. No notes in our study and no recorded facts in the coroners' reports suggest that such reasons existed among our population. Suicide-by-cop, when an individual's violent actions result in the use of deadly force by police officers, will be discussed in connection with those who died with impending legal action against them. While we do consider murder-suicide in interpersonal relationships, we do not have data on those who killed strangers and then themselves.

Since our study relied heavily on suicide notes, an explanation of our methodology with respect to the notes is important, as is a description of the nature of the notes. The notes came in various conditions. Occasionally they had splotches from blood spatter, which sometimes created difficulty in reading the words. Sometimes the person had been taking drugs, and those notes are especially incoherent towards the end. Not all notes were written on normal paper; e.g., some were on paper towels, mirrors, Christmas cards, and even their bodies. The notes were also not always in the form of letters, but might be in the form of a legal document or will. The notes sometimes addressed a particular person, and at other times were addressed to no one in particular. One person addressed the note to his dog.

We chose to leave all spelling, grammar and punctuation intact. When notes were printed or written in all capital letters we replicated that unless a person's printing made it clear they were not using capital letters for emphasis. We have not changed their prose to make it more readable or understandable, since we believe the communication left by the deceased must be interpreted as they left it to us. As we chose to make all case files including the notes anonymous, we changed those names. Our analysis and discussion of the cases and the notes reflect these name changes. While coroner cases are matters of public record, we felt real names did not add to our discussion of results as long as the characteristics of the person, which might include race and gender, or even religion, were clear in the reports. We also augmented or changed some incidental details of the cases when the anonymity of the person would be jeopardized if we did not. It was important to us to have case studies that preserved the essential humanity of the suicide victims and did not relegate them to mere objects of study. We did not change the names of public figures, however.

Some factors were unavailable to us. We had no method to establish in any reliable way the economic or social classes of all of the individuals in our sample. Even though we had addresses and were able to find the value of a house, e.g., the recession in 2008 meant values changed. We had no collective information about renters versus owners, about mortgagors versus outright owners, and so forth. Zip codes do not necessarily mean all who live within that area share economic and social characteristics. If we had evidence of wealth or social class from the notes or case records, we acknowledged it, but we have no statistics of our own. Any statistics about class come from other studies.

We also were unable to ascertain religion in most cases. While other studies show differences in both rates of suicide and attitudes towards it between Catholics, Protestants, Jews and Muslims, our data set usually made no mention of religion. In the counties we examined, most people identify as Christian, and the majority as evangelical Protestant. Catholics were the next largest group. In Montgomery County, 40.7% of the total population in 2000 belonged to religious organizations; in 2010, 44.5% (Montgomery County Metropolitan, 2014).

In the chapters, we variously refer to the people in this study as individuals or victims, but all killed themselves, and no distinction is meant by the use of alternative words. When referring to racial and ethnic groups we have used the terminology employed by the authors of the historical and psychological works upon which our study builds. There are various words used to describe the action of a person who takes his or her own life. These are "completed," "committed suicide," and "died by suicide." We elected to use "committed suicide" most often, because this is the common vernacular term. When we conducted this study of suicides that occurred between 2000 and 2009, the DSM IV-TR was used. The common severe mental disorders in our sample were based on the DSM-IV TR classification, but will be compared to the new version of Diagnostic Statistical Manual – 5th Edition (DSM-V) in Chapter 7, Severe Mental Illness, when we discuss mental illness.

Suicide records, even those with no note, are intimate documents, as much as a diary or letter. People are laid bare at death, and when they kill themselves, their secrets often get exposed. The people who died often felt alone, but most were not. They left behind grief-stricken relatives and friends and, frequently, stunned coworkers and neighbors. While we did not examine all obituaries, those we looked at did not mention the suicide. One victim's name appeared on an online suicide memorial site. One woman had nothing but a death notice stating when she died; several obituaries referred to the deceased's death as "sudden." Some had no services; others, private services; and still others, full-fledged funerals. As researchers, we were touched by these deaths, and we hope our investigation and this book will ensure that others learn from their suffering.

1

The History and Theories of Suicide

THE HISTORY OF SUICIDE

Historians have explained the historical changes in suicide and attitudes toward it by focusing on culture, religion, and science. As this book is comprised of our study of contemporary, midwestern Americans, examined with other contemporary studies from the western world, the historical focus will be on the peoples of North America who are of Native American, European, and African descent in the early modern and modern eras, for the trends established there. In most books about suicide, one finds only a minimal historical account covering the period from the ancient world to the present, usually focused on legal, religious and medical changes, but few give serious examination to changes in suicide practices, methods, and motivations. Although we are unable to devote many pages to its history in this book, having an understanding of the history of suicide is vital to the mission of this book to help to prevent it.

Beginning with the Protestant Reformation and the rise of literacy, scholars have been able to study suicide not just anecdotally but statistically. England began to keep records in parishes and counties, and the country began to take an interest in suicide (MacDonald & Murphy, 1990). The suicide note also became something of a new phenomenon with the publication of Goethe's *The Sorrows of Young Werther* in 1774. The protagonist in the novel, a sensitive and passionate artist, left a farewell note to his beloved that became a model for others (Minois, 1999). Suicide in the modern world became a subject of scientific inquiry. The communication of ideas about suicide in literature, art, newspapers, scholarly journals, public records, and the notes of the victims over the last 400 years provides us with a much fuller picture of suicide in this era than for any other time.

Over time, since the keeping of good records began in the 17th century, a strong continuity has existed in seasonal cycles of suicide.

Explaining Suicide.
DOI: http://dx.doi.org/10.1016/B978-0-12-809289-7.00001-4

1

In the northern hemisphere, research has found both more violent suicides, those in which guns or knives are used, and more female suicides in the most significant seasonal peak, April through June. Conversely, more male and nonviolent suicides occur in the lesser peak of October through November (Brådvik, 2002). Religious and economic indicators have been less stable and predictable. Any biological predispositions are beyond our ability to identify or analyze. One trend is clear: as religious prohibitions against suicide were displaced, suicide has moved from the category of self-murder, and thus a crime, to a disease of the mind. This is not to say that religious belief has had no influence in the modern age; many Christians still think that suicide relegates their souls to eternal damnation, even though their churches officially have abandoned such views (*Catechism of the Catholic Church*, 2nd ed., 1992; "On Mental Health Concerns and The Heart Of God," 2013).

America's history with respect to suicide can be divided into two periods: from 1492, when colonization began, to the post-Civil War years and Reconstruction to 1877; and from 1877 to the present. The years from 1492 to 1877 share some characteristics that are significant when discussing suicide. Until 1877, the United States was expanding, and for most of that period Native people were moved ever more westward, and finally enclosed on reservations. Africans and their descendants were enslaved until 1865, and thus constituted a special population; those who crossed on the Middle Passage ("saltwater slaves") had different experiences with death, including suicide, than those born on plantations or in cities in the United States and its territories. European settlers before 1877 were often engaged in colonization and the formation of new communities, even after the English colonial period ended, as they moved westward into newly acquired lands. The status of master could belong to white men before 1865, but not thereafter. Until 1877, the South continued to feel the effects of the Civil War, as it was under military occupation.

Moreover, between 1492 and 1877, the treatment of suicide in law and medicine changed little. It was in most of the colonies, and later states, a felony to kill oneself. Yet coroners could and often did find victims of suicide to be *non compos mentis*, or mentally ill, rather than "felonious" (Acts And Laws ... of the Massachusetts Bay, in New England, 1700; Jamison, 1999). Suicide or "self-murder" was considered a sin and crime similar to murder, adultery, and thievery, and often ministers condemned it as a willful act, but literature from the era also indicates that the clergy had begun to perceive a state of mind known as "melancholy" to be the cause of some suicides (Fox, 1709; Jamison, 1999).

After 1877, a society more recognizable to contemporary Americans began to arise. Indians had fought their last major battle at Little Bighorn in 1876; the reservation system was completed by 1890. African Americans were no longer enslaved, but a new system of oppression known as Jim Crow was emerging. Whites were no longer colonizing; immigrants who came after 1880 were settling in established places. The immigrant experience redefined whiteness and the so-called "American Dream."

Likewise, the treatment of suicide in law and medicine modernized. The rise of psychoanalysis did not eliminate the shame of suicide, but it did place it in the realm of mental disease or defect, which led to decriminalization and eventually to religious institutions changing some teachings on suicide. Feminist scholars have argued that the acceptance of suicide as the product of mental illness meant that it went from being a masculinized "act of will" to a feminized, passive act which turned those who killed themselves into victims (Gentry, 2006). Willful suicide was still considered sinful, but any act in which the individual was not responsible, because of mental illness for instance, was not considered sinful. The Catholic Church, which has one of the strongest stances on suicide, says in its current *Catechism* (para. 2282), "Grave psychological disturbances, anguish or grave fear of hardship, suffering or torture can diminish the responsibility of the one committing suicide." In this view, suicides are not to be condemned, but rather are to be pitied (Kheriaty, 2014).

SUICIDE FROM THE EARLY MODERN PERIOD TO THE POST–CIVIL WAR ERA

His homeland was changing. When he was a boy, Soranhes knew everyone in the lands around him. He was from the Huron village of Teanausteaiae, not far from Quebec. Now, in 1636, there were strange men, missionaries called "Black Robes," who had arrived in Huronia from France some years before. His son, Amantacha, went by the new French name of Louys de Saincte Foy, and he followed the teachings of the Jesuit priests. Soranhes himself had allowed the missionaries to instruct him in their beliefs, and he had even stopped eating meat on some days of the week in preparation for baptism. He had second thoughts, however, and never underwent their initiation, which disappointed them. He continued to meet the Jesuit priests in his travels, and they continued to try to teach him, but he preferred to live according to the way he always had. Then, much to his great sorrow, his son died. He fell into a deep despair. Le Jeune (1636) describes it as follows:

> One day, when he found himself alone in his cabin with one of his little daughters, he sent her to get a certain root that they call Ondachienroa, which is a quick poison. This child went for it very innocently, supposing that her father intended to make some medicine, as he had shown some slight indisposition. She brought him some, but not enough to suit him, and she returned for it the second time. He ate his fill of it; a high fever attacked him, and carried him off in a little while. But his relatives do not admit that he died in this way (Thwaites, XIII, 1896–1901, p. 27).

The first records of suicide in North America were provided by Jesuit missionaries who lived among the Native Americans in the Great Lakes region, Maine and eastern Canada. In 1636 Father Le Jeune recorded the death of Soranhes, a chief of the Huron people, saddened that he died unconverted and "miserably" (p. 27). Pierre de Charlevoix, who preached to the Miami and Potawatomie Indians, claimed that Indian children would threaten suicide if they were reprimanded in a way that offended their dignity or humiliated them. Charlevoix asserted that girls in particular could not suffer correction from their mothers, and he thought they were motivated primarily by revenge against their parents. Yet he did not cite any specific examples of actual suicide occurring among that population. Threatening or attempting suicide is not the same as completing the act (as will be discussed later), so it is difficult to know if the Native people of Michigan experienced a suicide problem (Axtell, 1981). In Maine, however, suicides were completed at a rate that alarmed Catholic observers.

Grief, dishonor, unrequited love or bad marriages did result in suicide. Among the Micmac, Jesuits witnessed what they thought was a suicide epidemic. In 1691, 50 years after colonization, Le Clerq wrote about the terrible spate of suicides in his mission. The eastern seaboard, according to other accounts, saw frequent suicides among both Algonquian and Iroquoian people. Le Clerq attributed their motivation for suicide to "affronts," especially those which "tarnish[ed] their honour and reputation" (Axtell, 1981, pp. 214–215). Like the Indians of Michigan, the Micmac used both poisonous herbs and strangulation to kill themselves. He described their melancholy as "so black and so profound that they become immersed wholly in a cruel despair" (p. 215). The priest espoused some sympathy for those who lost their true loves, but ultimately saw their deaths as examples of an impoverished, non-Christian culture. Nevertheless, his list of reasons for Micmac suicides resembles our own: humiliation from which there was no recovery, lost love, revenge, and grief. The Jesuits were learned men, and their taxonomies reflected both old religious categories and newer scientific ones. They were, though, oblivious to a degree about the many traumas that colonization inflicted on the Native people, such as the dramatic decline of their population from disease, the upending of gender roles, and the disruption to domestic life and the community caused by the fur trade. All of these situational elements could have been sources of severe depression (Pelletier, 1980). Ethnographer Fenton found that among the Iroquois, who like the Micmac were enmeshed in the fur trade, social disruption more than economic factors played the largest role in suicide (Fenton, 1986).

In many ways, what the Jesuits observed conforms to a theory advanced by modern scholars about relationship-related suicides and the concept of reciprocity. It is commonly understood by modern historians and ethnographers that Native Americans built their societies and relationships on reciprocity, whether it was in marriage proposals, in mourning wars to restore tribal numbers lost as a result of war or disease, or in trade with foreigners (Richter, 1992). Suicidologists have posited that when two parties engage in exchanges that are mutually beneficial based on a principle of reciprocity, it results in expectations that these benefits will be commensurate with what one party has given to the other. The exchange is predicated on fairness and equity. When one person in the relationship receives or perceives unfair treatment, distress and an attempt to restore balance results. It is possible that at least some of the suicides that took place in the eastern woodlands of North America in the 17th century were the result of something still prevalent today, a desire to correct an imbalance in a relationship (Davis, Callanan, Lester, & Haines, 2009).

In colonial British North America, suicide was generally seen as the problem of "the Other." Articles in colonial newspapers noted the nationalities of the suicides featured in their pages, people such as Frenchmen and Danes. They also described how certain cultures refrained from suicide, such as the Romans, or how even notorious convicts eschewed it as dishonorable. When rumors swirled that Englishmen had a high rate of suicide, colonial newspapers disagreed, positing that the French were far more likely than the English to kill themselves. ("London, April 6," *New York Gazette*, July 1, 1751; "Dublin, April 15," *Boston News-Letter*, July 10–17, 1740; "The Continuation of Our Last," *New York Weekly Journal*, Apr. 9, 1739; "London, October 13 Extract of a Letter from Paris, October 1, 1783," *Connecticut Courant*, Feb. 24, 1784.)

Yet the very first recorded possible suicide in New England was that of Dorothy Bradford, wife of William Bradford, and one of the original Pilgrims. On December 7, 1620, Dorothy "fell" off the *Mayflower* and into the icy waters off the coast of modern-day Provincetown, Massachusetts. Dorothy Bradford was the daughter of a member of the English Church of Amsterdam, and historians dispute whether her fall was an accident or a suicide. Some scholars claim she "jumped to her death" because she was "unable to reconcile her vision of utopia with the wilderness of the American shore" (Peters, 2014, p. 64), while others say no evidence exists to support the assertion (Galisteo, 2007). Bradford himself was silent about his wife's death.

Suicide as a result of religious despair was not unknown to the colonists. Jonathan Edwards, America's foremost theologian, recorded the death of his uncle, Joseph Hawley, who "laid violent hands to himself, and put an end to his life, by cutting his own throat" (Sederholm, 2012, p. 326). Edwards wrote that his uncle had suffered from "melancholy," but he saw in his uncle's death a more general despair, in which he imagined "the Spirit of God was gradually withdrawing from us" (p. 326). Edwards worried that more suicides would follow (Sederholm, 2012).

Edwards wrote of his uncle's death in 1736 during a religious revival, the first of the revivals now known as the First Great Awakening. After a little more than a decade, the zeal of the "awakening" was fading. One Tuesday in January, 1750, a man in Dorchester, Massachusetts, hanged himself at the cider mill. He was a very wealthy bachelor of about 40, but the newspaper had no information about his motives, observing only that it was the second suicide in a few weeks ("Boston," *New York Gazette*, Feb. 5, 1750). Then as now, suicide could occur in clusters. Point clusters are multiple suicides that approximate one another in both time and space and are often attributed to direct social learning from nearby individuals (Mesoudi, 2009; Stack, 2003). Newspapers, then as now, could play a dangerous role in suicide reporting, as clusters arise when suicides get attention. Today, details of suicide are held back in order to try to prevent clusters, but in earlier times, editors were unaware of the association between media coverage and suicide (Gould, Kleinman, Lake, Forman, & Midle, 2014).

"Well-to-do" Congregationalists in New England were not the only ones to experience melancholy. Enslaved Africans on the Middle Passage threw themselves overboard or refused to eat. The population most likely to commit suicide was older men, according to the records of slavers, but ships' logs show an African captive suicide rate of 7.2% (Snyder, 2010). In New England a female slave, working alone in her master's household, cut herself open, saying she wanted to go home. Many of the enslaved believed that suicide would return them to their home in Africa (Piersen, 1977). During the antebellum era, the abolitionist William Lloyd Garrison represented slave suicide as "fatalistic suicide," the result of cultural oppression rather than as an act of resistance (Bell, 2012). Historians have assumed, based on Durkheim's (1897, 2006) sociology of suicide, that once enslaved people were in America, community formation helped prevent suicide, but current research suggests that assumption may be incorrect. Snyder posited in her examination of "slave suicide ecology" that killing oneself could be a supreme act of resistance, but also material circumstances, psychological factors, and emotional reasons impelled some enslaved people to take their own lives (Snyder, 2010).

The master–slave relationship was a form of intimate relationship, and suicides that took place within that relationship are complex. Slavery ended in the United States in 1865 and in its last western bastion, Brazil, in 1888. After slavery, African–American rates of suicide were and remain lower than those of whites. For the period during slavery, however, it is impossible to have reliable data on a large scale. For the enslaved person, suicide may have been motivated by spiritual concerns, escape, resistance, or despair, but whites often interpreted it quite differently. White masters, depending on their relationship with the deceased, may have seen the suicide as a defiant act, often referring to the deceased as "willful" or "sullen." Other masters merely saw an act that cost them valuable property. If the master or mistress were familiar with the person, he or she may have understood the individual's motivation. A master could also face disgrace if his slave committed suicide, as it reflected badly on his ability to keep order in his household. Some whites attributed slave suicide to a biological predisposition, while others claimed to be mystified why an enslaved person would kill himself. White abolitionists like Garrison had a different perspective still, often viewing the slave only as a victim of oppression without agency (Silkenat, 2011; Snyder, 2010).

The slave narratives taken down by the Works Progress Administration (WPA) in the 1930s and suicide inquest testimony also provide insights into the perspectives of captives. Alienation and isolation played a significant part, as did honor. The disruption of traditional African gender roles and the separation of family members had a tremendous impact on the lives of captives. Women were especially vulnerable when their children were taken away (Snyder, 2010).

Masters and mistresses were also not immune from suicide (Kimball, 2003). While their suicides were not always related to their status or to the slaves themselves, some were. When masters' slaves were taken from them, they sometimes took their lives out of despair (Genovese, 1974). William Byrd III of Westover killed himself in 1777 to escape his financial ruin, when it became clear he would lose his plantation after his gambling losses depleted his fortune (Tyler-McGraw, 1994).

Before the Civil War, suicide was condemned both in the North and South in moral and religious terms. Antebellum newspaper accounts described the act as "horrific" or "terrible" (Silkenat, 2011, p. 25). Before the war, whites viewed those who committed suicide as "cowardly," "base," and eternally damned (Silkenat, 2011, p. 13). Durkheim (1897, 2006) recognized in his study of suicide that members of military organizations were likely to commit altruistic suicide, i.e., suicide intended to benefit others in the soldier's community, but he believed military men in general were not likely to kill themselves, because the military afforded men a social integration that protected them. Suicide among soldiers, especially after a war in which the human losses ran into the hundreds of thousands or millions, raised troubling questions in society. Historically high rates of suicide in the military were an anomaly, but in 19th-century Europe suicide rates among military populations rose above those of the general population (Braswell & Kushner, 2012). In the United States during the Civil War, suicide rates were not particularly high, but after the fighting ceased, they rose astronomically. According to Durkheim (1897, 2006), "the soldier kills himself at the least disappointment, for the most futile reasons, for a refusal of leave, a reprimand, an unjust punishment, a delay in promotion, a question of honor, a flush of momentary jealousy, or even simply because other suicides have occurred before his eyes or to his knowledge" (pp. 238–239). Yet for many of the Union soldiers who killed themselves after the war, the disappointment may have been so complex, it was hard to put into words. They had been fighting for ideas, the freedom of enslaved people, and the union's perpetuity. While real people were freed, for many northern white men, they knew no one personally who benefitted. It had been a cause, a glorious one, but afterwards they were tired, traumatized, and less triumphant than they had imagined.

Frueh and Smith (2012) studied northern troops' mortality, and estimated suicide rates for white men on active duty ranged from 8.74 to 14.54 per 100,000 during the four years of the Civil War. For black soldiers, who joined the war effort in 1863, the suicide rate was approximately 17.7 in the first year of their entry into the war. In their second year, however, no black soldiers killed themselves. In 1864 the suicide rate for white and black troops combined was 10.35 per 100,000. In the aftermath of the Civil War, the rate of suicide among white soldiers in the North surged to 30.4 per 100,000 in the year after the South's surrender, but for black soldiers it was only 1.8. Frueh and Smith found that alcoholism and nostalgia, a temporary depression that consisted of longing for home and comfort, were often present in the suicides of active duty soldiers, factors for whites that may have been exacerbated in the postwar period. Many white soldiers had been in the war for the entire four years. Black soldiers in the postwar period were a diverse group of long-free African Americans from northern cities and town as well as newly freed slaves or runaways whose main task was to reunite with their families. Black soldiers may have had a much greater sense of hope than white soldiers in the aftermath of the war.

No extant suicide statistics exist for Confederate soldiers. Following the Civil War, white southerners regarded suicide victims more sympathetically, and southern newspapers were less likely to condemn the act. Some historians claim a "suicide mania" occurred after the war. Indeed, many whites now saw it as "honorable" and even altruistic to kill themselves rather than face the destruction and usurpation of the plantation economy and way of life. The South, as an honorific and now militarized society, recharacterized suicide in terms that, while they did not quite ennoble it, relaxed condemnation of the deceased. The postwar suicide of ardent secessionist Edmund Ruffin, who had fired the first shot of the Civil War, was just the first to begin the transformation of southern attitudes (Sommerville, 2014, pp. 153–154).

In 1870 an article in *Appletons' Journal of Literature, Science and Art* called "Curious Facts about Suicide" laid out a series of observations: people who are more intelligent commit suicide more often than "primitive" people; Germans "are the most suicidal" followed by the French and the English, while the Irish were the least so; revolutions cause suicide ("Curious Facts," 1870, p. 319). A curious public was poised for the revolution that mental health would undergo in the next century and a half.

SUICIDE FROM THE POST–CIVIL WAR ERA TO THE PRESENT

Jennie Benson graduated from commercial school with a diploma in stenography in November, 1889. A pretty young woman from Rome City, Indiana, she had boarded with a family in Dayton, Ohio, while she was in school. Friends and family attested to her vibrant personality. By all accounts, Jennie was well loved and well regarded. One day in May, 1890 she took the train to Washington Court House. Jennie killed herself there, despondent, her family speculated, over the loss of the love, friendship and companionship of a young man from her home town. The reason for the suicide, though, remained a mystery, as no one knew for certain that the two had been lovers and the young man was respectable, not the type to seduce a young woman like Jennie. Was it unrequited love, or some more sinister motive that led this young woman to a death by her own hand? Jennie left a note for her landlady that only deepened the mystery: "You know little of my past life. You have not questioned me, and I have not informed you. When you know all do not judge me harshly." Jennie's landlord came to retrieve her body. The family was too poor to bury her on their own, so the citizens of the town took up a collection to bury her ("Unrequited Love," 1890).

Jennie's story touched the members of her communities in Indiana and Ohio, but it also became fodder for the *National Police Gazette*, a magazine that thrived on lurid tales of forbidden love, wronged women, and dramatic deaths. The article about Jennie was nevertheless sympathetic to her. Despite her note hinting of darker elements in her life, she was portrayed as a "determined" young woman who wanted an "honorable career" and who was pure of heart (p. 7). "There were other ways for her to make a living," the *Gazette* observed, "but she gave them no thought" (p. 7). Suicide, it seemed, could be an honorable way out, especially if prostitution were the alternative, and the deceased was a person to be pitied rather than reviled ("Unrequited Love," 1890). It had not always been that way. Two decades earlier the *National Police Gazette* had printed a story of a prostitute, Jennie Ball aka Jennie Metzger of New Carlisle, Ohio, in which it had also recorded the sad tale of the suicide of a once-innocent girl from a respectable family. In that article, a gentleman expressed a different sentiment, "She was only a prostitute" ("Only a Lost Woman," 1879, p. 3).

Suicide in the early modern and modern world underwent dramatic changes, both in the perception of its victims, the interest generated in its motivations, and the societal attempts to prevent it. Just seven years after Jennie's death, Durkheim (1897, 2006) wrote his groundbreaking work on suicide. Durkheim's attempt to see the individual motivations of suicide victims as part of their social context rather than as lone acts of sin or madness began to shift the way in which society treated suicide.

In the reunited United States, the population underwent a reconfiguration, as native whites and blacks adjusted to their new stations in life. The most dramatic change came among the newly freed African Americans, who constructed tighter, stronger communities, which served as a deterrent to suicide. Conversely, whites struggled with impoverishment and the diminution of power over blacks that had once been nearly limitless. Both the financial losses and the loss of control contributed to a rise in suicide for whites as well as a softened attitude toward the act of taking one's own life (Silkenat, 2011). The loss of power and privilege can be a risk factor for suicide, because the victim feels the weight of failure, and if the failure is so great as to seem irredeemable, there may appear to be no light at the end of the tunnel. While we cannot know the mindset of any person in the past who committed suicide with no note of explanation, suicides such as those resulting from failure or to escape inevitable pain can in part be the result of constricted thinking in which the person was unable to perceive an acceptable alternative to death.

By the turn of the 20th century, the South's situation was changing. It was an impoverished region with little industry or economic growth. Jim Crow segregated blacks and whites, and violence was extremely high. Suicide rates, though, were lower than the rest of the nation among both whites and blacks. This can be explained by the particular kind of power and privilege that southern whites lost at the end of the Civil War and gained after Reconstruction. Southern power and privilege was male, white, and legal. It rested in the law of racial difference, first in the slave codes that subjugated blacks by status, and later in the black codes that subjugated them by color. While wealthy white men had more power and privilege than poor white men, elites bound the white lower classes to them through an ideology of white supremacy supported by the law. Even when southern wealth was diminished after the war, the former leaders of the Confederacy found ways in which they could maintain white supremacy, albeit in a different way than during slavery. When masters had slaves, they exercised control by keeping a close watch over blacks. Slave quarters were not far from the master's house; everything could be seen. During Jim Crow and segregation, whites pushed blacks away physically but kept close watch on them nevertheless, drawing complex lines that people of color could not cross without punishment. In that way, southern men restored much of what they had lost during the war.

From 1920 to 1960, white southerners' suicide rate remained below that of northern whites. Even when suicide rates began to rise in the mid-1950s, the South did not surpass the north. The rate of suicide among black southerners also remained low—lower than that of blacks in the North, as well as much lower than white people. The southern states with the highest percentages of black people ranked lowest in both homicide and suicide in the 40 years before the Civil Rights Act of 1964 (Escott, 1988; Hackney, 1969). Poverty itself seems not to have been a risk factor for suicide. A precipitous fall in status and wealth, such as that experienced by elite southern whites at the end of the Civil War, was much more of a risk than the continuous presence of deprivation.

In the northern, eastern, and western United States, dynamic growth occurred after the Civil War, although frequent economic panics, wars in 1898 and 1917, and immigration created social instabilities. In the postbellum era in Massachusetts, suicides were often above 20 per 100,000 people, a number twice that of today. Also unlike today, suicide was openly reported in the newspapers; nearly two-thirds of known suicides appeared in Massachusetts newspapers, whose reporters speculated about suicide as a "contagion" (Logue, 2015).

White Americans in the late 19th and early to mid-20th century also faced a changing national identity. What we now think of as a monolithic and homogenous group (white Americans) was no longer that at all. After the Civil War, the number of immigrants to the United States rose dramatically. The native-born whites whose families had come to America in the 17th and 18th centuries found themselves confronting a new order. In some ways, these whites found more common cause with blacks, whose ancestors also had long antecedent roots in America, than with the Irish, German, Eastern European and Southern Europeans that entered America between 1880 and 1920. The relatively new field of "whiteness studies" has shed light on the ways in which new arrivals were classified as nonwhites, even though today their descendants certainly number among whites or "Caucasians." This distinction has implications for suicide studies, because minority populations who face collective trauma or hardship may have different behaviors than majority populations. Not only do they lack power and privilege, but they also lack the ability to extricate themselves from painful situations from which they wish to escape or to reverse failures. Suicide rates among native-born whites in this period were generally high, while for immigrant populations they were generally low. Few Irish and Italians killed themselves. Some immigrant groups, though, had high rates (Germans, Scandinavians, Chinese) and in cities like New York, Boston, and Philadelphia, the suicide rate for the foreign born was higher than for the native born. The suicide rate for New York in 1890 was three times greater for immigrants than for those born in the United States. By 1930, San Diego had the highest urban suicide rate in the United States, and more than 50% of the suicides there were immigrants (Kushner, 1984; Lane, 1979).

Why some immigrants had high rates of suicide and others did not is hard to explain. It seems unlikely that city life, poverty, adversity or discrimination or any other explanation suffices, when so many others of that group thrived in the United States. Kushner (1984), one of the foremost historians of suicide, posits a psychosocial approach is necessary to understand the trends. He suggests that one element the historian needs to understand is the particular group's attitude toward death, mourning and suicide. Germans, Danes, and Austrians, e.g., had a culture of disposing of the dead with little ceremony as quickly as possible with almost no mourning. Italians and Irish had a very different practice. Germans in America also assimilated very quickly, losing their language and customs faster than other groups. The Irish and Italians, on the other hand, more successfully recreated the culture of their homelands in the new world. Kushner speculates that those who suffered an extreme object loss (the death of a parent, spouse, sibling or child, or some other traumatic loss), may have been the ones who committed suicide. The difference in death rituals and successful preservation of one's culture related to suicide rates among the immigrant population.

Native Americans, too, underwent enormous social, political, and economic changes, and extreme loss of their culture. In the 20th century, various legislative schemes from the "Indian New Deal" to the Termination Act swung Indian policy in wildly different directions, but nothing alleviated the economic and often cultural poverty of the reservations (Hacker & Haines, 2005). If Kushner's (1984) psychosocial explanation of immigrant suicide is correct, it may apply to Native peoples as well. Few societies in the world have experienced more traumatic loss than American Indians. New research also shows that trauma can be passed on from mother to child, though the implications of that for suicide are as yet unknown (Kellerman, 2015).

Beginning in the 1970s, Native people instituted many steps to try to rebound, fighting for control of schooling and court systems, and engaging in economic development. Yet for all the progress, reservations remain places with chronic problems of substance abuse and high rates of suicide. No other population in the United States suffers the suicide rates of American Indians. According to the Indian Health Service, between 1989 and 1991 the Native suicide rate was 16.5 per 100,000 population—85% higher than the suicide rate of 11.5 per 100,000 for the rest of the United States. At the same time, Native deaths from alcoholism were 51.8 per 100,000 population—630% higher than the total US rate of 7.1 per 100,000 (Sandefur, Rindfuss, & Cohen, 1996; Snipp, 1997). In the most recent study of suicide rates by the CDC, American Indians had the sharpest rise of all racial and ethnic groups, with rates rising by 89% for women and 38% for men (Tavernise, 2016). These suicides, coupled with extraordinarily high rates of death by homicide and accident, are a collective problem, and not merely the result of individual decisions to end one's life. The problems faced by American Indians are likewise faced by other indigenous peoples around the globe, such as the Aborigines of Australia, and few nations have addressed this critical problem (Korff, 2016).

In the era between the Civil Rights Act of 1964 and the middle of the 1980s, African-American mortality from suicide rose more than 36%; among men, by 45%. Most strikingly, between 1970 and 1985, among adolescent males it rose 75% (Burr, Hartman, & Matteson, 1999). At a time when it seemed that blacks were moving toward electoral gains, increasing literacy and educational attainment, occupational growth and social progress, in fact a set of countermovements lessened the positive impact of these gains. Blacks were increasingly subject to arrest and incarceration. Large-scale unemployment still existed and young black men also experienced an increased risk of death by homicide. A white backlash also had to be contended with, over issues from schooling to jobs. The "war on drugs" did not simply result in the arrests of individuals; it destroyed black families and neighborhoods (Burr et al., 1999; Mauer, 2009). As lesbian, gay, bisexual, transgender and queer (LGBTQ) communities face backlash from civil rights victories, one wonders if they will see similar countermovements as the black community did, and thus whether they will be at risk for greater numbers of suicides. The role of having a functioning, healthy community protective of the well-being of its members has been and is essential to suicide prevention.

After the troubling rise in suicide among African Americans in the 1970s and 1980s, by the turn of the 21st century the suicide rate had dropped dramatically for African Americans; it was then the 16th-leading cause of death. From 1990 to 2003, 28,177 suicides were recorded among African Americans. The suicide rate was 7.15 deaths per 100,000 population in 1990, which fluctuated in the early 1990s but then declined after 1993 to 5.36 deaths per 100,000 in 2003 (Crosby & Molock, 2006). At the same time as the decline in suicide in the 1990s, there was also a 21.3% decline in the number of African Americans in prison for drugs (Mauer, 2009). Whether these simultaneous declines are related is not clear, but it suggests that perhaps less disruption and distress in black communities occurred as a result of the war on drugs than in the 1970s and 1980s, and better community health may have been related to a decline in suicides. Protective factors, such as high religiosity among blacks, may affect youth differently than older people, but historically and today the black churches have held an unparalleled place in the civic as well as religious life of the black community. The youth population, unstable and affected by mass incarceration that again rose in the late 1990s after a respite, still remained at greatest risk for suicide.

In 2000, reports announced the unexpected development that the rate of suicide among blacks was climbing. Suicide became the third leading cause of death among black males ages 15–19, after homicide and accidents (Poussaint & Alexander, 2000). Yet the most recent data show that between 1999 and 2014 only one racial group, black men, experienced a decline in suicide. At the midpoint, in 2007, the suicide rate for all African American males was 8.4 per 100,000, while the suicide rate for black females was 1.7 per 100,000 ("African American Suicide," n.d.). Part of the confusion in reporting whether suicide among black men was rising or falling has to do with age as well as the time surveyed. For the very young, especially children, the suicide rate did indeed rise between 1999 and 2012. It grew from about 1.8 to about 3.5 for every million African-American children. Adolescents and young adults experienced a rise as well. The rise contrasted with a decline among white boys of the same ages (Reuters, 2015).

The immigrant population today is a different one than in 1920, but it still faces the issues of assimilation, cultural adaptation and preservation that affected those coming to the United States in earlier times. Today, a different society greets them, but one not necessarily less hostile to cultural differences than of old. While schools and universities often celebrate diversity and increasingly are adding diversity requirements and multiculturalism to general education courses, the nativism and ethnic hardships that await immigrants are not less than they were in the past (Sanchez, 1997). Among young people, one study in the 1990s found that Hispanic students were more likely to have thought about committing suicide than their white or black counterparts (Jamison, 1999), but the suicide rate for Hispanics of all ages, 5.85, was slightly less than half of the overall US rate of 12.08 ("Web-Based Injury Statistics Query and Reporting System," CDC, 2016).

The latter half of the 20th century saw a number of important changes in the way that society at large, the medical profession and educational institutions approached the problem of suicide. Schneidman, who founded the Los Angeles Suicide Prevention Center, invented the field of suicidology, and established a Program in Thanatology, changed the way researchers studied suicide with the publication of his book, *Clues to Suicide* (1957). His study of suicide note writers in Los Angeles County, with Farberow, was one of the first to examine the communications of those who killed themselves (Schneidman & Farberow, 1957). Although he was interested in developing a theory of suicidal motivation and behavior, he also wanted to take practical steps to prevent it. Farberow and he realized that many suicide attempts were spontaneous and that if one could intervene in the window of suicidal ideation, one could save lives. Among other things, Schneidman was the originator of the suicide hotline (Dicke, 2009). Since that time a number of organizations in the United States are actively trying to prevent suicide. Universities have established awareness programs, and hospital protocols are in place to determine if someone is suicidal.

The United States today as a whole faces an alarmingly high rate of suicide. On April 22, 2016, a report by the CDC announced that suicide for almost all population groups had increased dramatically (Curtin, Warner & Hedegaard, 2016). The rate of suicide among white women rose by 80%. This followed on the heels of a report that said life expectancy in the United States had decreased for the first time in history, largely due to a surprisingly high number of deaths among non–college-educated, middle-aged white men. Another study showed that in 2005, unmarried middle-aged men were 3.5 times more likely than married men to die from suicide; unmarried women, 2.8 times more likely than married women (Tavernise, 2016). With rising rates in opioid and heroin abuse, which increases risk of death, and an increase in suicide, the United States is facing earlier mortality among its citizens, but this trend is not irreversible if the nation acts to circumvent it.

THEORIES OF SUICIDE

The most influential study of suicide in the modern era was *Le Suicide* (Durkheim, 1897, 2006). Considered the "father" of modern sociology, Durkheim has had a lasting effect on the way suicide is studied and analyzed today. His theory was simple in its framework, but not without intellectual complexity and nuance. In society, people are integrated into social networks, such as the family or the church, and they are also socially regulated, so that those networks operate according to norms. As long as one is integrated into the norms of one's own group, no conflict exists. When an extreme imbalance exists, however, it can lead to suicide. For example, when social integration is too high, i.e., when the relationship to the group is the highest value, one might commit altruistic suicide. When it is too low, one might commit egoistic suicide. When the level of social regulation is too high, i.e., when oppression is pervasive, it can lead to fatalistic suicide. The classic example is that of slave suicide. If the regulation is too low, it can lead to anomic suicide, the type often described as a "downward spiral." Durkheim also divided anomic suicide into categories of economic (what is happening to the economy) and domestic (what is happening at home).

Kurt Cobain, leader of the grunge band Nirvana, can be cited as an example of anomic suicide. A musician at the height of his career, worshipped by his fans, living in the economically volatile city of Seattle in the 1990s, and a father for the first time, Cobain experienced rising expectations (an upward spiral) that provoked in him feelings of deep self-doubt (a downward spiral). He wondered in his suicide note why he did not feel exhilarated making music anymore. "The fact is, I can't fool you, any one of you. It simply isn't fair to you or me" ("Cobain Suicide Note," 1994). His external economic environment was at the time depressed, though he himself was becoming wealthy, and his domestic environment was undergoing the profound change of parenthood (Cameron, 2005). Cobain is said to have suffered from bipolar disorder and addiction problems, factors which escalate the risk of suicide.

Durkheim used his theories of anomie and egoism to explain familial suicide (in which more than one member of a family kills himself). The family of writer Ernest Hemingway illustrates familial suicide as well as social suicide and suicide clustering. Social suicides involve numbers greater than one, and suicide clusters include interaction between or exchanges among the members of a group. Ernest Hemingway, his father Clarence, brother Leicester, sister Ursula, and granddaughter Margaux all committed suicide. Two of Ernest's sons had histories of mental health problems and perhaps suicide attempts (accidents from high-risk behavior). Margaux Hemingway lamented that as a family they were "dysfunctional." They committed suicide by various means, but experienced similar levels of social disruption from divorce, mental illness, and risky behaviors (Maris, 1997).

Durkheim's theory has shaped or influenced many of the theories that followed it, but current theories about the motivation for suicide also have disciplinary differences, with sociology, psychology, psychiatry, and neurobiology offering various theories. As with the example of Kurt Cobain, individuals who kill themselves often do so for complex reasons in complicated circumstances, in various physiological and psychological states. Durkheim (1897, 2006) was surely correct to examine extrasocial factors such as the inclinations, often culturally specific, that people have to kill themselves, as well as the physical environment in which people live. Since Durkheim published his theories, others have addressed these and other questions to posit theories of their own.

Most suicidologists adhere to a few assumptions, although they can disagree on various points. Perhaps the most significant is the presumption that the majority of people who commit suicide suffer from a diagnosable (though often undiagnosed) mental disorder, and that these disorders increase the risk of suicide. A figure of 90% is often quoted on suicide prevention sites ("Law Center to Prevent Gun Violence," 2016). This does not mean that people who commit suicide are insane or are recognizable as being in a group the media calls "the mentally ill," but rather that they have an underlying condition such as major depressive disorder, bipolar disorder, borderline personality disorder, or schizophrenia. It is important to note that the mental illness, while present, may not be causal. Indeed, causes such as the need to escape from legal or financial problems may not be accompanied by a mental illness, though underlying psychological disorders may also exist. Suicide-related behaviors (suicidality) are normally classified into three categories: ideations, communications or actions. For suicide to occur there must be an intent to die and a self-initiated lethal act. Suicide "attempts" that have no self-initiation with an intent to die or are not near-lethal may not be considered suicide-related behavior by some theorists (Van Orden et al., 2010). Identifying the risk factors that expose underlying motivations to commit suicide is necessary for constructing a model of causation (etiology). For a theory of suicide to have practical application, risk factors for suicide have to be taken into account and evaluation of them applied in a way that is consistent with empirically documented research.

Risk factors, while making it more likely that suicide will occur, are not themselves causal explanations for why someone committed suicide. Some common risk factors are mental disorders and previous suicide attempts, family problems, physical illness, social isolation, grief, unemployment or other financial stress, job stress, and legal troubles. We examine many of these in the chapters that follow in relation to motivations. Theories, however, offer explanatory frameworks for why people commit suicide. A person might have a risk factor and never have a single suicidal thought or engage in any suicidal behavior, whereas another person may appear to lack any risk factors and still kill herself. Suicide completion is more than the sum of risk factors.

Theories of suicide both describe and explain suicidal action. We examine here the most commonly cited theories in current literature. We address all of the theories for which we found some evidence in our study's population, as well as a few current theories for which we did not find evidence. It is not possible to give an exhaustive list or description of the numerous theories that have been proposed, but many theories share characteristics. They focus on suicidal behavior (psychology), cognition (psychology), social or anthropological conditions (sociology and anthropology), or the brain (psychology and neurobiology). We present these not in chronological order, but moving from behavior and thought to society, and lastly to physiology.

PSYCHACHE THEORY

Shneidman (1993) published a seminal article in which he theorized that psychache, i.e., unbearable psychological pain that might be described as anguish, hurt, soreness, or aching, was the cause of suicidal behavior. He proposed that every suicidal act reflected some specific unfulfilled psychological need. This theory was long in the making, since his work with Farberow in the 1950s (Schneidman & Farberow, 1957). He opined that each person's particular need leading up to the decision to take one's life might vary, as would the level of psychache that one could bear. Shneidman believed that what is at the heart of suicidal ideation is the belief that a permanent cessation of pain is the only solution.

Shneidman's theory was evaluated in studies of both university students and homeless persons. High-risk undergraduates demonstrated that psychache was associated with suicidal ideation. For general suicidal ideation and suicide preparation, these results were maintained even when depression and hopelessness were statistically controlled. This research was the first large-sample longitudinal study that evaluated Shneidman's psychache causal model of suicidality in general and with high-risk groups, and the findings supported his theory. Similarly, in a study of homeless men, who are 10 times more likely to kill themselves than the general population, the findings revealed that psychache was a stronger predictor of suicidal ideation than was depression, hopelessness, or life meaning (Patterson & Holden, 2012; Troister, Davis, Lowndes, & Holden, 2013).

INTERPERSONAL THEORY OF SUICIDAL BEHAVIOR

The interpersonal theory of suicidal behavior (Van Orden et al., 2010) developed from Joiner's (2005) theory of why people die by suicide. It posited that two interpersonal constructs—thwarted belongingness and perceived burdensomeness (and subsequently, hopelessness about these states)—were necessary elements that, when combined with the capability to engage in suicidal behavior, were fatal. In other words, they had the motivation, and they had the means.

Thwarted belongingness consists of a person's belief that he or she has no meaningful relationships with others, either because they do not care or because, while they do care, they do not really understand the person or his or her experiences. Social connections are absent or have been destroyed. Van Orden et al. (2010) proposed that "the need to belong is the need central to the development of suicidal desire" (p. 582). Thwarted belongingness is "a dynamic cognitive-affective state, rather than a stable trait, that is influenced by both interpersonal and intrapersonal factors" (p. 582). The motivating action and the thought process, in other words, have to come together in order for one to attempt suicide. For example, while an individual is married and raising children, one's sense of belongingness may be high, only to be substantially lowered when children move away and the spouse dies. Loneliness, violent abuse, physical isolation, or discordant relationships may all contribute to feelings of thwarted belongingness.

Perceived burdensomeness is a person's twofold belief that he or she makes no worthwhile contributions to society and serves as a liability to others. The person feels expendable and thinks the group with which he or she associates, often the family, would be better off without him or her. They have low self-esteem and blame themselves for what goes wrong. Joiner's studies showed that mere thwarted belongingness was not enough to raise the risk of suicide, but coupled with a sense of burdensomeness, individuals desired suicide. They then only needed a means.

Many theorists have noted that the capacity to commit suicide is separate from the desire to engage in suicidal behavior. The capacity for suicide refers to an individual's ability to overcome three things: a natural fear of death, a strong biological desire for survival, and an aversion to pain. According to Van Orden et al. (2010), "3.3 percent of Americans seriously consider suicide … 1.0 percent develop a plan for suicide, and 0.6 percent attempt suicide … only 0.01 percent of Americans die by suicide" (p. 580). The current population of the United States is nearly 320 million. Thus 10,296,000 will think seriously about killing themselves, but only a tiny fraction will. In 2010, 38,368 suicides occurred. What aligned for those 38,368 individuals so that they actually died? For Van Orden et al., the answer lies in the presence of thwarted belongingness, perceived burdensomeness and the acquired capacity for suicide. Joiner's theory is compatible with Schneidman's, but it adds explanatory categories.

THWARTED DISORIENTATION CONTEXTS

Naroll (1970), an anthropologist, sought to integrate psychoanalytic theories that focused on individual and often idiosyncratic explanations of suicide with sociological theories that examined social contexts. He hypothesized that suicide would be more commonly experienced in a society where its members were "socially disoriented," that is, in those who "lack or lose basic social ties." He thought this would particularly apply to indigenous societies. Naroll's theory resembled Durkheim's, but when Naroll confronted the fact that not all socially disoriented people commit suicide, he had to look for a psychological factor that made suicide more likely for a socially disoriented individual. Naroll proposed that it was the individual's reaction to "thwarting disorientation contexts," such that either the person or others weakened the social ties that had once been there. For instance, in the case of a divorce, whether one initiated the separation or was forced to accept it, a "thwarting disorientation" could occur. The thwarting needed both a social disruption and a person or persons to have caused it. In thwarting disorientation contexts, some individuals commit protest suicide, which Naroll defined as voluntary suicide committed in such a way as to come to public notice. Impersonal, natural, or even cultural events were not contexts for thwarted disorientation, but because societies differ in the extent to which they provide thwarting disorientation contexts, they will also differ in their suicide rates (Lester & Gunn, 2012).

In the behavioral theories, being thwarted, i.e., not having one's desires or needs met as a result of one's own actions or someone else's, is at the root of explanations for suicidal behaviors. These theories are often complex, and while empirical studies have been done, the concept of "thwartedness" is frequently that of the researchers, not those with suicidal ideation. The idea that one's needs are not being met and therefore one must do something as a result also involves some sense of entitlement on the part of the suicidal person. If one examines suicidal communication, especially if one factors in race, class, gender, culture, and the intersection of those characteristics (Canetto & Lester, 1998), and mental disorders such as borderline personality disorder (Lieb, Zanarini, Schmahl, Linehan, & Bohus, 2004), entitlement is not often present. Entitlement is not something all persons possess equally (Lerner & Mikula, 2013). Different kinds of entitlement are found: normal (expectations based on abilities and efforts are reasonable), psychological (believing oneself more deserving than others), narcissistic (high self-appraisals and demands are unrealistic), and aggrieved (believing oneself entitled to more than one is receiving) (Exline & Zell, 2009). In some suicides, such as those involving school shootings in which the killers then kill themselves afterward, researchers have found a sense of aggrieved entitlement resulting from "the culture of hegemonic masculinity in the US" (Kalish & Kimmel, 2010, p. 454). Any theory of suicidal behavior must either examine and assess different senses of entitlement among different populations to account for variables in "thwartedness," or it must seek a more basic and perhaps less complex explanation for what is at the root of suicide. While numerically more white men commit suicide in western culture than women or racial minorities, not all white men whose needs or desires are unmet feel entitled to have them met. Without such entitlement, it is difficult to say that thwartedness is always a causal element in suicide.

COGNITIVE THEORIES OF SUICIDE

Although Schneidman proposed a behavioral theory of suicide, he also identified cognitive constriction as a common cognitive state of those who kill themselves, preventing individuals in overwhelming pain from perceiving ways to solve their problems other than by death. Cognitive constriction occurs when a person focuses only on the pain he or she is feeling, or on the unbearable circumstances of life, such that no other part of life is visible. This can manifest as tunnel vision or dichotomous thinking. Not only is thinking narrowed, but it becomes centered on absolutes. To the person contemplating suicide, this thinking seems logical, because they can see no alternatives. It "makes sense" (Ellis, 2006). For example, one man in our study who left a note listed the many things that had gone wrong in his life. "I have tried to settle my problems by all other means ... but they have the same outcome, disappointme-This ... is the straw that broke the camels back ... my pain is just too strong." He became unable to see any option for the future that would not involve pain, so he resolved to die.

Although committing suicide takes action, it also involves thought, whether that thought involves an impulse or careful planning. Beck and

Lester (1976) developed a suicide intent scale to measure suicidal ideation in those who attempted suicide. Drawing on Beck's research about the relationship between depression and suicide, psychologist Baumeister (1990) theorized that escape was a primary motivation for suicide. When a person who has high expectations for himself or in a situation becomes enmeshed in life circumstances which are overwhelming, from stress or an insoluble problem or from a setback from which recovery is unlikely, the person may become suicidal. Baumeister's theory was nuanced. He argued that what caused the suicide was an attempt to avoid painful self-awareness by trying to reach "a state of cognitive deconstruction (constricted temporal focus, concrete thinking, immediate or proximal goals, cognitive rigidity, and rejection of meaning)" (Baumeister, 1990, p. 90). That deconstruction then allowed the person to engage in irrational and disinhibited thought. Once a person reached that state, suicide became possible as the escape from both the world and oneself.

The thought processes that underlay suicide, according to most cognitive theories, involve mentality, or a mode of thought, rather than intellect, which is the ability to reason or understand. In other words, when psychologists talk about cognition with respect to suicide, they are looking at a pattern of thought rather than its substance. All concur that such patterns of constricted thought are faulty. In modern, post-Enlightenment western philosophy, suicide is generally considered morally wrong and an irrational act. Thus, the idea that suicide could be rational meets with great resistance. In the 1980s and 1990s, scholarly articles appeared that raised questions about whether suicide could ever be rational. The trend has only grown stronger, though the proponents of rational suicide almost always limit their arguments to physician-assisted suicide cases that involve terminally ill patients who are cognitively aware and mentally competent. In these scenarios, patients are making the decision to die based on information and a rational assessment of their quality of life (Ho, 2014).

Other cognitive-behavioral theories employ a sociological model. Bandura's social learning theory (1986) proposed that learning occurs through observation and imitation, and suicide is thus a learned behavior from observation, imitation, or modeling, which as such involves attention, memory, and motivation. People both respond to stimuli and interpret them through observation, judgment, and self-response. In Bandura's classic research, children who saw another child punished for beating a Bobo doll did not beat the doll when they were provided the opportunity. Conversely, children who saw another child get rewarded for beating the doll imitated that behavior. In terms of suicide, individuals who observe someone rewarded for committing suicide (e.g., escaping pain, having a large memorial) may be more predisposed to suicide. Many cognitive theories combine with behavioral theories. Like Bandura and Schneidman, these theorists are searching for practical means to prevent suicide, so they focus on both thought and action.

HEREDITARY AND BIOLOGICAL THEORIES OF SUICIDE

For millennia, people have wondered whether heredity and biology played a role in suicide. When intergenerational members of one family killed themselves, like the Hemingways, it was natural for people to wonder about some transmitted inherited condition or acquired characteristic that led to suicide. Nowadays one might be more likely to hear people ponder whether a genetic predisposition might be present, or whether suicide is coded in the DNA. While popular misconceptions about heredity and biology abound, scientists have explored the question seriously about whether suicidality can be predicted by our physiology.

Several ways for biology to play a role in suicide are possible. A genetic defect or a physiological malfunction, like a neurological problem, might create the right condition for suicidality. Guintivano et al. (2014) argued that 80% of suicide, suicidal behavior and suicidal ideation comes from a variation in the region of the spindle and kinetochore associated complex subunit 2's (SKA2) genetic and epigenetic expression. They found that people who killed themselves had a lower expression of the SKA2 gene as well as a lower level of cortisol, a hormone which, among other things, helps the body manage stress. The study was immediately decried by Berezin (2014), who found the idea that one could take a blood test to detect suicidality to be absurd. Research into genetic influences continues but often to investigate the relationship between maladaptive behaviors and mental disorders. Thus, genetic research into the serotonergic system, for instance, which is implicated in mood disorders, may be helpful in understanding suicide, but not without also knowing about a person's environment, such as a history of trauma or abuse. Often teenage suicide is driven by impulsive or aggressive behavior, which may be related to abnormalities in serotonergic mechanisms. Dopamine has also been associated with impulsivity (Zai et al., 2012).

Another biological theory is that of de Catanzaro (1995). His ethological and sociobiological understanding of suicide first developed in the early 1980s but is rooted in ideas from the 1940s. De Catanzaro proposed that human suicide is an adaptive behavioral strategy that becomes increasingly likely to occur whenever there is a confluence of social, ecological, developmental, and biological variables factoring into the evolutionary equation. He also hypothesized that a threshold intelligence is necessary for suicidality, such that intelligence and suicide mortality would be positively related. He theorized that human brains are designed by natural selection to prefer ending one's own life when faced with conditions that spell doom, because this was best for our suicidal ancestors' overall genetic interests. Some studies have corroborated the hypothetical link between IQ and suicide, but others have either not found it or remain skeptical (Templer, Connelly, Lester, Arikawa, & Mancuso, 2007; Voracek, 2005).

While few experts adhere completely to de Catanzaro's theory today, there are proponents of other forms of biological theories. Rubinstein (1986) argued for a stress-diathesis theory. He proposed a biocultural theory of suicide, predicated on understanding the specific situational stressors and cultural factors that created a predisposition for suicide among certain vulnerable individuals. He hypothesized that some people are born with a genetic predisposition to mental illness and/or suicide, but not all of them will actually develop that mental illness or kill themselves. Others will experience situations in their lives that increase the likelihood that they will develop the mental illness or take their own lives. If their life situation is serious enough, the combination of environment and biology will lead them to the condition for which they were predisposed. Neither mental illness nor suicide was thus inevitable, but stressors increased their likelihood.

STUDYING SPECIAL POPULATIONS

Many of the behavioral theories and some of the biological theories of suicide have evolved out of studies of white men of European ancestry. In the last few decades, scholars have tried to examine the theories with respect to particular populations, including women, veterans, and LGBTQ (often without racial differentiation, although whites frequently predominate), African Americans and Native Americans. History, cultural experiences, and values shape suicide. Thus, the motivations that appear in one group may not be the same for those in another population. More importantly though, even if the motivations are the same, the cultural responses to suicide and its victims may vary, creating a very different suicide profile for particular communities. Much theoretical and empirical work remains to be done with respect to these and other understudied populations. If history and existing theories have taught us anything thus far, it is that some aspects of suicide are timeless, whether they are risk factors associated with human emotions or seasonal changes that affect mood, while other aspects vary with time and place. Finding a way to respond to the variable factors with preventive measures is a challenge, but by establishing and recognizing those elements which are predictable, we can achieve protocols for prevention.

In the upcoming chapters, we will see how some of these theories manifested in the 1280 people in our study. We will also examine in more depth those who are in special populations. We will propose a map for understanding patterns of suicide and a means of assessing risk, in addition to laying out a national agenda for prevention of suicide.

remain skeptical (Templer, Connally, Laster, Arikawa, & Thomas, Vasocek, 2005).

While few experts adhere completely to de Catanzaro's theory, today there are proponents of other forms of that idea.

Findings

Mike made entries on his calendar for each day of the week preceding his suicide, starting with "maybe" on the first day, several days of "not yet" and "yet" on the day he shot himself in the head. Mike had struggled with depression for years and had twice attempted suicide by slashing his wrists. His depression began after Mike was involved in an accident in which a child was killed. It was not his fault, but he always felt guilty and began to express his desire to kill himself. One morning he left to run some errands and when he had not returned by late that evening, his wife called the police. They found him in a shower stall at his workplace with a note addressed to his son which read, "Be a better Dad than me." He also left a note for his wife which simply said, "I love you."

DECIPHERING 1280 CASES

Considerable debate has taken place about using notes that victims of suicide leave behind to help us to understand suicidal behavior, since note writers may not be comparable to non-note writers. If they are not comparable, then conclusions made about note writers, based on information obtained from their notes, could not be generalized to non-note writers. Early research comparing note writers to non-note writers yielded conflicting findings. This was likely due to small sample sizes and cultural differences since the research was conducted in a variety of countries. More recent research suggests very few differences, if any, between note writers and non-note writers.

In a 2015 study, using a comprehensive state-wide database with information available on 2936 suicide victims, 18.75% of individuals left a suicide note. When comparing demographics and circumstances of the two groups, no differences were found between note writers and non-note writers (Cerel, Moore, Brown, van de Venne, & Brown, 2015). Demographics included information such as age, gender, race, marital status, and place at the time of injury. Circumstances of their suicides included mental and physical health problems and interpersonal relationship issues. Similarly, in another study comparing 621 cases of suicide on 40 variables, note writers did not differ from non-note writers, except that note writers were more likely to live alone and make threats of suicide (Callanan & Davis, 2009).

The coroner provided us with information related to 1664 cases. Each case had basic demographic information, such as age, gender, and method of suicide included in a spreadsheet and/or an investigator's report. We deleted 384 cases from the set the coroner provided for various reasons. In some cases we were missing a case file or critical information about the suicide or the cause of death was determined to be an accident or homicide. In other cases, the report said a note was left but we were not provided a copy of the note. We had a copy of the note for a small subset of individuals (174 or 14%) while 1106 individuals did not leave a note. (See appendices for a detailed methodology and a copy of the coding sheet we used in the study.)

Our ratio of note writers to non-note writers is comparable to what other researchers have found, but depending on the demographics of the population studied, one will find varying estimates regarding the percentage of suicide victims who leave notes. Rates range between 10 and 43% of suicide victims in the United States (Sinyor, Schaffer, Hull, Peisah, & Shulman, 2015). In a Tasmanian study, 33% of the sample left a suicide note. Researchers found that those who wrote a note were more often engaged in interpersonal conflicts but at the time of the suicide were alone. They had little medical or psychiatric care but were in psychological distress. They also tended to choose the most lethal methods for killing themselves (Haines, Williams, & Lester, 2011). Time and place are relevant as well, as percentages of note writers may be affected by literacy rates, cultural differences, and access to writing materials. Approximately 16% of all the people who committed suicide were note writers in a 1960 British study of Wales (Capstick, 1960), but in a 2006 Japanese study, 30% left notes (Kuwabara et al., 2006). Age may also be relevant; e.g., the elderly leave fewer notes than adolescents (Salib, Cawley, & Healy, 2002). In our study we had a population that spanned age groups, that had access to public education and was literate, and was diverse as to gender, race, ethnicity, and class. We had a number of people who killed themselves as a result of interpersonal conflict, but we also saw many who died to escape pain or situations.

Coroners obtain information for investigative purposes, not for research purposes (Rivlin, Fazel, Marzano, & Hawton, 2013). No standardized reporting format exists. The information collected even in one jurisdiction can vary. Some reports may be minimal, verifying the death and its suspected cause, while others contain extensive details about the weather, the condition and position of the body, and the mental, physical, and interpersonal history of the victim. These differences are due not only to investigator style, but also to the availability of information. We had basic information on almost every person. Gender was always recorded in the files or on the spreadsheet, but occasionally race or ethnicity was absent. Information that might have to be obtained from an informant, such as history of alcohol abuse, might not be included. If no mention was made of this type of information in the spreadsheet or investigator's report, we recorded it as "unknown." Reports were sometimes suggestive and might say, "the individual drank two bottles of wine before shooting himself," but unless investigators specifically mentioned a history of alcohol abuse, we recorded it as "unknown." This means that our numbers are likely underestimates of some information about our victims' experiences, because it was simply not available. Although cases with just investigator reports offered less information than the cases with notes, they provided a clearer sense of suicide patterns because of their sheer volume. In fact, we found, consistent with other research comparing note writers to non-note writers, virtually no differences (Callanan & Davis, 2009; Cerel et al., 2015).

We used the same coding form to record information about both note writers and non-note writers. The only exception was that for note writers, an additional section is included related to the characteristics of the note (see Appendix B, Coding Information). The basic coding form was divided into four sections: demographics, previous history, characteristics of the suicide, and motivation. Demographics included information such as the day of the suicide, season, living situation, and occupation of the victim. Previous history focused on legal, financial, or interpersonal problems, physical illness, drug and alcohol abuse, and previous suicide attempts. The location of the suicide, as well as the type of trauma, was noted in the characteristics of the suicide section. Finally, a motivation for the suicide was selected out of 11 main categories. In total, we examined 116 characteristics related to note writers and 33 characteristics related to non-note writers. We were able to compare note writers to non-note writers on the latter characteristics.

Since very few demographic differences between note writers and non-note writers were found, we combined the information for non-note writers and note writers to represent overall findings. When differences were found, however, we provided information for each group separately.

The average age of our victims was 45 with a range from 11 years old to 94 years old. In 2014, people ages 45 to 64 years old and those 85 years or older had approximately the same rate of suicide ("Suicide Statistics," 2014). The vast majority (92%) were Caucasian. These findings are virtually identical to Cerel et al.'s (2015), who found an average age of 46 years and approximately 96% of their sample was Caucasian.

In our sample, it was more common for a man to commit suicide (82%) than a woman. In 2013, 77.9% of all people who committed suicide were men. Moreover, white males accounted for 70% of all suicides ("Suicide

Statistics," 2014). More women in our sample wrote notes (20%) than men (12%). Some researchers have found the reverse pattern for note writing and gender, with men leaving more notes than women, while still others have found no differences. Cohen and Fiedler (1974) found 26% of women and 19.1% of men left notes while Cerel et al.'s (2015) results were consistent with 24% of women and 17% of men leaving notes. However, Cohen and Fiedler found no differences in the content of notes left by men and women nor were there differences in the content of notes left by men and women in our sample.

Just over 3% of our victims were identified as veterans, which appears low given the fact that a major US Air Force base is located in the vicinity so there is a high population of veterans in the area. Other researchers have found that veterans represented 19% of their sample (Cerel et al., 2015). Investigators of our cases may not have had access to veteran status, or they may not have thought it was worth noting. It is also possible that the presence of the military base was a source of support for veterans. In no case did anyone identify the impact of active duty as a major factor in his or her decision to commit suicide.

The most common methods used by individuals in our sample to kill themselves were firearms (51%) followed by asphyxiation (20%) and overdose (14%). Similarly, in 2013, the Center for Disease Control (CDC) found the most common mechanisms for suicide were firearms (51.5%), followed by asphyxia (24.5%) and poisoning (16.1%). The percentages in our study represented both note writers and non-note writers. Interestingly, Cerel et al. (2015) found overdosing and hanging to be equal among note writers while 18% of non-note writers hanged themselves and 11% used poisoning.

Most individuals in our cases killed themselves at home (74%) in their bedrooms (23.25%). Cerel et al. (2015) also found 77% of note writers and 83.15% of non-note writers killed themselves at home. When they did not kill themselves at home, they frequently were found in parks or cars. Perhaps the most unusual location was a church altar. We could identify the living situation for approximately two-thirds of the victims and they were fairly evenly split between living alone and living with a spouse, although we found that note writers were slightly more likely to live alone.

The highest percentage of suicides in our cases occurred in June (10%) with the lowest percentage (7%) in May. However, for note writers, both January and June were equally risky months. Note writers were more likely to kill themselves on Wednesday while non-note writers were more likely to kill themselves on Monday. Although the highest percentages of suicides occurred on the ninth and twentieth of the month, for note writers, the first day of the month held the highest risk.

There were virtually no differences between the percentage of note writers and non-note writers who expressed suicidal threats (19%) or ideation (14%) or had prior attempts (18%). These numbers are consistent with Cerel et al. (2015) who found approximately 19% of their sample expressed suicidal intent and 13% had a history of attempts. When added together, though, this means that half the victims had demonstrated or voiced their potential for self-harm. Often investigators noted that friends and relatives did not take the threats seriously. These family and friends may have been overcome by the chronic nature of the threats, as some individuals had threatened suicide for many years and had made numerous attempts. For others, suicide was more of an acute situation in which they were simply overcome by recent life events.

Almost a fourth (28%) of the sample had identified substance abuse issues, and 20% used substances just prior to their suicides. Callanan and Davis (2009) also found evidence of drugs or alcohol at the scene for 24% of note writers. The number dropped for non-note writers to 14%. Ten percent of our sample had been involved in some form of physically abusive situation in the past such as domestic violence, child abuse or sexual assault. However, non-note writers were more likely to have perpetrated the abuse than note writers and conversely, note writers were more likely to have been the victims of abuse than non-note writers.

Some variables existed between note writers and non-note writers that looked like they differed, but this was probably anecdotal. For example, it appears as if note writers had a greater percentage of depression (46%) than did non-note writers (37%), but since we had a note, we had more information available on note writers. Unless the investigator identified the victim's specific mental illness, we could not record it, so the percentage of depression for non-note writers is probably a bit higher than our data indicates. Other researchers have found 40–59% of individuals who commit suicide are depressed (Callanan & Davis, 2009; Cerel et al., 2015; Sinyor et al., 2015).

Given that a large percentage of the individuals in our sample were depressed, it is not surprising that the most common motivation for suicide (70%) was to escape painful life circumstances, such as physical or psychological illness. One-third of our victims had significant physical illnesses and over half (51%) were identified as having psychological illnesses. These numbers were slightly higher for note writers. Callanan and Davis (2009) also found approximately 28% of their sample mentioned long-term health problems.

The next most common motivation for suicide in our cases was interpersonal relationships (23%). Thirty-nine percent of our cases were identified as having interpersonal problems, and this number rose to 48% for note writers. These numbers are consistent with prior research findings indicating that approximately one-third of victims have interpersonal problems with either an intimate or nonintimate partner. Cerel et al. (2015) found that approximately 26% of their sample had intimate partner problems and another 5% had relationship problems that did not involve an intimate partner.

While reading the cases, we encountered a number in which the victim killed himself or herself in front of someone else, often an intimate partner. These witnessed suicides were not cases in which someone else was simply in the home, but rather ones in which the victim intentionally committed the act in front of someone. We found that 12% of victims killed themselves in front of someone, but that note writers were less likely to kill themselves in front of someone (3%) as compared to non-note writers (13%). The act of killing oneself in front of another was itself a form of communication, and thus a note may not have seemed necessary. Many of these cases also involved drug or alcohol use; e.g., one 20-year-old man had been drinking heavily when he found a gun in the home, said "Happy Birthday" to his mother, and shot himself in front of her. These cases will be explored more in this chapter on interpersonal issues as a motivation for suicide.

SUICIDE NOTES

Given the very few differences between note writers and non-note writers, it is likely the notes are representative of the sentiments and characteristics of both groups. Suicide notes are written for several purposes, including providing some explanation for the choice of suicide. Many notes were written for the clear purpose of reassuring survivors that the suicide was not their fault and that there was nothing they could have done to prevent it. Writers of these notes often apologized for the pain that would be caused by their loved one finding them. In cases in which no note was left, victims often took care to ensure that a family member would not be the one to find them by choosing a location such as a motel or park where a stranger would be the one to discover the body.

For the suicide note writers, this planned act of composing a final communication to others enabled them to communicate to survivors their emotional state and provided an opportunity for the individuals to justify their actions and put their affairs in order. Perhaps most importantly, many note writers attempted to mitigate the emotional burden that would be felt by survivors. Some note writers may have viewed the note as a means to have some element of control over others.

The content of the notes sometimes provided evidence that the suicide was not impulsive. These notes described the writer as having thought about suicide for days, weeks, months, or even years before carrying it out, and a substantial number described previous suicide attempts. Some notes included "to do" lists of steps leading to the suicide (e.g., "2:15-Take a shower; 3 PM-Crush pills") and a methodical check-off of items that were completed for as long as the writer could manage. Calendars were occasionally used to mark progress toward the suicide. One man wrote the phrase "Whack bang" on the date he shot himself and "funeral" on the date he believed his services would be held.

The medium of the suicide notes sometimes provided information about the writer or sent messages about the act. Suicide notes on hotel or motel stationery usually indicated the location of the suicide, and suicide notes on business or professional association note pads spoke of the writer's affiliations. Occasionally the medium used was simply a reflection of what was available to the writer. One young man wrote his note on a coffee filter; another spray painted his message on the floor of the barn where he killed himself; a woman wrote her message in soap on a bathroom mirror; and a father wrote the names of his children on his shirt with a magic marker. Sometimes the medium relayed its own message. With some obvious symbolism, one note was written on the reverse side of an antisuicide contract with a therapist where the writer had agreed to take various precautionary steps to counteract acute thoughts of suicide. Another was written on a Christmas card, leaving us to wonder if this was simply the only paper handy to the writer or if it was instead a statement that Christmas had been a disappointment.

Modern media were occasionally used for the final suicide communication. Some notes were generated on a computer and left beside the body, or a handwritten note was left that referred to a suicide note on an office computer. Some people announced their suicidal intentions in an e-mail or text message. Occasionally a packet containing audiotapes, videotapes, or electronic files was left at the scene or mailed to a family member or friend. We did not always have access to these "notes" but we included the ones that were in written form in the pool of people who left notes in an effort to distinguish characteristics of those who produced a final written communication and those who did not.

Some of the notes became difficult to decipher because of grammar or punctuation errors, misspellings or illegible handwriting. For individuals who had ingested substances, handwriting often became illegible as the substances took effect. The note from one person who had ingested 1.5 liters of vodka became less and less coherent until the note abruptly ended. Occasionally, parts of notes were illegible due to blood stains or spatter on the note.

The content of the notes sometimes gave us glimpses into the personality or talents of the writer. A few writers used handwriting or printing that was very precise, stylized, and even artistic. An occasional note was illustrated with drawings, usually depicting the writer's death and a few were sprinkled with humor (3%). One 39-year-old man who struggled with substance abuse issues wrote, "My body can go to science maybe they can find a cure for cirrossiss so people can drink with impunity

Ha!Ha!" Mike, the man discussed at the beginning of the chapter, apparently timed his suicide with the temperature of his beer and said, "Beer is getting warm. See ya." Humor is not common in notes. Foster (2003) also found only 5% of notes included humor.

We created our coding sheet for the notes after we had read a sample of notes and the previous research findings of other scholars. We then met as a team to generate a draft of the coding sheet which included characteristics of the notes but also the thoughts and feelings expressed by the note writers. We included any mention of life struggles or precipitating events and instructions and advice for survivors.

We tried to be as precise in our coding of notes as we had been with the demographics. Unless the note writer specifically mentioned a feeling, we did not record it. For example, if someone talked about how depressed s/he was but did not say, "I feel so sad," it was recorded as someone who was depressed but not as someone who was sad. We took this approach, because it was easy to read feelings into the notes and we wanted to be as objective as possible. However, this strategy likely led to underestimates of the feelings expressed and characteristics in the notes. Still, that said, our findings are consistent with other research.

OVERALL STRUCTURE OF THE NOTES

We examined a total of 350 notes from 174 writers. Most individuals (68%) left one note and an additional 14% left two notes. However, one individual left 20 notes and three more left over 10 notes. Since we were examining all 350 notes, the numbers following refer to the percentage of notes, not the percentage of individuals. Approximately one-fourth (26%) of notes were dated and about two-thirds were signed. Only a small percentage typed or word-processed their notes (7%) and only two individuals mailed them. Some quoted from various sources (6%), such as literature or music, to express how they were feeling.

Most notes contained organized thoughts throughout (92%) with a clear beginning, middle, and end, even when they were under 25 words long (15%). For example, one fiercely independent 91-year-old man, who was facing declining health, wrote, "To much pain. Can't take it no more. Love You All. God Bless." The majority (59%) wrote notes that were relatively short (26–300 words long). Sanger and Veach (2008) found 58% of their sample provided explanations for their actions and approximately two-thirds of ours did so as well. These could be brief, "Had a good life. It's my time to go," or detailed. Julian, a 25-year-old, chronically depressed man, whom we also discuss in Chapter 7, Severe Mental Illness, provided a comprehensive description of the rationale, preparation and timeline for his suicide. He listed over 20 reasons why he should die but had only one reason to live. His reasons ranged from politics to his broken phone to Britney Spears. He included pages and pages of his own poetry that he said should be made available to anyone who wanted to read it. He made a list, printed mostly in capital letters on lined notebook paper,

IF YOU DON'T DIE IN THE NEXT 48 HOURS YOU MUST:
GET A PHONE,
GET A JOB,
PUBLISH THE ZINE AND DISTRIBUTE IT,
FIND A WAY TO LIVE WITHOUT HOPE OR PRIDE
          TEN YEARS FROM NOW YOU WOULD INEVITABLY BE
in an insane asylum
in prison
drunk in a gutter
<u>unhappier</u>

Once individuals could justify their actions, and they were convinced suicide was the solution to their problems, they often developed thought constriction or tunnel vision (24%). Their thinking became rigid and narrow. Len, whose marriage and job had both ended, stated,

> However, this is no longer a matter of choice. Death has transitioned from an enticing notion to an irresistible compulsion. I simply abhor my very being—my tortured, twisted, weird, unfulfilling existence; and so I can <u>be</u> no more. I just have to turn off my thoughts—I <u>have</u> to. This is euthanasia, pure and simple. They shoot horses, don't they? ... But instead focus on the fact that I thought about it (suicide) far more days than I didn't and resisted on the basis of the moral implications and what it would do to the people I love ... My thoughts have become completely unbearable and I can't think of any other way to escape them.

Similar to the concept of tunnel vision is dichotomous thinking where an individual views him or herself and the world in black and white. Foster (2003) found in 12% of the notes in his sample the note writer discussed suicide as the only solution. In the notes in our sample, when dichotomous thinking was expressed (9% of notes), they often referred to the limited options individuals saw to change their life situations. One young woman's note reflected this dualism when she said, "I love you mom & Dad. I just couldn't take this anymore and I saw no other way out. Sorry!!!" At times, the combination of constriction and dichotomous thinking made it appear that the individual did not have control over his or her choice to commit suicide. Some individuals wrote a version of "I have no regrets only that I could not finish my life." It was as if someone or something else had control of their destinies, that death was inevitable. Thought constriction and dichotomous thinking were identified in approximately one-fourth of the notes. However, many of the notes simply were not long enough to include this pattern. More importantly, the intent of the note was not to convey one's pattern of thinking as much as it was to convey a message, thought, or feeling. Nevertheless, from the tone of the notes, it is clear that a vast majority of individuals saw no other way out of their situations.

Approximately two-thirds of the note writers addressed their notes to a specific person or persons, generally family members such as children (35%), parents (33%), spouses/partners (32%), siblings (13%), or other family (25%). One person wrote a note to his dog. Sometimes the note was addressed to a generic audience (18%) but for 53% of the notes, we could not determine the relationship between the note writer and the addressee and 5% had no addressee. The notes had a great variety of openings, but some similarities existed. Whether addressed to a specific person or not, many began,

"If your reading this it is probably not a good sign."

"If you are reading this letter that means I have decided to end my life because I feel Julie is going to file for divorce in September."

"Well if you're reading this, then I must be dead. Kind a hard to tell since I never had a life."

"I regret to inform you if you are reading this letter it is because I am dead."

CONTENT OF THE NOTES

Great diversity appeared in the content of the notes, and although the frequency of a certain topic varied, the content about that topic was often remarkably similar. In general, the notes are divided into three sections: very frequently occurring content (over 50% of notes), frequently occurring content (approximately a third of notes), and less frequently occurring content (less than 10%). However, when constructs are related, such as love, apology, blame, and forgiveness, they are discussed together, despite the fact that they may not occur with the same frequency.

VERY FREQUENTLY OCCURRING CONTENT IN THE NOTES

Love and Relationships

"Sorry I could not be more help to you but I will always love you both very very much. Please forgive me. Love Dad."

Love for others was clearly the most predominant message in the notes (76%). Even the 91-year-old man mentioned previously expressed love for others in his 13-word suicide note. Arguably, expressing love may have been a key motivation for writing the note. We will discuss motivation for the suicide in future chapters, but motivation for writing the note is often completely independent of the reason for the suicide. The vast majority of note writers wanted their loved ones to know that they had loved them.

Expressions of love for those left behind are common in suicide notes. Foster (2003) found 60% of the notes he examined had expressions of love for those left behind. Sanger and Veach (2008) found 48.6% of the notes in their sample specifically stated "I love you." Even though 76% of our sample expressed love for others, only 14% of note writers talked about being loved by others and 9% felt unlovable. The disparity between feeling love for others and feeling loved by others was disconcerting. The note writers were either trying to highlight that they did not feel loved or they simply forgot to mention it. Of course, many notes were written when the writer was extremely distressed because he or she had made a decision to kill himself or herself. Perhaps they thought it was too obvious to mention or simply forgot. Yet, some notes were written in the months or weeks leading up to the suicide, when they had plenty of time to consider the content. Moreover, note writers remembered to mention seemingly insignificant details in their notes (maintenance on the car). They were clearly addressing that which was important to them in the notes. However, what they did not say in the notes may be as important as what they did say. Only 14% of note writers said they felt loved by others, with 86% of note writers not mentioning feeling or being loved by others. It seems unlikely that this was simply an oversight but was rather a message they wanted to communicate.

A few note writers directly addressed not being loved but did not speculate about why they were not loved. One person said,

> If I hurt anyone, which I probably didn't, I'm sorry. It's just that it's my time to go now. As I sit here in this empty house I realize I am all alone. I don't have anybody. Nobody loves me; Nobody cares about me. I love you all but you don't love me … I came into this world naked and I will leave it naked. Forgive me, I Love You All.

Another wrote, "I really was never understood by anyone. I was <u>always</u> always <u>so so</u> alone." Although he did not specifically mention not being loved, one man made a list of all the people to contact after his death. The list was not very long, and he reflected, "Gee, that's a damn short list for someone who's been on this earth 52 years, isn't it? Kind of demonstrates the emptiness of my existence, no?"

Eleven percent indicated they were lonely which is similar to other studies (Foster, 2003; Sanger & Veach, 2008). Yet, some of these individuals isolated themselves. In his note, one middle-aged man talked about losing the love of his life in his twenties and then isolating himself from friends and family. He always declined invitations to family events, yet in his note, he thanked his cousin for all her support and extolled her virtues as a friend, parent and relative. He wrote,

> I've been <u>terribly</u> lonely and each passing year has brought more pain and despaire. Loneliness is a very bad place for a loving person like me to exist. I chose not to endure anymore. Please forgive me, please understand … I only wish I had

taken time to be part of and with your girls as they grew up ... I have no one to do it for me so I have prearranged my own funeral.

Although his cousin had reached out numerous times, he would not return cards or calls.

Another middle-aged man, who had lost his job and become a hermit, recognized his isolation but apparently did not understand that he could change it. He stated, "I am very sorry I did not reach out for help. That was stupid!" Others discuss their intentional isolation. One 25-year-old man who had not seen his mother and sister in six years wrote,

> This is hard because I know there are people who care and love me, yet I feel so alone, so isolated from the rest of the world ... Now I don't imagine to many people who will be affected by this but I sure there are a few. And to these people I am truly, truly sorry. I never meant to hurt anybody. I think that why I kept so isolated from the population, I don't want to hurt anymore than I have to.

Another man's journal entries detailed the months leading up to his suicide. One thing on his to-do list was to alienate himself from his friends. He intentionally started arguments with them and said things that would hurt them. He wrote,

> Trying to get rid of my friends is a heart breaking yet happy time ... .[talks about how he is doing this] I won't hear from them for a while. Just a few more people to go, then my family, then I will be free. FREE!! Ditch the bitch and fuck that life, there's no man happy that has a wife.

Although in some cases it appeared that the note writer had no support network, most had numerous people in their lives. Since the majority of note writers addressed their notes to a specific person or persons, presumably those were people they loved or for whom they felt an attachment. It is certainly possible these people did not love or express affection for the note writers. There are other explanations as to why note writers omitted expressions of love from others or feeling loved by others from the notes. Since some of the notes were very short, the writers only addressed a few basic sentiments such as their own love for others, a justification and, occasionally, instructions. The lengthier note writers may have intentionally left out feeling loved by others, but why remains unknown.

Others took responsibility for not being loved. Perhaps they were simply incapable of accepting the love. One woman who was sexually abused as a child said to her husband, "You loved me well. So well. In the end I couldn't love myself." Another woman knew she was loved but it was not enough. She stated, "Please make sure everyone knows it was NOT THEIR FAULT!!! I was loved and I know it. You were all there for me but I guess I needed more than any human being could be asked to give. I honestly and truly love you all." Still others had been in a very loving situation but lost the love of family and friends, frequently due to addictions. One writer with a gambling addiction put it quite succinctly, "I also didn't want to be such a big loser—but that isn't the case. I am a loser, I have lost the most precious things in life. I have lost my family, I have lost my pride, I have lost my own dignity." Even for the 14% who did feel loved by others, it was often not related to their suicides; it simply could not compensate for the pain or strife they felt. One man wrote, "I love everybody I just hate the world and the way people treat each other so I'm finished. Maybe its for the better."

Given the emphasis on love in the notes, it was not surprising to find a focus on relationships. Although some notes thanked partners for their love and support, over a third of the notes discussed interpersonal problems (39%) or the loss of a relationship (17%). The subsequent chapters on motivational categories will explain in more detail how characteristics of the notes fit in with overall motivational patterns. Chapter 3 focuses on interpersonal relationships as a motivation for suicide. Although the concept of unrequited love as it relates to romantic relationships will be discussed in that chapter, reading the notes leaves one with a sense of overall unrequited love, not just in their relationships, but in their lives.

Apology, Blame, and Forgiveness

"I don't think there's really any right way to start this except by saying I'm sorry."

Foster (2003) found 74% of his notes contained apologies or shame. However, Sanger and Veach (2008) found only 25.4% of notes contained apologies, but 33.3 asked for forgiveness. Given their professed love for others it was not surprising that many individuals felt a need to apologize for their actions. Most people did not want to hurt those they loved. Apologies were sometimes about the actual suicidal act, "If you hate me for what I've done. It's understandable but know that I am so, so, so truly sorry. Just remember that I love you all and will never hurt you again," or "Very sorry to put you through this." Others apologized for some aspect of the act. One elderly man who was in hospice care wrote, "Sorry, I just can't live this way any longer—I love all of you-sorry I lied about having a gun-Good bye Dad."

Apologies were not limited to the specific act of suicide. Many note writers apologized for actions throughout their lives. One man who struggled with alcoholism wrote, "I am sorry, I know sorry doesn't seem to have meaning anymore, but I am sorry I could not have been a better person." Often apologies were directed toward specific persons (43%). Most of one man's entire note was an apology directed toward his wife and children. He said, "I'm sorry for all I have done, to hurt you and the girls, and boys. Please forgive me. I love you." Other note writers (32%)

offered general apologies such as, "I'm sorry for tearing up so many lives. I've lost my way and don't know what else to do. Tell everyon that a man can mess up. Life is a bitch. You live and you love and sometimes its too much."

Apologies were often intertwined with other thoughts and feelings such as gratitude. Some focused on the inevitability of the suicide. One note writer said,

> To all those who offered support & compassion to me-and those who believed in me—I am forever grateful. In truth, you have kept me alive longer than I would have been w/o your support. There was nothing more you could have done for me. I understand that you are angry for what I've done. I have betrayed you, let you down in the worst ways. I am deeply, deeply sorry.

For others, apologies were tied in with the justification for the act. One individual said, "I'm sorry my mind and body couldn't take it anymore."

Sanger and Veach (2008) found 17.4% absolved others of blame or blamed themselves. In our sample, a similar percentage absolved others from blame (20%). One 29-year-old woman who was in the midst of a divorce and had suffered from lifelong depression said,

> It's not anyone's fault. I've been fucked up from the beginning. I've never been OK, I've never been good enough. I've never been normal ... I feel disgusting. I hate myself. I don't know how to change and I'll never ever be OK. Or normal. Or just acceptable. It's definitely no one's fault. Just I've had all I can bear.

Another man who was having financial and marital problems said, "This is nobody's fault but my own. I was out of control and didn't realize what I was doing until I crashed." Sanger and Veach (2008) found 8% of victims blamed others for their actions, similar to our findings (13%). Occasionally the blame was counterfactual, such as "If only you had ...," while other notes were very specific about to whom blame should be assigned. One 23-year-old man wrote, "I cant hold you and mom responsible all the way just 25/25 and the other 50 was my fault."

Since many of the note writers were apologizing for their actions and absolving others from blame, it is not surprising they were also seeking forgiveness. One-third of the notes included pleas for forgiveness. One person asked survivors to forgive another person and another note indicated the writer forgave someone, but in the vast majority of cases the note writer asked forgiveness for either their past behaviors or the suicidal act. These pleas were intertwined with many of the note excerpts already presented in this chapter. Even very short notes often contained a combination of love, apologies and requests for forgiveness. One middle-aged man facing the end of his relationship wrote, "I'm so sorry please darling forgive me and don't hate me because I still cherish the ground you walk on."

These pleas for forgiveness were directed toward survivors and toward God. Relationships played a central role in the lives of the note writers. Many talked about not wanting to be forgotten after death. They also wanted to be fondly remembered, which would hinge on forgiveness. As with apologies, often they followed their pleas for forgiveness with justifications for their actions. Cameron, a 47-year-old man struggling with questions of sexual orientation and suffering from both physical and psychological illnesses, apologized to his sister for leaving much of the care of their mother to her and added, "Please forgive me. I wasn't even living anymore ... I've always (well, not always) but most of my life thought of myself as a Christian, I've studied and read, but maybe I'm just a Nihilist, Existentialist at heart. Maybe there is no meaning to the universe." Those who asked God for forgiveness generally focused on the suicidal act. They sounded remarkably similar. One man who struggled with substance abuse and life-long depression wrote, "I've made my Rights with God and Pray He will have mercy on my soul and forgive me. I'm in his arms now."

Also, in a few notes the writer indicated he would never forgive someone. For example, one 22-year-old man who had spent the night arguing with his girlfriend wrote this,

> I know you think it was your fault but it wasn't I loved you but you treated me like shit and I will never forgive you for that I will take the hate I have for you to my grave. I loved you like no one else and you treat me like shit. But remember one thing I love you more than anyone else. You will be my wife in my grave.

This note, and the sentiment expressed in it, will be discussed in much greater detail in the section on interpersonal relationships as a motivation for suicide.

Overall, the apologies, discussion of blame, and pleas for forgiveness expressed by the note writers seem heartfelt. These individuals believed their lifelong patterns, or simply the act of suicide itself, caused pain and they were sorry. It was possible to see, even in their last acts, that many had been caring and considerate individuals. One man left a note for authorities telling them to be careful, because the gun he had used was not on safety and should only be handled by the officer in charge. Another man, who killed himself with a gun in a motel, was waiting until the morning to kill himself so he would not wake guests. He said, "It's about 3:15 A.M. & I'm trying to wait until 7 A.M. so I don't wake everybody up. I know how bad I hate to be woken up. I am also very sorry for anything that has to be financially taken care of or anything else. I'm sorry." One woman mailed a letter to her landlord asking him to come to her apartment but instructed him not to bring his son.

They also expressed their care and concern in other ways. Some note writers (22%) asked survivors to take care of another person or pet, while others (11%) said they would be "watching over" their loved ones. They were using the notes as a means to relieve others of blame. Although absolving or assigning blame may not have been the purpose of the note, for some note writers, who used precious space to add in this information, it was a critical message. It is clear that overall, many note writers were sorry, but they simply had to do this for themselves. As a 29-year-old man with multiple problems, including finances and relationship issues, said, "I am so sorry for being shallow and selfish and cowardly leaving...I know this is the easy way out but it's the only way I know. I just can't go through with the everyday struggles both physically and mentally."

Escape

> I'm sorry, I can't take this mental illness any mor. I love you.

Escape was both a theme in the notes and a motivation for suicide so it will be discussed at length in Chapter 4, Escape as a Motivation for Suicide. Approximately one-fourth of notes (15%) discussed a need to escape unspecified pain. Other notes were more specific and focused on health-related problems, including mental illness (22%), physical illness (14%), medications (10%), or an acquired disability (9%). Foster (2003) also found 10% of note writers discussed physical health and/or symptoms. Not surprisingly, those who mentioned wanting to escape pain were older (50 years old) than those who did not (44 years old), and this difference was more pronounced when it came to physical pain (54 versus 44 years old). The illness or pain was often compounded by concerns about future debilitation.

James was a 50-year-old ex-Army Ranger and former Marine who injured his neck and spinal cord parachuting out of a plane. He had been through several surgeries and was taking numerous pain medications. He was depressed about his decreased mobility and had run out of pain medication. He wrote,

> My spinal disorder is worring-as they told me one day it would be to painful to move or get around. I can't work and Social Security doesn't pay enoug to live on. Ever day is the same—just looking at a T.V. scene—watching fantasy and make believe—or seeing other people live an active-fun and fulfilling life with family and friends. Even when someone is here I feel alone and out of place...All I ever wanted was close friends and family—it wasn't meant to be...I can't—I don't have it in me to ask for any help....

Those discussing a need to escape psychological pain were approximately the same age as those who did not discuss it. Many had struggled with mental illness for most of their lives and it had become unbearable. Susan, a 25-year-old woman who had struggled with anxiety and depression her whole life, wrote a note to her father and then asphyxiated herself in his garage. She told him,

> I just want you to know that I love you and even through all the anger I loved you. I'm sorry I couldn't fulfill your aspirations for me. I'm sorry I won't be there for you when you need me as you were there for me...I just lost my way and became too afraid of my own anger, too afraid of always feeling this empty....I'm sorry that I add this burden to your life. I'm sorry I couldn't be a stronger person. Of course, even in death I have one last favor to ask of you-[to take care of her pet]...

Like James and Susan, some individuals wrote about not wanting to become a burden in their notes (7%). While Susan felt she already had been and continued to be a burden, James did not want to become a burden. However, their concern over being a burden did not seem to be the impetus for their actions, but simply provided additional support for their decision and a confirmation that what they were doing was necessary and right. Foster (2003) also found 7% of note writers discussed being a burden to others while Sanger and Veach (2008) found 25.4% mentioned this concern.

For some individuals, their need to escape came from a combination of problems, such as the onset of depression over a cancer diagnosis. Some notes also described a need to escape an array of problems, which included illnesses, financial concerns or legal entanglement. Some talked about needing to escape their pain but did not specify its source. One woman wrote, "Dear Mom: I love you but my life means nothing to me anymore. It's not your fault, you were the best mother in the world. But life is full of pain." Whatever the reason, a large percentage of note writers needed to escape from something.

Instructions

> I don't want a funeral. Just put me in a hole. Cremate me and throw my ashes in a dumpster. Please. I am so sorry I ruined your life. Please find it in your heart somehow to forgive. It's not your fault.

Instructions are common in notes. Foster (2003) found 36% of notes included instructions. Sanger and Veach (2008) found 69.6% of notes included instructions related to financial affairs (28.3%), final affairs (26.1%), and other issues. Most of our notes provided instructions for survivors (64%), although only a few of the notes (3%) were merely instructions without any other content to the note. Instructions included the disposal of the body (22%) or funeral arrangements. One woman wrote a very bitter obituary and left instructions not to change it in any way. After her name and the date it read, "She leaves behind a living hell to go be with God. I want to thank my family for helping a weak mind and body to get to this point. You took so much and gave so little. I reached out to all of you, where were you?"

Instructions about funerals were sometimes quite detailed, naming speakers, preferred readings, or the music to be played. In a few cases the writer identified specific people that he or she did not want to attend the services. Other notes had instructions regarding the allocation of property (25%) or managing affairs such as bills that needed to be paid (24%). Often these notes included bank account information and the location of particular documents. Occasionally the suicide note included a formal will or a self-written obituary.

Instructions were also left for whoever found the body. These instructions assured law enforcement that this was indeed a suicide and not a result of foul play (7%), or forbade emergency personnel to attempt to resuscitate them (7%). Some also were heartfelt requests such as, "To The Authorities Who Find Me. I beg you—do not embarrass my family (especially my Son) by putting this in the Newspapers."

For some note writers the purpose of the instructions was simply an effort to put their affairs in order so as to ease the burden of survivors. For others, it appeared to be an attempt to maintain control over things after their deaths; e.g., one woman who was going through a bitter divorce instructed her relatives to try to take custody of her daughter away from her soon-to-be exhusband. She wrote, "Please do everything you can to have her [daughter] live with you."

FREQUENTLY OCCURRING CONTENT

God and Religion

"I leave this life with some sadness and grief, but on the other hand, I have a great curiosity to know what's on the other side. And, I have a faith that tells me that it's a better place and the loved ones who've gone before me will be here to greet me and we'll be together and be happy. In that regard, I'm looking forward to it."

Approximately one-third of the note writers mentioned faith, religion or God in their notes. References to God were more prevalent than to faith or religion. Most note writers hoped God would forgive them for their actions. Other individuals were angry with the hand that God had dealt them in life. One wrote,

I am so tired of hurting. I know it's selfish and I said I never would but this whole life sucks. From being abandoned at birth UNWANTED to today. I give up. I never could figure out why God hated me so much-but he wins. I LOSE. I'm not fighting any more. Nothing to fight for. Just more and more PAIN.

Although not angry, one man, who was struggling with reconciling his homosexuality with his religious upbringing, wrote a lengthy note to his sister. In it he explained, "And then there's the gay thing. Even though I know it's wrong, I would rather have a relationship with a man who loved me and wanted to spend his life with me than a close walk with Christ. I guess my fate is sealed."

A subset of the notes were letters addressed to God; e.g., one 27-year-old man who was struggling with the end of a relationship said, "Dear God, I love you so much. But I feel as if I'm all alone. I feel as if I have no one. So I had to take my own life. I want to be with you. Because you are all I have. Your the only one that truly loves me and I want to be near you. Please take me home with you. Please forgive me if I am committing a sin…See you soon!" Although his note ends as one might cheerfully sign a postcard, his sentiments show a deep and genuine desire to connect with God. The possibility of being with God and ending his aloneness was better than facing the prospect of beginning a new relationship.

A few note writers discussed God in an abstract way, often intertwining spirituality and death. One wrote, "As human beings, our highest calling should be knowledge of God. Death is an uninterrupted path to the spiritual platform. Naturally it occurs in a fleeting moment." However, one note writer expressed the bottom line for many individuals. He said, "For everyone else—only God can judge me now."

The Afterlife and the Morality of Suicide

"Life is not worth it. I will take my chances on the other side."

Twenty-nine percent of note writers pondered the afterlife. Among those people, most felt something positive would happen (40%) or were uncertain (33%). A small percentage thought the afterlife would be negative (15%) or neutral (13%) for them. A few were a blend of uncertainty, but hoped for a positive result. One 24-year-old man wrote, "And as much uncertainly as I have about what will happen to me, I really do hope we are all together eventually. I will be waiting to make you smile."

Those who anticipated a positive future often talked about reunions. In fact, overall 21% of note writers discussed reunions that would happen. Some of these reunions referred to their already deceased relatives (6%): "I'll tell everyone that we once loved hello." Others discussed eventual reunions with those who they were leaving behind (10%): "If Mommy is correct, and there is a heaven, I will see you there…Study hard, smile often & I will be looking down, watching over you."

Their anticipated afterlife was often intertwined with an assessment of their lives and their views on the morality of suicide. Overall, 14% of notes discussed the morality of suicide. Paul, a 52-year-old man who had struggled with depression his whole life, was on the phone with a friend when she heard a bang and his breathing became labored. When police arrived they found a note that said, "Please try not to be too angry with me and please try not to hate my memory. On the whole, I think I was a good and moral person and in spite of the unspeakable cruelty of this act, I honestly don't think I had a mean, inconsiderate bone in my body."

Advice

"Be true to yourself–and those you love. Be happy in yourself and show the love to those who are close to you. Life is a very precious thing."

This advice was written by Roger, a 41-year-old man who was depressed over his financial situation. He was about to file for bankruptcy, because he had gambled away the family savings. His wife was unaware of their financial situation. Roger's advice was to be happy, when he clearly was not, and he recognized life as a precious thing just before he took his own.

Precipitating Events

"My life sucks. The world sucks. People suck. Today I plan on shooting myself but with my luck the gun will probably missfire life's a bitch then you die. There are alot of factors that have effected my choice to do this the death of my girlfriend and my best friend. The deciding factor is the people upstairs they have threatened me followed me, kicked in my door and constantly harassed me. I really don't know why...I'm disabled and I am not able to fight them on my own...But I can have no peace where I live and am not able to move so I guess this is it. Anybody that ever cared about me is dead I have no one to turn to."

Twenty-two percent of notes mentioned precipitating events that drove the writers to commit suicide. Case after case documented a recent trauma that appeared to lead to the suicide. Usually these were significant events such as the loss of a job, a distressing medical diagnosis, an arrest or impending jail sentence, a financial crisis, or a breakup with a spouse or boyfriend/girlfriend. However, in some cases the precipitating event seemed trivial to the reader or observer. For example, a girlfriend described an argument at a bar with her boyfriend in which she chided him for drinking too much. After they went home, she left with a stated intention of returning after allowing him time to sober up and cool down. When she came back later and found that he had shot himself, it was a great surprise to her since she did not view the argument as having been serious at all.

The pattern of trivial precipitating incidents held especially true for adolescent suicides. For many teens in our sample, seemingly minor setbacks—arguments with parents or friends or punishments at school for rules violations—served as the impetus for suicide. For example, a teenager who received a traffic ticket went home and talked to his mother about his distress over the ticket. After a brief conversation, the boy seemed to calm down but he then went to his room and hanged himself. His mother was completely shocked; she had not recognized the intensity of his feelings about the incident nor how it might have interacted with other problems in his life to cause him to seek such a drastic solution.

More striking were the many people who indicated that there was not a precipitating event or acknowledged that some event was simply the last straw but not the real reason for their decision. The following notes reflect the writers' self-awareness:

> "I hope no one is disappointed in me. I am sure you will all know the story even-tually, but everyone remember that this situation was the trigger, not the reason, I killed myself."
> "I decided in Sept. 2007 life was no longer worth living. I liquidated all my assets and decided to end it when they ran out. They ran out."
> "There were recent events that allowed me to reach this state of suicidal depression, but they are not to blame. The rest of my life has been nearly-suicidal depression, just waiting for something to give me a push. I'm taking advantage of the situation while it exists."

LESS FREQUENTLY OCCURRING CONTENT

In addition to the preceding content, we assessed each note for any other issues the note writers deemed were important enough to put in a note, as well as emotions they expressed in the note. In general, the issues they referred to were those which contributed to their life stress and in turn led to the suicide. The most prevalent issue was some form of legal involvement, which may be one of the most underestimated risk factors for suicide.

Callanan and Davis (2009) found approximately 9% of their sample was accused of a crime or wrongdoing and approximately 12% were fac-ing a financial crisis. Similarly, approximately 7% of Cerel et al.'s (2015) sample had a recent criminal problem and 2% had a recent noncriminal legal problem. At least 19% of our sample were entangled in criminal or civil processes, with individuals facing criminal charges ranging from child pornography to rape to sexual assault to robbery. Although at first we were not coding for arrests related to driving under the influence (DUI), we saw so many of them that we went back and began noting these cases. Also, in some cases the individual somehow involved the police in his or her suicide; e.g., a man called the police and indicated he was about to take his life. In most of these calls, no intervention could take place. It was more a notification for the police to come and pick up the body. Some individuals engaged the police in car chases or gunfire in an attempt to commit suicide-by-cop. Other individuals committed suicide in their jail cells while awaiting a hearing. In most of these cases, they did not leave a note. However, it was clear that the cause of the suicide was their legal entanglement. Finally, some legal cases involved civil issues such as custody or divorce. In many of these cases the suicide victim had been embroiled in a bitter custody dispute. In others, he simply could not face the prospect of a divorce. These cases will be examined in greater detail in the chapter on legal issues.

Although infrequent (10%), some note writers discussed work- or school-related problems. Callanan and Davis (2009) also found work issues were only mentioned in 11% of notes. Although certainly cases exist where the main impetus for suicide has been bullying in the workplace or school, for most of our cases these were simply additional stressors and not the main reason for their decision. One woman wrote,

> .....It has nothing to do with you. There was nothing you could do. I was so unhappy. There was no happiness anywhere. I was so alone. 45. No husband. No man in sight. No child. No friends to hang-out with, have fun with. No money. House I never could fix up. A house where I was disrespected. A nice car. Great parents. A great niece and Aunt. A job that keeps me stressed.....I've made numerous mistakes on the job lately. One that might have civil consequences -----. ...I battle sadness, depression and aloneness everyday....I love you both with all my heart. Thank you for being my parents....Forgive me for leaving this yucky house to be cleaned. The truth is I tried but I was too sad to finish cleaning it first....I'll always love you. I hope I see you on the other side. Love Daughter

It was impossible to determine how frequently job loss contributed to the suicides. Clearly, the origin of the legal involvement was often the loss of a job, which led to financial stress resulting in bankruptcies, foreclosures, evictions, marital distress, and sometimes criminal behavior. Some note writers provided these details but others could only focus on their present angst.

Although infrequent, some note writers discussed the impact of an abusive relationship (5%), discrimination or oppression (5%), a recent death (2%), or body image (2%) on them. However, similar to their jobs and school, these did not appear to be the predominant cause of the suicide but more often represented one of the many stressors in their lives. One woman, who was dealing with health issues from obesity, financial distress, chronic depression, and the loss of her career wrote,

> I have been very depressed for many years & this is because my family background is abusive. I experience abuse everyday & most days multiple times/day & multiple types of abuse. My death will end all of the 'crap' in my head. It is difficult to live with all of the memories. I have been thinking of suicide daily for several years & with me loosing my house this is the final straw.

Emotions

The predominant emotion expressed in the notes was love, but they also expressed a myriad of other emotions. Given the large percentage of note writers who were depressed, it was not surprisingly to find emotions expressed in the notes that were hallmarks of depression. Common emotions were feeling like a failure (17%), or feeling tired (12%), sad (9%), hopeless (7%), guilty (7%), or ashamed (5%). Foster (2003) found 21% of note writers discussed feeling hopeless or that life was not worth living. When adding those two feelings together, 22% of our sample expressed them. Their failures sometimes related to specific circumstances, or a relationship or endeavor, but more often the feelings of failure reflected assessments of their lives. On the back of the antisuicide contract that he had agreed upon with his therapist, one 22-year-old wrote,

> I am a disappointment...I have been a failure in my own eyes my entire life. There is nothing that I excell at. There is nothing where I am the best. I have not ever completed anything of any importance. I am not a good friend. I am selfish. No one ever seems to care about me and if they do it seems self-fulfilling. That is how I treat people so that is how I should be treated in return...Why should I hang around and continue to make myself miserable? **I HATE MYSELF**. Fuck it I'm out.

Despite the fact that most people are just beginning to launch their lives at 22 years old and have not yet had a chance to excel, this man already felt like a failure.

Perhaps because of this sense of failure, note writers frequently indicated that life was not worth living (15%) or they were ambivalent (7%) or apathetic (2%) about their deaths. "This is not something I want to do, it's something I have to do. Lord knows I love you girls and I don't want to leave you, but as it has been pointed out in so many ways, by so many people I'm not good at anything as your father spent almost nine years telling me." Another person did not discuss her failure but was clearly apathetic about her death. She wrote, "I don't want to die but I feel dead already."

A few note writers expressed joy (5%) or relief (3%) and some talked about the peace they would feel after they died. One 41-year-old man was separated from his wife, but when they attended their son's wedding he asked her to come by to talk the next day. When she did she found his body and a note that read, "I'm sorry but I can't take it anymore. I don't want any one to feel sorry for me but I am finally at peace. I love you all." James, the ex-Army Ranger discussed previously, wrote, "It's hard to let go of this life—because you can see—hear—taste and feel it all. What is death—I fear it because I don't know—what lies ahead, at least there will be no more pain—just rest and peace of mind—may I find friends—happiness or something better. I'am afraid-and alone with this feeling of hopelessness." Similarly, others spoke of feeling free. One 57-year-old woman wrote, "I have finally found a way to finally free myself. I have felt depressed for so long—now it is time to go. I'm sorry for causing you all this inconvenience...God Bless You. You are a fine man. I don't know how you turned out so good. Must have been prayers."

Although we only occasionally found a note writer who expressed anger (4%), when we did, the magnitude of the anger was striking. One middle-aged woman who had worked as a nurse hanged herself in the family garage one afternoon. She left this note,

> My children are grown & don't need me. I am not in my grand children lives. I have no friends, I don't go out, I don't have a job because you wanted me to leave the job I liked because of insurance. I am in debt up to my ass paying for all your Drs, medicines, lawyers etc. I wish I would have left you years ago...I told you I wish I was dead-I chose the time & place. HAPPY ANNIVERSARY...DO NOT TAKE THIS OUT ON THE KIDS...I guess now you'll get off your ass, stop drinking & smoking your weed and stop being a loser. GET A JOB. You act like an old man-try living-I wish I had....No services of any kind-Nobody was there while I was alive, I'll be damned if they need to be there when I'm dead.

FUTURE STUDIES

Although we created a very detailed list of the content and emotions we thought would be in the notes, some things we did not anticipate. When we encountered these in the cases, we recorded them so we could provide some direction for future research. In general, they related to risk factors and the note writer's psychological state.

There is no doubt that substance use and abuse are risk factors for suicide. However, gambling was another addiction that was noted frequently and set in motion a chain of events that led to suicide. The pattern was similar to substance abusers—the addiction led to the loss of jobs, family, and control. Although the other personal and legal consequences for these addictions may have varied, the end result was the same. It is important to determine how much of a risk factor gambling is for suicide. Clearly an increased risk of suicidal behavior exists among gamblers (Moghaddam, Yoon, Dickerson, Kim, & Westermeyer, 2015). It is unclear how many suicides involve gambling, however, and how that relates to overall motivational patterns.

Many note writers were concerned that they not be forgotten and pleaded with survivors to keep their memory alive. One person wrote, "I will finally be at peace—please don't ever forget me—I love you so very much!" A 42-year-old man who was an intravenous heroin user and suffered from chronic pain wrote, "Take care of yourself and these kids. When they get older they will forget me as I'm sure everyone else here will do to. Good luck." Others were worried about their legacy, or how they would be remembered. Several talked about how they did not want to be remembered for seeming like a coward or as a selfish person because of their actions. Some felt they were, in fact, being cowardly and selfish. One note writer said, "I am so sorry for being shallow and selfish and cowardly leaving...I know this is the easy way out but it's the only way I know. I just can't go through with the everyday struggles both physically and mentally." Another note writer detailed why his actions were not selfish or cowardly. He said,

> Dear family & friends,
> Mom & Dad please let anyone I know read this if they want. Thank you!
> Let me start by saying I'm sorry. I'm sure that doesn't help but I don't know what else to say. I know some of you, or all of you are probably going to be mad at me at some point. And I'm sure some people are going to say I was a coward or I'm only thinking about myself. I hope to address these feelings in this letter. Because I'm not a coward or selfish. Some of my friends know I've been battling these feelings for a long time. A lot of people don't know this, but my first suicide attempt was .....but surviving did not destroy the pain in my head. Not a lot of people even know I have this pain because I do not talk about it. Maybe that is part of my problem. But as far as everyone being angry with me about this, I understand. But, #1 I am not a coward. I've never been fucking scared of one thing in my life. And #2 I'm not being selfish. Being selfish is what I did to Alice. I cannot live with the pain I have caused her.

We were unable to determine if or how these victims differed from the other victims, since we did not identify these factors until we completed our data collection. As with gambling, it would be interesting to determine how these concerns related to motivation. It is expected that individuals who are concerned with their legacies are more likely motivated by interpersonal reasons for the suicide.

MOTIVATIONS

No recent attempts have been made at a typology of individuals who commit suicide, and none that is derived from an extensive database comparing both note writers and non-note writers, using both a qualitative and quantitative approach. After we had examined the content of the notes and files, our next step was to develop motivational categories through data-driven analyses. We then compared these to motivational systems in the literature. In the end, we delineated 11 categories and assigned each case to one. For note writers this was based on their note and the file but for non-note writers we had only the file information.

The categories included relationship issues, alienation, failure or inadequacy, guilt, escape, spiritual concerns, revenge, altruism, abuse, oppression or discrimination, and finally, bereavement. Overall, four of the categories received support and two of these categories accounted for more than 90% of the motivations for suicide. They were: *Relationship* (23%, killing oneself in response to a relational conflict, abandonment, or divorce) and *Escape* (70%, need to free oneself from psychological or physical pain, financial distress, legal problems, or other adverse life circumstances). Two other categories, *Failure/inadequacy* (motivations related to low self-esteem, worthlessness, self-pity, hopelessness, or self-hate), and *Bereavement* (suicide in response to bereavement issues) emerged as the next highest categories. However, bereavement, failure, and other motivations totaled to less than 7% of the cases.

Each of these categories has different patterns associated with the suicide; e.g., the demographics and histories of the individuals are different as are the characteristics of the suicides and the notes. The next chapters are organized around these motivations and how identification of them can lead to more successful prevention and intervention.

Suicide Motivated by Interpersonal Relationships

Linda was approaching her 40th birthday when she learned that Michael, her husband of seven years, was involved with another woman. Linda had struggled with depression and low self-esteem since adolescence. When she learned about Michael's affair, she attempted to kill herself by overdosing but was unsuccessful. This plunged her into an even deeper depression. Michael moved out and for months they attempted to work things out, but finally he came over and told her he wanted a divorce. They talked for several hours, and she cried most of that time. The next morning Michael called to check on her, and she was still very upset. He asked Linda if she had any suicidal ideation, and she told him that she did not. She told him she would probably just fail as she had the last time. The next day, after several hours of attempting to reach her and receiving no response, Michael went to check on her. He found her hanging from one of the rafters with a dog leash wrapped around her neck. In her note she said, "I hope you can forgive me one day. Without the love in my life, and with all the rejection issues, and my constant lack of confidence—I saw no other way.
"I am grateful to you all
"I love you."

One theory of suicide focuses solely on interpersonal issues. As discussed in Chapter 1, The History and Theories of Suicide, Joiner (2005), an academic psychologist and expert on suicide, has proposed that two predisposing stressors increase the risk of suicide: thwarted belongingness, a painful mental state resulting from wanting to connect with other people but being prevented from doing so, and perceived burdensomeness, i.e., the sense that one is a burden to loved ones. In addition, the individual must have an acquired capacity for self-harm, or an ability to circumvent one's survival instinct. Although many of the note writers in our study who had problems with interpersonal relationships expressed some sense of thwarted belongingness, very few discussed being a burden or indicated they considered themselves to be burdens. Lester and Gunn

(2012) found similar results in their analysis of suicide notes. When note writers did discuss being a burden, it was independent of the relationship. However, thwarted belongingness, through break-ups and divorce, was commonplace. Independent of depression, a recent divorce increases the odds of suicide 1.6 times, while the long-term strains related to the divorce increase it 1.3 times (Stack & Scourfield, 2015).

For 218 people (17%) in our original sample, the motivation for suicide was conflict in interpersonal relationships. When we eliminated cases from the overall sample where the motivation for the suicide could not be determined, that number jumped to 23%. In an analysis of violent deaths using data from seven states, "problems with a current or former intimate partner contributed to 27.9% of suicides" (Patel et al., 2006, p. 723). When a relationship was the motivation behind the suicide, in the vast majority of cases (92%) it involved intimate partners. Three subgroups emerged within the intimate partner group: unrequited or lost love (45%), abusive relationship (30%), and unknown cause (24%).

SUICIDES RELATED TO INTIMATE PARTNERS

Unrequited or Lost Love

The most typical pattern in this category, and the one represented by Linda, involved unrequited or lost love (90 people). The victims ranged in age from 16 to 60, although most were under 45 years old (76%) with an average age of 37. Most were white (92%) and male (91%), and they killed themselves by gunshot (52%), asphyxiation (29%), or overdose (16%). One individual killed himself by stepping in front of a truck. At least 21% were under the influence of drugs or alcohol when they killed themselves. Similar to Callanan and Davis's findings (2009), our victims were much more likely to leave a note if they were not using alcohol. For this group, suicides were most likely to occur on Monday (21%) and least likely to occur on Friday (8%). The majority of individuals killed themselves at home (77%). No one committed murder-suicide, but 21% killed themselves in front of someone. However, of those who killed themselves in front of someone, only two of them left notes.

It was unknown whether 51 of the 90 individuals had ever expressed suicidal ideation or made threats, but among the remaining 39, 19 had threatened suicide, 9 had ideation, and 5 had both thoughts about suicide and had made threats. Linda, and at least 13 other individuals, had previously attempted suicide. Among the 39 individuals who were identified as having a mental illness, most were depressed (85%), while some were experiencing symptoms of bipolar disorder or schizophrenia. It is not possible to determine exactly how many individuals were coping with other stressors in their lives, but some investigators' reports mentioned drug abuse (21%), physical illness (17%), legal problems (17%), or financial problems (4%).

Approximately one-fourth (24%) of the individuals in this group left notes, often addressed to a specific person (73%) such as an intimate partner (64%). Over one-third left more than one note (41%), writing separately to parents (37%), children (32%), siblings (14%), friends (14%), and other family members (23%). In their notes the victims' thoughts were organized (91%) and most talked about their love for others (91%) and their interpersonal problems (77%). Many provided a justification for their suicide (68%). For example, in the only double suicide in our entire sample, the couple wrote a joint note and stated,

> Were tired
> We can't make it work so were done
> Maybe we can rest now
> Love all of you.

The only other widespread theme in the notes was apology. Over half of the notes (55%) contained apologies to a specific person. One 46-year-old man, depressed over his impending divorce, repeatedly said he was sorry to his wife and children. Specifically, he directed the following to his wife, "Why have you turned into one of the most cold hearted people I have ever met. We had two beautiful children together and you did not understand how important all 3 of you were to me... I'm very, very, very sorry for what I have done, but this was out of control what the court and you did to me." Some notes (50%) either contained an additional general apology or just a general apology. One middle-aged white man, who died of intoxication from multiple drugs and carbon monoxide poisoning, wrote, "I'm sorry but I just couldn't cope with life anymore. And I'm sorry about the mess I'm leaving for all of you." A third of the note writers cited a cause for their suicide, and in every case it was the end of a relationship.

Approximately one-fourth of the notes (27%) addressed God and another third addressed the afterlife, most often with positive or uncertain feelings: "I don't know if I will go to heaven or not but I ask god for His forgivness." Not surprisingly, God was often intertwined with the afterlife, sometimes in chilling ways. Andrew was 44 years old when his wife, Carol, and children moved out of the house. After they left, he told both Carol and his neighbor that he was going to kill himself. About a month later he called his best friend, told him that he loved him, then went to the patio at the back of the house and shot himself in the head. He left numerous notes throughout the house and they are excerpted here. One read,

> Dearest Carol, I was afraid this would happen. You shut yourself off from all the people like Patty and Denny who would have guided you in God's way, and that

would have counseled us together. I prayed so much for God to help you see my changes and know they were permanent. But I guess you kept your eyes closed to it all.

Regardless, I could never hate you Carol, I love you with all my heart. Everyday without being with my soulmate is an eternity, and I simply can't take the pain any longer.

You know Matt wondered from the start if you were trying to drive me to suicide. I never wanted to believe that about you though...But for me to have went through a divorce would have been wrong in so many ways.

First, it is against God's will. You and I vowed to each other before God, to stay together till death do us part. That vow has become very important to me lately. And I cannot allow man's laws to override that.

I will love you forever Carol, and I will always be your best friend and soul mate...Our only future now hopefully will be in heaven

Along with Andrew's note was a diary of sorts. In it he spent dozens of pages reflecting on why Carol left, begging her to return and apologizing profusely. He talked about his "anger issues" and how both Carol and their marriage counselor told him that he needed to mature and stop being a "third child." He also discussed how he had begun reading a book on codependency that she left in the house, paying special attention to the parts she underlined. He said he had changed and was doing chores and attending church services to become a good "Christian husband." And then he asked, "What can I do to show you it is safe to come home?" Carol was afraid to talk to him. When he realized she was not coming home, he wrote the notes, which have a much different tone than the diary. In the note, it was Carol's fault for shutting herself off from friends that would have counseled them to stay together, with no awareness that maybe she was shutting herself off out of fear. Then he intimated that she drove him to suicide and ended suggesting that their only future would be in heaven. The note reflects his conceptualization of heaven, not hers. He suggested Carol had been manipulative and yet one can read his note as an attempt to manipulate her. His words insinuated that she was to blame for his actions.

The length of the notes in our sample varied but many were over 150 words long (49%) with another forty-one percent 26–150 words long. In almost a third of the notes, evidence of constriction or of a rigid and narrow cognitive pattern appeared, with words like "I cannot live without you." Approximately one-fourth (22%) left instructions, most often about how to dispose of their property or their bodies and about managing affairs.

What is interesting about the notes is not so much what they do focus on but also what they do not address. Three note writers (out of 22) mentioned having psychological pain, three unspecified pain, and two physical pain. Few discussed feeling tired (23%), ambivalent (18%), loved (14%), lonely (14%), like a failure (14%) or worthless (5%) or that life was not worth living (9%). They rarely discussed issues like the morality of suicide; problems at school, on the job or with the law; or feeling shame, hopelessness, sadness, joy, guilt, relief, apathy, or burdensomeness. No one talked about being abused or having trouble with body image, and none expressed apathy. They also did not use humor in their notes. However, in a "P.S." one person did say, "Here is some smokes Rita you will need them." Some either absolved others for blame (18%) or blamed others (14%), or gave advice (14%). Although no one explicitly stated he or she was angry, it was implied in a few notes. One woman's entire note read, "Arnie thanks for ruining my life After what he has done Arnie deserves nothing," while another woman wrote, "I am sorry to ruin your life Luke. I loved you." Finally, one man wrote, "I told her I would never sign divorce papers. I am a man of my word." In other words, the focus of these notes is on the relationship, not on illnesses or other life problems such as legal or financial issues.

In addition to the content, the tone and characteristics of these notes sharply contrasted with those written by individuals who were motivated to commit suicide to escape pain. Those motivated to commit suicide due to lost or unrequited love wrote notes that were longer, more detailed and contained more innuendo than those written by individuals who were escaping pain. In reading these notes, one has the sense that some felt too sensitive for this world. One note referenced the lyrics from a popular song "Vincent," about the life and suicide of the Impressionist artist, Vincent Van Gogh. The quoted verse, "this world was never meant for one as beautiful as you," expresses a lack of belongingness (McLean, 1971). Others were simply unable or unwilling to let go of the relationship and move on with their lives. Conversely, notes written by those escaping pain were shorter and more definitive, with a central focus on the pain, not on the relationship.

One explanation for relationship suicides can be found in reciprocity theory. Davis, Callanan, Lester, and Haines (2009) examined suicide notes left by individuals they believed were motivated to kill themselves because of relationship issues. They suggest that when one person in an intimate partner relationship feels they have been treated unfairly, or are not receiving benefits that are equal to their investment, the norm of reciprocity has been violated leading to "reciprocity imbalance." Suicide can become a means of restoring balance. They discussed four modes of adaptation: suicide as retreat, suicide as exploitation, suicide as retaliation, and suicide due to exploiter guilt. Those individuals who were using suicide as a retreat were most similar to those in the lost or unrequited love category. In general, the notes did not express ill will toward the intimate partner, but rather the person saw suicide as the only way to stop the pain they felt from the relationship. Their notes were similar to ours with apologetic tones and requests for forgiveness.

Some notes in our sample suggested that the suicide may have been exploitative. The imbalance in the relationship felt by the individual who wrote the note was characterized by the victim continually taking advantage of the other person or leaving them "in a mess" (Davis, Callanan, Lester, & Haines, 2009). Suicide became the only way to restore balance. Some note writers explicitly discussed being sorry for leaving a mess. It was not unusual to read words like, "Please forgive me. This is the last mess of mine you will ever have to clean up..." By and large, though, the motivation for their suicide was not relationship issues but to escape from the mess that had become their lives. This often included legal and financial difficulties. In addition to evidence of tunnel vision, this note expresses the victim's dual realization that the consequences of past actions will be too much to bear and remorse for creating a situation that could not be untangled:

> I really don't want to do this, but I don't feel like I have any options. I've got myself in such a mess & theres no one who can help me. I'm afraid, I'm alone. I know a lot of people are concerned about me, but they all see me self-destructing. I have no hard feelings toward anyone. I have felt like I've been punished more than I should have been. Most of my problems though were my own fault. I don't blame anybody for this. Not even me. My life just got out of control and one bad break or decision was followed by another.

In short, very little support was found for using suicide exploitatively, but individuals were clearly using suicide as a retreat from relationships.

Although a large percentage of the people who committed suicide in our overall sample did not do so exclusively because of interpersonal problems, it appears that those individuals who call hotlines are more likely to discuss interpersonal issues. When the content of calls to a suicide hotline were examined, a few themes—loneliness, social isolation, and interpersonal/family problems—accounted for the majority of calls (Barber, Blackman, Talbot, & Saebel, 2004). Males were more likely to discuss relationships that had ended while females were more likely to discuss current relationship problems, especially abuse. Unfortunately, the actions of perpetrators in abusive relationships may be too spontaneous for hotlines to be of any help. This could explain why the number of calls hotlines received was almost equally distributed between males and females. Females call but males act, especially in abusive relationships . However, males also give warning signs which go unheeded by friends, family and the criminal justice system.

For those individuals who are seeking to escape other adverse life circumstances, such as physical pain, a hotline may not provide a supportive outlet. However, a hotline can help alleviate pain from loneliness or social isolation. It can also help direct victims toward resources. For these callers, who resembled those individuals in our lost or unrequited love category, it was critical that those who staffed hotlines worked to reduce their feelings of social isolation and loneliness. However, these strategies may be completely ineffective when abuse is a part of the relationship.

Abusive Relationships

Paul and Emily had been married for six years and had one child. The relationship became physically abusive shortly after the birth of their child. Although he had never directly threatened to kill Emily, he had told mutual friends that he planned to do so and they had related this information to her. She left and obtained a temporary protection order (TPO) against Paul. In the space of a month, she had called the police twice when he violated the TPO. Each time, he parked his van a block from her apartment and sat in the driver's seat watching. Once, he was arrested, and the other time he was admitted to a hospital so his mental health could be evaluated. During that same time period, he attempted suicide by taking an overdose.

They had a court hearing related to their divorce on Thursday afternoon. On Friday morning, as Emily prepared to leave for work, she noticed he was again sitting down the street. She called police but when they arrived there was no one in the driver's seat and the van was locked. However, an empty gun case and shotgun shell box were on the front seat. As they approached Emily's house to search the premises, they heard a shotgun blast from the back of the van. They forcibly opened the vehicle and found that Paul had shot himself in the head.

The second group of suicides (61 cases) which were motivated by relationships with intimate partners involved emotional or physical abuse, and some ended in murder-suicide. In these cases, the perpetrator of the abuse was the person who committed suicide, not the person who was abused. Only five people left notes (8% as compared to 24% for those in the lost love group), and one of them wrote the note after he had murdered his girlfriend.

Ray and Pam were already married to others when they met at work and began dating. After a year, Ray moved in with Pam, but their relationship was contentious. A pattern developed. They would argue and Ray would move out for a period of time, and then they would reconcile and he would move back in. Although Pam had been abused by the husband she left, no records existed of any domestic violence with Ray. Late one evening, after another round of fighting, Ray wrote Pam an angry note that said, "I've had it with your cruelty and viciousness. You treat me like shit. You run my ass down or see how mean you can be. Well I'm not Walter and won't take it from anyone." However, this note ended with Ray saying he was leaving to work on someone's truck, and it does not appear he intended to kill Pam. Ray did go to work on the truck. The next morning he killed Pam, wrote another note, and killed himself. In the second note he apologized for messing up so many lives. Even with no prior domestic violence, clearly anyone who kills an intimate partner is abusive. It is unlikely that Ray was never abusive, even if he had never abused Pam. Most men who murder their spouses and commit suicide have a history of domestic violence against their previous partners. Yet one study found that 41% of men who killed their partners had no history of prior violence with the women they murdered (Dobash, Dobash, Cavenagh, & Medina-Ariza, 2007).

The suicide victim's ages in the abusive group are similar to those in the lost love group discussed previously, with a range of 19 to 71 and an average of 39 years, although most were under 50 years old (77%). Most were males (90%), but this group had slightly more ethnic diversity, with 82% Caucasian and 16% African American. Although we could not determine if 69% were using drugs or alcohol at the time of the suicide, we could confirm that 26% were using substances.

Aside from the vast difference in the percentage of people who leave notes, several things clearly distinguish this group from those committing suicide due to lost love. Thirty-four percent committed murder-suicide in the abuse group while no one in the lost love group murdered anyone. Not surprisingly, the method of suicide also changed, with the percentage of victims using a gun increasing 17%, from 52% in the lost love group to 69% in the abusive group. This decreased the percentage using some form of asphyxiation to 26%. All other methods had less than 5%. While only 17% of those individuals who were in the lost love group had legal problems, 39% of these individuals had legal problems, often from violations of TPOs. Finally, over a third killed themselves in front of someone (38%) while only 21% of victims in the lost love group killed themselves in front of someone. Moreover, six people in the abusive group did not murder anyone but their acts were particularly callous. Each of these cases warrants further consideration.

In two of these cases, the victims returned home from a night of drinking and woke their intimate partners. One man then said, "you're gonna watch this," before he placed the gun under his chin and fired. The second man threatened his intimate partner, then said, "I'm going to show you how much I love you," before shooting himself. In a similar case, a woman who had been arguing with her husband told him to "watch this." Her teenage children did not witness the shooting but heard the exchange from an adjacent room. Another man threatened his wife, then fled before police arrived. The next morning he was hanging from a tree limb outside her window. One woman, who had been dating a man for five months, became incensed when he told her he was dating another woman as well. While he was away, she snuck into his house, turned on his truck and asphyxiated herself. Her naked body was found in the driver's seat of his car.

Perhaps the most disturbing case involved emotional abuse. Missy and Alan had been married for nine years and had three children, who were 8, 7, and 5. They had been in marital counseling for several months, but Alan had met someone else and moved out. Missy began writing in a journal as soon as he left. In it she indicates that God's vengeance will come upon him for having an affair and expresses jealousy and hate toward his new partner, all the while begging for him to come back and telling him she cannot live without him. At times she wrote in the third person. She stated,

> I am giving you what you want, your freedom. I have always loved you. Always…. These kids love you. Please don't let them forget me. I hope you'll never forget me either. You could be such a wonderful man when you wanted too…It hurts so much to love someone so deeply that doesnt share the same love for you. I can't for the life of me understand why someone would treat someone that they know loves them so much so bad. I wish he would realize how much he means to me and how deep my love is for him…I just want this marriage to work. I love Alan soo much with all my heart & soul. He is my heart. I don't want to do this with out him. This family means the world to me…I have reflected on, especially the past. How stupid & immature I acted over things. Honestly I'm surprised it lasted this long. I acted so childish. My behaviors were totally unacceptable. I guess I have pushed him away in a big way. I know alot of this is my fault. Trying to control what we watched, trying to control everything was just stupid. Tearing up things because I was jealous and insecure. All of that is just dumb. And all of the bitching and nagging, damn I wouldn't want to be around me either…
>
> That woman is so unattractive and old looking. And she can hardly speak…..I'm actually insulted….Well the both of you pulled us apart. You & her are bringing your own souls to ruin. And you'll never inherit Gods Kingdom…She is a low life dirty whore to be messing around with a married man…I dont see how you could live with that. Knowing you won't recieve ever lasting life in the new system. You wont see your daddy again. But this is the path satan set out for you & you took it Alan. And for that you will definately feel Jehovah's Vengeance…I just want us to continue on this journey together…Just sitting back and reflecting on all the crap I went through in this marriage, thinking about how I wish I coulda beat him to the punch I wish I coulda left him. I just want him to feel the pain & heart ache I'm feeling…

After she wrote the last sentence in that entry, an appreciable shift occurred in the journal. She moved to a new page and wrote a suicide note. Thinking that she could have "beat him to the punch" seems to have impelled her toward suicide. The tone of her writing changed and she began to write explicit instructions for her funeral and burial. She said,

> I wanted to grow old with you. You made my life hell alot of the time but I loved you…Please out of respect for me and the kids please break off your relationship with that woman…I know you been with her. All these nights away from home. Come on. But I still love you. My heart will always belong to you. Please take good care of my kids and visit my grave. I want my obituary & head stone to say Mrs. <u>Missy Roberts</u> and make sure I have my wedding rings on…bury me with pictures of you and the kids … … I hope she's happy I am out of the way.

She told her husband she forgave him, and chastised him to get himself right with God and to take care of "her" kids. She reiterated, "I just couldn't take you being with her. If you really love me then you'll leave her."

Missy hanged herself in the closet of her bedroom and her 8-year-old daughter found her. When her daughter screamed, all of the children entered the room and saw their mother hanging in the closet. Finally, one called for help. Although she did not actually kill herself in front of someone, killing herself in her home when only her children were present virtually insured they would find the body. Both her actions and her suicide note indicate the control she was attempting to exert over her relationships.

It was unknown whether 40 out of the 61 individuals in the abusive group had ever expressed suicidal ideation or made threats, but 17 had threatened suicide, and two had ideation and had made threats. At least eight other individuals had previously attempted suicide. Among the 14 victims who were identified as having a mental illness, most were depressed (64%). It is not possible to determine exactly how many individuals were coping with other stressors in their lives. However, the investigators' reports mentioned for some drug abuse (21%), physical illness (10%), or financial problems (3%).

For this group, suicides were most likely to occur at home (57%) on Monday (21%) and least likely to occur on Wednesday or Saturday (10%). Since many of the couples were separated, the weekend would likely be the best opportunity to see each other, especially if they were sharing custody of children. Sunday would also often be the day that transfer of the children would occur. These suicides were much more likely to occur in the winter (34%) when people are spending more time indoors together. In contrast, only 18% occurred in the spring. The season and days of the week stand out, as historically and in our own sample most suicides take place in the late spring (June) or early fall and on Mondays (Jamison, 1999). Miller, Furr-Holden, Lawrence, and Weiss (2012) found that Monday and Tuesday had the highest frequencies and rates of deliberate self-harm, both fatal and nonfatal. For month-of-year rate comparisons, April and May had the highest frequencies and rates of nonfatal self-harm. Fatality rates varied with minor monthly variation, but had peaks from February through May and in September.

This group presents a much different profile than the individuals who lost the love of a significant other. In general, these suicides are much more spontaneous, which explains the lack of notes and the use of guns. Although guns were also used in a high percentage of planned suicides, they are also the means of choice in spontaneous suicides in the United States, because two-fifths of all white American households have one, as do one-fifth of all black households (Morin, 2014). Relationships that involve physical and emotional abuse generally involve issues of power and control. The fact that almost half of these individuals killed themselves in front of someone, usually their intimate partners, represents a very different kind of control. It is almost as if they realized that although their partners and relationships were out of their control, they could still control one last thing: how they were remembered. Killing themselves in front of someone burned an indelible image in the memories their partners had of them.

Only one research study has been published on witnessed suicides. McDowell, Rothberg, and Koshes (1994) examined 1183 cases of suicide among Air Force personnel and their families. They found 50 cases where the suicide was completed in the physical, visible presence of another person. They proposed that these cases fit into a taxonomy with four categories: Russian roulette, violent divorce, homicidal rage, and reciprocal abandonment. We found no Russian roulette cases but we were using a nonmilitary population, which may account for the difference. The homicidal rage cases were murder-suicides and will be discussed at length later in this chapter. Reciprocal abandonment refers to cases where the individual feels "cut off and isolated from all that is important to them and responds in kind" (p. 219). The violent divorce cases are most applicable to the present discussion. They indicate that in these cases, "The wish to kill becomes sublimated by a wish to *punish*, which the victim accomplishes by forcing the spouse to witness the trauma of his or her death, leaving its memory like a Trojan horse in the spouse's psyche. The act is always violent and often impulsive, usually with diminished restraint fueled by alcohol" (pp. 217–218). McDowell et al. (1994) further suggest that the suicides convey a message to the witnesses that they are responsible and the victim wants them to suffer. Although we can never know the exact reasons an individual chooses to kill himself in front of another person, especially someone he indicated that he loved, a clear relationship appears to exist between physical and emotional abuse and these suicides.

Recall that Davis, Callanan, Lester, and Haines (2009) suggest four modes of adapting to relationship reciprocity-imbalance, including using suicide as a retreat, exploitation, retaliation, or to alleviate exploiter guilt. Suicides as retreat and exploitation were discussed in the last section. Committing suicide for retaliation "gives such individuals an unfair advantage in the relationship; they literally have the 'final word'" (p. 487). Davis, Callanan, Lester, and Haines found that the notes written by those who were determined to be using suicide as retaliation were full of blame and crafted so that surviving individuals would feel responsible and suffer guilt and remorse. Consider one mother's note to her son: "I know you hate me. I'm not alowed to see my grandGirls. Thanks to you I killed myself." Or Missy's words from previously, "I wish I coulda beat him to the punch. I wish I could have left him. I just want him to feel the pain & heart ache I am feeling...."

Although we had only a few notes to examine, the actions of the individuals spoke much louder than words. Consider the man who was killing himself out of love for his girlfriend ("I'm going to show you how much I love you") or the number of people who killed themselves in front of their partners. The focus of intervention in these relationships needs to be on the power, control, and abuse in the relationship and has to occur at the first signs of relationship imbalance. Power and control can also be accomplished through suicide threats, ideation, and attempts. Although threats should always be taken seriously, the victim can use these to control the relationship in many ways; e.g., his partner may stay in the relationship to prevent the suicide from happening, even though she no longer wants to be in the relationship. Ultimately, if she does leave the relationship, and the victim kills himself, she has to live with this knowledge. This is why the best intervention in these cases is to obtain professional help for each individual.

In theory, there should be some examples of suicide related to exploiter guilt in the abuse category. In exploiter guilt an individual becomes aware that s/he has exploited another and suicide becomes the only way to restore balance. This exploitation could have occurred over months or years or been a one-time occurrence. Although we did see a few examples of this, as in the case where one man raped his girlfriend and then killed himself out of guilt, it was rare. Exploiter guilt would require an individual to have a combination of tremendous self-awareness and to have engaged in exploitation. Generally, we found those who had been exploitative were not self-aware but rather self-centered. They were less accepting of responsibility and more likely to blame others and act out of retaliation.

Unknown Cause

Jimmy had been arguing with Molly, his live-in girlfriend, when she left the room to answer the phone. Moments later he emerged from their bedroom, placed a handgun under his chin and fired. According to Molly, they had frequent arguments, but prior to the shooting, there was nothing unusual about this specific quarrel. She had no idea why Jimmy killed himself.

In the final group of suicides which were motivated by relationships with intimate partners, it was difficult to determine the exact motivation for the suicide. In part, this was because no one left a note. All of these cases were precipitated by some interpersonal situation, usually arguments. However, in other cases the individual killed himself in response to other interpersonal stresses. One middle-aged man, for instance, killed himself because his wife was dying of cancer.

As in the other categories, the victims were mostly men (82%), white (94%), and ranged in age from 19 to 83 with an average age of 38. All three groups also had similar percentages of suicidal threats (24%) and ideation (14%). In some ways this group resembled the lost love group, including the low percentage of murder-suicide (2%) and parallel percentages in the method of suicide (54% guns and 34% asphyxiation). However, this group had the highest rate of known substance use prior to the suicide

(32%) as well as the highest percentage of substance abuse history (30%) of any group. This is especially significant given the paucity of information available on these individuals. In other words, the rates were likely even higher. They also had the lowest levels of health and legal problems. This reaffirms that interpersonal relationships were likely the cause of the suicide but the exact nature could not be determined. However, substance abuse was probably a contributing factor. Finally, the highest percentage of these suicides occurred in the fall (35%), when family celebrations occur. The lowest percentage was in the winter, unlike the lost love and abuse groups, so extended family may have been part of the catalyst.

Suicides Motivated by Other Interpersonal Relationships

It was really hard for Ashley to determine where it all started. Since high school, she had struggled with substance abuse and depression. When she met Jacob, life was just one big party. However, when she became pregnant, Jacob sobered up and tried to convince Ashley to do the same. There were periods where she was clean, but there were more lapses than not. After six years and two children, Jacob left and took the children with him. He obtained full custody and moved out of state. Despite everything, Ashley adored her children and wanted at least joint custody. However, she began to use more drugs and her depression deepened. Eventually she lost her job, because she simply stopping going. She moved out of her parents' house and began living in a motel. Shortly thereafter, she began expressing suicidal ideation to her family and friends. Ashley had a history of medical problems so it was relatively easy to plan her overdose since she had access to numerous medications. In her note, which was not addressed to anyone in particular, she said, "First of all, I want to appoligize for being such a huge burden on all of you! I talked to my kids today & they seem to be doing great! My dad told them that it is baby talk if they say mommy or daddy. It has to be mom or dad. So I guess I wasn't the best mom after all! I miss them so dearly-no one could imagine. My mom tells me she's tired of hearing me cry all the time. That's all I know how to express myself! Sorry for hurting so bad.... And let them [her children] know how much I loved them & will always look over them! I'm sorry I'm leaving you to hurt like this, but I'm tierd of suffering & being such a failure. I told everyone that if I didn't have them by Christmas I'd be gone. I love you all!"

A small subset (8% of the total category) existed of individuals who were motivated by interpersonal relationships that were not with intimate partners. These most frequently involved children or multiple family members but cases also involved parents, grandparents, or siblings. Although a few cases were seen with conflict relating to children involving lost custody, like Ashley, it was more likely that adult children were involved. For example, one man's adult children removed their mother from his care due to his substance abuse. In another typical scenario, the individual had a conflict with numerous family members, generally due to his actions. When it became clear that Carl was molesting his 8-year-old granddaughter, he was asked to move out of his son's home and ostracized by the rest of the family. Instead of packing, he went in his room and shot himself.

Only 17 individuals were in this subset and only two left notes, but it still has some distinguishing features. Most notably, 82% of these deaths occurred in the summer (29%) or fall (53%), often connected to family celebrations. Given this, it is not surprising that approximately one-fourth (24%) killed themselves in front of someone, and there were two murder-suicides which will be discussed in more detail in the murder-suicide section. This group had the lowest rate of depression (35%) and substance use prior to the suicide (18%) but they were the most likely to have physical illness (29%). Like Ashley, some of these individuals may represent the "perceived burdensomeness" that Joiner (2005) discussed in his theory. This would explain why the suicides occur in close proximity to family gatherings, when their burdensomeness may be more obvious to them.

All of the groups in this chapter highlight the pivotal role of interpersonal relationships in many suicides. In fact, one of the stressful life events (SLEs) that is a significant predictor for both lifetime and incident suicidal ideation is the onset of serious problems with a neighbor, friend, or relative (Wang et al., 2015). However, these problems may be interwoven with qualities that are common in those who have a depressive disorder, making it impossible to determine if depression leads to interpersonal problems or vice versa. In any case, both depression and interpersonal problems can lead to reduced social support. For many individuals, social support serves a protective function, helping to inhibit suicidal behaviors.

Murder-Suicide

Darrell and Amber had been married for 11 years and the police had been called to their home over 30 times related to domestic disputes. Their daughter, April, was seven years old and their son, Tyler, was two years old. Despite numerous attempts to work things out, including family therapy, and substance abuse and batterer's treatment for Darrell, the violence was becoming more frequent and unpredictable. Amber filed for divorce and acquired a TPO. Darrell was forced to move out. One Saturday morning, April went to visit a neighbor and upon returning found her mother in the closet, bound and gagged. Her father told her not to touch her mother and began barricading the doors. After a few hours of doing drugs and watching television, her father passed out on the bed. When April removed the gag from her mother's mouth, she told her to sneak out a window and run next door to her paternal grandmother's house and have her call the police. The grandmother did not want to see her son arrested so instead she called relatives who eventually agreed they needed to call the police. In the meantime, Darrell had awakened and was pouring gasoline all over the house.

The police arrived and tried to break down the barricade but were forced to retreat when flames began shooting from the house. When they were able to enter the home, they found Tyler and Amber burned and unconscious. Tyler died at the hospital a short time later, but Amber lived with extensive damage to her lungs and burns over half her body.

Darrell and Amber represent a typical murder-suicide with TPOs, domestic violence and intimate partners as victims. In our sample 35 cases involved murder-suicide or attempted murder-suicide. In 5 cases, the perpetrator intended to commit murder, but the victims, like Amber, survived the attempts on their lives, often with long-lasting consequences. For these reasons, the attempted murder victims are included in the murder-suicide group. Many were impulsive crimes but oftentimes there were warnings that went unheeded.

Some debate exists as to how to refer to a person who kills someone else, then kills himself or herself, and the deaths are connected. The perpetrator obviously has not been convicted of murder but this term has been used in the common nomenclature and will be used here. Murder-suicide has been defined as a murder that occurs within one week of the suicide (Marzuk, Tardiff, & Hirsch, 1992). Although this range can be debated, it is unnecessary to do so for the current discussion because in all of these cases the murder and suicide occurred within 24 hours of each other. This discussion will also not focus on rampage killers who target victims who are strangers.

Although murder-suicide is relatively rare in the United States, with an incidence rate under 0.001 (0.1%) (Eliason, 2009), approximately three men murder a current or former female partner every day (Vagionos, 2014). Most of the victims in our sample were wives or girlfriends or ex-wives or ex-girlfriends (86% of cases). Warren-Gordon, Byers, Brodt, Wartak, and Biskupki (2010) found in 69% of their cases the victim of homicide was a wife or girlfriend while 0% were husbands or boyfriends. In a few cases there were additional victims, generally children or boyfriends. Motivation for the suicide could be determined for 27 cases with 24 of those clearly motivated by difficulties in an intimate partner relationship. Divorce or separation is a common precipitating factor in murder-suicide (Eliason, 2009). Not surprisingly, we found interpersonal problems were reported in 74% of the cases and almost two-thirds of all cases involved a history of domestic violence towards their victims.

Marzuk, Tardiff, and Hirsch (1992) proposed a typology of murder-suicide that included amorous jealousy, declining health, filicide-suicide, familicide and extrafamilial murder-suicide. Amorous jealousy most often stems from a relationship, like Darrell and Amber's relationship, which has been chronically chaotic and marked with domestic violence and jealousy. The trigger is often rejection with the threat of withdrawal or estrangement. A new love interest may be involved, but the jealousy might be related simply to withdrawal of affection. Murder-suicides related to declining health are similar to altruistic or mercy killings and generally involve elderly couples. Filicide is the killing of one's own child while familicide is the killing of most, if not all, members of the family. Finally, extrafamilial murder-suicide is the killing of those outside of the family such as employers or teachers, often in an act of vengeance. While the majority of our cases involved an intimate partner motivated by amorous jealousy, in some cases a child killed a parent (once for declining health), a parent killed a child (filicide) and an adolescent killed most of his family (familicide), including his mother, grandparents, and a family friend. None of the intimate partner cases, not even one with an 86-year-old perpetrator, were precipitated by declining health but rather all involved interpersonal problems. No case would be classified as extrafamilial.

The perpetrators in our sample were mostly white (86%) and men (89%). The average age of the perpetrators was 43 and, while approximately two-thirds were under 50 years old, there was a range from 18–86 years old. These numbers are consistent with other findings. Marzuk, Tardiff, and Hirsch (1992) report that the average age of offenders in three United States studies was 39.6 and 93–97% of offenders were male while 50–86% were white. In a more recent review of the literature, Eliason (2009) found most perpetrators were men between 40 and 50 years old and that depression was the most common diagnosis in cases of murder-suicide. History of mental illness could only be determined for six individuals in our sample. Five of those were depressed, and one was unspecified. Although substance use and abuse was difficult to assess, at least five individuals were described as having a history of substance abuse and five had been using substances on the day of the murder-suicide. Eliason reviewed a study suggesting that 30% of perpetrators tested positive for alcohol and 22% were intoxicated at the time of the suicide.

Bossarte, Simon, and Barker (2006) found that in cases of murder suicide, many of the perpetrators had some form of legal involvement. In our sample, 34% were dealing with legal problems, such as assault, kidnapping, divorce proceedings and violations of TPOs (it was unknown whether the other 66% were involved in any legal issues). One 56-year-old man stabbed his 22-year-old girlfriend outside of the grade school where his wife was teaching and then entered the school, stabbed his wife 14 times in front of her fifth-grade students, then shot her. She had filed for divorce, after 30 years of marriage, due to his domestic violence. He had been making threatening calls to her for weeks and she had obtained a TPO, which he had violated. Although his wife died, his girlfriend survived the attack.

This is actually an aberrant case as 78.5% of murder-suicides occur in a private home (Warren-Gordon, Byers, Brodt, Wartak, & Biskupki, 2010). Most of the murder victims in our sample were killed in or around their homes (80%), and many perpetrators killed themselves in front of others (37%). In McDowell et al.'s (1994) study of witnessed suicides, researchers concluded that "the witnesses (other than the victim) are incidental. They play no role in the central drama and their presence is as much a matter of happenstance as anything else" (p. 217).

The vast majority of perpetrators (89%) used guns when committing the murder or the suicide, or both. Similarly, Warren-Gordon et al. (2010) found a high percentage (77%) of perpetrators used firearms. The murders were most likely to occur on Monday (22%) followed by Sunday (20%), and least likely to occur on Friday (9%) or Saturday (6%). Murder-suicides were more than twice as likely to occur in the winter (32%) than in the summer (14%).

Only four women committed murder-suicide. Two of the four women committed the murder for altruistic reasons. Charlene signed her mother out of an assisted-care facility on Christmas Day and took her to a family gathering. Despite the fact that Charlene's mother was in the advanced stages of Alzheimer's disease, and could not even recognize her, she always made sure her mother attended family events. As the day was winding down and the rest of the family was in the kitchen cleaning, Charlene shot her mother in the head and then turned the gun on herself. The other woman who had altruistic motives killed her son. Seven years prior to killing her son, she had been in a car accident which left her with a severe head injury. She left a note for her surviving children which mostly contained instructions but also said, "What can I say except my life has been rough & I am so tired. My mind is not right and I can't go on like this anymore. Liam (the child she killed), he stays sick and never feels good. He has so many problems. For so many reasons this is best."

Only three people left notes and two of them were women. The other woman left a note explaining why she was killing her three children, ages 5, 4, and 2. Again, most of her note contained instructions, but then she stated, "I know you wont understand why, but I just can't go on anymore. I'm so tired of hurting. I know I'm going to hell, but life is a living hell." There are very few other indicators as to why this woman killed her children. However, as she was a single mother with three very young children and no resources, it is likely life felt overwhelming. Additionally, mothers who purposely set out to kill their children, particularly multiple children, are also frequently dealing with mental health issues (Meyer & Oberman, 2001). This woman killed her children eight days after she had purchased a hand gun.

The third person to leave a note was a 50-year-old man who was struggling with mental and physical health issues. He wrote the note after he killed his 73-year-old stepmother, whom he said hastened his father's death by neglecting him after he had a stroke. In the note he indicated where police could find her body, then said, "Ice cold woman. If I ever got sick to die, I would kill her. Eye for an eye. So I did this crime. She was evil. So her day to go." These cases were aberrations both in the relationship the victims had with the perpetrators and the fact that the perpetrators left notes. The last person to leave a note was Ray, discussed previously, who killed his intimate partner.

In another case murder-suicide did not occur, although the perpetrator considered it. Shaun had a long history of unrequited love with the intended victim. In his note he said,

> I loved you I think truely the second I saw you. I know you were repulsed by me at first and wanted to leave. I was so glad you stayed, after you got to see me for who I really was. I truely don't know what to say to you now. We have had a rough 4 years some good yet so many bad times. Love will make us all do crazy things. Staying together for so long was the craziest of all I guess....Madeline (their child) became what I lived for. I lost you along time ago, but I didn't want to admit it to myself. You probably won't get it. You have always treated me like a child. You never showed me any respect at all. Yet you demanded for yourself.
>
> Blame for all of this is mine. I should have ended us a long time ago, but I never had the courage.
>
> I'm so tired of all the argueing. I have thought about doing this several times and have thought of taking you with me. Madeline was what stopped me from anything. I love her dearly.

Shaun was found dead in his truck in a shopping mall parking lot. On his right arm he had written "Forgive me" while on his left arm he wrote "Worthless." His love for their daughter served a protective function.

Unfortunately, having children did not prevent others from killing their partners, sometimes in front of their children. Serena awoke at 2:30 one morning to the shouts of her drunken husband outside of their apartment. The police came and cited him for public intoxication, releasing him to her custody. They began to argue and he shot her in the chest with a shotgun, then put the weapon under his chin and shot himself. At 3:00 a.m. their 11-year-old daughter, who had witnessed the whole episode, called the police to report the deaths of her parents.

One case provides a unique perspective on murder-suicide. Don, 54, and Karen, 52, had been married three years and had occasional disagreements about finances. In the last month Karen noticed that Don had become increasingly depressed and withdrawn. He even said at one point, "I should just blow both our brains out." Karen did not take this seriously and one morning as they argued Don retrieved a gun, told his wife he was going to follow through with his threat, and forced her to write a "farewell note." After the note was written, Don left the kitchen with the note and walked into the living room, and Karen fled out the back door. As she ran to a neighbor's house, she heard a single gunshot. The note lists numerous friends and family then reads, "I love all of you & so does Don. I don't understand why Don thought this was the only way this could be. I can't say how I feel in such a short time—but I hope you all know. I love you <u>so very</u> much. I guess this is goodbye. Be happy in your lives & know you have always had a special place in my heart. Love you, Karen. Hugs and kisses." It is unclear whether Don allowed Karen to leave or shot himself after he knew she had left and he had lost control of the situation. Although this is ostensibly "their" note, Don really provided little input. Perhaps he stepped out of the room to consider the content of the note and it distracted or dissuaded him from killing Karen. Maybe, as in the case of Shaun, the love Karen expressed for others made Don consider the impact of his actions. Alternatively, maybe Don had no intention of killing Karen but received some sort of sadistic pleasure in making her write the note, believing that she was about to die. In any case, Karen escaped unharmed.

Joiner (2014) argues that perpetrators of murder-suicide decide on the suicide first, then commit the murder for "virtuous" reasons which represent distortions of one of four interpersonal virtues: mercy, justice, duty, or heroic glory. The case described previously in which Charlene murdered her mother and then committed suicide would be considered mercy. When justice is the virtue, an individual murders someone who has wronged him or her. The man who killed the stepmother who had neglected his dying father did so because she had wronged both his father and him. These two virtues represent the most common types. However, duty involves acting on responsibilities to others. The mother who killed her three children may have done so out of duty. Some mothers who kill their children do so because not doing so would result in harm to the rest of society; e.g., they believe their children are defective in some way and not killing them would have a negative impact on society. Finally, some commit murder-suicide to obtain glory for themselves. Joiner uses the example of the Columbine High School shooters, whose goal was to kill more people than were killed in the Oklahoma City bombings.

These are interesting conceptualizations, and Joiner examines each of them in great detail in his book. Many people do decide to kill themselves first and then plan the murder. However, some of the more spontaneous murder-suicides described here are difficult to fit into Joiner's framework. Although murder-suicides generally involve interpersonal problems and domestic violence, they represent a small subset of cases. It is much more likely that interpersonal problems and domestic violence will end in *either* a murder or a suicide but not both. Similar to other cases described in this chapter, risk factors or warning signs exist.

In all cases, the perpetrator and victim were in some kind of relationship, usually as intimate partners. It was the threat of the end of this relationship that precipitated most of the murder-suicides. In these relationships the perpetrators, generally men, had been controlling and often engaged in verbal or physical abuse. In almost every case, there was easy access to guns. In most cases, even in filicide cases, the perpetrators were young, usually under 40 years old. Although it is impossible to determine the exact prevalence of substance abuse and depression, these were present in at least five of the cases.

In an article in the *New Yorker*, Rachel Snyder cited some often-quoted statistics stating, "Between 2000 and 2006, thirty-two hundred American soldiers were killed; during that period, domestic homicide in the United States claimed ten thousand six hundred lives" (Snyder, 2013, p. 35). Risk factors for murder-suicide are similar to those present in intimate partner homicide (Campbell et al., 2003). In an effort to reduce intimate partner homicide and murder-suicide, domestic violence high-risk teams have been created to coordinate agencies and assess the risk for lethal violence (Snyder, 2013). Danger assessments allow teams to determine who is at the highest risk for intimate partner homicide and provide more support for potential victims while placing greater restrictions on batterers. Prior to this, the only recourse for women to remain safe was to house them (and generally their children) in shelters, cutting them off from family, friends and often employment. This isolation and lack of ability to work often created both financial and emotional hardship. Under danger assessment systems, it is the batterer that is restrained, not the victim. Police may confiscate guns, increase drive-by observations of the victim's house and work, deny bail or monitor the batterer through the use of a GPS. Training in and adoption of this model have increased.

CONCLUSIONS

Conflict in interpersonal relationships, specifically with intimate partners, was the motivation for approximately one-fifth of our cases. As Joiner (2005) suggested, many of these people wanted to connect with others but were unable to do so, resulting in a thwarted belongingness. However, two main subgroups emerged: those who committed suicide because of lost or unrequited love and those whose suicide was part of a more abusive relationship. For these groups, the suicides may have represented different ways of achieving balance in a relationship that had become imbalanced. When individuals committed suicide due to lost love or thwarted belongingness, the suicide allowed them to retreat from a painful relationship. On the other hand, for those who had been abusive in a relationship but had lost control because their intimate partner had left them, the suicide served more as retaliation. Extreme versions of this culminated in murder-suicide. Since these motivations and relationships are very different, the needs of the victims and interventions would also differ. While those suffering the loss of a love may benefit from the interpersonal support provided by a suicide hotline, such support would not prevent the more spontaneous suicides which frequently occur in abusive relationships.

Not all interpersonally motivated suicides are represented by these two groups. Another subgroup may emerge from the suicides that were due to interpersonal conflict with intimate partners, but in which the motivation could not be determined. However, with additional information, it is likely that many of these individuals would be accounted for by the present motivational categories, lost love, and abuse-related suicides. Suicides that are due to interpersonal conflict with other family members represent other dynamics and may be tied to perceived burdensomeness.

Escape as a Motivation for Suicide

When wondering why anyone would consider suicide, interpersonal issues are frequently considered a primary factor. From *Romeo and Juliet* to the film *It's Kind of a Funny Story* (2011), popular culture is flush with examples of individuals who kill themselves because of lost or unrequited love. One movie is even called *Love and Suicide* (2006). Despite this, the most prevalent motivation for suicide in our sample was to escape pain. We could not identify the motivation for 344 individuals in our overall sample, but 658 of the remaining 936 people (70%) were escaping from pain. The source of the pain was psychological (32%), physical (18%), legal (8%), financial (3%), or a combination of many of these things (39%). When cases were sorted into these groups, clear patterns emerged.

ESCAPING FROM MULTIPLE ISSUES

When Jim was in high school he used to cut himself just to feel the pain. He said, "When you are first born and through childhood you are happy, you bounce back from so much mentally and physically, you have pure goodness. As you get older you start to realize that life is pain, and we are all wired for pain. You spend your time thinking of the future but when you get there all you think about is the past. NO ONE is ever truly happy at any time. Life is pain and anyone who says differently is trying to sell something."

Eventually he began to burn himself as well. He wrote, "I have now heard the sound of my own flesh burning. When I put something red hot, and I do mean glowing red against my skin, it makes a crackling sound, like rice crispy's. Yum. Only this makes me feel relaxed." Jim was both obese and a heavy smoker. At 22 years old he had a massive heart attack which left him debilitated and depressed. He also had permanent heart damage, which made his dreams of being a firefighter impossible, so he decided to go back to school. At school, drinking

Explaining Suicide.
DOI: http://dx.doi.org/10.1016/B978-0-12-809289-7.00004-X

73

replaced his self-mutilation as a way to alleviate some of his social anxiety. He stated, "Drinking is a temporary relief to my pain, so is cutting and burning (not to big on burning)." However, his drinking made it impossible for him to keep up with his classes, and he was placed on academic probation. Jim moved back in with his parents and began working at a local grocery.

Jim had always considered suicide. He wrote, "All my life I have thought about suicide. How I would do it, where I would do it, I always have thought about it but I have never planned it or even started to think or consider planning it. For the last month or two I have started planning it. This is a huge difference from before because I don't just want to do it anymore, I am going to do it." One afternoon Jim came home from work, went to his room, smoked some pot and perused some pornographic magazines. Then he pointed a handgun at his faulty heart and pulled the trigger. In his note Jim said, "2 rules to life. 1. There is always a victim. 2. Don't be it. I am tired of being a victim."

Ed was a contractor who lost his small business when the bottom dropped out of the economy. Although he applied for many jobs, he could not find employment. He suspected that because he was in his late fifties, no one wanted to hire him for a manual labor job. He was upset that he could not provide for his wife and four daughters and this eventually led to depression. He dealt with the depression by withdrawing to his bedroom where he would remain for long periods of time. He began having physical problems and was diagnosed with high blood pressure. Ed refused to take his medications and had a stroke. When he was discharged from the hospital, he began threatening suicide. On one occasion, he left the house with a gun which he placed under the seat of his car. Fearing for his safety, his wife called the police, and Ed was arrested for carrying a concealed weapon. A few weeks later his 14-year-old daughter came home from school and found him dead on the couch. He had taken an overdose of pain pills, then shot himself in the head. In his note he said, "Too this end, I give up this life. Despite everything I've done the best I could. I am just too tirid to keep on 'keepin on.' No I don't feel sorry for myself. Its just a good day to die. What has taken me so long is to try doing it without leaving a mess for the girls to find. I love you."

Jim and Ed represent the largest group within the escape category, those who had killed themselves to escape multiple problems (258 people). These individuals are similar to the other escape categories in that they are trying to end some pain or psychache, but unlike other escape categories, not one precipitant is identified. For example, in the physical escape category, the primary precipitant is pain related to some physical cause. Individuals in the escape multiple group were struggling with pain from numerous stressors including any combination of physical, psychological, financial, legal, or interpersonal problems. For Jim, these were lifelong stressors but for Ed, unemployment led to a downward spiral that resulted in a pain too great for him to handle. Sometimes the spiral takes years but other times, such as with legal involvement, it can take days.

Similar to our overall sample, and every subgroup, the victims were mostly Caucasian (94%) men (82%) who killed themselves at home (76%). The average age was 47 with a range of 11–89 years old. Although it may be hard to imagine how an 11-year-old could have a multitude of problems that caused unbearable pain, the confluence of circumstances, misery, an inability to envision an end to the pain, and a lack of appropriate and sufficient help can push even young people into suicide. Jordan, the youngest person in the sample, suffered from seizures, allergies, and asthma for most of his life. He recently had been expelled from school for behavioral problems and was referred to therapy for his depression. For years, Jordan had been saying that he wanted to die. Unfortunately Alice, his mother, was having difficulty finding a mental health provider that accepted her insurance. One day Alice went to the grocery and when she returned she found Jordan "sleeping" in his closet. She did not notice the tie wrapped around his neck. Later, when he did not come down for dinner, she realized something was wrong, but it was too late to revive him. Like Jordan, each of the very young children in our sample had a long history of multiple problems.

Some of Jordan's problems were representative of the other individuals in this group. At least half had physical problems (50%) or substance abuse problems (50%), or both. Twelve percent spoke of their disabilities in their notes. In addition, approximately three-fourths (73%) had identified psychological problems such as depression (80%), bipolar disorder (5%), schizophrenia (1%), multiple diagnoses (8%), or miscellaneous other diagnoses (5%), such as anxiety. One-fourth had previously attempted suicide, 24% had made threats and 22% had suicidal ideation. When these victims wrote of their psychological pain, it sounded remarkably similar. Their feelings were expressed in the strongest terms.

Christy began abusing drugs in high school. At 42 years old she was in a near-fatal car accident that left her with facial distortions and a physical disability. Although she was able to break free of her addictions, she was severely depressed. In her note she said,

> I can no longer tolerate the pain I feel & have felt for many years. I am referring to the emotional pain which has only increased since I stopped using drugs. I contemplated using again but I know in my heart that drugs would only compound the problems so that was not an option. My facial injuries make me feel grotesque...I isolate myself because I cannot stand for people to see me. My depression is paralyzing. I hate being on disability. I want to work & be a productive member of society. I am not in any kind of trouble. I am also in a great deal of physical pain.

Paul and Suzanne had been high school sweethearts. When Suzanne was diagnosed with breast cancer, they vowed to fight it together. Unfortunately, she died just before her 50th birthday. In the 12 years after her death, Paul struggled with depression and attempted suicide several times. His depression was so severe that he was on disability. A few months before he committed suicide, Paul began a new relationship but they broke up because Paul could not move beyond his depression. He wrote, "I have begged God over and over for years to please take me home out of my mental anguish, and yet here I am. Why does God torture me? Why doesn't he help me??"

Christy exemplifies the interpersonal problems that many individuals (47%) were dealing with in this group and 37% spoke about in their notes. Christy isolated herself but other people talked about lost or unrequited love in their notes. Although some of these endings were recent, many, like Paul, were still suffering years after the end of the relationship. One man described the loss saying,

> Eighteen years ago I loved a woman so completely and so perfectly I thought I had found my life long love and so did she. After five years together she went out of town on business and came home and left me without any explanation whatsoever. I was stunned and heartbroken. When she left a part of my soul left with her. Whatever from deep deep inside me left was, it has never returned and my soul has remained empty since August 5th 1984. It has been 18 years since a pretty woman has touched my hand or put her arms around my neck and said "I love you."

Although there are many stories similar to this relating to the loss of a partner, rarely did interpersonal problems that involved domestic violence occur in this group (5%).

Other interpersonal problems were not due to lost romantic relationships, but caused instead by strained interactions with family members. Lori was conflicted about whether to press charges against her daughter, who had stolen $1000.00 from her, thus causing a financial crisis. Lori struggled with mental and physical health issues as well, and while she was hospitalized for her depression, her daughter stole her credit card. The last straw was when Lori learned her insurance would not cover her hospital bill. She wrote,

> ...Finding out that I do not have good insurance I could of never gotten out of this debt....my mind is not the same. its a chemical imbalance & God will understand. Rember the way I used to be. Please. Love always, Nicole. I will be looking down on you & be your guardian angel Remember me when you see a goldfinch....I just can't take the physical or mental pain anymore. I do not want to end up in the mental ward...Mia, I was so tired of you wishing me dead & cutting me down, & stealing from me That I hope your happy that you took everything from me.

Overall, financial (41%) and legal (35%) problems were almost as prevalent as interpersonal problems among those trying to escape multiple issues. In their notes, 24% talked about financial problems while 18% referred to their legal problems. Inadequate medical insurance was occasionally a complicating circumstance, as with Jordan and Lori. Oftentimes, as with Lori, the legal and financial issues were intertwined with interpersonal, physical, or mental health problems. Occasionally, other problems were mentioned in the notes such as employment (16%) or school (6%).

Fifty-one people in this group (20%) left notes and most of those (61%) left only one note. Most notes (63%) were addressed to a specific person and were signed (59%). Some evidence existed of tunnel vision or constricted thought processes (29%) and/or dichotomous thinking (14%) in the notes. For example, an elderly man with multiple health issues wrote this note to his wife of 50 years, "I did not want to do it this way, but all other alternatives scared me. I did not want to postpone it any longer on account of finances, and I was getting so bad. I could not even read anymore. It will take you awhile to adjust but it looks like you will have a good future. 'Your Loving Husband.'"

Most people talked about their love for others (75%), mentioning their children (41%), partners (39%), parents (33%), siblings (16%) or other family (27%), and friends (22%) in their notes. Fourteen percent said they felt loved by others. It is not surprising then that many (63%) felt a need to provide some justification for their actions, sometimes identifying a precipitant (20%). Some directed apologies to specific individuals (47%) while others offered general apologies (33%) or asked for forgiveness (37%). They absolved others from blame (24%) but sometimes blamed others (18%).

Some note writers specifically said life was not worth living (25%) or they needed to escape (35%). Paul, in his early sixties, said, "I just couldn't take any more of my nothingness life. It was beyond horrible." Adam had struggled with substance abuse and physical illness since he was an adolescent. In his second year of college he was expelled when he assaulted his roommate during a night of heavy drinking. He said,

> I'm sorry things turned out this way, but shit happens. Some can say that they have it worse, and that might be true...but it is in the eye of the beholder as to how it is. I have had many good times in my life...I have also had many bad times...to many to overpower the good. The fact is that recently (and by recently I mean the past few years) ALL things have caused pain that I do not want to endure....To my family, do not think that this has anything to do with you casue it doesn't...I'm just sick and tired of the disappointment life cont. to bring me. I'm sick of paying for life (syn, insulin). I have tried to settle my problems by all other means...but they have the same outcome, disappointment.

However, even if the note writer did not explicitly discuss the need to escape, or say that life was not worth living, the overall tone of *all* the notes reflects these sentiments. Some instead referred to their physical (27%) or psychological pain (31%) or just talked about unspecified pain

(12%). Still, never was just one source of pain cited, but many, often of interrelated origins.

When note writers did refer to the afterlife (31%) it was often in relation to their present circumstances. One man in his midforties said, "To my family, I am very sorry, I know you have been through enough. Life is not worth it. I will take my chances on the other side!! I love you all. ME. I just wanted help, It is overwhelming (LIFE) I'm sorry." Some talked about God (26%): "May God have mercy on my soul. I have not been the best. I am so lost. I am so weak...And to all don't grieve, my Father has prepared many rooms for me." A small number envisioned God watching over loved ones (13%). Some despaired that there was no God. "I just wished there was a God to help me in these final moments of loneliness," one man lamented in his note. He then shot himself in his vehicle in the parking lot of his sister's apartment building.

Others spoke of reuniting with loved ones who were already deceased (8%) or after those who are alive have died (14%). A few pondered the morality of suicide (20%). They also left instructions (69%) regarding how to dispose of their property (29%) or their bodies (29%) or managing their affairs (29%). Some made requests to take care of others (25%) and occasionally advice was offered (22%). Some told police that this was a suicide (12%) or insisted on no attempts to resuscitate (8%). A few people used quotations from songs or books in their notes (10%).

Other feelings were mentioned in the notes. It is not surprising that some note writers felt tired (18%), lonely (16%), sad (16%), joyful (8%), hopeless (10%), worthless (10%), guilty (8%), and/or like a burden (14%) or failure (10%), as these feelings are relatively consistent with the need to escape. Only one or two people talked about feeling ambivalent, apathetic, or ashamed. For the most part, they were unwavering in the course of action that they had decided upon. In fact, a few expressed relief. Unlike the anger that was present in so many suicides which were driven by interpersonal relationships, only a few individuals expressed feeling angry.

Even the suicidal acts are in stark contrast to those who were motivated by interpersonal relationships. In our research, those who killed themselves to escape pain were less likely to use violent means such as guns or knives than nonviolent means such as poison or hanging. Those who killed themselves for interpersonal reasons more often used violent means. Thirteen of these individuals killed themselves in front of another person; three committed murder-suicide and two of the victims were not intimate partners. Guns were much less frequently used (45%) and more victims died by asphyxia (28%) or toxic substances (22%). Asphyxia was three times more likely to be from ligature or hanging than from carbon monoxide. Hanging is certainly not as impulsive as using a firearm and sends a very different message. Consider the case of Zack.

After high school, Zack started going to rave parties and experimented with LSD and ecstasy. Then he met Lisa. They fell in love, married and had two children. However, Zack could not give up his raves, and eventually he and Lisa split up. Zack also could not hold a job, because he always showed up late for work. When his car broke down he bought a used car from a friend but after weeks still had not paid him the money. Eventually, the friend went to the police and Zack was issued a summons. Zack wrote notes to his family and his new girlfriend, then asked a neighbor to give her the package of notes. He returned home, used a ladder to secure a rope over the rafter in his living room, tied a noose around his neck, put duct tape over his mouth, and kicked the ladder out from under him. When his girlfriend received the package she called the police.

Presumably Zack covered his mouth so no one would hear him struggling or perhaps so no one would come to his aid. However, it may also have been symbolic as to how Zack felt during the last years of his life, silenced by his problems and life itself. Certainly, for some children and adolescents, like Jordan, hanging may be the most readily available option, but for most people in this group, many other options existed. Perhaps they wanted to feel life slip away from them, again symbolically representing what it has felt like over the course of time. Maybe, like Jim, who was described at the beginning of the chapter, they wanted to feel the pain in death, the way they felt it in life.

Overall, individuals who killed themselves to escape multiple problems felt suicide was the only solution. Some feared where the future would lead them; others felt life had simply become too exhausting. In the words of one victim, "I'm just so tired, tired of the pain and just tired of the struggle. Every day I go out and pretend, I pretend nothing is wrong when deep down all I want to do is leave."

Suicidal action can be a seasonal affliction. A popular perception is that people are more likely to commit suicide on holidays like Thanksgiving and Christmas (Jamieson, Jamieson, & Romer, 2003). A number of studies have addressed the question of seasonality in suicide, but one study focused on the differences between violent and nonviolent suicide. Maes, Cosyns, Meltzer, De Meyer, and Peeters (1993) found that seasonality was present in violent but not in nonviolent suicide. The number of violent suicides increased with age and was more prominent in men. According to the study, "The violent suicide chronograms of younger and elderly persons were quite distinct in the occurrence of peaks in March–April and August, respectively, and lows in December–January" (Maes et al., 1993, p. 1380). In our group, 31 people (12%) committed suicide in June, while 14 people, or 5%, died in December. Many people killed themselves late in the month, near the 20th (7%). Forty-three (17%) killed themselves on Wednesday.

The notes often reflect no sense of season or time. It is as if the cyclical rhythms of life that are so often marked by holidays followed by ordinary days have blurred into one form of time, eternal misery. Each day, no matter what day, was one faced with trepidation. "I cannot go on with this awful dread that fills each day," one man wrote mournfully. "I have lost all will to live. I have lost all the elements needed to survive in work, love and life. I am so sorry for what this will do to my most wonderful children to which I am so blessed and my sister who has been great." He died in early September. One 43-year-old woman suffering from diabetes and psychological pain drove her sports car, without braking, into a tree. She left a note that said, "I have given up on love, trust, faith & hope & dreams. There really is no such thing anymore & that's sad. Im certainly not worth any tears but I doubt if anyone is sad anyway. So I guess that's it." She died in mid-September. A man went to his storage shed, full of the stuff of his life. In his note, he said material possessions never meant much to him, but events unfolded that were going to result in him losing everything. "If I don't do this I see nothing but jail, misery & a slow painful death for the remainder of my life....Don't be sad for now I am released...I've been carrying a big ball of guilt, shame, embarrassment hopelessness and worthlessness in my gut." He hanged himself in mid-December. In none of these cases was there a mention of the time of year. The days of pain were ongoing, unending sameness.

ESCAPING FROM PSYCHOLOGICAL PAIN

Virginia had struggled with depression for most of her life. When she met Bill she thought he would be her knight in shining armor. They married when she was 23 years old and had four children during the first decade of their marriage. Virginia did not realize until after they were married that Bill could not control his drinking. When Virginia quit her job to take care of the children, it increased the strain on both their finances and their marriage. Bill became verbally abusive and Virginia, who had already been taking medications for her depression, became anxious as well. Finally, she took the children and left Bill. She found single parenting difficult, but not as difficult as living with Bill. Virginia relied on her mother to help her with the children, but when the children were teenagers her mother suffered a stroke and died. Virginia's depression worsened, and she began seeing a therapist.

After her family was raised, Virginia rented a small apartment and continued to work. She was a political activist and had even published a book, but these accomplishments did not assuage her psychological pain. She told her friends and co-workers that she had begun dating again and that she and her boyfriend were moving in together. However, no one ever met her boyfriend and some even questioned his existence. As the date of their cohabitation neared, Virginia told friends and co-workers that her boyfriend had been called away because of a family emergency. Shortly after that, she wrote notes to her family, drove to a park, and took an overdose of medications. In one note she said, "I fought the depression &

anxiety since the 70's. I just don't want to deal with this anymore. I'm tired. Even as a child I've thought about not <u>living</u>. That may be hard to believe but it's true."

Life was crashing down on a number of different fronts for Jim, Ed, and Christy, who were described in the previous section. For individuals who commit suicide to escape psychological problems, one main source of distress exists, their mental illnesses. Like Virginia, most of the people in this category struggled with mental illness for a very long time. Although the average was 43, ages ranged from 12 to 82 years old, with over 70% under 50. The three youngest people in the sample were 12, 13, and 14 years old, and they were all diagnosed with bipolar disorder. Virginia thought about dying when she was a child; these children acted. Others talked about having feelings of wanting to die since they were children. One man said, "…but I still felt in my heart this was my fate because no one dies unless its ur time too…It was my fate callen now I understand why I was thinking about death when I was a little kid. Now I understand why I felt out of place as a kid when I felt weird some times about life because I was completly lost and was suppose to stay this way my whole life now I no why I felt this way and thought this way it was the shadows death."

This group had 208 people, making it the second largest subcategory within escape. Similar to other groups, most of these individuals were Caucasian (88%), but this is the first group where the gap between the percentage of men (68%) and women is not as large. Women are approximately twice as likely as men to be depressed, and depression is the most prevalent diagnosis among those who commit suicide (Mayo Clinic, 2016). This is the first group where the number of men and women leaving notes was equal.

Twenty-four individuals left notes, which represented 12% of the group. For the most part, the notes were short and to the point. The majority left one note (75%) and they were under 150 words long (58%). They generally mentioned their struggles and professed their love for others (75%) and some said they felt loved by others (17%). They mentioned parents (33%), children (29%), partners (17%), other family (21%), siblings (13%), and friends (8%). Most had a specific addressee (67%) and were signed (58%). Overall, the victims' thoughts were organized (88%), and very little evidence of tunnel vision (8%) or dichotomous thinking (4%) appeared.

The percentages of people who provided a justification for their actions is almost the same as in the escape multiple group (71%) and so is the percentage who asked for forgiveness (33%). Generally, they asked for forgiveness from God. One woman's entire note read,

> To my dear family. I love all of you so very much! Please take care of each other! I hope I have been a good wife, mother and grandmother! I just can't fight this depression any more. Please forgive me! I hope our Lord will find in his heart to forgive me. Love to all of you!

Another note read, "I just can't go on anymore. I've thought about this for a very long time. But now I feel I can follow through. I just hope God can forgive me. I've been wanting to go home for a very long time."

In comparison to the escape multiple group, fewer felt a need to apologize to specific individuals (25% vs 47%), offer general apologies (25% vs 33%), absolve others from blame (21% vs 24%) or blame others (8% vs 18%). There really was not anyone to blame and nothing for which to apologize, since they had an illness that they could not control.

Other than their psychological issues, they had few other identified problems. In general, they were not in legal (4%) or financial trouble (7%) and only one identified as having job problems while none had school problems. Ten percent of note writers in this group mentioned legal trouble in their notes, while 15% mentioned financial issues. Whereas almost half of the escape multiple group were dealing with interpersonal problems, only 29% of this group were having these issues, and there were very few (3) reports of domestic violence. Only one person talked about interpersonal abuse in her note. Even the percentage of physical illness (26%) was approximately half that of the escape multiple group. For these individuals, it was all about the pain of their mental illnesses.

Although the majority of individuals were depressed (61%), 15% had multiple diagnoses, 11% had bipolar disorder, 6% had schizophrenia, and for the rest the actual mental illness was not specified in the report. Some of the victims with mental illness had made previous suicide attempts (37%) or threats (25%) and had suicidal ideation (25%). It is not uncommon among people with mental illness to use substances frequently to self-medicate, and almost a fourth had problems with substance abuse (Bolton, Robinson, & Sareen, 2009).

No overwhelming themes appeared in their notes other than the need to escape (46%) and acknowledgment of their psychological pain (46%). One man who had struggled with lifelong mental illness and then separated from his wife described his pain as follows, "There is an emptiness, a hurt, pain!!! I can't describe, I don't have the word to explain, agony-rip, tear my flesh, HURT, HURT. Forgive me." No one talked about physical pain, although some talked about unspecified pain (13%). Over one-fourth (29%) mentioned interpersonal issues and 33% talked of God, the afterlife (17%) or the morality of suicide (17%). Three thought suicide was immoral but discussed reuniting with the living after they died. One imagined watching over his loved ones. Interestingly, two out of ten of the women who wrote notes were retired surgical nurses.

When considering how short these notes were, and that most everyone mentioned love for others and almost half talked about the need to escape, the remaining content was sparse and not consistent across notes. A few of the note writers said that life was not worth living or that they felt like a failure or that they were lonely. Only one or two people mentioned feeling tired, guilty, shame, burdensome, hopeless, worthless, ambivalent, relieved, angry, or joyous. One person discussed being discriminated against. No one said they felt apathetic, talked about dissatisfaction with his/her body image, a recent death or having a disability.

When they left instructions (50%) they talked about taking care of others (25%), managing property (17%) or other affairs (13%), or disposal of the body (4%). When they gave advice (33%) it was generally short and simple, such as "U got to stay strong and learn quick or U die so be smart about every move u make." Virginia told her son to "Stay the way you are."

The methods that these individuals used to kill themselves were very similar to those used when individuals were motivated to escape multiple problems. Guns were only slightly more predominant (39%) than asphyxia (28%) and overdose (25%). Those who asphyxiated were three times more likely to die by hanging than by carbon monoxide. Most of the suicides occurred at home (82%) and only 13% were reported to have been using substances prior to their suicides. The most prevalent days of the week were Monday or Friday (19%) and the least prevalent was Wednesday (10%). Six percent killed themselves in front of someone, and there was no murder-suicide.

At least two of the women who wrote notes, including Virginia, had been lying to friends and relatives about major issues in their lives. After her death, it was confirmed that Virginia had been lying about her relationship status. One woman in her late twenties was lying to her relatives about having cancer. She had told her family and boyfriend that she had cancer, yet it was determined that this was a fabrication. All her loved ones remarked that she was very secretive about her health matters. In her note to her parents she wrote,

> For so many years now I've felt so depressed and all alone. I've never been able to shake these feelings! Words cannot describe how I've felt. I feel like a failure. A train wreck waiting to happen. I've spent most of my life pleasing others and doing things for them. It's time now that I do something for myself—I just need an end to my misery. I love you—I love all my family—but sometimes that's not enough to keep someone going—I'm so sorry—Please always remember this has nothing to do with anyone but myself. I just can't fight these horrible feelings that I have.

In her mind, her suicide was something she was doing for herself.

In fact, in some notes the note writer seemed to think that the impending suicide was just one more thing in her day. Jessica, 57, had struggled with depression her whole life. When her husband went out to a movie, she wrote a note, took an overdose of her medications, then lay down on her bed clutching a crucifix to her chest. When her husband came home he found her in that position. The first part of her note read, "Pete Warwick wants you to work tomorrow." The font for the first part of the note is much larger, suggesting she may have written it earlier before the medications took effect. Then in the second part she wrote, "I love you with all my heart forever and Trish & Carly too but I can't go backward again. I can't make it through. God forgive me. I love you forever and always Jessica I'm sorry I failed you." It is almost as if this was just a routine part of her day. Did she write the first part and then decide to kill herself or did she know she was going to kill herself when she wrote it? If she knew, it is almost as if she had no awareness that her husband would likely not be working the next day because his wife had just died. Or maybe she thought her death would not be important enough to keep him from work.

The prevailing sense in these notes is that the note writer is done with life and has made an indisputable decision to die. When Harry turned 65 years old he retired from his trucking job and had a lot of free time. Despite the fact that he was in Gamblers Anonymous, and had always struggled with his addiction to gambling, he decided to try his luck once more. In three months, he had gambled away $225,000. He wrote a letter to his friend who was the executrix of his will and told her of his intentions. The note to her was mainly instructions but he also said, "I have been so depressed for so long I really feel no need or want, to go on." Enclosed with the note was a second note that Harry wrote to his dog apologizing for abandoning him and wishing him well. When she received the letter she called police, and they found Harry dead from a gunshot wound to the head. It is difficult to determine if Harry's gambling problem led to his depression or his depression led him to gamble, but the end result was the same.

In short, the notes and actions of people in this group are unambiguous. They had simply had enough of life and wanted to die to escape the psychological pain. Some had received interventions and some had not. Others, like Harry, thought they had put their demons behind them, but they had not. They could never envision a time when they would have control over their own lives. As one person said, "This was my fate to be lost my whole life and die young... I never had control of my life so I wanted to have control of my death...I picked this date months before believe me it was hard to hold on this long."

In November 2012, Christine O'Hagan attempted to kill herself but was interrupted when her daughter called home (O'Hagan, 2014). Although she knew she needed help, she was afraid that in doing so she could lose her job or family and that she would be stigmatized for having a mental illness. She prayed that she would die. She said, "The pain had to stop. I'd been through some painful moments, but nothing was comparable. I survived skin cancer as a preteen and live with lupus. I gave birth without pain medicine or epidurals. I've been hurt emotionally and mentally and never felt anything like this before. So when my children left for school for the day, I called in sick to work then said what I thought would be a final prayer for peace." After her attempt, Christine revealed that she was diagnosed with generalized anxiety disorder, major depression, and obsessive-compulsive disorder. She received the right combination of medications and therapy and, with the support of family and nonmedication strategies, such as exercise, she is doing well. When she thinks back she says, "Now, all these months later, I understand what I could and should have done differently. I could have asked for help. I should have reached out sooner. I might have recognized that what I was feeling was biological and not my fault. This was not a weakness or a character flaw."

Christine's story stresses both the importance of reaching out for help instead of becoming isolated and confronting the stigma associated with mental illness. In and of itself, a mental illness, and the loss of control associated with it, can be paralyzing. However, when no one is there to help or normalize the symptoms, it can be painful and terrifying as well. The fear and pain is compounded by the social stigma from having a mental illness. When someone is diagnosed with a physical illness, such as diabetes, a wealth of social support exists. Yet when someone receives a diagnosis of schizophrenia, even if people want to help, there is a general lack of knowledge as to how to help. This absence, or in some cases inaccurate knowledge, and the plethora of misinformation about mental illnesses which is communicated in the media and even in popular culture such as films, enhances the fear of people with mental illnesses. For example, after a recent spate of mass shootings, House Speaker Paul Ryan suggested legislation to increase funding for the care and treatment of mental illness. He stated, "One common denominator in these tragedies is mental illness" (Huetteman & Pérez-Peñadec, 2015, p. 1). Although the increase in funding for the prevention and treatment of mental illness is long overdue, it shifts the blame for mass killings onto those with a mental illness. The vast majority of those diagnosed with a mental illness are not violent, and not all those who shoot others have a diagnosis of mental illness (Swanson, McGinty, Fazel, & Mays, 2015). It is no wonder that those who suffer from mental illnesses fear "coming out" to friends and family. In his note, one person said, "… no amount of money or girls or friends or family or cars could have made me not crazy again.…I had a mental problem or was crazy u Know That was killing me on the inside that's why I gave up because like I said before I couldn't win I allready lost. I couldn't live with peoples ridicule anymore my own family laughing at me callen me crazy, That was killing me cuz I know I couldnt do nothing about it…I was'nt scarred to die so don't worrie. I was more prepared For Death Than Life." Given the pain of mental illness, and the stigma associated with it, it is clear why death becomes a preferable alternative.

Living with any mental illness can be difficult, but when psychosis is present, which can appear in people struggling with illnesses like bipolar disorder or schizophrenia or be induced by some drugs, it can be especially painful (Black, Winokur, & Nasrallah, 1988; Tarrier, Khan, Cater,

& Picken, 2007). Tammy, who is discussed further in Chapter 7, Severe Mental Illness, suffered from auditory hallucinations. "I just can't take it anymore the voices in my head R driving me crazy Ive had them sence last Ester Don't let Casey do that to anyone else." Some felt they were no longer in control of their actions. "I worry that the demons are trying to possess me. P. N. I can't keep battling this." Others believed that death was the only way to drive out the devil that lived inside. "I don't want to live with the devin inside me. I don't want to be set up after everything over. Please tell everyone the truth. I love you all."

ESCAPING FROM PHYSICAL PAIN

Louie and Marilyn had been married for 54 years and had two wonderful daughters. Shortly after his 78th birthday, he began having severe stomach pain and vomiting. They were shocked to learn that he was in stage four of pancreatic cancer. He began chemotherapy but the pain increased, and Louie became despondent. One morning Marilyn woke, showered, dressed and checked in on him. After she left the room, he wrote a brief note, placed the bathroom rug on his side of the bed so that he would not make a mess, then laid down on it. Marilyn was in the kitchen preparing breakfast when she heard a loud "bang" and found her husband in their bed with a gunshot wound to the head. He left a note that said, "I'm going crazy I hurt so bad, try to forgive me for taking my life. I know it's not right, I'm pushed to the breaking edge...I love you." Although Marilyn knew they owned a handgun she did not think her husband had the strength to retrieve it from the upstairs bedroom where it was kept.

Without a doubt, health concerns can have an impact on suicidal behavior (WHO, 2014). Individuals who killed themselves to escape physical illness (118 people) have their own unique characteristics. Like other groups, they were mostly males (88%) and white (97%), but they were older, with an average age of 68 and a range of 34–94. In fact, 88% were over 50 years old. Very few of the notes or investigators' reports mentioned legal (<1%), financial (3%), job (0%) or interpersonal problems (4%), substance abuse (6%), or abusive relationships (<1%). Instead they all talked about physical illness and some note writers, like Louie, targeted the illness as the precipitant for the suicide.

Physical illness is a critical motivating factor for suicide (Shiratori et al., 2014). For example, suicide risk increases in the 90 days following a diagnosis of malignant cancer (Bolton, Walld, Chateau, Finlayson, & Sareen, 2015). Although some research has linked discharge from a psychiatric hospital to increased risk of suicide, the link between discharge from a general hospital and suicide is just beginning to be explored. Dougall et al. (2014) found that individuals who killed themselves were 3.1 times more likely to have been discharged from a general than a psychiatric hospital. Moreover, "higher percentages of people died by suicide 3, 6 and 12 months after last discharge from general than from psychiatric hospitals" (p. 267). Physical illness is recognized as a risk factor for suicide in older populations. Harwood, Hawton, Hope, Harriss, and Jacoby (2006) conducted psychological autopsy interviews relating to over 100 victims who were 60 years old or over. They found that the most frequent life problem associated with suicide, a contributory factor in almost two-thirds of cases, was physical illness. Pain contributed to the suicide in approximately one-fourth of their sample.

Many of the investigators' reports and some notes discussed recent medical involvement such as a visit to the physician or a hospital admission. One 85-year-old man, whose lung cancer had metastasized to his bones, had just had a portion of his femur removed. In his note to his children, he wrote, "Carrie, Sissy, Nelly, it does not look very good for the outlook of my leg the way it is healing. Yesterday I had a spell of coughing of my chest. Not so bad now but I'm having a problem of breathing. I also have a problem of eating. Nothing taste right. Hard to eat enough to keep me going. I do not like the way things are. I therefore am thinking of checking out. I hope that you fellows will forgive me. I hope that god will forgive me. Dad." He later added, "5:30 PM I'm so sorry fellows, I think I have lived long enough." He left notes throughout the house informing his children how to settle his affairs and dispose of his property and then shot himself while sitting in his wheelchair.

Other note writers did not discuss a recent admission but were dreading a future admission. Sam was only 34 years old but was obese and a heavy smoker. After suffering numerous painful gallbladder attacks, he had his gallbladder removed. Unfortunately, he developed a hernia and had three more surgeries. He became depressed over the continuing pain and the need for yet another surgery. He wrote a note to his father and said, "I love you, and I am sorry…Truly. Please understand, I am in pain, Great [unintelligible] pysically & emotionally—I don't want any more surgeries or pain." Then, he overdosed on his pain medications.

The vast majority of individuals who were trying to escape physical illness killed themselves at home (89%), using guns (80%). When we could determine where they were living prior to their deaths, it was fairly evenly split between living alone (34%) or living with a spouse/partner (37%), while a few were living with adult children. None of them committed murder-suicide and only 6% killed themselves in front of someone else. A small percentage were reported to have been using substances prior to their deaths (6%).

Some people had expressed suicidal ideation (15%) or made threats (19%) but only 6% were reported to have made previous attempts. It is likely there were few attempts because prior to their diagnoses, these individuals had been contented with their lives and were not trying to escape from anything. Approximately one-third (34%) of the investigators' reports spoke of an additional psychological illness, usually depression (93%). However, for most of these people, the source of depression was their physical illness. For example, Anthony suffered a stroke when he was 76 and after that he had difficulty sleeping and eating. In a year he had lost over 70 pounds and could only tolerate eating chicken. He was depressed about his physical illness and told his wife that he did not know how much longer he could take it. In the middle of the night, he went outside their house and shot himself by their garbage cans. His note read, "Maggie Sweetheart-My Nerves have snapped—Never thought I would do this but I can't take any more of this punishment!! I see no help in getting well...Love you dearly and everybody else." The suicide was directly a result of the physical illness. Although depression may mediate the link between physical illness and suicide, even when mental illness is factored out, still an increased risk of suicide exists.

In a small subset of cases, generally among the older victims, physical illness resulted in a loss of independence and triggered considerations about future housing options. For example, Gordon was 75 years old and had suffered from severe chronic obstructive pulmonary disease (COPD) for several years. He had just spent a week in the hospital and was settling back into his home when his sister suggested that he consider moving into assisted living. He told her he would rather die than move into assisted living. Ten days after his discharge, he sat down in his favorite living room chair and shot himself in the center of his chest. His sister had asked a relative to remove the gun from his home almost a year before Gordon took his life. Harwood et al. (2006) also found that the possibility of moving into an assisted care facility, or with adult children, precipitated suicide in their sample.

Gordon's story is emblematic of two problems family and friends may have when confronting a situation like this. "I'd rather die" can be a colloquial expression; many more people say it than carry out a suicide. Recognizing what patients are saying when they assess their own pain and understanding the impact of severe pain on desire for death, from the patients' own words, can provide a framework for a clinician to intervene, though it may be more difficult for a family member or friend (Coyle, 2004). It can be awkward raising the issue of getting psychological help. Likewise, seeking to remove firearms or other means of killing oneself from a home can be a hard discussion to have. Gordon's sister recognized the danger of having weapons in the home, but she did not act decisively enough to remove them. Perhaps she could not under the circumstances. Organizations like the National Alliance on Mental Illness (NAMI) sometimes offer classes to teach communication or offer other services to facilitate conversations with people suffering from mental illnesses, including depression brought on by circumstances.

Although no large differences in the day of death were apparent, more people killed themselves on Saturday than any other day (19%), unlike the prevalence of Monday for other groups. Perhaps this is related to the lack of medical care available on the weekends. Additionally, more deaths occurred in the spring (32%), particularly April (14%). The fewest deaths occurred in the fall (19%). It may be the contrast between the renewal of life in the spring and their continuing pain which precipitates a desire to die.

Not only did the demographics and characteristics associated with these suicides differ from those motivated by interpersonal reasons, but so did the notes they left. A total of 17 people, or 14%, left suicide notes. This is typical for our overall sample, but it is much less than those motivated by lost love and much greater than from abusive relationships. In general, the notes are less dramatic than those written for interpersonal reasons. For instance, not one person talked about feeling lonely, relieved, angry, ashamed, apathetic, or worthless. No one discussed feeling like a failure, forgiving oneself or others, watching over others, or having problems in their relationships. Only one person mentioned feeling guilty or ambivalent or sad. There were no quotations or poems and no humor. However, over two-thirds mentioned their love for others. A little over one-third showed thought constriction; they simply saw no other way out and they provided justification for their actions (71%). Most did not mention an afterlife, although some (29%) mentioned God.

The notes were short (71% were under 150 words), and most wrote only one note (82%). The focus of the notes was more on escaping (59%), physical pain (41%), disability (35%), medications (18%), unspecified pain (29%), psychological pain (12%), and that life was not worth living (24%). One entire note read, "Kelly, Phone 000-0000 I couldn't stand the pain any longer. Thanks for all you done for me. Love, Brandon." This man had colon cancer and had recently had a colostomy which left him with increased pain and discomfort.

The pattern that emerges here is in sharp contrast to those who killed themselves for interpersonal reasons. Aside from some basic demographics, such as gender, very few similarities exist. Their notes are short, simple, and straightforward, with no assignment of blame. They are older individuals who are not experiencing secondary problems such as legal issues; rather the primary problem is their declining health and its impact on their quality of life. Their interpersonal relationships are good, with no sign of revenge. When friends and family are mentioned in notes, the expressions are full of love, not bitterness, and frequent requests for forgiveness appear. They also differ from those who are attempting to escape from legal and financial problems.

ESCAPING FROM LEGAL AND FINANCIAL CRISES

Legal Crises

Steve was 18 years old when he and his friends held up a liquor store. They were not apprehended immediately but when the surveillance video aired on television, police were tipped off to Steve's identity within a week. In the meantime, Steve and his friends decided that since their robbery was successful, and they had not been caught, they would rob a convenience store. Steve was arrested and convicted on the liquor store robbery and was scheduled to appear in court for sentencing in a week. He was facing 3 to 8 years in prison on the liquor store robbery, but the judge delayed sentencing to allow Steve to attend his high school graduation. Steve went to his parent's house then told them he was going to work on his car in the garage. When he had not returned for dinner they found him hanging from a tree in the woods near their home.

Benny robbed a convenience store of $8,000 then fled in his car. When an all-points bulletin was issued and he was spotted by the sheriff, he pulled into an abandoned parking lot and, as police closed in, shot himself in the head.

Legal and financial issues were woven throughout our sample and are discussed extensively in the chapter titled "The Intersection of Suicide and Legal Issues." However, in the next two sections we focus on those 73 cases where legal or financial issues were the main precipitant for the suicide. Many of the cases resembled Steve and Benny's circumstances where a person was running from police or was in a jail cell. Although they may have had other problems, often substance abuse (34%), it was the legal situation that prompted the suicide.

In contrast to those escaping physical issues, those escaping legal issues were relatively healthy. Very few people were identified as having physical (8%) or mental illnesses (12%). Although some had made previous suicide attempts (14%), only 2% had suicidal ideation and 6% had made threats. Approximately one-fourth (24%) had interpersonal problems with 14% identified as the perpetrators of domestic violence. Only 2% were identified as having financial problems.

Ninety-two percent of the victims were men and 82% were Caucasian, with 14% African American. Although the age range seems very large (17–91), only one person was over 69 years old. The average age was 37 years old. Both the 91-year-old man and the 17-year-old boy panicked after minor traffic accidents and took their lives. No pattern appeared as to month, but almost three times as many occurred in the summer (37%) when compared to the fall (14%). The least likely day for these suicides to occur was Sunday (8%) and the most likely day was Monday (20%).

This is the only category where more suicides were committed by asphyxia (48%) than by guns (40%). This probably has to do with the fact that almost 40% occurred in a prison or jail cell where no other means was available. The method of suicide is clearly influenced by accessibility. However, some research supports that suffocation among those who are middle-aged (40–64 years old) is more likely to be used in suicides that are related to jobs, or economic or legal factors (Hempstead & Phillips, 2015). A total of 65% occurred away from home but again this number may be higher due to those who were incarcerated and it may also explain the small percentage of people who were using substances prior to their deaths (12%). Twenty percent killed themselves in front of others, usually the police.

This group had 50 people and, not surprisingly, only three wrote notes. Because of this, it was impossible to observe patterns among the note writers. Although other note writers discussed prison or jail, usually it was one part of overall problematic circumstances. Presumably, for the people in this group, the threat of prison or jail was greater than their fear of dying.

Financial Crises

Mitchell recently retired and then invested his life savings in multiple rental properties. Unfortunately, a few of his tenants fell on hard times and could not pay their rents and he could not seem to find renters for his other properties. In addition, someone who was visiting one of his properties had fallen on a broken sidewalk and was suing him. He had known about the sidewalk for six months but did not have the cash to repair it. Due to this negligence, his insurance company was claiming his policy was not valid.

For the last several years Mitchell had been in a stable and loving relationship with Joan. He was very health conscious and did not have any substance abuse problems. He had never spoken of or attempted suicide. However, Joan noticed that he had become increasingly despondent over his financial situation and he feared he would lose his home. When Mitchell did not respond to Joan's texts for two days, she called the police. Mitchell had used one of the guns from his collection to shoot himself in the head. His daughter was shocked to learn of her father's suicide. Although she was aware of his financial problems, she never expected he would take his own life.

In our overall set of cases, at least 14% of victims were identified as having financial problems. However, for the people in the present subset, financial problems were identified as the main precipitant for the suicide. A total of 23 people were in this group and although what led up to their financial crises varied, the repercussions were similar.

Mitchell is representative of a small group of people who had bad business ventures. A physician had poured all his money into his practice but could not afford his home mortgage and was being foreclosed upon. Another man had invested both his and his mother's savings into a bar that was failing. One woman owned a small shop and resided above it. When it became apparent she would lose both, she attempted to kill herself. When police arrived she told them she wanted to die because of her financial troubles. Although she was not successful on this first attempt, she was successful on her second. Others were people who had lost their jobs due to the economy or had been the victim of a crime or scam. Mitchell's fear that he would lose his home is common and the actual loss of a home is a key factor in the decision to commit suicide. In 2014, Houle and Light found a relationship between actual home foreclosure and suicide. Specifically, when a home was foreclosed on and repossessed, suicide rates increased, especially among people ages 46–64. A slight increase in suicides occurred for those aged 30–45 and no relationship for those over 64 or under 30. This relationship was independent of other economic factors such as unemployment. The authors suggested that for those in the 46–64 age group, who were close to retirement age, the loss of a home has a profound impact on their physical and mental health.

For the most part, these were people who did not have other problems in their lives but their financial problems were overwhelming because they had cascading consequences. Less than 5% were identified as having had previous suicide attempts or problems with drug abuse or interpersonal relationships. Only 13% had physical illnesses, although 39% had psychological problems. However, all 39% were depressed, generally from their financial situations. Similarly, 22% had legal problems which were rooted in their financial problems. In short, these individuals resembled those in the escape-physical group who were living relatively contented lives until their financial problems began. Even their demographics are similar to the physical group. Their ages ranged from 37 to 72 with an average age of 52. Hempstead and Phillips (2015) found an increase in suicides among middle-aged individuals between the years 2005 and 2010, and they attributed this to deteriorating economic conditions.

Many reached out for help. Approximately 22% threatened suicide while another 22% expressed suicidal ideation. When one individual told his sister he was contemplating suicide she told him that he should pray to God but she did not alert anyone. These individuals could not see any other way out of the situation. One man, whose financial investments had depleted his savings, wrote, "I have no regrets only that I could not finish my life." He clearly could not envision any other options. The reality is that he could have continued his life, but he could not grasp this.

Other people had gambled away all their assets and now had nowhere left to turn. Most had alienated friends and family who were tired of lending them money. One person had not paid child support and was forced to move in with relatives in order to make the payments and stay out of jail.

Only two people (9%) left notes and they were both less than 50 words long. Neither of them was addressed to a specific person. One has no salutation but has two sentences of instructions and then the words "Had a good life it's my time to go." This middle-aged man had lost his high-paying sales job and had been unemployed for over two years. He was now facing foreclosure. The other note writer was filing for bankruptcy and for most of the note he expresses his love for his friends and relatives but indicates that "somehow my pain has overcome me."

Individuals motivated by physical illness or financial reasons were most likely to use guns to kill themselves (70%), whereas there was more diversity in the methods of those motivated by escape from psychological or multiple issues. The next most predominant method was asphyxiation (13%) followed by overdose (9%). No one committed murder-suicide and no one killed himself in front of another. Only two people were using substances before they killed themselves. Most were men (87%) and Caucasian (91%). The vast majority killed themselves at home (83%) during the months of January and July (22% each), the start of the year and the start of the fiscal year. Almost three-fourths (74%) of the deaths occurred on Monday, Tuesday, or Friday.

CONCLUSIONS

The majority of people in our sample were attempting to escape. For some, that escape was from actual physical or psychological pain. For others, the escape was related to circumstances which they believed were too difficult to ever overcome. The unknown of death was preferable to the knowns of life.

Many of these people were facing their circumstances alone. Sometimes this was by design but other times they had alienated friends and family. Also, some individuals feared reaching out, especially those struggling with a mental illness, due to the possible impact it would have on their lives. No doubt there were others, such as those having legal or financial difficulties, who were too humiliated to share their circumstances with others. Without social support, it is easy to develop tunnel vision and only see one solution to problems. For a moment, imagine that your doctor just gave you some bad news about your health but you had no one with whom you felt you could share this news. Furthermore, you could not process treatment options with anyone other than your health care providers and no one was there to help with caretaking or assistance. In other words, you are not only being confronted with this upsetting news, but you also have to deal with how alone you feel in life. Suicide becomes an option not only for the escape it provides, but also for the relief.

You no longer have to worry about solutions to your problems or your aloneness. This does not mean all of these individuals were alone, but they felt alone and they wanted to escape. Escape means to break free from confinement or control. These individuals felt they no longer had control over their lives but believed by killing themselves they would gain control. The key to successful prevention and intervention lies in finding other ways to give them back control.

Grief and Failure

Joyce struggled with depression for most of her adult life and had been under the care of a psychiatrist for years. Now she was in her fifties and had developed a number of physical conditions, including high blood pressure, high cholesterol, and a heart arrhythmia. Joyce had one daughter, Carolyn, who spoke with her every day on the phone and visited on weekends. Joyce had never expressed any suicidal ideation until Carolyn was killed by her husband. She had suspected Carolyn was being abused by her husband, but Carolyn would not discuss it with her. Joyce attended the funeral and almost immediately began talking about suicide. She told her brother she was going to kill "some people" and then kill herself. Two weeks after the murder, she began calling her psychiatrist and leaving what he called "desperate" voicemails. Although he returned the calls within an hour, Joyce did not answer the phone. He requested a welfare check and when the police entered her residence, they found Joyce dead from a gunshot wound to the head. On the end table near her chair were pictures of her daughter, her grandchildren, and a newspaper clipping about her daughter's murder which indicated that Carolyn's husband would be charged with murder.

The vast majority of cases we examined were motivated by interpersonal issues or were individuals trying to escape painful circumstances, as described in the previous two chapters. However, there was a small group (60 people or 5%) who committed suicide for other reasons. Most of these people were either dealing with grief issues (31 people) or felt like a failure in life (22 people). There were also some people who spoke of feeling guilty (4) or alienated (2). Finally, there was one person who believed suicide would make someone else's life easier (altruism). Joyce provides a representative example of someone who killed herself out of grief.

Explaining Suicide.
DOI: http://dx.doi.org/10.1016/B978-0-12-809289-7.00005-1

DISTINGUISHING UNCOMPLICATED AND COMPLICATED GRIEF

Grief is a term used to describe emotional, cognitive, functional, and behavioral responses to a loss, such as a death (Zisook & Shear, 2009). Following the loss of a loved one, most people experience normal or uncomplicated grief. Uncomplicated grief usually begins with an acute phase and proceeds to integrated or abiding grief. The acute phase is characterized by intense sadness, preoccupation with thoughts of the deceased, and difficulty concentrating (Zisook & Shear, 2009). There may be "shock, anguish, loss, anger, guilt, regret, anxiety, fear, loneliness, unhappiness, depression, intrusive images, depersonalization, and the feeling of being overwhelmed" (p. 68), which may be intermingled with positive feelings about the deceased. The length of acute grief can vary based on many things including the individual, the significance of the loss, and whether the loss was expected. In the acute grief phase, daily routines are often disrupted. Most individuals begin to shift to integrated grief within 6 months. In this phase, there may still be sadness related to the deceased, but the preoccupation has lessened. There is also healing, adaptation, rebalancing, and a reengagement into life's activities. It is not that the deceased is forgotten, but the loss becomes integrated into the individual's new worldview. Grief may at times become more prominent, e.g., on the anniversary of a death, but it is not as pronounced as it was during the acute phase. Most people experience uncomplicated grief while others (7–20%) develop complicated grief (Carmassi, Shear, Socci, Corsi, & Dell'osso, 2013).

When someone remains in acute grief for a prolonged period, without shifting to integrated grief, complicated grief generally results. Complicated grief is also known as traumatic or unresolved grief. Complicated grief is intense grief that is associated with impairments in work, health, and social functioning (Zisook & Shear, 2009). A yearning for the deceased is often experienced, as well as anger, bitterness, shock, and/or a continuing disbelief that the person has died. Individuals experiencing complicated grief may be preoccupied with thoughts of the deceased and avoid reengaging in life. They may also feel that by moving on with life, they are being disloyal to the deceased. Feelings of excessive loneliness, purposelessness, and emotional detachment from others can also be present (Latham & Prigerson, 2004). Prolonged complicated grief can lead to negative physical outcomes such as high blood pressure or heart problems. Not surprisingly, individuals suffering from complicated grief have higher rates of suicidal ideation than do bereaved people experiencing uncomplicated grief (Szanto et al., 2006).

Quintessential Case of Bereavement

Bill and Linda were high school sweethearts and married shortly after they graduated. They were unable to have children and chose not to adopt, but they were very active in their community and their church. Bill worked as a police officer, and Linda worked for the police department. They were virtually inseparable. When they retired, they bought a home in Florida and spent summer months in Ohio. They were enjoying life. Shortly after they celebrated their fifty-fifth wedding anniversary, Linda was diagnosed with ovarian cancer. Linda fought the cancer with every treatment that was available, but after 18 months she died. Bill was devastated and for two months told friends and neighbors how depressed he was feeling. One morning a neighbor saw Bill leave his house carrying a long object. When Bill had not returned by late afternoon, she called police requesting a welfare check. On the dining room table in Bill's home the police found his will, power of attorney, and the names of next of kin. They also found a piece of paper with "Bird Island" written on it. Bird Island was not accessible by car but the police boated out to it where they found Bill, dead from a shotgun blast to the head. He did not leave a note, but near his body there was a picture pinned to the tree. In the picture, Bill and Linda were smiling, enjoying a vacation together.

When one considers who would kill himself or herself out of bereavement, Bill and Linda represent the quintessential case. It had only been 2 months since Linda died, so Bill was still in an acute phase of grief, but it seems he could not integrate the death into his new worldview. In other words, he could not envision a life without Linda. Zisook and Shear (2009) found that when a bereaved spouse was older than 50, over half (57%) with complicated grief had suicidal ideation. To a certain extent, this is supported by our findings. The age range of those killing themselves because of grief was 23 to 85, but approximately two-thirds were over 46 and the average age was 57 years old. Ten were grieving the loss of a wife, and four had lost a husband. However, there were more people who had lost someone other than a spouse than those who had lost a spouse. Eight had lost a parent, evenly split between mothers and fathers. Eight had also lost a child, six sons and two daughters. One had lost a sister and one had lost a brother, while three had lost a friend. Finally, one person lost his guide dog. Some people had lost more than one person. Interestingly, two people had lost a loved one to suicide.

Similar to our overall sample and every subgroup, the victims were mostly men (68%) and Caucasian (94%). Although two women used knives to kill themselves, most used guns (39%), asphyxia (26%), or overdose (26%). No one committed murder–suicide and only two people killed themselves in front of someone, one by jumping from the top of a building. Most were home when they killed themselves (74%).

By and large, these were not people who were experiencing other life problems. Legal or financial problems or domestic violence were not mentioned in any case. This does not mean that no one had these problems, but rather that they were not significant enough for an investigator to mention. Aside from dealing with the loss of a loved one, only two people were identified as having interpersonal issues. A few people had physical illnesses (23%) but almost everyone was identified as dealing with mental health issues, mostly related to their loss.

The death of a loved one can trigger or worsen mental disorders (Carmassi et al., 2013). Mental health concerns were identified by investigators in 28 out of 31 people and for the other three people mental health status was not addressed. In only six cases did the investigator identify that the mental illness was present before the death of a loved one. Since the mental illness frequently arose from the loss, it is not surprising that 25 people were depressed. In addition, one person was diagnosed with bipolar disorder; one person with multiple disorders; and one person with dementia. At least 19% had a history of drug or alcohol abuse, and the same percentage were drinking or using drugs prior to their suicides. Twenty-three percent had previously attempted suicide, 27% had made threats, and 24% had expressed suicidal ideation.

The highest risk period for suicide due to bereavement is in the 2 years following the loss but the risk remains elevated for 5 years after the loss (Szanto et al., 2006). It was impossible to determine how long it had been since the loss for 35% of our cases, because the investigator's report simply said "recent death" or did not mention a time frame. For three (10%) it had been less than a month, for seven (23%) it had been one to six months, for two (6%) it had been seven months to a year and for eight people (26%), it had been more than a year. One woman killed herself on the anniversary of her husband's suicide, which he had committed on her birthday.

For our sample, almost half of the suicides (48%) occurred during the summer months (June, July, and August), particularly June (23%). Many memories are made during the summer as families and couples go on vacations and relax together. Perhaps the idea of spending a summer without their loved ones was just too overwhelming. Additionally, almost half killed themselves on Sunday (23%) or Monday (26%). Sunday and Monday can be difficult days for many people as they face the challenges of a new week. Frequently weekends are spent with friends or loved ones but the week can be long and lonely. Oftentimes it is the routines of the week that become too difficult to face alone. The loss of a partner/spouse means an individual may be facing life ostensibly alone, but for some the loss of other family and friends creates just as significant a void. As the victims struggled to cope with the loss of the person they loved, they often gave clear signals of their peril and distress.

The day after Memorial Day, Scott drove to the cemetery with Tina, his girl-friend, to visit his mother's grave. His mother had recently succumbed to pancreatic cancer. Scott felt that, at 58, she was too young to die, and that she had died too fast. Diagnosed in October, his mother died in January. In the months after she died Scott was depressed and had been talking continually about suicide. During one suicide attempt, his gun was confiscated by the police.

On this visit to the cemetery, Scott left his girlfriend in the car and grabbed a cold beer from a cooler in the trunk. He walked over to the grave, where he sat down. Ten minutes later Tina saw him rise, then heard a muffled sound, and watched Scott collapse. When she arrived at the grave, she found Scott unresponsive and bleeding from the chest. Although she called for help, Scott was dead on arrival at the hospital.

The relationship between the griever and their loved one may affect the severity of grief symptoms. Approximately half of our sample lost someone other than a spouse. These included siblings, friends, and a guide dog. Yet, the biggest groups were those who had lost a child or a parent. Only one person in our sample left a note. In the note, he talked about being reunited with his son and said to his wife, "I tride to be a good man for you but wen I lost my son it changed."

It is common for parents to experience many of the symptoms of complicated grief following the loss of a child (Zetumer et al., 2015). These may include shock, disbelief, anger, and guilt. Zetumer et al. compared parents with complicated grief to nonparents with complicated grief. Parents experienced significantly more yearning, preoccupation, anger, bitterness, shock, and disbelief than nonparents. In addition, they experienced more caregiver self-blame and were significantly more likely to indicate that they felt they should have done something to prevent or ease the death than nonparents. Finally, parents were more likely than nonparents to have suicidal ideation, such as a wish to be dead, and engage in more indirect suicidal behavior following the loss.

Losing a child, even an adult child, can be devastating to parents. In general, parents are the primary caregivers to children and establish their first attachment patterns (Bowlby, 1969). For most parents and children, attachment is lifelong. It continues to dictate the parent–child relationship, but also becomes a template for other relationships. Part of the responsibilities of a healthy parent–child attachment includes protecting the child from harm. There is also a societal expectation, especially for young children, that parents will protect their child from harm. Even children themselves look to their parents to protect them from harm. When a child has died, parents often feel they have not fulfilled their parenting responsibilities. Whether the death was accidental or medical, parents may feel responsible for it or for the death process. Most parents expect their children will outlive them and when they do not, the grief becomes complicated.

Losing anyone with whom one has had a deeply satisfying relationship is a risk factor for complicated grief (Zisook & Shear, 2009). Other risk factors include a history of mood or anxiety disorders, poor health, multiple important losses, adverse life events, concurrent stress and a lack of social support. Even the quality of care that a loved one receives at the end of life is related to caregiver suicidal ideation. Abbott, Prigerson, and Maciejewski (2014) found that if caregivers perceive that the quality of care their loved ones received at the end of life was poor, there is an elevated risk of suicidal ideation in bereavement. That hypothesis was especially true for those who had a spousal relationship with the deceased and for those who had suicidal ideation before the death. Most caregivers want to feel as if they did all that they could, and poor quality of life at the end of life may leave them with lingering doubts and guilt.

The process of grief, like coping, is very personal. Someone with no risk factors, such as Bill, can develop complicated grief, while others who have all the risk factors may not. Just as there are identified risk factors, there are also identified protective factors that attenuate depression. Prigerson, Frank, Reynolds, George, and Kupfer (1993) found that older individuals who had lost a spouse were less likely to develop depression, or developed a less severe depression, if they received social support and mastered life events. Given the pivotal role of social support, it was not surprising to see investigators' reports which referred to conditions suggesting a lack of social support. Victims were clearly telling people they were in distress, yet often their signals, and even threats, were ignored. This is not an attempt to disparage the people who did not respond to these signals and threats. It is impossible to know how worn down these people were from their own grief and from possibly responding to the victim's repeated suicide attempts, threats or ideation. Still, victims may have viewed this lack of response as representing the absence of social support.

Prevention and Intervention

In most of the cases of suicide that were precipitated by bereavement and complicated grief, the individuals were not experiencing other life problems. Overall, the loss itself created an imbalance and made life unbearable. Consider the case of Joyce from the beginning of the chapter. Although Joyce had some physical and psychological challenges, she was not considering suicide. Domestic violence had led to Carolyn's death, and Joyce was unable to protect her child from harm. Joyce was clearly angry, as she told her brother she was going to kill some people, but there was more than anger. Her psychiatrist referred to her messages as "desperate." There is no doubt that she was despairing and likely distressed. Joyce had a very close relationship with her daughter, and she likely missed her calls and her company. Her previous mood disorder, the loss of social support, physical illness, and her guilt over not being able to prevent her daughter's murder put her at risk for suicide. Like many individuals discussed in this section, Joyce did reach out, but she was too distraught to continue on or even wait for help.

There are ways to assess whether someone who has experienced a loss is at risk for suicide. One way is to assess them on the risk factors outlined previously. For example, if someone has struggled with mental illness throughout his/her life, the risk for complicated grief is heightened. However, in addition to assessing for the risk factors outlined, an Inventory of Complicated Grief was developed to identify those individuals who may be suffering from pathological grief (Prigerson et al., 1995). This would not likely have helped Joyce, since she killed herself so quickly after Carolyn's death. However, had Bill or Scott been assessed, their results would have indicated that intervention was needed. Funeral directors, who are often the first point of contact for a bereaved person, are sometimes prepared to offer grief counseling or recommend programs in the community. Larger funeral homes sometimes employ grief counselors (Worden, 2008). While they may come too early in the process to identify complicated grief, they may be able to prevent it from occurring by routinely recommending assessment to their clients.

Suicide among bereaved caregivers must also be addressed. Enhancing the quality of palliative care would reduce the risk of suicide among caregivers, although this would not have affected every case. Hospital-based care models have traditionally been focused on cost and are not patient centered. New models, such as community-based, nonhospice, palliative medicine programs have addressed symptoms, psychosocial and emotional wellbeing, and caregiver and patient satisfaction. As palliative care continues to evolve, the focus on the individual's quality of life at the end of life may be enhanced. In the meantime, assessing caregiver satisfaction may provide important information about caregiver risk for suicide.

It may seem that the suicides precipitated by grief fit better in the interpersonal motivations for suicides section, but they were qualitatively different. As opposed to many of the interpersonal cases, no longstanding conflicts or rejection issues in the relationships were identified. In fact, the individuals who died were generally beloved. Also, no history of unrequited love was present. The deceased and the suicide victim usually had a mutually loving relationship. It was the death, not the relationship, that caused the suicide. Therefore, the goal of intervention becomes trying to find ways to rebalance an individual's life after the loss. This may involve establishing or reestablishing positive social support and encouraging them to focus on the things that enhance their sense of self-sufficiency or mastery (Prigerson et al., 1993). It may also mean helping individuals to create a worldview that both includes their memories of their loved ones but allows for their own personal evolution to continue beyond their deaths.

FAILURE

Nick was a junior in college when he wrote, "I HATE MYSELF. I CAN'T ACCOMPLISH WHAT I WANT TO DO...I DON'T EVEN KNOW WHAT I WANT OR WHAT I WANT TO DO...I AM LOST. I HAVE NO VALUE TO THIS WORLD. I AM EXPENDABLE. ANYTHING THAT I CAN DO, SO MANY OTHER PEOPLE CAN DO TOO...I FEEL LIKE A CARD HOUSE BUILT OF FAILURE. NOT PUBLIC FAILURE BUT PERSONAL FAILURE. I AM FAT, LAZY, ENJOY ONLY THINGS THAT BENEFIT ME."

Nick had struggled with depression during his life. Recently, he had shared his suicidal ideation with his therapist who had him sign a "suicide contract." The contract explicitly stated what Nick would do if he felt suicidal, such as calling his therapist. Nick lived off campus in a fraternity. One night he and his roommates were watching movies and drinking. He went up to his room about midnight and two hours later his roommate found him hanging in a closet. Nick had also taken an overdose of sleeping pills. There were small amounts of cocaine and marijuana in the room.

On the desk was a suicide note, which was written on the back of Nick's suicide contract. There was also a journal. In the note he said, "I HATE MYSELF... ..STEPPED OUT OF REALITY. STEPPED INTO A DREAM. —BYE— NICK. 100 TYLENOL PM +31 CVP SLEEP TABLETS. GOODNIGHT. I AM A DISAPPOINTMENT." The last lines in his journal were, "WHY SHOULD I HANG AROUND AND CONTINUE TO MAKE MYSELF MISERABLE? I HATE MYSELF. FUCK IT I'M OUT."

Nick is an example of someone who killed himself because he felt like a failure. In our study, we counted failure as a motivation for suicide only in cases in which the deceased left a note where it was explicitly mentioned or where details from the investigator's report made it clear the person felt like a failure. For example, the investigator's report detailed the results of interviews with family members who indicated the deceased had always felt like a failure or described some aspect of the scene or body that made it clear the person felt like a failure. One woman wrote words or phrases all over her body such as "Worthless," "Trash," and "Big Ugly," and then hanged herself from a rafter in the living room.

Another investigator's report referred to a notepad with what appeared to be scribbles and doodles. The scribbles sounded like a to-do list and read, "Death, Kill Yourself, Suicide Edicius, Cash Check, Make Resume, WP, Shut up, Less talk is better, Talk is cheap, Trying is the first step toward the failer, Can't be afraid to fail, if you don't want to succeed, Get By Liven or get busy dien. Why, no friends, no job, no part of society, better off, Don't want to go on Another 40 years. Nobody likes you." Edicius (suicide spelled backwards) is a popular term on certain websites. Numerous poems have the title "Edicius," too many to list. It is also the name of an Indie Rock group and a French death metal group. Some of the lines were from popular culture: *The Simpson's* hapless father figure, Homer Simpson ("Trying is the first step toward failure") and *The Shawshank Redemption* ("Get busy living or get busy dying"). Also, a drawing showed a person hanging by a noose from a rafter and the words "Brooks was here" were carved into the wood. That phrase was also a reference to *The Shawshank Redemption* and the character, Brooks, who killed himself shortly after getting released from prison. Brooks was unable to adjust to the outside. Alone and out of place, he hanged himself from the wooden beam in his shabby hotel room after carving his name for posterity. Not surprisingly, this person killed himself by hanging.

At first, it was difficult to discern the difference between failure and escape. After careful examination, it became clear that the tone of the "failure" notes was different, as were the circumstances of the person's life and death. For those who killed themselves because they felt like a failure, the source of the failure was internal, whereas with escape it was external. For example, some note writers explicitly stated that they had failed at everything in life. Nick wrote, "I have been a failure in my own eyes my entire life." People in the escape category may have failed at something specific and external, such as their finances, but they did not necessarily see themselves as failures. They might state, "I can't take this anymore," but it referred to specific circumstances. People who were trying to escape felt helpless, but people who felt like failures felt hopeless. They had a sense of doom, an inability to see a light at the end of the tunnel. They weren't just trying to escape specific circumstances; they were trying to escape life altogether.

Although a precipitant was present for everyone, the significance of it was different for those who were attempting to escape versus those who felt like a failure. Those who were attempting to escape felt they had lost control of the situation, and their decision to kill themselves was often impulsive. Those who felt like a failure had thought about suicide for a long time, and the precipitant was simply the final straw. Nick talked about the multiple failures in his life, including relationships ("I suck @ them") and school ("I have always been picked on in school. It is a cruel place.") When he spoke about suicide, it was almost as if he found it comforting. He said, "It is the one consistency in my everyday activities. I think about it all the time. You know how men think about sex like every minute, or something like that?, well I think of suicide and killing myself the same way."

When people viewed themselves as failures, it was a long-term assessment, so it was not surprising to see that many (65%) were and had been depressed for a long time. They saw themselves as alone in their suffering. Similar to every other category, this group had mostly men (86%) and they ranged in age from 20 to 52 with the average age 35 years old. Out of 22 people, 18 left notes (81%). This high percentage may be due to the fact that, as mentioned earlier, a note was generally the only way to identify someone who committed suicide due to feeling like a failure. In their notes they referred to feeling like a failure (84%), worthless (28%), shame (28%), guilt (17%), hopeless (11%), or that life was not worth living (11%). Virtually every note contained some statement referring to the person's failure or lack of self-worth. It may be of some significance that 11 of the suicides in this group (50%) occurred in 2008 and 2009, during the greatest economic downturn since the Great Depression of the 1930s. As we have no information about the economic circumstances of most of the victims, we cannot be sure of any causation or relationship.

Donny was 45 years old and lived by himself in an apartment in a white, middle class, suburban neighborhood near Dayton, Ohio. He had a history of depression and had just lost his job in December. He had attempted suicide before, but this time he knew he would follow through. "Well, I'm surprised I didn't do this sooner," he wrote. "I had the lowest self-esteem in the world." He died in his bed of an overdose in mid-January. His sister told police he had become increasingly withdrawn.

Sonya also died of an overdose. She was recently divorced but still having phone contact with her ex-husband. It was one day after a conversation with him that her mother discovered Sonya's lifeless body in bed. Next to her were pill bottles and a note. "It is not anyone's fault," her note began. "I've been fucked up from the beginning. I've never been OK, I've never been good enough. I've never been normal... It's definitely no one's fault. just I've had all I can bear. I'm done I'm done I'm done," she wrote, with no period after "done." She loathed herself. "I feel disgusting. I hate myself. I don't know how to change and I'll never ever be OK. Or normal. Or just acceptable." She pleaded for them to understand. "It's an immature decision," she reflected, "but I really am doing all that I can and its never good enough. I'm so so tired of feeling like a reject. I'm just fucked up. I hurt so much and I hurt all the time. It's no one's fault. It's no one's fault."

Alone, depressed, not without loved ones but nevertheless withdrawn from others, Donny and Sonya were typical of one quarter of those who died feeling like failures.

Letting others down was a predominant theme in several notes. "Sorry I couldn't make you proud," wrote one 21-year-old man. He left many notes to several family members, and then shot himself while in his apartment. One woman in her late fifties was found clutching a crucifix with both hands, having taken an overdose of pills. In her note, she told her husband she loved him and apologized for her action. In a P.S., she wrote, "I'm sorry I failed you." A white man in his early thirties hanged himself in a wooded area. He sent his mom a message before he killed himself, warning her about his intentions. "I am such a disappointment to you and everyone else so I'm sorry and I love you." Then to his father he wrote, "I know you have tried to be there for me and I sorry to let you down." A 40-year-old man who hanged himself wrote to his wife, "I have let you down; I have done this in such a way that I can't even look at myself in the mirror. I didn't do my job taking care of you—and for that I am so very very sorry." These notes demonstrate three dimensions to "failure suicide" which were identified in an earlier study: self-perception of competence/failure, another's support (succorance) of the individual's efforts, and the individual's perception of what others think of his competence/failure. In some of these cases, the individual's aspirations may have exceeded the individual's capability. The aspirations or expectations may have been the individual's own or those imposed by others. It's possible a dysfunctional cycle developed in which high expectations were followed by a lack of success, then followed by a lack of support (or perceived lack of support). The individual then may have believed that in the eyes of the person whose approval was desired, the individual was a failure (Folse & Peck, 1994). This culminated in the suicidal act, very much as Durkheim (1897, 2006) predicted.

Others cast themselves very specifically as losers who were unable to face themselves. In addition to believing he let his wife down, the previously discussed 40-year-old hanging victim added, "I also didn't want to be such a big loser—but that isn't the case. I am a loser, I have lost the most precious things in life. I have lost my family, I have lost my pride, I have lost my own dignity." One 31-year-old man hanged himself in a motel room from the shower curtain rod. He said, "I've done to many bad things in my life and I can't look at myself. You will understand one day." Sonya expressed her exasperation at repeated failure: "I'm just so tired of trying my best and things here working out never being good enough." Another man who hanged himself from a water pipe in the basement of his apartment pleaded, "Please beleive that I love you all so so much And that I'm sorry I was such a shitty dad and lover." The idea of being a loser demonstrates the adoption of an identity that can affect behavior. The person who believes himself or herself to be a loser differs from the aspiring person who does not succeed. The "loser" engages in a thought process that may lead to apathy and a perceived inability to act differently.

Those who let others down and those who believe themselves to be losers are small subsets of those who feel like failures. Another subset is those who were "screw-ups," who could not do anything right. Their notes demonstrated a sense of fatal inevitability. "I just can't take be 47, broken down, and nothing to show for my life anymore." They felt predestined to be where they were. "I wish I could go Back and Change everything We All Know I Cant So I am sorry to bring pain to everyone. My life has no meaning any more all I do is drag everyone around me down." Sometimes that sense of predestination haunted the future. "Please don't let our boys F-up & turn out like we did." They also lacked an ability to cope. "I just can't deal with all the mistakes I've made." Moreover, they often expressed themselves in broad, general terms. "I've screwed up my life I don't need to screw his up too." Others also believed they had no ability to help or change the pattern. "You have been so good to me and I allways fuck up."

Many people who felt like failures had myriad problems. One middle-aged man who had numerous health problems was depressed because of a recent divorce. He called his ex-wife to tell her he was going to kill himself. She called his parents, who called 911. He shot himself, and left a note that read, "Sorry that I did this to everybody but I candle handle feeling like shit everyday and being a disappointment to everyone."

Outward appearances could belie internal identifications with failure. One man in his late twenties worked in law enforcement for the state. What he felt inside was that he "let down" those he cared about and "the more anyone tried to help, the more guilt I felt when I kept failing." He shot himself while on patrol just after being in touch with a dispatcher.

The pain these victims felt was palpable. "This is what I feel is best. A world without me in it," wrote a man who killed himself with carbon monoxide poisoning. He had a job, but had broken up with a girlfriend the week before his death. "I noe this hurts to bear. I'm tired as always be labeled a failure...I tried so hard to hold onto my life, but this time I cant do it. No more. I've only failed everyone and for that I'm sry. All I wanted was to make everyone happy, but I can't." He had an alcohol and drug abuse problem linked to chronic back pain, but when his girlfriend broke up with him because of the substance abuse, it engendered feelings of failure so great that he locked himself in his car in his garage and turned on the engine.

In their notes, some individuals referred to the pain they felt, whether it was unspecified (22%) or psychological (17%). Sonya, discussed previously, was a college graduate who worked in healthcare and was still attending school for additional certification. She had long been depressed and was recently divorced. The divorce proceedings were contentious, and her ex-husband was awarded custody of their 5-year-old daughter. Although Sonya had visitation rights, these visits were marked by bickering between the parents. One weekend when her daughter was with her ex-husband, Sonya decided to end her life. She had stockpiled an array of medications and ingested dozens of pills while drinking beer. She left a journal and a suicide note detailing her thoughts and her experience of pain. She said, "It just never seems to leave. I'm always in such pain. Something is definitely wrong in my brain. I'm ready to be done here. I don't know what awaits me, if anything, but I've had all I can bear and I want the pain to stop....I was so tired of feeling down. I am hoping to go peacefully asleep. I've suffered enough." Other than pain, people talked about feeling love for others (83%), ambivalent (17%), loved (17%), apathetic (11%), angry (11%), lonely (11%), and tired (11%). No one talked about feeling joy, sadness, or relief. One person felt like a burden.

In all of the notes, the victim's thoughts were organized and most provided a justification for what they were doing (83%). For example, one man wrote to his son, "Please try to understand that this has nothing to do with you. Daddy has a lot of problems." Only two (11%) mentioned the precipitant cause. In some notes there was constriction or dichotomous thinking (33%). The most frequent stressor mentioned was interpersonal problems (50%). They did not mention a lot of other problems although two mentioned financial issues, one mentioned legal issues and one person mentioned school problems. No one mentioned job problems or abuse.

When most people mentioned blame, it was both to blame (28%) and to absolve people from blame (33%). Over half (61%) wrote a personal apology to someone specific, and many wrote a general apology (44%). One-third (33%) asked for forgiveness and another 11% asked that someone else be forgiven. When they talked about forgiveness, oftentimes it was to ask God for forgiveness. When they talked about the afterlife, there were equal percentages of positive, negative, and uncertain terms. Two people (12%) talked about watching over their loved ones, two talked about looking forward to being reunited in the afterlife and one person talked about being reunited with a deceased relative.

Most people left only one note (78%) with 50% under 150 words. The others were 151–300 words (17%) or over 300 words (33%). In their notes they mentioned parents most often (56%), followed by other family members (50%), children (44%), siblings (28%), partners (22%), and friends (17%). When they left instructions, these related to managing property (39%) or affairs (22%), and caring for someone or something (22%). They (44%) provided general advice or life lessons such as, "Be the man I know you can be," or "Try to forgive her (Mom) she messed up. She loves you." There was no use of humor or quotation in any note.

This group of people was unusual in several other ways, the most striking of which was the method of death. Aside from the escape legal group, where some had restricted access to means, this group had the largest percentage (41%) who chose to kill themselves by asphyxiation, and all but one of these was via hanging. In many other countries, but not in the United States, hanging is one of the most frequently used methods of suicide (Ajdacic-Gross et al., 2008). For example, in England, 55.2% of men and 35.9% of women commit suicide by hanging. It is possible that these individuals viewed hanging as more painful and felt they were so worthless that they deserved pain. However, much debate is ongoing about whether hanging is more or less painful or quick than other means. Additionally, in their notes not one person spoke of feeling a need to be punished, but rather they talked about needing to stop the long-term pain. In other words, they had been punished enough. It is also possible that hanging is symbolic of how they felt, unable to speak or articulate their pain.

British researchers conducted interviews with 12 men and 10 women who had survived a near-fatal suicide attempt, 8 of whom had attempted hanging (Biddle et al., 2010). Those 8 all concurred that they had expected that hanging would be certain, rapid and painless with little awareness of dying. They believed hanging would not damage their bodies and that it would be less horrifying for others. Materials for hanging were easy to obtain. The majority saw hanging as easy to accomplish, with no need for special knowledge. The interviewees who did not choose hanging believed that it was not foolproof and could be both messy and difficult (Biddle et al., 2010). For people in the United States, it is not clear how much information about hanging they possess. However, hanging is, with firearms and drowning, one of the most lethal forms of suicide (Spicer & Miller, 2000).

In almost any room of the house, numerous materials can be used to construct a noose, from electrical cords to curtains. For someone who is depressed and lacking energy, hanging is relatively effortless. Since materials are so accessible, and because it is a relatively silent death, hanging is very difficult to prevent. It also has a comparatively high success rate. Interestingly, it may be that individuals who feel like a failure use a method where they are virtually assured success.

No one in this group committed murder–suicide and no one killed him/herself in front of another person. In addition to being depressed (65%), two were diagnosed as bipolar (10%), one had multiple diagnoses, and three were diagnosed but their disorder was not specified. At least 41% had problems with drug or alcohol abuse and a few had physical illnesses as well (23%). Twenty-three percent were using substances when they killed themselves. Some had expressed suicidal ideation (14%) or threats (18%). Many of the people who felt like failures experienced multiple layers of pain that added to their inability to bear their perceived failures.

Failure is in some ways a state of mind, but it is also situational and circumstantial. When a person loses a job, or repeatedly loses multiple jobs, or does poorly in college, failure is not just a perception. It is happening, even if those to whom it is happening cannot figure out why. With failure comes a loss of self-esteem, but failure can spread its tentacles beyond the self, and it can cause the loss of relationships and prevent new ones from forming. Most of the time the people in the "failure" group saw the failure coming. Some even felt rather used to it, though it still hurt. But in some situations failure sneaks up; a successful person suddenly finds himself or herself abused, intimidated, undermined, sabotaged, or exploited in an unexpected way. It's called bullying.

People who commit suicide as a result of bullying may at first appear to want to escape pain. Those who were escaping pain, however, did not feel like failures, but rather wanted to escape specific circumstances, as we discussed previously. Targets of bullying internalized what was happening to them and blamed themselves. They believed they had failed and felt a sense of doom.

In bullying situations, failure can result from an interpersonal relationship conflict between the bully and the bullied; it can also then cause other relationships to fail. Failure creeps into the bullied person's life in insidious ways. Nick, the college student, bemoaned in his journal how he was bullied at school. Years later he could not shake the way it made him feel. Others in our study had problems at work; at least one was bullied at work. It is worth a look at the problem of bullying and why suicide could be a result.

WORKPLACE BULLYING: AN EXAMPLE OF COMPLEX FAILURE

The temperature that autumn had averaged around 55 degrees, not bad for October. But it had poured rain, a total of five inches for the month. It only rained relentlessly like that every few years. Roberta held the handgun to her chest. It was nearly three o'clock in the afternoon on a Monday, and the children would be getting home from school soon. She felt terrible that they would find her, that in addition to everything else, the kids would remember her like this. She signed her note "Mom" and pulled the trigger of the gun.

"Hold onto this paper. Don't let anyone know about it or see it," Roberta instructed her eldest daughter. Concerned that the autopsy might reveal drugs in her system, she informed her girls that the only drug she had taken was valium and the only chemical she had been exposed to was a pesticide fogger. "If there is anything else then I have inadvertently taken it—without my knowledge. Remember what I have told you about the department last year and this year. Leaving my Mountain Dews unattended at my desk and in booking may have been how other drugs have gotten into my system if there are any present."

In her note, she expressed regret about lost relationships, including her nine-year failed marriage to their father, and her loss of trust in other people. "Trust…is a hard thing to live without in life." She told her children how much she regretted having to commit suicide, but she simply had no choice. "[A]s it has been pointed out in so many ways, by so many people I'm not good at anything…" Although Roberta never used the term, and perhaps had no words to express what was happening to her, she was being mobbed, and she had come to believe her colleagues were trying to poison her. Mobbing is a form of workplace bullying, when more than one person targets another. Roberta felt she had been in a "battle" in which she was the only one fighting on her side. She was surrendering.

Bullying is a subject that has been much in the news. The suicides of 15-year-old Phoebe Prince at a Massachusetts high school and Tyler Clemente, a university freshman at Rutgers whose private love affair with a man was filmed and circulated by his roommate, gained national attention, because they showed the vulnerability of young people who are subjected to bullying (Associated Press, 2011). Bullying in schools has been the subject of legislation in some states. The public, though, generally considers bullying a "school" problem. In the last decade, the media have reported on suicides as a result of workplace bullying or cyberbullying of adults, and legislation has been introduced in 31 states and territories of the United States to make it illegal. In some western countries and Australia, it is already illegal. Australia took the dramatic step of criminalizing workplace bullying (Yamada, 2004).

Workplace bullying, whether in person or online, includes behavior that is intimidating or abusive, results in work sabotage, or exploits a known psychological or physical disability in an attempt to harm the person who is targeted. In the United States bullying is distinguished from illegal discrimination or harassment in the workplace, because those are defined by federal and state laws and protect people based on their status, such as race, religion, and sex. Bullied targets are not chosen because of their status, and the abuse they suffer is not the traditional quid pro quo or disparate treatment of discrimination or harassment law. Since much of the bullying behavior includes psychological abuse, it often does not fall under state workplace violence statutes either. Because employment is often essential to all aspects of a person's life, from financial security to friendships to internal self-esteem, workplace bullying can be completely devastating and leave its targets feeling, like Roberta, as if they have failed in all aspects of life (Yamada, 2000).

Between 2003 and 2010 in the United States, 1719 employees committed suicide in their workplaces, but no study has been conducted on the reasons for those deaths (Nielsen, Einarsen, Notelaers, & Nielsen, 2016). A 2012 poll of 516 self-identified targets of workplace bullying conducted by the Workplace Bullying Institute revealed that targets had contemplated suicide (29%) and some planned how to commit it (16%; Namie & Namie, 2012). It isn't known what percentage of targets who completed the survey, if any, eventually committed suicide. The Namies compared the results of the 2012 poll with results from a scientific survey they had done in 2003 and found they aligned, but the 2012 poll had asked more detailed health questions. Half (49%) of targets reported being diagnosed with clinical depression, and nearly one-third (30%) with posttraumatic stress disorder (PTSD), though few reported using addictive substances. What came to the fore was their attitudes and ways of thinking. Many (41%) said they could understand how a person could be driven to hurting or killing those who had bullied them, though the number of those who had formulated a plan to hurt or kill others was about the same percentage (14%) as those who had planned suicide. The vast majority of bullied targets said they felt betrayed by coworkers (74%) and were now distrustful of institutions (63%). More than half (59%) experienced hypervigilance and 50% had intrusive thoughts, but the top negative effect of the bullying was the anticipation of the next negative event.

EXPLAINING SUICIDE

Negative events often do occur for targets in the aftermath of their bullying, such as losing friends, housing, future job opportunities and so on. Yet sometimes the anticipation of negative events, even without any actual occurrences, was enough to cause overwhelming anxiety and thoughts of suicide among bullied individuals. A recent study (Nielsen et al., 2016) matches some of the Namies' findings. They found that suicidal ideation was clearly present in targets of bullying after they had been bullied. The odds for having suicidal ideation were 2.05 times higher among bullied people than among those not bullied.

Annette Prada was a state employee in New Mexico. After experiencing bullying at work for years, in the form of verbal abuse, intimidating emails, and finally demotion, Annette killed herself. Her colleagues testified that she was the most competent worker in their division. She had even been promoted to bureau chief. When the next opportunity for promotion came up, Annette was passed over because she had asked for more money. That's when the bullying began. Annette's daughter said that her mother was "only two years away from retirement. She tried to stay strong." Annette also had health problems. As older workers face the possible loss of employment which may affect their housing and ability to retire, it can feel like a failure, especially if the employment had been long, as with Annette, who was a 22-year veteran in her office (Matlock, 2012).

In the wake of a suicide, families and friends also frequently say they did not understand the severity of what the person was telling them. They often responded that the person should just retire, if that were an option, or that he or she should find a new job, not realizing that by that point, the target had almost certainly formed a belief that he or she would never work again or have a future (Namie & Namie, 2009). Suicide because of workplace bullying also elicits some harsh responses from those who read stories about it. When stories appear in newspapers or in online forums, it is not uncommon to see comments that disparage the deceased target as weak, incompetent or crazy. The comments often cite the writers' own terrible job situations and seem to be a way they can distance themselves from the suicide victim through ridicule.

Online commentary has indeed become its own form of bullying known as cyberbullying. Targets can be any age. Indeed, the targets themselves do not even need to have an online presence. Social media sites like Facebook, Twitter, and Instagram and newspaper sites do have reporting systems for cyberbullying, but other platforms such as chat rooms may have fewer or no controls. In all instances, though, the sites do not intervene unless the posts are reported. Sometimes, the sites themselves can become the forum for cyberbullying, not in comment sections, but in pages set up for the express purpose of bullying someone.

Thirty-one-year-old Nicole Mittendorf was a stunningly beautiful woman, a fact noticed by coworkers and, as it turned out, people on the internet whom she did not even know. She worked as a firefighter in Virginia, a traditionally male job. Nicole's body was found one Thursday in April in a national park after she had been missing for six days. A suicide note was found in her car. Nicole was the victim of vicious comments on a forum set up ostensibly for discussing firefighter and emergency personnel issues, but which in reality was used for disparaging women in those professions. Comments about women's promiscuity and discussions of their bodies, looks, and sex lives abounded (Hensley, 2016).

What makes cyberbullying so pernicious is its public nature on the one hand and the anonymity of the commentators on the other. A single comment or incident can suddenly become hundreds of texts, posts, and comments that "go viral" and spread even to strangers. Those who are young may be especially vulnerable to suicide, but no one is immune from the shame and humiliation that such bullying inflicts upon the target. Targets then often isolate themselves, exacerbating the effects of being shunned. As with workplace bullying, the target's entire social network can crumble quickly. Feelings of failure are multiplied, and it can become impossible for the target to see a way out (Kowalski, Limber, & Agatston, 2012). It is clear that intervention for this group needs to involve treatment or support for the emotional and cognitive effects of bullying.

INTERVENTION

In our overall findings, and throughout all categories, the psychological diagnosis most associated with suicide was depression. For individuals who felt like a failure, this was often a condition they had struggled with for most of their lives. Unlike other individuals who were responding to a death and were bereaved or were trying to escape circumstances, such as physical pain, individuals who felt like a failure had been struggling for years. Their pain and agony are evident in their notes. Most specifically said that they felt like a failure, but others referred to worthlessness, shame, guilt, hopelessness, or simply said that life was not worth living. Bolton, Belik, Enns, Cox, and Sareen (2008) found that "the depressive symptom most strongly associated with a history of suicide attempts in both men and women was feelings of worthlessness" (p. 1139). In addition, chronic symptoms of depression (over 13 months) increases the risk of suicide (Spijker, de Graaf, ten Have, Nolen, & Speckens, 2010). Not surprisingly, Spijker et al. also found that suicide was associated with feelings of hopelessness. Feelings of hopelessness likely develop and worsen over the chronic course of depression when no relief is found from the symptoms and pain.

It is difficult to point to a specific intervention or prevention for people who kill themselves because they believe they are failures. It is generally a chronic condition and therefore often difficult to identify something pivotal that tips the balance for them. They simply reach a point where they are sick of feeling this way and things have to change. Carrie Fisher, the actress best known for her portrayal of Princess Leia in the *Star Wars* series, has documented her long struggles with addiction and mental illness in two autobiographies (Fisher, 2008, 2011). In *Shockaholic*, she poignantly discusses how she became so depressed after the death of a friend that she ultimately relapsed and turned to drugs to cope. She states, "You see, even after decades of therapy and workshops and retreats and twelve-steps and meditation and even experiencing a very weird session of rebirthings, even after rappelling down mountains and walking over hot coals and jumping out of airplanes...I remained pelted and plagued by feelings of uncertainty and despair" (Fisher, 2011, p. 4). Eventually, she decided to try electroconvulsive therapy (ECT). She describes the decision as follows:

> I believed that this treatment was an extreme measure primarily administered as punishment to mental patients for being crazily uncooperative. But it turns out that if you're in sufficiently agonizing shape, you—or maybe not you, but, for example, I—will finally sob, 'Fuck it. Let's say it even *does* turn out to be a punishment, which I doubt very much that it will, but if it did it couldn't be much more horrifyingly harsh than what I'm barely able to endure now, so what are you waiting for?! Go on! Do it! Do it before you don't have a mind to change (pp. 4–5).

This is the same reasoning that appears in the notes of those who killed themselves because they felt like a failure. The distinction is that Carrie Fisher opted for trying a new treatment approach as opposed to ending her life. She indicates that having a child served as a protective factor for her. Having a strong support system could make the difference between choosing alternative, and perhaps frightening, treatment options, and suicide.

It was not unusual to read a statement in the investigator's report that indicates, "The decedent had a long history of depression and had threatened suicide to his wife, brother and sister." In other words, for most of these victims, friends and/or relatives knew they were struggling with thoughts of suicide or mental health issues. However, simply suggesting that family or friends be more supportive and take these threats seriously is short-sighted. These support systems had usually been hearing suicidal ideation or threats for a long time. Loved ones can reach a point where they become numb to the threats and fatigued from numerous trips to emergency rooms and hospitals. Like Nick, many of these individuals were seeing mental health providers and family and friends had turned responsibility over to those people. In fact, mental health providers will tell family and friends not to try to handle someone who is suicidal but rather to get them into treatment. However, even providers may have difficulty detecting the subtle changes that indicate someone has become suicidal.

Perhaps the best prevention might be to educate friends and family about the warning signs of suicide, and even more importantly, how to build resilience and enhance protective factors to prevent suicide. These include helping the individual to stay connected with loved ones and aiding them in trying out new problem-solving approaches. This may mean considering new treatment options or adopting new ways of dealing with stress or conflict. It is also vital to provide support for family and friends who may become exhausted, frustrated and even bitter. They not only need help in dealing with the current circumstances, but they will need a well-established support system if they have to handle the suicide of a loved one.

If asked to envision the "type" of person who would commit suicide, many people would envision someone who has been described in this section: a person who feels like a failure. However, according to our findings, these individuals represent less than 1% of the sample. It could be that our numbers underestimate the actual prevalence, since many people do not leave notes and that is where feelings of failure are most often expressed. However, it could also be that our numbers are correct and this is, in fact, a small subset. Although Nick may seem to embody the quintessential suicide, this is likely illusory. This happens with other shocking and misunderstood behaviors. For example, people often associate postpartum depression with a mother killing a child but, in reality, that is rarely the case; it simply receives more media attention than other reasons mothers kill their children (Meyer & Oberman, 2001). We want to believe that a mother must be "mad" (or "bad") to kill a child but, in fact, more mothers kill their children through neglect, by abuse or with intent. However, if they are mad or bad then we can convince ourselves that we would never do it. Connecting suicide to mental illness and feelings of failure may be the "safe" way to perceive it. It becomes distant then, something most people cannot envision themselves doing because they do not have a mental illness. However, our findings suggest suicide is more often in response to specific external stressors and that makes anyone a potential victim.

OTHER CATEGORIES THAT WERE NOT WELL SUPPORTED

In total we derived 11 categories from preexisting literature and research. We have already discussed interpersonal relationships (see chapter: Suicide Motivated by Interpersonal Relationships), escape (see chapter: Escape as a Motivation for Suicide), bereavement (this chapter), and failure (this chapter). Approximately 95% of our cases fell into those categories. Some categories received no support and a few received weak support. No support was found for the idea of killing oneself for spiritual reasons or to end life in order to gain entry into an eternal life/existence. Also, no support was found for killing oneself because of feeling discriminated against or to leave an abusive situation. Some people had a history of being abused and spoke of it in their notes, but no one indicated that the motivation for his/her suicide was a current abusive situation. For example, two women met our definition of abuse, experiencing unwanted physical contact or being subjected to emotionally harmful intimidation, but the abuse occurred 30 years before the suicide. The precipitant for the suicide was to escape from current psychological pain which resurfaced when their daughters reached puberty and the perpetrators attempted to renew contact with the victims.

Similarly, although revenge/retaliation was a part of other suicides, the motivation was interwoven with relationships and the relationship was the driving force, not the revenge/retaliation. Those cases are discussed in the chapter on interpersonal relationships as motivations for suicide.

As for the other categories, only four people killed themselves out of guilt, two who committed suicide because they felt alienated, and one who killed herself for altruistic reasons. Each of these smaller categories will be briefly discussed here.

Guilt

Frank came from a large family. Although his dad and one sibling had already passed away, he had several siblings still living nearby, and his mother had worked in the community for years. He was 44 years old with a daughter from a previous relationship. He attended two evangelical churches, one of which identified itself as reforming and Jesus-centered. Holiness and unity were the themes of the church movement. He liked sports and even did a little coaching.

Frank and his girlfriend had been having relationship difficulties for months. While on the phone one night she suggested they spend some time apart, but Frank wanted to talk to her about this in person. He went to his girlfriend's house, and they began to argue. Frank threw his girlfriend on the bed and raped her. The next day he wrote a brief note that said, "I'm sorry for my action's! I can't live with myself. Please forgive me. My insides are just full of guilt!" Then he hanged himself in his garage.

The motivation for Frank's suicide was unambiguous. Everything else was stable in his life and the previous quotation represents most of his entire note. The other three individuals who killed themselves due to guilt were just as clear-cut. One man wrote a long note to his girlfriend which read, in part, "I just couldn't believe I hurt someone I love as bad as I hurt you. I'm truly sorry. It was not me that did that. That is why I cannot live with myself. Because I know I could not hurt you & I still did." In his note he never stated what he did to his girlfriend, but frequent passages similar to this one discuss how he felt about it.

Two other individuals were included in this category but neither of them left a note. They were both in their fifties when tragedy struck. One man was the driver in a fatal car crash which killed his wife. For 5 years he struggled with depression and guilt related to her loss, and then one day he shot himself in the temple. The last person had a long history of physical and mental health problems and suicide threats but no attempts. One weekend while she was babysitting her grandson, who was a toddler, he ingested a large quantity of her medications. He was taken to the hospital by the grandfather but the grandmother remained at home with a relative. According to the relative, the grandmother was very distraught about the accident. When the relative stepped out to go to the convenience store, the grandmother took all her remaining medications. Although she died, the child lived.

Not much can be extrapolated from only four individuals, especially since two did not leave notes. It is impossible to compare them to other categories. Half left notes and one note was very long, while the other was very short. In general, things appeared to be relatively stable in their lives. It was an event that was precipitated by their behavior, or lack of it, that sent them reeling. All of them had remorse over doing or failing to do something that led to the injury of another. Even if it was accidental, their remorse over the event triggered their suicides.

Research on guilt as a motivation for suicide is limited and much of what is available focuses on veterans. Kopacz, McCarten, Vance, and Connery (2015) examined sources of guilt in veterans who sought chaplaincy services. Approximately 12% of their sample reported they had experienced suicidal ideation sometime during the prior 2 years while the rest had not. They divided their sample into "ideators" and "nonideators." They then determined how frequently each of the groups experienced guilt and the sources of that guilt. Participants were asked, "How often do you feel guilty over past behaviors?" Of those who were identified as "ideators," almost 59% said they felt guilty very often as compared to approximately 22% of the "nonideators." When asked the sources of the guilt, overall the four most common sources were life, God, family, and the military. Their research was designed to provide information about the frequency with which guilt is connected to suicidal ideation in a military population and the sources of guilt. Future research may identify exactly what is meant by the constructs they identified. For example, when participants felt guilt about "military," what specifically were they referring to? It could be construed as survivor's guilt or guilt over having to kill others. Perhaps most importantly, this research suggests that, although guilt as a motivation received very little support, it may warrant further consideration within a military population.

Alienation

Tom was a married man with one son, Tommy, Jr. After high school he served in the military and then returned home to settle down amidst the many relatives he had in the area. He had a good job in the building trades. His wife, Beverly, was a professional in the health care community. They belonged to a local black Christian church.

Tom and Beverly had experienced marital problems for years and although they had been in counseling many times to repair their relationship, it never worked. Finally, Beverly told Tom she was going to file for divorce. They had been living separately and their son was residing with Beverly. The night she told him she wanted a divorce, Tom became intoxicated and came to her house at four o'clock in the morning. When she left for work, he was passed out in the living room and she left him to "sleep it off." That afternoon he called her and told her that he intended to kill himself. Beverly called the police and told them what Tom had said and that he did own a gun. When police entered the home they smelled gasoline but they did not find Tom. They called a SWAT team and an hour later the team found Tom sprawled on the garage floor dead from carbon monoxide poisoning. In the note he left for his son he said, "Oh! Tommy, I love you so much. Please forgive me, this hurts so much Tommy. I need you more than you need me. It sounds stupid, but it's true, because all I love is you. I love you so much little buddy please forgive me, please. I'm so alone. I feel completely by myself."

Tom was just one of two people whom we determined killed themselves due to feeling alienated, and they both left notes. The other person talked about how he had recovered from his addictions and yet still no one came to visit him. He indicated that this hurt and he was "going Home to heven." Both note writers referred to feeling isolated from family, friends, intimate partners or society.

For the two individuals in this category, alienation was not just one more thing, but rather the motivation for their suicide. As with guilt, not much research has been done on alienation as a motivation for suicide. Basically, motivations for suicide are just not that simple. However, recent research published in Croatia which is titled, "Parental Alienation and Suicide in Men," may offer some insight into Tom's actions (Sher, 2015). Sher indicates that:

> Parental alienation is defined as a mental state in which a child, usually one whose parents are engaged in a high-conflict separation or divorce, allies himself strongly with one parent (the preferred parent) and rejects a relationship with the other parent (the alienated parent) without legitimate justification. Parental alienation is anomalous, maladaptive behavior (refusal to have a relationship with a loving parent) that is driven by an abnormal emotional condition (the false belief that the rejected parent is evil, dangerous, or unworthy of love) (p. 1).

Sher suggests this alienation may be connected with suicidality, especially in men.

Similar to guilt, relatively no support exists for alienation as a lone motivation for suicide. However, it may be that certain populations are more at risk, such as recently separated parents. Even if it is not a motivation, alienation is a risk factor that frequently occurs in victims.

Altruism

It was right after her 66th birthday when Frances found that it was becoming difficult to find the right words to express herself during conversations with friends and family. She attributed this to menopause, but later found she became confused, disoriented and lost while driving. She decided to look up the symptoms of Alzheimer's disease and found that out of ten early symptoms, she had nine. She also had a family history of Alzheimer's disease and cared for her mother and grandmother as they died from it. Frances had always struggled with anxiety and depression, and she was paralyzed with fear over the possibility of having this disease. She would not even make an appointment with the physician to have any testing completed but instead relied on her self-diagnosis. She lived with her husband on a farm and after he went to work one day she wrote him a brief note that read, "Honey, Don't grieve for me. I feel like I'm getting Alzheimers. I love you & don't want to be a burden." Then she shot herself in the chest with a handgun.

Durkheim (1897) referred to altruistic suicide as death as a duty or honor. We had no cases where someone killed themselves out of duty or honor. Durkheim associated this type of suicide with those in the military. One who serves may feel the need to kill himself, when his service is no longer of value or he cannot perform it ably. In civilian life, an analogous situation can occur, which Durkheim also labeled altruistic, when someone is motivated to kill herself to help others. Some people in our sample spoke of not wanting to be a burden in their notes, but it was a small part of the note and not the impetus for the suicide. Frances was the only case where the motivation for the suicide appeared to be to spare someone from having to deal with a burden. To us, this represented an unselfish concern for the welfare of others, an altruistic reason for the suicide.

According to Durkheim, altruistic suicides are perceived by the victim as supporting the social order and meeting with cultural approval. The military is an area in modern society in which these suicides persist. One may also find them in highly traditional societies. One reason altruistic suicides may not have appeared more often in our study is that they tend to occur in social groups where a low value is placed on the individual (Stack, 2004). The United States, and western culture as a whole, places a high value on the individual, but in rural, traditional farming communities, individualism may be less valued among women than in urban areas. Frances lived in a rural community and was of an older generation. In a traditional society, women, not men, are the caregivers, but Frances had no woman to look after her.

In our sample, although altruism may have played a small part in why some people committed suicide, especially those escaping physical or mental pain, the deciding factor was not related to a motivation to help others. It was not even one of the main considerations. People enduring physical pain killed themselves to escape the pain and relieving any burden to others was simply an added benefit.

CONCLUSIONS

All of the motivations discussed in this chapter represent a very small proportion of individuals in our sample. We include them because other theorists had suggested them as motivations for suicide. It is important to note that many suicide motivations are time and culture specific. While these motivations may have been more prevalent in another time or are more prevalent in another culture, at this point they are surpassed by other categories which are more robust. Still, we felt it was important to describe the specific patterns that can be seen within both the bereavement and failure categories, which can provide information about risk factors. More importantly, for individuals in both categories, social support may be the most important preventative factor.

6

The Complexity of Suicide Motivation

In Chapter 2, Findings, Chapter 3, Suicide Motivated by Interpersonal Relationships, Chapter 4, Escape as a Motivation for Suicide, and Chapter 5, Grief and Failure, we examined what motivated individuals to take their own lives. The 174 individuals who wrote notes actively sought to express their thoughts, desires, or emotions. They wanted to leave instructions, apologies, and explanations. Those direct communications helped inform us as to what motivated them to take their own lives. There are other forms of communication that also reveal much about motivations for suicide for note writers and for those who left no note. These communications are the actions of the dead. What they did and how they did it, in conjunction with their written words, create a clearer picture of modern suicide, despite its complexity.

A motivation is what impels the person to commit suicide; a risk factor is a common denominator among those who commit suicide. Thus, financial difficulties may be a motivation; bankruptcy may be a risk factor. In the psychological, psychiatric, and sociological literature, motivation has been the biggest question for researchers hoping to explain suicide, while risk factors have been the focus of prevention and intervention. It is imperative to understand that these are relational, and that any suicide is a complex intertwining of both motivation and risk factors, as well as mental state.

Two main reasons for committing suicide emerged from our data, with a vast majority—approximately 95%—doing so because of interpersonal relationships gone awry or because of a desire to escape something. While a few other motivations such as grief or failure appeared, these were uncommon. But there were other patterns that appeared across motivational categories that related to behavior. We then wondered if effective intervention and prevention might depend on the patterns we found.

Explaining Suicide.
DOI: http://dx.doi.org/10.1016/B978-0-12-809289-7.00006-3 **121**

CHAOS IN LIFE AND INTENT TO DIE

We found we could divide suicides across two dimensions, chaos in life and intent to die. Patterns of impulsivity and volatility (*chaos*) represented one dimension. Individuals were on a continuum from high to low chaos. For example, those in the interpersonally abusive relationship group, those escaping multiple problems, and those escaping legal or financial problems had a high amount of chaos in their lives, while those who were bereaved or escaping physical pain had a low amount of chaos in their lives.

The second dimension was *intent*, demonstrated by the level of lethality in the method used to kill themselves, as well as in their expressed sentiments if they wrote notes and in their aggressive or passive behaviors. For example, those escaping physical pain or in abusive relationships had a high predilection for death and tried to ensure lethality through the choices they made. Conversely, there were other groups that showed patterns of ambivalence and uncertainty about their suicides. Those who suffered psychological pain, grief, and failure felt despair and resignation, but their behaviors suggest that, as a group, they were less determined to end their lives. If we combine the dimensions, four quadrants emerge (Fig. 6.1).

The diagram in the figure shows four quadrants. In the upper left quadrant are the motivation groups that showed a strong desire to die, based on lethality, words and behaviors, and planned their deaths. Those who wanted to escape physical pain, e.g., had relatively stable lives. They were simply in terrible pain. Had they not been physically ill and unable to cope with the illness, it is unlikely many, if any, of them would have killed themselves. Thus, they are placed on the far end of the chaos line, nearest to stability, but high on the intent line. Their high use of guns (80%) and the content of their notes indicate they definitely wanted their lives to end. In the middle of the upper left are those in interpersonal relationships who lost love or had unrequited love. They experienced some chaos as a result of their loss and so are closer to the center on the chaos line, but they also often planned their suicides and were not as impulsive. They did, however, want to die and chose guns and hanging. Most of this group shot themselves in the head, indicating little ambivalence. Closer to the center, but still in the upper left quadrant, were those in the escape psychological group who had a higher intent to die, but who were otherwise similar to the others in the same quadrant. They were as a group living somewhat chaotic lives, usually because of their mental illness, but were not otherwise extremely volatile or impulsive.

In the upper right quadrant, highest on the intent scale and highest on the chaos scale are those in abusive interpersonal relationships. These

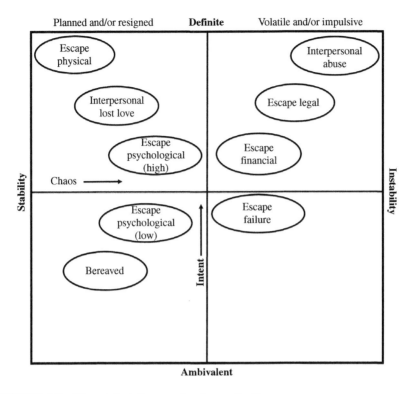

FIGURE 6.1 Chaos-intent diagram showing motivation groups.

people were definite about their desire to die, and they often killed themselves with little, if any, planning. Those escaping legal problems shared the impulsivity and instability of those in abusive relationships. Closer to the center, with less chaos but with high intent, were those escaping financial problems. This quadrant represents the highest usage of guns and violence towards others. In many ways life had spiraled out of control for the individuals in this quadrant.

In the lower right quadrant is only one group, failure. These individuals often spent a long time thinking about what they believed were their messed-up lives, and when they decided to die, they had given it considerable thought. They had not necessarily planned their actual deaths a long time in advance, though, and they used guns much less often than those in other categories. They chose asphyxia more often, and their words often betrayed regret that they were unable to do better in life. Their lives were chaotic, to a degree, because they had multiple difficulties and felt a lot of emotion, but they were not the most volatile.

The lower left quadrant represents the two groups that demonstrated the most ambivalence about wanting to die and who had the least amount of chaos in their lives. In the case of the bereaved, they are close to the stability line. Grief unhinged them and made life unbearable, but in most other ways their lives were stable. If it were not for the death of their loved ones, they probably would not have wanted to die. Among those escaping psychological pain, there was less frequent use of the most lethal means but often there had been multiple attempts or a history of suicidal ideation. They are near the center. Their deaths were not mere accidents, but the pain and instability they felt was pronounced.

Below we will examine and discuss some of the qualities that the various groups have and theories that may help interpret how those qualities relate to suicide. We have included figures, in the form of circles divided by characteristics, to show group composite images with the most noticeable qualities appearing in the diagram. The circles show the relative importance each quality played in making up the group's dynamic based on comparative percentages.

INTERPERSONAL RELATIONSHIPS AND GENDER DYNAMICS

Men made up the overwhelming majority of suicide victims (82–91%) in every category we examined, although the percentage was lower for those who wished to escape psychological pain (68%) and those who were grieving (68%). Of all those who suffered from unrequited or lost love or who were in abusive relationships, nine out of ten were men. It was men, overwhelmingly, who wanted to escape physical pain, legal entanglements, financial problems, and psychological pain.

The statistics paint a picture of male suicide that is quite striking. In popular culture, we often caricature men as unable to function well in intimate relationships, but for a significant group of men, this is no laughing matter. In matters of love, loss and intimate conflict, some men will take their own lives. But which men? There were two theories of masculinity articulated in the late 20th century that explored men's power and privilege, or lack of it, in their cultural contexts. Hegemonic masculinity and hypermasculinity explained how men gained and maintained power over other men and women, on the one hand, and defined manliness on the other (Hooper, 2012). The two can also work in tandem, and they may explain the high rate of suicide among men.

Hegemonic masculinity refers to a social construction of power in which men who embody the norm of masculinity, whatever that is for a particular culture, establish and keep power over others (Hooper, 2012). In other words, if men are supposed to be heads of households and breadwinners, there will be a range of masculinities on a continuum that will incorporate or reject those qualities. A very hegemonic man will perhaps be the sole breadwinner or at least the top earner in the household; he may be the disciplinarian in the family, the keeper of the finances, the one who controls the way the household works. A less hegemonic man may cede some control of those things to his partner/spouse. On this continuum at the other end, one may find men who have no interest in being the breadwinner, who enjoy childcare, and who leave the finances to the spouse.

Manliness is not an immutable or unchangeable trait. Among some classes and subcultures in America, for instance, men who are comfortable outside of traditional gender roles and who are inclusive and nurturing are considered more manly and desirable than those who have physical prowess or who exhibit a desire to dominate others. In a country as diverse and as large as the United States, manliness traits can be exactly the opposite among different classes, geographic regions, or racial or ethnic groups. Attitudes about manliness and masculinity affect more than personality. They can help or impede one's path through life. Certain constructs of masculinity are harmful to men's health if men will not use services, especially medical or psychological, out of a belief that to do so is weak. Hegemonic masculinity can have some positive elements. These men often feel a great sense of responsibility toward others and will often pitch in to help others, but in some instances this can take a negative turn, if men believe they cannot fulfill those responsibilities or that others will be better off without them (Southworth, 2016). In extreme cases, men who place a high value on being "the family man," whose identities are completely intertwined with their families, and then who cannot withstand the pressures, often financial but also interpersonal, can go on to commit familicide (Auchter, 2010).

Men who are hypermasculine believe manliness is characterized by violence, risk-taking, endurance of pain, and demonstrated superiority over women. According to both Schneidman (1957) and Joiner (2005), as well as other theorists, to die by suicide a person must be able to overcome the natural fear of death and be willing to endure its pain. Hypermasculine men already see fear of death as unmanly; they are likely to be involved in activities that involve pain, such as contact sports, and they are often involved in domestic violence. Inflicting pain is something they have become accustomed to. Their own masculine gender norms might make them especially susceptible to suicide. Moreover, hypermasculine men often think that talking about or expressing one's feelings is unmanly, so they are unlikely to be able to resolve problems, communicate their distress or ask for help. Just as German men were the immigrants most likely to kill themselves in the early 20th-century United States because of their emotional reserve and lack of cultural rituals to help them assimilate, modern men in hypermasculine subcultures are at risk. Studies have shown that hypermasculine men exhibited depression, psychological distress, and some suicidal ideation, whether they were straight or gay, black or white, or young or old (Fischgrund, Halkitis, & Carroll, 2012; Granato, Smith, & Selwyn, 2015).

Moreover, in our suicide data, the second and third highest use of guns occurred in the men who were in the abusive interpersonal relationship group (69%) and the unrequited or lost love group (52%), respectively. The CDC found that 55.4% of all male suicide victims used guns to kill themselves, and we found 51% did (CDC, 2016). The CDC also noted, however, that the number of men using guns had declined since 1991, when it was 61.7%. It may be that hypermasculinity and hegemonic masculinity, with their attendant violent or dominant behavior, are in decline (Curtin, Warner, & Hedegaard, 2016). Men's beliefs about masculinity, and the behavior rooted in that mentality, may be directly related to suicidal behavior. It is also possible for women to have traits that are associated with hegemonic masculinity or hypermasculinity, because these traits are personality characteristics across the gender spectrum. Women can be high risk takers, dominant over other women and men, and violent.

Stallones, Doenges, Dik, and Valley (2013) studied suicide in Colorado from 2004 to 2005 and found that men who worked in farming, fishing, and forestry (475.6 per 100,000) had the highest age-adjusted suicide rates, and a higher number used firearms (50.18 per 100,000). Among women, workers with the highest suicide rates were in construction and extraction (134.3 per 100,000), and in those occupations, most people died by hanging, suffocation, or strangulation. Roberts, Jaremin, and Lloyd (2013) found that in Britain there was a high rate of suicide among farmers, coal miners, seafarers, construction workers, and other manual trades. These were not the only occupations with high risk. Access to the means to kill oneself also explains high suicide rates in some professions (doctors, pharmacists, veterinarians). Occupations with greater numbers of suicide changed from the 1970s to the 2000s, from professionals and farmers to all manual occupations, largely because efforts at prevention had been directed at occupations with high risk in the past (Roberts et al., 2013).

Men who are hypermasculine or who accept a patriarchal, hegemonic masculinity as the normative standard are not necessarily "he-men" in the physical sense. Their physical appearance can be of any body type. Much more significant are attitudes and behaviors that subscribe to certain values: extreme stoicism in the face of pain, perhaps an overdeveloped sense of duty and responsibility, and a willingness to take extreme risks. While many psychologically healthy men are not ones to bare their souls, are loyal and responsible, and enjoy sports or other activities with some risk involved, hypermasculine and hegemonic masculine men will be on the far end of the masculine spectrum and will overvalue these qualities. Hypermasculine men also will exhibit violent behaviors. The men and women who share these traits or who value behaviors associated with the traits may be at more risk of suicide, especially if they are involved in relationships that have turned abusive.

Abusive Relationships

One winter night a 32-year-old white man was sitting in jail on a domestic violence charge. A little after 11 p.m. he was discovered in his cell hanging by a sheet. Not long before Valentine's Day, a 42-year-old white man hanged himself after he and his wife had a domestic argument. One spring evening a 38-year-old black man jumped from a highway overpass after being involved in a domestic violence incident in his home. One autumn day a 34-year-old white female, who had been incarcerated for domestic violence, hanged herself in her cell.

Every day of every year in all seasons there is a suicide related to domestic violence. Karch et al. (2009) estimate as many as 30% of all suicides may be related to domestic violence.

Interpersonal violence, most of which is domestic violence, is by its nature an event that can turn lethal. In 2013, homicide was the second leading cause of death for both white and black females between the ages of 15–24, the fourth leading cause of death for black women between the ages of 25–34, and the fifth leading cause of death for white women aged 25–34 (CDC, 2014). Nearly 12,000 people in the United States were murdered in intimate partner homicides by current or former male partners between 2000 and 2011. Twenty percent of domestic violence homicides were not intimate partners themselves, but family members, friends, neighbors, persons who intervened, law enforcement responders, or bystanders. Seventy-two percent of all murder-suicides involve an intimate partner; 94% of the homicide victims of these murder-suicides are female (CDC, 2014). Not all of the deaths that result, though, are murder victims. Many of those who die as a result of domestic or interpersonal violence in their lives die by their own hand. Over one-third of the men in our sample who committed suicide in interpersonally abusive relationships also killed someone else.

The men who killed themselves in interpersonal violence situations were generally young to early middle-aged. They were usually physically healthy and were at a time in their lives when they should have been at the peak of their earning opportunities. They were at the age to be raising children, if they so chose. Yet something went terribly wrong for these men.

As our findings showed, they mostly used guns and frequently they committed the act in front of someone else. Most often it was at home, but it is striking how many were elsewhere. Only one other group, those in legal entanglements, killed themselves less often at home, and that was because they were either in jail or sometimes fleeing police. In many cases, the men chose public places for their suicides and chose not to die alone. Two-thirds had been cited for previous domestic violence. The intermingling of public demonstration with private, intimate violence characterized the interpersonally abusive relationship group more than any other, although those escaping from multiple problems had some similar public expression of their private pain. They were trying to communicate, but less through words and more through actions.

These were men who had never expressed any suicidal ideation before their suicides and only 20% had been diagnosed with psychological illness. They were not seeking help for their problems from professionals. In their final notes some of them articulated their psychological pain, but a large proportion could only say they were in some unspecified pain. They hurt but did not, perhaps could not, say why. Violence is a reaction toward a source that is causing pain. It can be directed outwardly or inwardly. Those who act violently in their interpersonal relationships believe someone close to them is causing them pain and deserves punishment. They are either unable to express it verbally or words provide insufficient relief.

While the interpersonally abusive relationship group was more impulsive than other groups, occasionally there was some planning. It was often shorter than those in psychological pain or other categories. Their notes and behavior, when interpreted together, reveal patterns of emotion and thought. Fig. 6.2 represents the dominant characteristics of the group.

The most noticeable emotion they never acknowledged was their anger, which was explosive. They did not feel shame or sadness, and they never felt they were worthless or failures. People failed them, not the other way around. They blamed others, not themselves. They felt no guilt. They wrote about joy, hopelessness, tiredness, loneliness, their love for others, and being loved by others, but as they did so, seething underneath was anger. Love and anger were so balled up together, one articulated in words, the other in violent action, that they were nearly synonymous. Sometimes these individuals did extend an apology for killing themselves, either generally or to another person, but usually not to the person at whom their anger (and their love) was directed. The men in the group appear to have been highly certain of themselves, given what they were about to do, and so it is perhaps not surprising to find tunnel vision and dichotomous thinking. It was all or nothing for them.

This way of thinking about love is often something romanticized in literature, movies, television, and music. Both men and women may internalize the message that love at its most passionate is violent. That passionate love is also one aspect of their lives that many people do feel

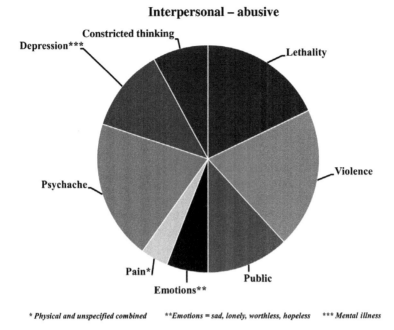

FIGURE 6.2   The interpersonally abusive relationship group composite image.

entitled to, even when they may not feel entitled to much else. "Don't let anyone ever make you feel like you don't deserve what you want," Heath Ledger's character resolved in 10 Things I Hate About You (1999), a modern remake of Shakespeare's The Taming of the Shrew, in which a man makes a noncompliant, rather unpleasant ("bitchy") woman become his subservient, sweet lover. Even in movies with a healthier message about love, the idea that one should not be able to live without a particular person is ubiquitous. "I didn't come back to tell you that I can't live without you," Jennifer Aniston's character in Rumor Has It (2005) tells her boyfriend. "I can live without you. I just don't want to." In movies like Ghost (1990) or Wuthering Heights (1939, 1970 (in this version, Heathcliff kills himself), 1992, 2012) love persists beyond the grave. Popular media are not responsible for making people think a certain way. In many ways, they reflect what people already think, but they then reinforce the message that relationships are eternal, even if someone dies. When people in an abusive relationship internalize the message that passionate love means conflict, they are often supported in that belief by their social circle. Beres (1999) referred to this as the "subtle romanticization of control" (p. 195). Some of the men in the interpersonally abusive relationship group believed they would be reunited with their intimate partners after death.

A Comparison of Interpersonal Relationships

Men in the unrequited or lost love group (Fig. 6.3) shared many of the characteristics with the abusive group, but they expressed more ambivalence about death and had a greater sense of blameworthiness. Both groups mentioned forgiveness, but the abusive group mentioned it almost twice as much as the unrequited love group, usually to ask for forgiveness from a person other than their intimate partner. They had similar contricted thinking patterns, but more of the men in the unrequited love group had had suicidal ideation prior to the suicide attempt that ended their lives, and they suffered more from depression.

Unrequited love can sound like an old-fashioned phrase, but it is a problem that many people in contemporary society face and struggle with. The pain is quite real. Research demonstrates that people feel an emotional wound in the same way as they feel physical injury. A "broken heart" can feel exactly like that. Kross, Egner, Ochsner, Hirsch, and Downey (2007) found that emotional pain activates the same part of one's brain as physical pain. Baumeister, Wotman, and Stillwell (1993) estimated that 98% of people have suffered from unrequited love or lost love at one time or another. As a result the person feels sad, lonely and hopeless, as well as ashamed. The persistence of these feelings distinguishes the people in the unrequited love group from other people and

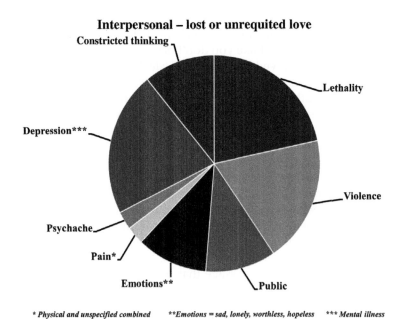

Interpersonal – lost or unrequited love

FIGURE 6.3   The interpersonal lost or unrequited love group composite image.

from individuals in the abusive group. Those who experience unrequited love, while distinguishable from those in interpersonally abusive relationships, are not wholly dissimilar from them. While physical abuse may not be present, or is present to a lesser extent, the men who experience unrequited love can be emotionally abusive, controlling or manipulative. The suicides in the physically abusive group were not done quietly. In one case, after having a fight with his wife, a man locked himself in a camper on his property. The police had been called, and upon arriving they asked the man to come out. He refused, so the police obtained a key and unlocked the door. As they began to enter, the man took a fire extinguisher and sprayed the police, throwing it at them to keep them out of the camper. The police used mace against the man. He then grabbed two knives and started toward the police officers. They backed away and the man began to stab himself. He closed the camper door. When the officers finally got back in, the man had stabbed himself in the chest with two different four-inch blades a total of ten times. Many of these cases had elements of graphic violence and were terrifying to the witnesses.

When Oliffe et al. (2014) studied murder-suicide, they concluded that hegemonic masculinities, which value power and aggression, were implicated in the majority of cases. Among the domestic violence cases, these men had "failed to gain or sustain" their dominance over the family or establish themselves as financial breadwinners according to the masculine norms in their communities. In the workplace and school shooting cases that were also examined in that study, problems with masculinity were present.

Intimate partner violence is a problem for women that transcends all races and socioeconomic statuses, but not all women have the same experience. While 82% of the suicide victims in this group were white, 18% were not. Thirty-nine percent had legal problems. We must look to one other category to get a clearer picture; the other category which had the highest percentage of nonwhite suicides was those escaping legal entanglements. African-American men are hardly present at all in some groups, like those escaping physical pain, but in the group of interpersonally abusive suicides and legal entanglements they comprise not quite 18%. The literature also documents that interpersonal violence has a higher impact on African-American women than on white women; African-American women were assaulted by partners at a rate 35% higher than white women (Taft, Bryant-Davis, Woodward, Tillman, & Torres, 2009).

African-American men have been the hardest hit by the rise in mass incarceration over the last 30 years. It is also a community affected disproportionately by unemployment and poverty. There is high religiosity among African Americans, but these religions, Christianity and Islam, tend to be patriarchal. Indeed, a higher emphasis may be placed on the role of men in the family and community, because of a long history of white oppression that specifically denied such power to black men. During slavery, enslaved men could not be married to their partners and had no control over their children, who could be sold away from their parents. After slavery ended, black men often embraced patriarchal values and reasserted their manhood by reclaiming control over their families. Black men in the United States traditionally subscribe to hegemonic masculinity (hooks, 2004). The relatively high presence of black men among suicide victims in the interpersonally abusive group compared to their presence in other groups is thus not surprising. This group's close links to those escaping legal entanglements, both in racial makeup and the presence of hegemonic masculinity and hypermasculinity, means that black men in these categories are at a higher risk for suicide than they are across all other categories, and intervention and prevention need to be afforded to these men.

There is no doubt that hegemonic masculinity and hypermasculinity are problems for men of both races. While it would be too much to say that these theories of masculinity explain suicide in the interpersonal relationships category, there is evidence to suggest they played a role in many if not most of the cases we examined. We are not saying that men need to be more like women. There are already more versions of what it means to be a man, and what it means to be manly, that run counter to the hegemonic narrative. The Good Men Project, e.g., is a social media and website presence that invites men to share their experiences and to read about manhood and fatherhood in ways that are supportive and positive (The Good Men Project, 2016). Founded in 2009 by Tom Matlack and James Houghton, the Good Men Project aims to be a "national conversation" about masculinity and men's experiences. Orienting men, especially young men, to that conversation is an important first step in making them healthier psychologically.

Not all men who commit suicide, and certainly not all women, fit into classifications of hypermasculinity or hegemonic masculinity. While men's preponderance in a motivational category like interpersonal relationships is firmly established (Van Orden et al., 2010), it is less clear what type of man or woman commits suicide to escape, or whether gender or race matters at all in this category.

ATTITUDES TOWARD DEATH

While those who committed suicide to escape were also predominantly white men, gender, and race intersected in noticeable ways. White men made up the majority of those who wanted to escape, but women were present to a larger degree than they were in other categories, such as those who wanted to escape psychological pain (32%) and those who were escaping multiple things (18%). African Americans and other racial and ethnic minorities (almost all of whom were men) were overrepresented in those escaping legal entanglements (18%).

It is important to recognize this difference, because these are the escape categories that represent the greatest risk for nonwhites and women. It is also important to look at categories in which whites were almost exclusively at risk, like those escaping physical pain. All but 3% of the 119 people in our study who killed themselves to escape physical pain were white. At first that number may not seem extraordinary; white men are the majority in every category. However, it signifies that there is a very different attitude about end-of-life issues between whites and blacks. A study on black and white attitudes towards physician-assisted suicide demonstrates different belief systems between the two races about the end of life and may indicate attitudes that factor into suicide (Lichtenstein, Alcser, Corning, Bachman, & Doukas, 1997). For instance, blacks prefer aggressive medical intervention to preserve life in cases that might be fatal far more than whites (Lichtenstein et al., 1997), but they will not use palliative care or hospice facilities where patients go to die (Winston, Leshner, Kramer, & Allen, 2005). Furthermore, whites historically have made up a higher percentage of those who supported physician-assisted suicide since the question was first researched. Over the decades, a gap of nearly 20 percentage points on acceptance of physician-assisted suicide persisted between whites and blacks even as support for it rose in both groups (Lichtenstein et al., 1997).

In order to understand why the gaps existed, Lichtenstein et al. (1997) examined differences in religious beliefs and religiosity between blacks and whites, and found that religiosity was the strongest predictor of lack of support for physician-assisted suicide. The African-American religious community's belief in preserving life is particularly strong regardless of denomination. Almost all black churches are evangelical, espousing an often fundamentalist interpretation of the ten commandments. Lichtenstein et al. also found that African Americans have a greater distrust of the medical community, in part because of the infamous and well-known syphilis experiments on black men at the Tuskegee Institute in the mid-20th century. The underutilization of end-of-life and palliative care has been attributed in part to the incompatibility between the hospice philosophy of accepting death when cure is no longer possible and African-American religious, spiritual, and cultural beliefs as well as distrust of the medical establishment (Winston et al., 2005). Previous research on African-American suicide revealed that pastors in black churches universally discouraged and condemned suicide even as a means to escape pain from a terminal illness (Early, 1992).

It would be incorrect to suggest that whites lack religiosity or do not take religious beliefs seriously, but differences in church culture may have a bearing on their willingness to commit suicide to end physical pain. Evangelical Protestant churches dominate the United States (25.4%) and Ohio (29%). Yet 22% of people in Ohio are unaffiliated with any religion, and only 67% of Ohioans believe in God with certainty. A slight majority of Ohioans (56%) think religion is important to their daily lives. Perhaps most significantly, 58% never participate in studying anything about their religion (Pew Research Center (Pew Forum), 2016a,b). They lack knowledge of scripture or doctrine, and thus may be unaware of church teachings on suicide. Could differences in religiosity between whites and blacks, as well as differences in attitudes toward end of life issues, explain the whiteness of the escape from physical pain group?

There is evidence, though not conclusive, that religious affiliation, devotional practice (piety) and belief can have a positive effect on mental well-being, though to what degree and for whom is debated. Ellison (1995) examined other research on southern blacks to see if black churches had an impact on depression, which is the mental illness most associated with suicide. According to Ellison, researchers have found that both public and private religious involvement appear to be more important for holding depression at bay for blacks than for whites. Public religious activities help with social integration and with social status. Since blacks have had fewer opportunities for both of those things in secular institutions, the black churches have played a significant role. Also, black congregations sponsor more social service programs than most white churches and disseminate more information related to health and crisis intervention (Ellison, 2015). We can't know for certain if any of the people in our study were churchgoers or what their personal religion practices and beliefs were, but if blacks and whites in Ohio are similar to those in other states, then understanding the role of religion in helping depression can benefit both groups.

The Pew Research Center (Pew Forum, 2016a,b) reported that 32% of Ohioans had very clear ideas about what is right and wrong, while 66% thought right and wrong depended on the situation. Pew also found that 77% expressed a belief in heaven, slightly higher than the national average of 72%, while 17% did not and 5% were unsure; 63% believed in hell. If those escaping physical pain represent a cross-section of white adults in middle America, and there is evidence to think they do, they may have been among the growing number of white Americans who see no moral or ethical impediment to suicide when it is done to end physical pain (Fig. 6.4).

Effect of Pain

Those escaping physical pain wanted very much to die. They chose highly lethal means, such as guns, and they stayed home where they had privacy. They made sure they were alone. They did not appear to want to be saved from death. Yet we cannot dismiss their suicides as simply the most rational choice. In some instances that might have been true, but much could have been done to make these lives worth living in the time

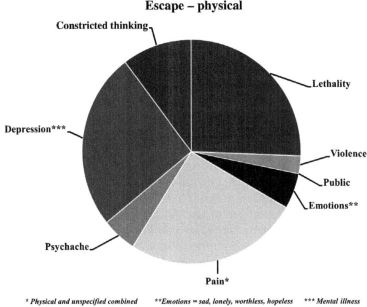

Escape – physical

* *Physical and unspecified combined*   **Emotions = sad, lonely, worthless, hopeless*   *** *Mental illness*

FIGURE 6.4   Escape from physical pain group composite image.

they would have had left had they not killed themselves. Greater access
to medical and psychological care, especially on weekends, could have
helped some of the victims in our group. Better pain management might
have helped those with chronic but not fatal illnesses. More attention on
the part of family and friends to remove firearms possibly could have prevented some of these suicides. Communal living situations in which there
was less isolation might also have obviated the suicidal situation. These
deaths were motivated almost solely by a desire to alleviate physical
pain, but in these cases medical, psychological and perhaps even familial
resources often failed. The reasons for those failures are complicated, and
frequently have to do with funding, and other issues we will discuss in
Chapter 10, Conclusions and Implications. A well-planned, well-funded
effort to help prevent suicide among the sick and elderly may save lives—
lives worth living.

While little ambivalence may have existed for those who wanted to
escape physical pain, that was not true of those wishing to escape psychological pain. That group can be split in two—high and low intent—
because nearly half (low) chose methods that were less lethal, such as
overdose or carbon monoxide poisoning, and reflected more ambivalence
in their notes and behavior than the other half (high), who chose guns or
asphyxiation by hanging. More specifically, overall 23% died by overdose,

7% by carbon monoxide, 3% using an unknown means, 2% by drowning, 2% by falling (jumping to one's death), and less than 1% by suffocation, train, or vehicle, while another 25% died by handgun, 10% by shotgun, 5% by rifle, and 19% by hanging. One person killed herself by carbon monoxide and overdose. Otherwise there appear to be few differences between high and low intent. Their psychological pain was unbearable for all of them.

There were more nonwhites (12%) and women (32%) among those escaping psychological pain than in other groups. The individuals were also quite distinct from those escaping physical pain. They were more engaged with suicide, having made previous attempts and having suicidal ideation, yet some of them were less sure they wanted to die. They shared the greatest similarity with those in the grief and failure groups. The escape-psychological, grief, and failure groups had the fewest gun deaths and had similar percentages who killed themselves by overdose and asphyxia. While it can be difficult to know for certain or to measure accurately how much someone wanted to die, lethality has become a measure for researchers (Haw, Hawton, Houston, & Townsend, 2003).

Intent can also be inferred by looking at words and actions in addition to lethality. Only 13% of note writers in this group said life was not worth living, as compared to those who were escaping multiple problems (26%) or physical pain (24%), suggesting that more people in this group could still imagine a life worth living. They also had the least amount of constricted thinking of any group, suggesting that they had not become convinced that death was inevitable. In Figs. 6.5A and B one can see that lethality is the only substantial difference between the high and low intent subgroups, which is why in Fig. 6.1, at the beginning of the chapter, both subgroups reside near the center of the diagram.

A number of possible interpretations of this information exist. As sufferers of psychological pain, they may have been more introspective than those in other groups. Indeed Schneidman (1999) describes psychological pain as "the introspective experience of negative emotions such as anger, despair, fear, grief, shame, guilt, hopelessness, loneliness, and loss" (p. 287). He called this "psychache." The psychological pain associated with severe depression is often perceived by its sufferers as worse than any physical pain that the individual has experienced (Mee, Bunney, Reist, Potkin, & Bunney, 2006). Psychache makes up a large portion of the group composite images of those escaping psychological pain, with both high and low intent (Figs. 6.5A and B), and of those in the interpersonally abusive group (Fig. 6.2), but it makes very little appearance in those escaping physical pain (Fig. 6.4).

There were differences between women and men that essentially correspond to the high and low intent subgroups. Women did not use guns. While we might conclude that this is simply a gender preference, it may

(A) **Escape – psychological (high)**

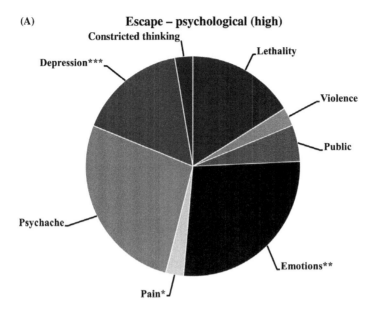

* Physical and unspecified combined   **Emotions = sad, lonely, worthless, hopeless   *** Mental illness

(B) **Escape – psychological (low)**

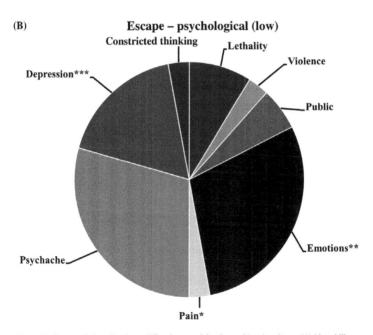

* Physical and unspecified combined   **Emotions = sad, lonely, worthless, hopeless   *** Mental illness

FIGURE 6.5   (A) Escape psychological pain (high) and (B) escape psychological pain (low) group composite images.

be more than that. As we saw in the introduction, the rate for women taken to the hospital for a suicide attempt was nearly twice that of men, but the death rate for suicide among men was four times higher than for women (Daniulaityte, Carlson, & Siegal, 2007). Women are twice as likely as men to suffer from depression (Nolen-Hoeksema, 2001), but it is possible more of them get treatment for it than men (Weissman, 2014). Women who complete a suicide after previous attempts do not usually escalate the violence or lethality of the suicide method, but men do (Brådvik, 2007). It may be that women escaping from psychological pain are simply more ambivalent about death than men in the same category when they decide to commit suicide.

REASONS FOR LIVING

Those who killed themselves over grief and failure shared many characteristics with the psychological escape group. Predominantly white, there were more women in these groups than in other groups. They used few guns, and most died by asphyxia and overdose. Almost three-quarters of the time they killed themselves at home. Nearly a quarter had physical illnesses, and the rate of depression of those in the failure group were similar to those in escape-psychological.

The similarities of their characteristics may have something to do with the fact that the number of women in these groups was proportionally high in each. Likewise the people in these groups tended to have one problem. For those in psychological pain, that was their major impediment to living. Many people experiencing grief had no compound major problems. The loss of their loved one made life unbearable (Fig. 6.6).

Those in the failure group did often have multiple problems, at least to outward observers. However, it may be that "failure" itself was the singular problem in the eyes of the victims. Maybe life did not seem completely worthless to the people in these groups because they really only had one problem that, if gone, would have made life worth living. Their choices of means other than guns to die suggests ambivalence. It is possible that had some life-affirming events or social supports been present to counter the grief or failure, some of these suicides might have been prevented.

Having a reason to live that supercedes the reason to die is frequently identified as a protective factor (see discussion in Chapter 9: Protective Factors and Resilience). Many of the victims in our sample who suffered from psychological illness, grief, or failure identified the absence of a reason for living as the problem. "We are ruined, our marrige and our financial situation… I have given up on love, trust, faith & hope's & dreams," mourned a 42-year-old woman who had diabetes and

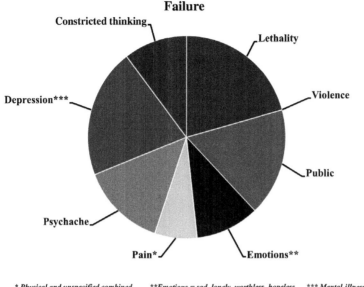

FIGURE 6.6   The failure group composite image.

psychological problems. Nick was searching for a reason to keep going, but none appeared: "I have been a failure in my own eyes my entire life. There is nothing that I excel at. There is nothing where I am the best." A 30-year-old woman who was tired of "being such a failure" made it clear that it was her failure as a mother that was propelling her toward death. She had just lost custody of her children. "I miss them so dearly—no one could imagine."

Outside observers cannot always tell what might be a person's reasons for living. The individuals in our study left behind children, parents, spouses, siblings, friends, and pets whom they loved. Loving others may be one person's reason to live and not another's. Three-quarters of note writers mentioned love for others. The issue is not whether others could find a reason for living in the suicide victim's circumstances, but whether the suicidal person could. In the psychological escape, grief, and failure categories, they were able to identify reasons for living (marriage, being good at something, parenting), but having those things eluded them. People in other groups were unable to identify reasons for living. Thought processes were critical. Constricted thinking, such as tunnel vision or dichotomous thinking, may affect one's ability to be able to identify a reason for living (Jobes & Mann, 1999). In those escaping multiple problems, financial problems and legal problems, we can see the effects of constricted thinking on their loss of a reason to live (Fig. 6.7).

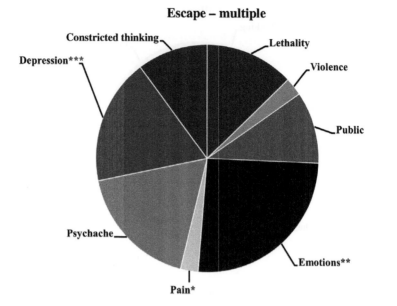

FIGURE 6.7   Escape from multiple problems group composite image.

Effect of Overwhelming Problems

Those who were escaping multiple problems might be expected to straddle the categories in escape we have just discussed, but in fact, they were quite distinct. This group, like the interpersonally abusive relationship group (Fig. 6.2), was highly volatile and impulsive in a way the other escape-psychological (Figs. 6.5A and B) and physical (Fig. 6.4) subgroups were not. If we look at their rates of interpersonal problems, physical and unspecified pain, physical illness and legal and financial problems, as discussed in Chapter 4, Escape as a Motivation for Suicide, we see lives that seemed to be a "mess." They also had the highest rate of negative emotions in their suicide notes, and exhibited constricted thinking. Like those in the interpersonally abusive relationship group, they could not see a way out of their misery. Their lives were falling apart and, in their minds, they were out of options. They felt they had no choice but to die.

Those escaping multiple problems also face challenges in getting help because of a combination of circumstances that surround not just the number of issues but their complexity. Constricted or rigid thinking may precede the onset of planning the suicide and may be the usual way a person with multiple problems thinks. In other words, the constricted thinking is typical for them. That pattern of thinking may be shared with the person's social milieu, where many have poor problem-solving skills. This might be especially true for adolescents who rely on their peer group more than on professional help. Moreover, expertise in all the problem areas is not likely to be found in any single individual who is present to help the person. The person who can provide psychological counseling is unlikely to be equipped to provide financial counseling. Referral to someone else may seem to the suicidal person like adding to the set of problems. A mindset of help-negation, i.e., the refutation of all help-related suggestions for myriad reasons ("I can't, because..."), can set in among multiple parties, the victim and family or friends, as the problems mount. Help-negation can increase the risk of suicidality (Deane, Wilson, & Ciarrochi, 2001; Joiner, Walker, Rudd, & Jobes, 1999). This is a group that gives mixed messages about wanting help and resists accepting it, not purely out of obstinacy, although it can be perceived that way. Often there is a confluence of reasons for the help-negation that includes constricted thinking, mental illness, substance abuse, and myriad personal issues. This category cuts across race, gender, and class lines.

It may seem difficult to imagine a more complex category than those trying to escape from multiple problems, but those trying to escape legal problems is arguably more so. Like the interpersonally abusive group (Fig. 6.2), those escaping legal problems (Fig. 6.8), while predominantly

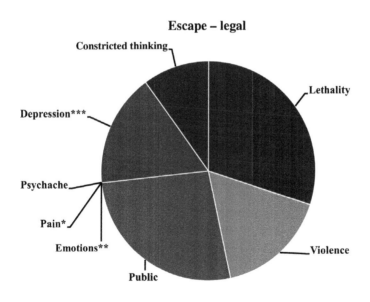

Physical and unspecified combined   **Emotions = sad, lonely, worthless, hopeless*   ***Mental illness*

FIGURE 6.8   Escape from legal problems group composite image.

white and male, had a significant number of minority individuals. Also, like both of the interpersonal subgroups, the average age at death, 37, was younger than in other groups. The only group with a younger average age was the financial problem group at 35. Some individuals in this group had hypermasculine traits, including risky and violent behavior.

The largest number of deaths occurred by asphyxia, which reflects the high number in jail. Those who had access to guns used them. In some ways, those escaping legal problems had multiple problems, but they only died because of their legal problems. Like those escaping multiple problems, those escaping legal problems had complicated lives. They exhibited some of the same high risk and violent behavior seen in the abusive relationship group, but a few were caught up in circumstances that simply became overwhelming and no reason for living more significant than their problems was on the horizon.

Only three of the people escaping legal problems left notes, so we have no way to determine the emotional states or other subjective factors for people in this category. More telling of their mindsets, perhaps, is the nonverbal communication among the 50 people in this category. In one case, police spotted a van driving erratically late at night and attempted to pull the driver over. Instead of complying the driver kept going for over an hour and 40 minutes, through several jurisdictions, over "stop-sticks" designed to puncture the tires of the vehicle. Eventually, the driver was forced to stop when his tires went flat. As the police officers approached the van, the driver put a handgun to his head and pulled the trigger. Individuals in this category resisted arrest, and after arrest hanged themselves, or as police approached spontaneously shot themselves. Citations for DUI often revealed problems with alcoholism. One 22-year-old woman who worked at an Air Force base killed herself after she was caught buying alcohol for a minor and getting a DUI. A large bottle of whisky was found in her dormitory room. While only a small number had addictive substances in their bodies at the time of their deaths, over a third had substance abuse problems. Suicide appears to have been an impulsive reaction to circumstances rather than a considered desire to die, but the individuals in this group, although impulsive, used highly lethal methods and clearly intended to die.

Despite the fact that incarceration rates have risen for all populations in the United States and in some countries in Europe since the 1980s, suicide rates in jails have decreased in many countries, including the United States (Fond et al., 2016), as we will discuss further in Chapter 8, The Intersection of Suicide and Legal Issues. Hayes (2013) found that suicides were evenly distributed across time, from the first few days of incarceration to over several months of imprisonment. Arrest and incarceration generate a host of problems, from the tangible, such as legal bills, to the ethereal, such as feelings of shame and guilt. But those who find themselves in legal trouble have something that those in other kinds of trouble often do not have, a definite day of reckoning from which there is no retreat (Fig. 6.9).

Financial problems sometimes also have days of reckoning, such as a foreclosure or a bankruptcy, though in some cases the problems seemed continuous and unending. Some of the decedents had gambling problems, a high-risk behavior, and had accumulated large gambling debts. Those seeking to escape their painful circumstances have the similarity of seeking escape, but they are not all similar with respect to how and why they commit suicide. Their motivation, escape, is also affected by their risk factors, which include their mental health and their belief systems or mindsets, such as constricted thinking. Those who sought to escape legal and financial difficulties did have one distinction from the interpersonal group or those in the other escape categories. They, more than others, faced systemic problems rather than personal problems. The trends of mass incarceration or the recessions that occurred in 1999–2000 and again in 2008–09 were forces beyond the control of these individuals. While their behaviors may have landed them in trouble, their ability to resolve their problems was made worse by circumstances over which they had no influence and perhaps which they did not even understand.

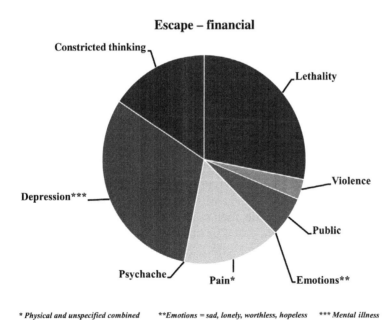

Escape – financial

Constricted thinking

Lethality

Violence

Depression***

Public

Psychache

Pain*

Emotions**

*Physical and unspecified combined **Emotions = sad, lonely, worthless, hopeless ***Mental illness

FIGURE 6.9   Escape financial problems group composite image.

CONCLUSIONS

There are very different characteristics among and between groups of people who kill themselves. Prevention and intervention must be tailored to fit the groups. There are essentially two subgroups in the interpersonal relationships group, the unrequited love suicides and the abusive relationship suicides. For men in both subgroups, losing control in the relationship was the impetus for the suicide. Yet for the unrequited love group, the response was to turn inward; their suicides were predicated on loss. They may have internalized ideas of hegemonic masculinity in which they believed they ought to have been in control of their relationships, but most often they were not violent towards others. For these men, interventions that involve counseling make sense. As we noted in Chapter 3, Suicide Motivated by Interpersonal Relationships, hotlines may be of value since reaching out to someone may help break the isolation that they feel as a result of their loss.

For those in the abusive subgroup, the suicide is not a turn inward, but a turn outward. Even when the situation is not murder-suicide, the events are frequently aggressive, public and terrifying. Hotlines and counseling are not interventions that these men would accept, so other interventions must be devised. In Chapter 8, The Intersection of Suicide and Legal Issues and Chapter 10, Conclusions and Implications we propose some possible solutions.

Those who kill themselves for escape represent the most complex group to help, and indeed prevention and intervention have no one-size-fits-all model. When Baumeister et al. (1993) advanced his escape theory, he proposed that those who killed themselves to escape would exhibit a heightened sense of perfectionism, self-loathing when failure is present, negative emotional affect, high self-awareness, cognitive destruction, and disinhibition. Yet those qualities do not hold true for our escape umbrella, nor for the individual subgroups. There are demographic differences among those who die to escape problems.

Those who want to escape physical pain may be, in some cases, beyond help. This group more carefully planned their suicides and took steps to ensure there would be no intervention. They were not ambivalent in their wish to die. At the same time, their suicides were in response to situations that were not all inherently fatal or miserable.

For those attempting to escape psychological pain, prevention and intervention are very complex. There seemed to be ambivalence about dying among some of the people in this group. If a large number of individuals in any group wanted to be prevented from killing themselves, it appears to have been these. Yet, there was often no precipitant, so that a time to intervene was not necessarily obvious to family, friends, or even professionals such as social workers, counselors, or doctors. Since members of this group had been diagnosed with psychological problems, they had in fact sought help, but what existed was not continuing to work. Those suffering from grief or failure were similar to those escaping psychological problems. In none of these groups were the individuals trying to hurt others. Their actions were all directed inward, and the very quietness of these victims may have staved off intervention.

Those escaping multiple problems are also among those hardest to help, but not because they refuse to reach out. All the evidence points to this group reaching out or behaviorally acting out to get help. Yet because the set of problems is so complex, those who could help them often don't know what to do first. For example, people suffering from depression and alcoholism have what is a called a "dual diagnosis." Psychologists and social workers will often tell the alcoholic to get treatment for the alcoholism first, because it is impossible to treat the depression while the individual is still drinking. Yet the difficulties of getting treatment for the alcoholic abound. Many "treatments" are simply 12-step programs, which are not evidence based and sometimes have no professionals involved. For individuals who are clinically depressed, an Alcoholics Anonymous (A.A.) group may not provide sufficient care, although one study has indicated that membership in A.A. does decrease suicidality (Hashimoto & Ashizawa, 2012). In Europe treatment for alcoholism almost always involves medications to stop cravings, but in the United States, it rarely does (Jonas et al., 2014).

For people with multiple problems, all of which bear down on them at some point and snowball, the idea of tackling one at a time may appear overwhelming, both to them and to those who could help them. For all parties involved, the victim and those close to the victim, it may appear that death is the only way to stop the downward spiral. Thus, others share the constricted thinking or poor problem-solving affects of the suicidal individual, and may also perpetuate help-negation. Studies have documented that help-negation occurs for both professional and nonprofessional sources of help (Yakunina, Rogers, Waehler, & Werth, 2010). This cycle must be broken among all parties in order for the person to survive.

Those escaping legal and financial problems also resemble the escape multiple, but have some slight differences. The individuals in these categories also show some hypermasculine or hegemonic masculine qualities, like those in the interpersonally abusive relationship category. Yet the fact they were caught up in external economic and political forces may have exacerbated their problems.

A central question in all of the suicidal acts was whether and to what degree the victim was suffering from mental illness. In the next chapter, we explore mental illness and its role in causation.

7

Severe Mental Illness

In the preceding chapters, we have examined the motivations of those who killed themselves and discussed the emergence of patterns among those groups. Motivations, risk factors, and patterns of suicidal behaviors do not tell the whole story. Mental illness underscores most of the suicides. Where it was not explicitly cited in a report or note, we did not include it, but doubtless many victims suffered from mental illness that was undiagnosed or undisclosed. Underreporting can be the result of a lack of education and training on the part of investigators. To some extent it may also reflect the stigma that still follows mental illness today. It often goes unreported (Bharadwaj, Pai, & Suziedelyte, 2015).

SEVERE PERSISTENT MENTAL ILLNESS AND SUICIDE

Mark was 43 years old and living with his parents. He had always had emotional and behavioral problems. Because of his instability, he was not able to maintain employment. Mark also had difficulty in his interpersonal relationships. He started isolating himself and would not engage in conversations with anyone, because he believed they were all against him. At times, he would become noncompliant with treatment and then would abuse alcohol. A year before he died, during one of these periods of volatility, he castrated himself. After that, Mark never recovered physically or emotionally. Because he had a history of previous suicide attempts, his family had taken precautionary measures, removing anything that could be potentially harmful to him such as sharp objects, medications and firearms. However, Mark had recently begun unfailingly taking his medications and was becoming more social. In fact, his parents thought he was stable enough for them to take a brief respite. Mark's sister lived a few blocks from the parent's home, and they asked her to check in on Mark every few days while they went to winter in Florida for a few weeks. As soon as they left, Mark stopped taking his medications and grew increasingly despondent and paranoid. When Mark did not

Explaining Suicide.
DOI: http://dx.doi.org/10.1016/B978-0-12-809289-7.00007-5

147

respond to his sister's calls for several days, she went over to check on him. She found him dead on his parent's living room sofa. Apparently Mark had tried to kill himself by cutting his neck with a hacksaw but he did not succeed. However, he had acquired a rifle, which he then used to shoot himself in the head.

Mark's severe and persistent mental illness was one of the many factors that put him at risk for completing suicide. Although the investigator's report did not specify Mark's diagnosis, his psychological problems had clearly affected his daily functioning for a long time. Severe mental illness (SMI) or severe persistent mental illness (SPMI) are commonly used terms to describe mental conditions that are complex in nature and require comprehensive and ongoing treatment. SMIs or SPMIs include mental, emotional, or behavioral disorders which interfere with a person's daily functioning. In 2014, approximately 4.1% of adults in the United States were living with SMIs such as depression, schizophrenia, or bipolar disorder ("Behavioral Health Trends," 2015). An estimated 90% or more of those who complete suicide have had one or more mental disorders (Bertolote & Fleischmann, 2002). In one study of elderly people who killed themselves, researchers found 97% of the suicide victims fulfilled criteria for at least one DSM-IV Axis I diagnosis, usually recurrent major depressive disorder (Waern et al., 2002). Understanding motivations for suicide cannot be complete without understanding the ways in which mental illnesses interact with other risk factors and triggering events.

Some of the common suicide risk factors that have already been noted for individuals with diagnosed mental disorders are impulsivity, a sense of hopelessness, social isolation, drug and alcohol abuse, physical, legal, financial or interpersonal problems, a history of previous suicide attempts or physical or sexual abuse in childhood, and family history of suicide. Additionally, suicide risk also increases when a person experiences major changes in life circumstances such as the loss of a loved one, the end of a relationship, or the loss of a job. Usually, the individual lacks the coping skills and social support to deal with the stress (Fawcett et al., 1990; Hall, Platt, & Hall, 1999; World Health Organization, 1999).

Among our overall sample, 656 of 1280 cases were identified as having psychological problems. Not all of them had SMIs. Similar to our overall sample, they were generally Caucasian (92%) and male (77%). The average age was 45 with a range of 11–91. The most common methods used to commit suicide were guns (45%), asphyxia (28%), and overdose (21%). Most killed themselves at home (78%). They had other struggles in life, primarily physical illnesses (40%), interpersonal problems (37%), drug use (30%), financial problems (17%), and legal problems (14%). Some had made previous suicide attempts (26%) or threats (21%), while 20% had suicidal ideation. Only 20% sought some psychological help for their mental health condition.

Overall, those suffering from SMIs were nonviolent toward others, with only 4% involved in domestic violence and 7% killing themselves in front of others. Victims were most often diagnosed with depression (75%), bipolar disorder (7%), schizophrenia (2%), multiple diagnoses (9%), or miscellaneous other diagnoses (7%). We had no one diagnosed with a personality disorder. They were likely underreported. One hundred and seven people in this group (16%) left notes. In an era when the media routinely couples mental illness with violence, largely because of sensational mass murders, it is important to remember that most often when mentally ill persons use violence it is only upon themselves (Price & Khubchandani, 2016; Taylor & Gunn, 1999). Moreover, while mental disorders are present in the majority of suicide cases, most mentally ill people are not suicidal and do not commit suicide (Law Center to Prevent Gun Violence, 2016).

Depression

Julian was 25 years old and had been depressed for the past four years. He was not seeking any help or treatment. He was also unemployed, had financial problems, and was struggling to publish some of his writings. Julian was also on probation for theft charges. His parents became concerned when his girlfriend broke up with him, and he started isolating himself. When his father had not heard from him for a few days, he asked the police to do a welfare check. When the police went to his home, Julian was not at his apartment, and his car was not in the garage. Four hours later, his father called the landlord and asked him to check on Julian. Julian was found in his garage seated in his car which was still running. He was unresponsive and by the time medical help arrived, it was too late. Julian left notes and pages of his unpublished writings listing, among other things, the reasons he should live and the reasons he should kill himself. These reasons (which we have arranged side by side) included the following:

REASONS TO DIE (IN CASE YOU LOSE YOUR NERVE)	*REASONS TO STAY ALIVE*
YOU HAVE NO FREEDOM	*KEEP EVERYONE ELSE MARGINALLY HAPPY*
NO ONE LOVES YOU	
YOU ARE A WRECK OF A PERSON, YOU NEED THERAPY	
YOU HAVE NO MONEY	
YOU DON'T WANT TO WORK	

YOUR WRITING IS WORTHLESS

*YOU WANTED TO DIE FOR OVER TEN
YEARS*

THE AMERICAN CULTURE

NO ONE COULD LOVE YOU

YOU COULDN'T LOVE ANYONE

YOU BROKE ANOTHER PHONE

*YOU'RE GOING TO HAVE TO PUBLISH
THE ZINE*

THEY'RE ALL EVEN SICKER THAN YOU

YOU CAN'T CRY

POLITICS

*YOU CAN'T CARE ABOUT LIFE, YOU HAVE NO
MOTIVATION*

YOU ARE A NAIL, NOT A HAMMER

THERE IS NO GOD

*YOU CANT ESCAPE YOUR OWN
PERCEPTIVENESS*

BRITNEY SPEARS

SPACE

NONE OF THIS IS REAL

*GOOD CREDIT IS YOUR MOST
VALUABLE ASSET*

YOU ARE ALONE.

Julian also left the following note:

Bobby,
    I am sorry to do this to you and Abby (and everyone else). But this is the right thing
for me. This is my one true love, death. I am sad and little afraid, but it will be over quickly
and permanently. Nada y pues nada. I don't give a fuck what happens to my writing, but I
thought making it available to you might make things easier for you. You can share it with
whoever. You don't have to read any of it, but if you want some explanations, many can be
found in my three hundred poems and the essays in particular. There were recent events that
allowed me to reach this state of suicidal depression, but they are not to blame. The rest of
my life has mostly been nearly-suicidal depression, just waiting for something to give me a

push. I'm taking advantage of the situation while it exists. If you need me I'll be fishing with Mr. Hemingway. Or just dead, I don't know. The password to all my stuff, as you know, is "common."

Your friend,
julian

P.S. You can have my computer or my guns or whatever else.

In the new *Diagnostic Statistical Manual of Mental Disorder*-Fifth Edition (DSM-V, 2013), depressive disorders are separated from bipolar and related disorders. It lists four main depressive disorders: major depressive disorder (clinical depression), persistent depressive disorder (formerly dysthymia disorder), disruptive mood dysregulation (diagnosed in children and adolescents), and premenstrual dysphoric disorder. Julian was experiencing clinical depression. While feeling sad, "blue," despondent or dejected are normal reactions to major life events, such as the loss of someone or major health problems, or can be a side effect of medical treatment, clinical depression is much more severe. Someone who is experiencing clinical depression will usually experience a mood disruption that affects his or her thoughts, feelings, behaviors, and overall well-being. During this state, the person might feel persistent sadness, anxiety, hopelessness or pessimism, helplessness, worthlessness, guilt or irritability. He or she finds it difficult to enjoy or engage in previously pleasurable activities. Other symptoms include an increase or decrease in sleeping or eating, feeling tired or restless, difficulty concentrating or making decisions, moving or talking more slowly, forgetting things, and the person may even attempt, think or plan suicide. The person can also have physical symptoms such as aches or pains, headaches, or cramps (DSM-V, 2013).

Clinical depression affects different people in different ways. Some people experience only a few symptoms while other may experience many symptoms. The severity, frequency, timing, and duration of symptoms depend on the person. Clinical depression can be caused by a combination of genetic, biological, environmental, and psychological factors. Clinical depression often begins in early adulthood (Depression, 2015). When depression occurs in middle adulthood or among older adults, often it can be connected with other serious medical illnesses, such as cancer, diabetes, heart problems, or chronic pain (de C. Williams, 1998). Some other risk factors include other co-occurring psychiatric disorders, a family history of depression, or medication usage. Clinical depression can be precipitated by stress due to a major change or trauma such as the death of a family member, divorce, or loss of a job (Depression, 2015).

Depression is a serious illness that individuals may not want to admit to themselves, or that family and friends may not understand. It is always important to seek professional help (Depression, 2015). Individuals with clinical depression are at a 25 times greater risk for suicide than the overall population (American Association of Suicidology (AAS), 2014). The AAS reports that in individuals with untreated depression, the lifetime risk of suicide ranges from 2.2% to 15%. Fifty percent of the people who commit suicide suffer from clinical depression (AAS). Comorbidity of depression and anxiety may create an even greater risk of suicide than depression alone (Bronisch & Wittchen, 1994).

Although in the general population, women and girls are twice as likely as men to suffer from depression (Jamison, 1999). In our sample of people who committed suicide, those who were identified as depressed were mostly men (81%) and Caucasian (94%) with an average age of 46 (in a range of 11–91 years old). Most killed themselves at home (78%), most frequently on Mondays (19%). Many of them experienced physical illnesses (40%), drug abuse (32%), or interpersonal (37%), legal (14%), or financial problems (19%). Almost one-fourth (23%) had previously attempted suicide, threatened to hurt themselves (33%) or expressed suicidal ideation (29%). In 35 cases (7%), individuals completed suicide in front of others and 5 were murder-suicides (1%). The most common methods of suicide were firearms (49%), followed by asphyxia (27%).

Eighty people in this group (16%) left notes and most (65%) left only one note. It is likely that individuals who are experiencing depression have been contemplating the act over a long period of time, as opposed to acting impulsively, as seen in other psychiatric disorders (Anestis, Soberay, Gutierrez, Hernández, & Joiner, 2014). Most addressed their notes to a specific person such as children (32%), parents (31%), family (30%), and partners (28%). Harry, discussed in Chapter 4, Escape as a Motivation for Suicide, wrote an entire note to his dog, Seneca. In it he said:

> By the time Darla reads this letter to you, you'll have an idea something's different you'll be scared & confused, but you're smart enough to know how much I've loved you and would never put you in harm's way. My number one priority was finding you someone who will love & cherish you...This for now, will not be perfect, there is no puppy door & the yard is not fenced but I have given her the money, to do both...
> I know you're afraid of the two big dogs, but try to be brave, and become friends. This will be a whole new world, you're entering...
> Take care of yourself, my little man. Try not to hate me, for having to give you away.

Harry agonized over his decision to leave his dog, and he prayed about it at church. The note never mentions his death, only his leaving. His depression, mentioned in a separate letter to a friend, was hidden underneath layers of love and gratitude to his dog.

Most individuals, like Harry, provided a justification for death (56%) and expressed their love for others (70%). Sometimes, the victims mentioned God (32%) and gave a justification to God about why they were taking their lives. Additionally, individuals talked about their interpersonal problems (40%). The underlying tone of individuals who discussed their interpersonal problems was often characterized by tension, negative affect, and hostility. Evidence of tunnel vision or constricted thought processes (23%), and/or dichotomous thinking (11%) also appeared in the notes. Sometimes the constricted thoughts resulted in individuals discussing their inability to see or generate other options, feeling out of control, or expecting that their future outcome would also be out of their control.

Kim was a 46-year-old woman who had a history of depression, chronic back pain and arthritis, and was known to abuse prescription drugs. She was diagnosed with major depressive disorder and had attempted suicide a number of times. She took an overdose of her prescription pills and left a note for her two daughters saying, "This was the only way; I've made a big mess out of too many lives. Just let me go. I love you."

People in this group identified a precipitant (21%) and directed apologies to specific individuals (33%) or general apologies (28%). They asked forgiveness for themselves (26%) and sometimes gave advice (22%). They were more likely to absolve others from blame (18%) than to blame others (11%). One middle-aged white man left a note to a friend he had just been talking to on the phone, "This development is no one's fault and no one is responsible for it but myself, just as there is no single catalytic trigger event, but extensive accumulation of failures, disappointments and dead-end (no pun intended)."

Some note writers suffering from depression specifically discussed their need to escape (28%). Janis was a 30-year-old woman who said, "I am sorry to bring pain to everyone My life has no meaning anymore all I do is drag everyone around me down. I am such a disappointment. I dug myself a hole so deep I cant get out this is my only way to have piece of mind." Some referred to their psychological pain (25%) or physical pain (18%) or just talked about unspecified pain (17%). While many people who consider suicide seek to escape something, those who were clinically depressed expressed the weight they felt going through life.

Those who suffered from depression were less impulsive than those with other mental illnesses (Anestis et al. 2014), which meant they could plan for the aftermath of their deaths and instruct others. A few left instructions regarding how to dispose of their bodies (26%) or their property (25%), and how to manage their affairs (22%). Others asked that survivors take care of friends or family (21%). For example, Gina left a note to her friends and family with the following instructions:

At my funeral, I'd like many of my photo's on display—pets, people, places...I'd like all my painting & crafts to come back together on display once & for all. If Hugh can find the series of tapes he made for my wedding back in 1994, I'd love those to be played at the reception, & copies made for my dearest friends—if they'd like them.

If its appropriate for a therapist to do so, I'd like Iona Metcalf to give the eulogy, and Sheila knew me best of anyone, and could speak on my behalf, as well.
All my vital organ can go to those who need them...
PS. I'd like just a small marker by a tree that says 'Fly, be free.'

A few of them also left quotations, giving advice, referring to favorite songs, and sharing poems in their notes (6%). One person wrote, "The most important thing in life is relationship—do anything you can to protect & preserve them. Don't judge the 'gentle spirit' as being weak—for therein lies humanities greatest strength. Please take care of the earth, its animal, and each other." Gina paraphrased the song, "Vincent," writing, "This world was never meant for one as beautiful as me." Many of these quoted songs or poems were sad, referenced suicide in some way, or focused on themes of things coming to an end. On one man's list were "Sittin' on the Dock of the Bay," by Otis Redding and "Hear My Train A Comin'" by Jimi Hendrix, next to crossed out songs that he had written. The connection to lyrics, music, and lost dreams was present in several notes.

Some note writers mentioned explicit sentiments in their notes. Specifically, they talked about feeling loved (15%), like a failure (15%), tired (13%), sad (12%), that life was not worth living (11%), hopeless (8%), lonely (8%), and ambivalent (8%). Some of these feelings are relatively consistent with the presentation of clinical depression. When individuals expressed these feelings, the overall sentiment was that there was no way out and no hope left.

In her novel *The Bean Trees* (1989), Barbara Kingsolver wrote, "There is no point treating a depressed person as though she were just feeling sad, saying, 'There now, hang on, you'll get over it.' Sadness is more or less like a head cold—with patience, it passes. Depression is like cancer" (p. 232). Cancer is a serious illness, but it is not always fatal, and neither is depression. For the individuals in our study who were clinically depressed, it became impossible for them to find hope. Some had come to the end of their rope because they had been through several bouts of depression, and it was the repeated nature of it that ground them down. It is common for relapses in depression to occur, even with the use of antidepressants. Evidence exists that cognitive therapy may reduce relapse rates (Paykel et al., 1999; Teasdale et al., 2000). For those suffering from depression, consistent treatment, coupled with maintaining social support and having a reason for living, is the key to maintaining wellness.

Bipolar Disorder

Len was a 50-year-old salesman who had been diagnosed with bipolar disorder in his early thirties. He had mood swings that included both mania and depression and a history of prior suicide attempts. Len had been inconsistently taking his medications, preferring to self-medicate with alcohol. He was separated from his wife and was living alone. Recently he had lost his job, which had led to financial problems. Because of this, Len felt that he was not a good provider for his wife and his daughter. All of this led to a state of agitation, and Len was unable to sleep for several days. One night while he was awake, he decided to end his life. The day he killed himself, Len was on the phone and was speaking to his daughter. He asked her if she would help with his memorial service and when she said yes, she heard a shot followed by her father gasping on the phone. Len had shot himself in the chest. He wrote this letter before he took his life.

I AM FULLY MEDICATED, SO MY BIOLOGICAL ISSUES ARE NOT TO BLAME FOR THIS. HOWEVER, BEING MEDICATED DOES NOT ALTER THE FOLLOWING, INESCAPABLE FACTS:

I CAN'T even pay my rent in full at the start of any given month.

I CAN'T meet my moral responsibility to give Cindy ample financial help.

I CAN'T even really afford this shithole of an apartment, much less a decent place.

I CAN'T afford a decent car...

I CAN'T afford a decent, normal social/dating life.

I CAN'T offer a woman an acceptable explanation for my lowly circumstances.

I CAN'T be a worthy half of a real relationship.

I CAN'T sleep through the night and so.....

I CAN'T escape my tortured thoughts which ricochet incessantly off the walls of my brain.

I CAN'T get a grasp on my swirling, slippery thoughts.

I CAN'T concentrate or focus.

I CAN'T absorb and assimilate what I need to know to do my job effectively.

I CAN'T even begin to organize and prioritize my tasks at work.

I CAN'T manufacture even a scintilla of self-confidence, enthusiasm and optimism necessary to sell effectively, and therefore...

I CAN'T let go of pronounced feelings of inferiority and worthlessness.

I CAN'T untie the knots in my stomach.

I CAN'T stop shaking on the inside.

I CAN'T stand the unfailingly sick, abysmal feeling that accompanies waking up from a fitful night's sleep.

I CAN'T derive any true enjoyment from anything.

I CAN'T keep faking it anymore.

I CAN'T take this weird, solitary, unfulfilling existence for even one more day.

Bipolar disorder (BD) was once known as manic depression. BD is a mental disorder described by mood changes that fluctuate from periods of intense high mood states (mania) to extreme low mood states (depression). Those with BD often die prematurely. At one time, the higher premature death rate among people with bipolar disorder was attributed to a higher rate of suicide and accidents. More recently, researchers discovered that suicide and accidents only partly account for the higher premature death rate (National Institute of Mental Health, 2016). Emerging evidence shows that the majority of early deaths among people with bipolar disorder come from medical conditions (Roshanaei-Moghaddam & Katon, 2009). Nevertheless, suicide rates are 20 times higher than in the general population (Tondo, Isacsson, & Baldessarini, 2003).

Symptom patterns differ for every individual diagnosed with bipolar disorder (Ostacher, Frye, & Suppes, 2016). In a manic episode individuals may be erratic and irritable with extreme changes in energy, activity, sleep, and behavior. As we can see from Len's list, he experienced these symptoms. His job as a salesman may have benefited from periods of mania if they were not out of control, since mania may include talking fast and an elevated mood, lending an air of excitement to conversation. Yet the person experiencing mania may also jump from one idea to another, have racing thoughts, be easily distracted or overly restless, be unable to sleep and have unrealistic beliefs related to one's abilities. They may also behave impulsively and engage in pleasurable but high-risk behaviors, such as unsafe sex.

In the depressive episode, they may experience feelings of being sad or tired and a lack of interest in activities they once liked. They may have problems with concentrating, remembering and making decisions, and become restless or irritable and experience changes in eating, sleeping or other habits. They often have increased thoughts of death and suicide. Individuals may have a mixed episode, in which they experience both mania and depression within a week's time (Ostacher et al., 2016). Among the 45 cases of people with BD in our study, 18 cases specified that the person had episodes of both mania and depression. A hypomania episode is similar to a mixed episode, but it has less extreme mood swings and is shorter in duration (Ostacher et al., 2016). Individuals diagnosed with BD often experience a multitude of problems due to their mental illness.

Sandra was a 45-year-old woman who was diagnosed with bipolar disorder. She refused to take medications and self-medicated with alcohol. Sandra had been divorced from her husband for over five years, and attempted suicide multiple times in that period. Sandra isolated herself and avoided people and problems. She was facing foreclosure due to her financial problems and was worried about the ramifications of an incident where she assaulted a state trooper. Sandra also suffered from multiple medical issues such as diabetes, hypertension, and obesity. Additionally, Sandra recently experienced multiple losses. Her sister, who was also diagnosed with BD, committed suicide and her father died unexpectedly. Then, her niece died of a drug overdose. In addition, Sandra's son was being deployed to Iraq where he was to be stationed for the next two years. Sandra decided to hang herself, and left a note to her boyfriend. "Baby, I'm sorry I just can't survive the mess I've created. Please forgive me. I love you. This is nobody's fault but my own. You & my family have done everything to support me. I love you. Please tell my family I love them. Love, Sandra."

Sandra's illness and the many problems that stemmed from it meant that her life was full of stress in addition to the other symptoms of BD. In our sample, 45 individuals (7%) were diagnosed with BD. It is likely, based on the documented risk of suicide for persons with BD, which is 20 to 30 times greater than in the general population, that there were more who suffered from it (Pompili et al., 2013).

Three individuals with diagnosed BD left a note. The demographics of this particular sample are similar to our overall SMI sample consisting mostly of Caucasian (93%) and male (62%) victims. However, this category has a higher percentage of women than other categories. The average age of people in this group was 39.

In unipolar disorders, like depression, women out number men two to one (Kawa et al., 2005). Gender, once thought to be irrelevant to BD discussions because of its equal distribution, has been shown to matter. Women's first experience of BD seems to occur as depression, while men first experience mania. When women have mania they are more likely to be hospitalized. Women also have more rapid cycling and experience more mixed mania (Kawa et al., 2005). Men with BD may be more likely than women to have substance abuse issues. The abuse of substances is itself a mental disorder and when combined with BD, it is sometimes called a "dual diagnosis." In our sample 33% of patients with BD also had substance abuse problems. Sandra, who was self-medicating with alcohol, struggled with maintaining treatment for her BD. Dual diagnoses are notoriously hard to treat, as discussed in Chapter 6, The Complexity of Suicide Motivation.

Sometimes substance abuse can trigger symptoms of BD. Twenty percent of those with BD in our study consumed substances before or while they completed the suicidal act. Not surprisingly, as opposed to the overall sample and the SMI sample, the most common method of committing suicide in BD cases was overdose on some toxic substance (40%). Most people with BD have easy access to prescription medications, including antidepressants, mood stabilizers, antipsychotics, antianxiety medications and, too often, opioids.

Nearly half of the people diagnosed as bipolar were trying to escape psychological problems and had attempted suicide in the past. A little more than a fourth had expressed suicidal ideation and a fifth made threats of suicide in the past. Sandra's and Len's problems are representative of people diagnosed with BD. Less than a quarter of the people in our sample diagnosed with BD had interpersonal problems, and fewer still had legal or financial problems. In three of the cases of individuals with bipolar disorder, they took their lives in front of others. Many individuals who are diagnosed with BD act impulsively, so it is not surprising to find a smaller number of notes.

Schizophrenia

Arthur was 42 years old and had a longstanding history of schizophrenia, paranoid type. He was known to create problems in the apartment building where he resided. Oftentimes, he was caught pulling the fire alarm and kicking neighbor's doors. He was known to the police officers in the neighborhood. For the most part, he said his behaviors were commands made by the voices that he kept hearing. Eventually, Arthur could not take the voices and took his life by jumping from a tenth-floor apartment window.

Fred was 50 years old and lived in a group home. One day he was found wandering and reported that he was hearing voices which were telling him to jump off a bridge. He was taken to the hospital and admitted to the psychiatric unit. When the staff went to call him for dinner, Fred was found unresponsive in the bathroom. He had wrapped the bedsheet around his neck and tied it to the handicap railing. Fred had a long standing history of schizophrenia and had attempted suicide every time he was hearing voices and was not taking medications.

Saul was diagnosed with paranoid schizophrenia when he was 20 years old and had been living with it for another 20 years. He resided with his brother and had been especially unhappy for the past week. Saul thought that people at work, and his neighbors, had been saying he was the devil. He was employed as a maintenance worker but had not been to work that week. On the day he completed his suicide, Saul waited for his 10-year-old son to leave for school. A few hours later, Saul's neighbor dropped by after he was unable to reach him by phone. Saul was found unresponsive in the living room. He had overdosed on his prescription medications.

While Arthur, Fred, and Saul's stories differ, they were all diagnosed with schizophrenia, which increased their risk for suicide. Schizophrenia is one of the most chronic, disabling psychological conditions. It has a broad range of symptoms including hallucinations (auditory, visual, or other type), unusual or strange ideas, disorganized speech, and difficulty distinguishing between what is real and what is imaginary. In order for an individual to be diagnosed with schizophrenia, he or she must exhibit two or more of the symptoms (DSM-V, 2013). Twenty to forty percent of individuals diagnosed with schizophrenia have attempted suicide (Harkavy-Friedman, 2007), while 4% to 10% complete the act of suicide (Martin-Fumadó & Hurtado-Ruíz, 2012). Not all symptoms of schizophrenia increase the risk of suicide. Hallucinations, for instance, are associated with a reduced risk of suicide, but a history of depression, prior suicide attempts, drug misuse, fear of mental disintegration, poor adherence to treatment and recent losses all increased the risk for suicide among people with schizophrenia (Hawton, Sutton, Haw, Sinclair, & Deeks, 2005).

In our sample 14 individuals were diagnosed with schizophrenia. While research suggests that substance abuse is usually linked to suicide risk in people diagnosed with schizophrenia, only 23% of our sample had a longstanding history of substance use/abuse problems (Hawton et al., 2005). Furthermore, no one in the sample had consumed any substances at the time of their deaths. Three individuals experienced interpersonal difficulties, two individuals had attempted taking their lives in the past, one person expressed suicidal threats, and one person attempted to kill himself in front of others. Also, none had legal problems, although some had a history of abuse. The means by which individuals completed the suicide were also similar to the overall SMI sample. However, the individuals in our sample completed the act during summer (43%), and mostly on Thursday (36%), as opposed to the overall SMI sample. Christodoulou, et al. (2012) found autumn and winter were more common seasons for the suicides of those diagnosed with schizophrenia, but noted that some studies have shown a rise in suicide associated with psychiatric illness in the summer and a rise in economically motivated suicides in the winter.

Schizophrenia is an illness with distressing symptoms for the sufferer and often for others. It usually, though not always, manifests for the first time in late adolescence to early adulthood, and there seems to be little if any difference in age of onset between the sexes (Eranti, MacCabe, Bundy, & Murray, 2013). Its onset is sometimes so sudden that family members and friends react with disbelief, and may even deny the person needs psychiatric help. Schizophrenia is a psychotic disorder, and when it takes over a person it wreaks havoc on their senses, their emotions, their reason and their ability to act (Jamison, 1999). Both sufferers and observers can find its symptoms terrifying.

Kerry was 60 years old and living with her sister. She was diagnosed with schizophrenia in her forties and was in the Supplemental Security Income disability program (SSI). Three months prior to her death, she had to move in with her sister for support, because of her medical problems, including diabetes and a heart disease. On a recent birthday none of her children called her or visited her. During her last appointment with her psychiatrist he told her that her symptoms from schizophrenia were not going to improve and she just had to learn to "deal with it." Kerry's sister knew that she was unhappy about having to move in with her, and about finding out that she was not going to improve. Yet she had never heard her sister make any suicidal statements or threats. However, when Kerry's sister returned home after running errands one day, she found Kerry unresponsive in her chair. She had overdosed on her prescription pills.

Kerry was at risk for suicide, because she was deeply depressed about her prognosis. It is not uncommon for people diagnosed with schizophrenia to find it hard to cope with their symptoms. For others, the suicide act can be a response to delusions. Delusions in the individuals diagnosed with schizophrenia are false beliefs based on psychotic thinking about external reality. Hallucinations, in contrast, are false or distorted sensory experiences that appear to be real. While hallucinations can be more frightening, both hallucinations and delusions are dangerous to the individual. Delusions, however, create a greater risk of suicide in people diagnosed with schizophrenia (Hawton et al., 2005; Kelleher et al., 2013).

The only note left in this sample was from Ben, a 26-year-old who was diagnosed with delusional disorder. Though Ben had been under psychiatric care for a long time, he did not adhere to his treatment plan.

He was suspicious of his family and friends and believed that a few of his family members were conspiring against him. In fact, he believed that he was under surveillance seven days a week. At times, he believed his parents were part of a plan and were drugging him, so he refused to take his medications. He became more and more secretive and suspicious. Even though Ben never discussed any suicidal thoughts, nor attempted or made suicidal threats, he killed himself. Ben left a note for his father in large handwriting, the few words stark against the white paper, "I LOVE YOU ALL I LOVE YOU ALL I LOVE YOU ALL IM SORRY... I DON'T KNOW WHAT I DID, BUT I DIDNT DESERVE ALL THIS. IT WAS REAL." When his father found the note, it was too late, Ben was found hanging in the bedroom closet with a dog leash wrapped around his neck. The note written by Ben was short (i.e., less than 25 words), expressed love for others, and provided a general apology. It was not surprising that the majority of individuals in this category did not leave notes. Research has found that people diagnosed with schizophrenia commit suicide with greater violence and lethality and are more likely to commit suicide without warning (Fenton, 2000).

Chad was a 46-year-old man with a history of depression and schizophrenia. Chad had been suffering from schizophrenia since he was a teenager. Chad had attempted several times to kill himself. Once, he walked out onto a bridge with the intent of taking his life, but he was talked out of it by the police. Chad's parents had a restraining order issued against him, because he was abusive towards them. The last his parents knew he was living in New York and was homeless. Chad returned to Ohio and committed suicide by walking into a river. A nearby fisherman heard a sudden splash and saw Chad going under water just off the shoreline. When they retrieved the body, police found empty bottles of his prescribed medications in his pocket.

In Chad's case, it was unclear whether he suffered from schizophrenia and later developed symptoms of depression, or whether they existed concomitantly. He may have been diagnosed first with depression and then developed symptoms of schizophrenia. In any case, depression is common among individuals who are diagnosed with schizophrenia, and it is likely to increase the risk of suicide (Hawton et al., 2005). In our sample, nine cases had schizophrenia co-occurring with depression. Similar to the overall sample of individuals who were only diagnosed with schizophrenia, the individuals in this group did not leave any notes. We cannot know their thoughts and feelings, but the case files reveal a history of painful struggle.

Multiple Diagnoses

Tammy was 65 years old and had a history of schizophrenia, bipolar disorder, hypertension, hyperlipidemia, hypothyroidism, and breast cancer. She was a retired nurse who lived by herself and received disability benefits. Tammy did *not adhere to her treatment plan and her brother and daughter checked on her regularly in an attempt to make sure that Tammy was taking her prescription medications. The night before she killed herself her brother spoke with her and felt something was wrong. He said it seemed as though she was having a conversation with someone while he was talking to her on the phone. The next day after she did not return his calls, he went to check on her. He found Tammy on the bathroom floor with numerous prescription bottles and with two suicide notes. In one note, Tammy wrote, "I worry that the demons are trying to possess me, Arlene. I can't keep battling this, Arlene I am sorry to leave such a mess."*

Tammy was coping with the challenges caused by multiple diagnoses, and all of them were difficult and complicated. Comorbidity was not only a risk factor in suicide attempts, but it heightened the risk of lethality (Kessler, Borges, & Walters, 1999). In our sample, the people who had multiple diagnoses included individuals with dual diagnoses or diagnosed with comorbid disorders. Comorbidity refers to individuals who are diagnosed with two or more mental health disorders. Approximately 79% of individuals who are diagnosed with a lifetime psychiatric disorder are dealing with complications arising from multiple diagnoses (Farmer, Kosty, Seeley, Olino, & Lewinsohn, 2013). Sixty individuals in our sample were identified as having comorbid diagnoses. Sixteen of these individuals left notes.

The number of men (53%) and women (47%) completing suicide were almost equal in this sample, and two-thirds had attempted suicide in the past. Almost one-fourth had expressed suicidal ideation or threatened to hurt themselves. Two-thirds were also dealing with physical illness and problems in interpersonal relationships. Less than a quarter had a history of drug use and only a few had legal and financial problems. The most common means of completing suicide was overdose (37%), followed by guns (33%). Twenty-two percent consumed alcohol or some type of substance at the time of their deaths. Nearly half of these individuals committed suicide to escape from psychological problems.

Eighty-one percent of the note writers in this group provided justifications for their suicides in their notes. Their notes were full of apologies, general and personal, as they shared their interpersonal problems. They overwhelmingly spoke of their love for others, and nearly half talked about God. Some of them gave advice. More than half of them talked about escaping, especially psychological pain (31%), and indicated that suicide was the only solution to their problems (38%). They asked for forgiveness (38%), and absolved others from blame (25%).

Jeannette placed the letter to her landlord in the mailbox. She told him to bring his keys, and not to bring his son.

Physically and mentally I can't work any longer and have no money left, just lots of bills. I love my husband but can't live with him. We have been separated 8 years and he never loved me and hates me now. He has his own problems. My elderly

EXPLAINING SUICIDE

dog, Buddy is with him and probably won't live much longer. I can't bear to lose him too. He is my heart, I am also losing my parents [Illegible] their health and I can't comprehend not having them. I love all my family and beg their forgiveness but I know they really won't forgive this ultimate act of selfishness. I don't <u>want</u> to hurt anyone except for myself but I don't have any other choice. I have no place to go and no way to take care of myself... I just can't live with depression and anxiety or deal with the multiple losses in my life... God forgive me.

Jeannette Saunders.

In her notes, Jeannette talked about her struggles with depression and anxiety. In this excerpt, she provided a justification for her actions. Like many in our sample with depression, she also mentioned God, asked forgiveness from others, and expressed how suicide was the only solution. At the foot of her bed were a half-full bottle of vodka and empty bottles of the antidepressant amitriptyline, an antianxiety pill called alprazolam, and methocarbamol, a muscle relaxant often used for back pain. Comorbidity is itself a risk factor for suicide, but patients also often have numerous drugs that can have bad interactions with one another. In this case two of the drugs caused severe drowsiness, and none was supposed to be consumed with alcohol.

Those note writers with comorbidity were also likely to plan their suicides and not be impulsive. Half left instructions in their notes, mostly discussing managing affairs (38%) and the distribution of their personal property (31%). Additionally, 50% included specific requests in their instructions. Many notes paid attention to financial details. Jeannette reminded her landlord that her lease provided for a 30-day grace period before her things had to be removed. One man gave precise instructions for his ex-wife and daughter to be taken care of and wrapped up his own financial affairs:

> As far as the house is concerned, Mimi's name is on the deed to it, so she can do as she pleases with it. Let her know to put Babs on her automobile policy. She is currently on mine. Please cancel the appointment with Dr. Neiderman to avoid being charged. I've paid everything I was billed so far. I'm leaving about 70 signed check to help cover upcoming expenses. Farewell. (Thanks for trying, Mom)—Xavier.

Xavier then ingested more than a liter of vodka and some medication, in addition to poisoning himself with ethanol.

The most frequent co-occurring conditions with depression were anxiety (37%), unspecified mental illness (18%), schizophrenia (15%), and dementia (7%). We found one person diagnosed with depression and attention deficit disorder (ADD), one individual diagnosed with depression, bipolar disorder, and attention deficit and hyperactivity disorder (ADHD); and one individual diagnosed with depression, anxiety, and unspecified mental illness. While these cases were not high in frequency, it is quite common to have individuals be at risk of complications arising with two or more diagnoses.

Dementia

Depression and anxiety can be co-occurring conditions in the aged (Beekman et al., 2000). Between 2010 and 2030, all of the "baby boom" generation will age past 65. The old age dependency ratio will grow from 22% to 35% in that period (Vincent & Velkoff, 2010). Older adults with depression often experience cognitive difficulties. Depression is also common during dementia, with reported prevalence rates of up to 86%, and may even be the first sign of a dementing illness (Wright & Persad, 2007). A study of the elderly (55–85 years old) in the Netherlands found that comorbidity of depression and anxiety was highly prevalent: 47.5% of those with major depressive disorder also met criteria for anxiety disorders, whereas 26.1% of those with anxiety disorders also met criteria for major depressive disorder (Beekman et al., 2000).

Solomon was 60 years old and had suffered from depression for a long time. In addition, he had conflictual relationships with many family members. When he was diagnosed as being in the early stages of Alzheimer's disease, he became afraid and felt life would not be worth living. His father had attempted suicide after being diagnosed with Alzheimer's disease. One day, after leaving his son's residence, Solomon went to his farmhouse, which had been vacant for months. Later that morning, a passerby reported the farmhouse was on fire. After the flames subsided, Solomon's body was found in his bedroom and his dog, who was always with him, was found in the bathroom. Solomon had shot his dog and then shot himself with a handgun.

Alzheimer's disease is the most common type of progressive dementia in older adults. Other types of dementia include vascular dementia, Parkinson's disease, Huntington's disease, Pick's disease, Creutzfeldt-Jakob disease, AIDS dementia, alcoholic dementia (Korsakoff's), dementia due to head trauma, and mixed dementia. Although each of these forms of dementia is distinguishable, with its own symptoms and pathology, all forms of dementia affect one's memory, thinking, and social abilities, which interferes with the ability to complete daily activities (Alzheimer's Association, 2013).

The connection between increased risk of suicide in those who are diagnosed with depression and dementia is not well-documented. Some studies found a low incidence, especially when compared with the higher risk of suicide in those with comorbidity of depression and substance abuse (Waern et al., 2002). There is evidence that Alzheimer's disease does increase a "wish to die" and suicidal ideation (Draper, MacCuspie-Moore, & Brodaty, 1998). A study of veterans by the Department of Veterans Affairs found the majority (75%) of suicides among that population occurred in those with a new dementia diagnosis, and the individuals in the study who died by suicide were significantly more likely to have been diagnosed with depression.

Anxiety Disorders

Cameron's life was no longer the same after he returned from serving his country. He could not find a job and did not have steady relationships. He had a long history of depression, anxiety, Crohn's disease, diabetes, and impotence. One day, Cameron went to the local Veteran's Affairs (VA) Hospital to seek other treatment options for his Crohn's disease. After the appointment, Cameron went to an inexpensive motel near the hospital and checked in. When he failed to check out of the room, the manager went to his room. He found Cameron on the bed unresponsive. When the police arrived, Cameron was already dead. He had left a suicide note addressed to his sister and with it was an empty bottle of his prescription pills. In his note, Cameron wrote,

> Dear Penny,
> ...I loathed what I had become, unable to even look in the mirror anymore. My mind was tormented from day until night. Death was all I could think about...I've let so many people down, you, Mom...and others who saw something in me and acted like I was okay...I don't know why I do the things I do. Maybe I am crazy; I just don't think coherently anymore.
> And then there's the gay thing. Even though I know its wrong I would rather have a relationship with a man who loved me and wanted to spend his life with me than a close walk with Christ. I guess my fate is sealed.
> I just can't take being 47, broken down, and nothing to show for my life anymore. Please don't hate me, please try to understand. I just feel like I've become this sick cosmic joke...I've so much more I want to say, but what's the point? Whether or not you believe it, or even care for that matter, I love you and am glad you were my sister.

It's not unusual for someone with an anxiety disorder to also suffer from depression or vice versa. Anxiety is a typical reaction when one is faced with uncertainty. Anxiety is not always a disorder. It often helps an individual to find a way to retreat from a situation or to get ready to face difficult life events. For a person affected with an anxiety disorder, the worry or fears are not temporary and usually worsen over time. All anxiety disorders involve persistent, excessive fear or worry that interferes with daily activities. Comorbid depression and anxiety are highly prevalent conditions, and there may even be genetic and neurobiologic similarities between them. Patients with panic disorder, generalized anxiety disorder, social phobia, and other anxiety disorders are also frequently clinically depressed. Nearly 85% of patients with depression also experience anxiety; comorbid depression occurs in up to 90% of patients with anxiety disorders (Gorman, 1996).

Among the 21 cases of people diagnosed with an anxiety disorder in our sample, the anxiety disorders that were often mentioned were generalized anxiety, panic, posttraumatic stress disorder (PTSD), and agoraphobia. In some of the cases, the relationship between the anxiety and depression was unknown to us. Eleven individuals, over half of the sample, left notes. Sometimes, comorbidity is one of the chief reasons that anxiety disorders go unrecognized and untreated (Gorman, 1996). The overlap of symptoms associated with depressive and anxiety disorders makes diagnosis, research, and treatment particularly difficult. Early recognition of the multiple conditions is key to successful treatment of patients with mixed depressive and anxiety disorders in order to develop comprehensive treatment.

Miscellaneous Other Diagnoses

In our study we occasionally found cases that were not easily compared to others, because there were so few with a particular diagnosis. For example, attention deficit hyperactivity disorder (ADHD) is a condition frequently diagnosed in children and adolescents. Researchers have found a relative risk ratio of 2.91 compared to United States national suicide rates in general, but if ADHD is combined with depression or a conduct disorder, the risk goes up (Impey & Heun, 2012), especially for young men (James, Lai, & Dahl, 2004).

In our study two boys, one with ADHD and one with an unspecified mental illness who had been prescribed Adderall, hanged themselves. Jamal was 11 years old and had a history of ADHD. Over the weekend, when his parents were doing different household chores, his father came to the carport to do some work in the garage. When he opened the door he found Jamal hanging from a rafter. Jamal never expressed suicidal ideation, nor had he ever attempted suicide. However, Jamal was impulsive and had had a recent conversation about death with his mother, but it did not suggest that he had any suicidal intent. Timmy was one of five children removed from his home by Children's Services, and he was placed in a group home. Although he was only 12 years old, Timmy was known to have behavioral problems and had been prescribed Adderall. Timmy threatened suicide when he was disciplined, but he never attempted to hurt himself. On the day he took his life, Timmy was sent to his room for breaking a minor rule. When a resident went to find him for dinner, he opened the closet and found he had hanged himself. In Jamal's case, it is impossible to determine whether his ADHD was a factor in his suicide. In Timmy's case, his removal from his home and his family could have played a role in his suicide, but as he was on medication typically assigned for attention disorders and other problems, we don't know what else might have contributed.

A third young boy had Asperger's syndrome. One day at his private high school, Nathan was confronted by a member of his school's administration who noticed that his shirt was not tucked in. He was asked to go to the guidance counselor for violation of the school dress code. Although his mother attempted to explain to him about the school dress code, Nathan was devastated and could not be consoled. Nathan grabbed the dog leash and ran out towards the back side of the house. His mother just thought he needed some time to himself. She later found that Nathan used the dog leash to hang himself from a tree.

Like many parents, Nathan's mother did not expect him to have such a drastic response. Asperger's syndrome is a complex disorder. Not only does it impair social interactions, but it is a source for nonverbal communication problems. Little research exists to affirm that Asperger's is a risk factor in suicide (Fitzgerald, 2007). It is important to consider and evaluate the extent of a child's inability to cope with his current situation, his level of impulsivity, and his constricted thoughts, all of which may have factored into Nathan's decision.

Among the 46 cases in this category of miscellaneous other diagnosis, the majority were identified as having a mental illness, but in 40 cases the diagnoses were unspecified. A total of seven people, or 15%, left suicide notes. The vast majority of note writers expressed love for others and discussed the psychological pain they felt, and all of them gave justifications for completing suicide. Similarly, in this category more than half the note writers discussed their fear of failure, asked for forgiveness for themselves, and left instructions, mostly for managing property, and nearly half gave advice.

CONCLUSIONS

The presence of any kind of mental illness can increase the risk of suicide, but the most prevalent mental illness found in completed suicides is clinical depression. It is sometimes the case that family and friends question that statement. They may have seen their loved one improve just before the suicide. Many will have noticed the darkest times for the victim were in the winter months, and as spring approached they seemed happier. Depression is complicated and for that very reason, it is imperative that anyone suffering from it get professional help and treatment. It cannot be assessed by whether a person feels happy on any given day. It is possible that in the very depths of depression the person is too impaired to take an action like suicide, but as the depression lifts, yet before it has passed, he takes his life. It is also possible that the decision to commit suicide provides a sense of relief that appears to observers like improvement.

Significant problems can arise with patients receiving adequate treatment, especially when they seek care from hospitals. In 1999 a large study was conducted on over 6000 suicide cases to see if the victims had had mental health care. Nearly a quarter of all suicide victims had visited hospitals or mental health treatment facilities within one year of their deaths. One quarter of these committed suicide in the first three months of being in contact with these services. Sixteen percent of those who visited hospitals were psychiatric patients, and some deaths occurred in the hospital (Appleby et al., 1999). Much has changed in United States healthcare since

1999, but access to good mental health care has not necessarily improved. Patients and those who provide support and care are sometimes failed by the system.

That said, no one should ever try to treat a mental illness without proper training. A suspicion of psychiatry and psychology exists among the general public, not only in the United States, but in many western countries (Sartorius et al., 2010). Yet the peril of leaving a mental illness untreated is great. Many of the people in our study who had diagnoses resisted or stopped treatment. Individuals who do this are referred to by doctors as noncompliant. To a lay person, this can sound judgmental. Noncompliance is not just a patient throwing a tantrum and refusing to take medication, and the term is not a judgment. Professionals understand that the person may dislike taking medication, or the person may believe she no longer needs it. The person may also find medication and treatment hard to obtain. Noncompliance is a danger zone, though, and it may increase the risk of suicide. Families and friends should urge those with mental illnesses to continue treatment, if possible with a therapist or doctor with whom they have a trusted relationship. Resources discussed in Chapter 10, Conclusions and Implications may help people in need of services to find them.

8

The Intersection of Suicide and Legal Issues

Eric had a long history of alcohol abuse. It was the primary reason his wife left him, taking their four children with her. However, instead of seeking treatment, Eric began drinking more. As he was weaving home from the bar one night, he was followed by police, who stopped him and, when he failed the sobriety tests, cited him for DUI. Eric was an administrator for a school district and when the news broke that he had received a DUI, he was put on leave. Eventually, he was able to return to work, but he was placed on probation. It was difficult to arrange transportation to work since his driving privileges were suspended and he lived in a rural area, so he started driving. Six weeks later, he was stopped again. He was cited for driving under a suspended license, and he received a second DUI. This time he would likely receive a prison sentence.

Eric had tried to quit drinking on many occasions but always failed. He did not think it was possible to succeed. He had already lost his family. Now, he would probably lose his job. From his perspective, it would be difficult to retrain for another job as he was nearing retirement age. He thought there was only a slim chance that he could stop drinking. There was an even slimmer chance that his family or job would take him back after he got out of prison. He wrote that he despised and feared prison. Game over. He purchased a hand gun, wrote notes to his wife and children, and the day before his court appearance, he drove to a park and shot himself in the head.

It is difficult to avoid encounters with the legal system. Most of us have experienced moving violations or car accidents or civil situations involving the courts, such as divorce, or probate of an estate. It is thus not surprising to find that the sample with which we are working included individuals who were involved in legal processes. However, for many of the individuals in this sample, the legal processes were not just a part of life, but had become overwhelming. For some, the legal process represented the main reason they were contemplating suicide. For others, it was simply "one more thing." Some were criminal cases that involved

Explaining Suicide.
DOI: http://dx.doi.org/10.1016/B978-0-12-809289-7.00008-7

felonies or multiple charges and would likely result in loss of freedom through time in prison, and some were civil cases such as foreclosures and bankruptcies that would result in major life disruptions. There were also traffic violations and minor car accidents that would only be inconveniences to most people. For all of the individuals in this group, though, their legal involvement took center stage in their lives.

CRIMINAL INVOLVEMENT

The link between legal involvement and suicide risk is just beginning to be explored, and generally the focus has been on criminal offending, especially relating to those who commit suicide in jails or prisons. According to Schiff et al. (2015), who used data from the National Violent Death Reporting System, the four most common precipitant events for middle-aged men (35–64) without substance abuse problems or a diagnosed mental illness who committed suicide were intimate partner violence (58.3%), criminal/legal problems (50.7%), jobs and financial problems (22.5%), and health problems (13.5%). Of those who had legal problems, 41% had attempted or committed a homicide, and the victims were usually their intimate partners or family members. Suicide attempts among those who have had a recent arrest, yet remain in the community, are much more common (2.3%) than suicide attempts in the general population (0.4%), and even more common for those who had multiple arrests (4.5%; Cook, 2013). A key factor is the recent nature of the legal involvement. Previous legal involvement does not, in and of itself, seem to represent an enhanced risk.

Approximately 19% of our sample had had recent legal involvement. Of those, 77% were involved with the criminal justice system. The criminal cases represent about 14% of our total sample, and the figure is in line with one national estimate suggesting that "approximately 18% of the U.S. adult population at risk of suicide had recent criminal contacts in the year prior to death, making criminal courts and the criminal justice system an important focus for prevention efforts" (Cook, 2013, p. 771). As we have seen, the most prevalent crimes in our sample were related to interpersonal issues. Crimes involving substance use, abuse, or addictions were the next most pervasive.

CRIMES INVOLVING SUBSTANCE USE, ABUSE, OR ADDICTIONS

Driving Under the Influence

In September 2014, Michael Phelps, the most decorated Olympic athlete of all time, received his second DUI citation. Ten years earlier he had pleaded guilty to his first DUI charge and was sentenced to probation. A requirement of his probation was to talk to high school students about alcohol. This time, Phelps was also charged with speeding and crossing a double yellow line. After that, he said he felt he was in a dark place and did not want to be alive anymore (Michael Phelps, 2015). His license was suspended, and Michael went into inpatient treatment. He was fortunate that he was once again put on probation. However, the fact that Michael Phelps considered suicide after his DUI suggests how devastating it can be. The greatest success may not be enough to counter the stigma of a DUI; indeed, status may enhance it.

Of all the legal issues, DUIs may represent the most overlooked risk factor in suicide. Little research has been done on the topic, but one finding indicates that as the rate of car accidents related to DUIs increases, so does the suicide rate (Hourani et al., 2006). In our sample, 36 cases of suicide mentioned DUIs as a precipitating event. This represented approximately 3% of our sample, but likely other cases existed where we were not aware of the DUI, because it was not mentioned in the coroner's report or in the note. Ninety-two percent were men who ranged in age from 23 to 69. Although the average age was 46, more than two-thirds of the sample were over 40 years old. Most of the victims used guns (50%), followed by asphyxia (31%), and toxic substances (19%). Approximately two-thirds killed themselves at home.

There were blue-collar workers and professionals, including a judge, a lawyer, a retired physician, and a coroner's office investigator. We were able to determine the motivation for all but one individual. Although a few were motivated by relationship problems (8%) or felt like a failure (3%), the vast majority were attempting to escape from legal (14%) or psychological (3%) problems or, like Eric, a multitude of problems (70%). The psychological problems were not always specified, but when they were, most individuals were reported to be depressed. They were also struggling with medical (36%), interpersonal (39%), or financial issues (20%). It is not surprising then that in their notes, they spoke of "messing things up" or being out of options. One note read:

> I really don't want to do this, but I don't feel like I have any options. I've got myself in such a mess & theres no one who can help me. I'm afraid, I'm alone. I know a lot of people are concerned about me, but they all see me self-destructing. I have no hard feelings toward anyone. I have felt like I've been punished more than I should have been. Most of my problems though were my own fault. I don't blame anybody for this. Not even me. My life just got out of control and one bad break or decision was followed by another. It just got too bad to even talk about. I don't want to spend the holidays in jail or in an institution. I'm sorry but I have been punished enough. Thanks to all who helped me last this long. Especially Sidney Kahn and Samantha Little, and my kids. They didn't give up on me when they should have. I know I can never repay them for all they have done. I pray they will someday be rewarded. I'm sorry to the ones I let down, but the more anyone tried to help, the more guilt I felt when I kept failing. It's been a very strange and interesting life. Lots of Joys and Sorrows but too lonely for too long.

Similarly, another individual spoke about her mess but also spoke of her exhaustion: "Please forgive me. This is the last mess of mine you will ever have to clean up... I love you & I'm sorry. Suicide is selfish and devastating act. But little by little, bit by bit, I've been worn out."

For many of these individuals, the DUI was simply the last straw. Eric's was a typical scenario. He received a DUI, which would likely lead to a career loss, financial concerns, and the possibility of prison. It was simply too overwhelming to overcome a lifelong addiction and all the consequences from the addiction. Another individual's note read:

> Sorry. I wish I was better. I am not. You deserve a better person. I am just not strong enough. I love you with all my heart and always will.....I am sorry I let you down....I think I am a good person but I have too many challenges. It is too much for me to deal with alone... I am sorry for all the trouble I have caused. I know you will have to deal with a lot. I just can not go on dealing with losing you and all the other problems I have caused. I know that it is not your fault, it is all me.

Others were more succinct: "I can't fight anymore too much on my head." In each of these notes, from the longest to the shortest, the sense of "too much" was clear. Coupled with a drinking problem and the legal issues, all of the other problems became a tidal wave of difficulty.

For at least one-third of our DUI sample, it was not their first DUI offense. One person had received two DUIs in one day while another received two DUIs within a month. One individual was in a treatment facility for his drinking. For these people, it is likely that in addition to the loss of a driver's license, the consequences would include time in jail, prison, or a treatment facility. The coroner's reports stated that many non–note writers had indicated to friends that they would kill themselves before going to jail. One note writer said:

> MY LAST DAY ON EARTH
> Present circumstances have let me to make a decision for my future. I have the option of going to jail or basically rot in jail for an undetermined amount of months. Basically I am looking anywhere from 6 months, up to a year.
> I have pondered on the idea of either committing suicide or do my time in jail. I think I'll do away with my life and rot in Hell, where I'll probably wind up any way. I don't think that I'll be able to handle any amount of jail time. I'll go probably nuts and loose it mentally.
> Therefore I made up my mind to do away with my life. The only being that I'll have to answer to will be the ALMIGHTY above. I think that I'd rather answer to HIM, then the assholes here on Earth.

In a report summarizing CDC data on over 10,000 suicide victims, approximately one-third of their toxicology tests were positive for alcohol (Parks, Johnson, McDaniel, & Gladden, 2014). About half of our DUI sample were drinking or abusing substances when they killed themselves, probably to make the task easier. Some of them had just been escorted to their homes by police and immediately killed themselves, so they were still drunk. While researchers have examined the suicides of those taken to jail, no comprehensive study exists of suicides after police have taken someone home. One recent British study observed community-based offenders on a "criminal justice pathway," not those in jail, and found they were at increased risk of suicide (King et al., 2015).

Most individuals killed themselves within 24 hours of their arrest or shortly before their court appearances. If they did not kill themselves immediately, some may have used that time to get their affairs in order, then killed themselves before a decision could be rendered or a warrant could be issued for their failure to appear. Others may have experienced a period of mounting stress that they found they could not handle; tunnel vision may have set in. Once in jail, it becomes much more difficult to kill oneself, and the options become limited.

Given these patterns, there are obvious points of intervention. Since receiving a DUI is clearly a risk factor for suicide, one potential initial point of intervention is through the arresting officer or at the police station. A police officer would not want to tell someone who has been arrested for a DUI, and is likely drunk, that apparently a relationship exists between DUIs and suicide. Yet police could routinely provide contact information for crisis intervention options before releasing someone. In fact, police should do this routinely on all arrests. Additionally, holding an individual until he is sober or has a responsible party who will stay with him until he is sober, should be standard policy. Training police to recognize suicidal risk factors, as well as suicidal ideation and behavior, and to act as intervention teams, is practiced in some jurisdictions, but mainly in the form of pilot programs or grant programs (Draper, Murphy, Vega, Covington, & McKeon, 2015; Sareen et al., 2013). Mastrofski and Ritti (1996) found that whether police officers enforce DUI laws is more affected by supportive organizational management than by their personal attitudes. Training matters. By implication, officers trained to behave in a way attentive to suicide risk toward DUI offenders might lower the risk.

If suicide can be prevented during those first 24 hours following arrest, the focus should then shift to listening to the individual's dialogue with others. When someone has received a DUI, particularly multiple DUIs, he or she may begin to develop tunnel vision and talk about seeing no way out of the situation. At least a third of our DUI sample—and this finding is supported by other research—made suicidal threats or expressed suicidal ideation, but these were dismissed by friends, family, and even some professionals (Parks et al., 2014). Individuals may also talk about prison and their fears related to incarceration or punishment. At this point, it is critical to break the cycle of all-or-none thinking and help the person to examine options.

Cook (2013) also found a risk of suicide among those who had recently received a DUI and suggested that prevention efforts should be broadened to include the period between arrest and arraignment. In our sample, the 48 hours before court appearances represented an especially critical period. For those who had not committed suicide immediately following the arrest, the day of or day before court appearances were the next most lethal period. Cook suggests developing assessment tools, based on already existing data, to identify individuals who come into contact with the criminal justice system and are at high risk of suicide. Once they are identified, then more interagency cooperation with mental health and substance abuse programs is needed.

In many other cases substance use or other addictions played a key role in the commission of a crime, but were not the reason for the arrest. The backdrop of substance use, abuse, and addiction can be seen in some of the following criminal cases.

Other Crimes

Norbert had a gambling problem, and his credit card debt became astronomical. When he failed to make minimum payments, he was sued by the company, resulting in garnishment of his wages. Norbert worked at a retirement community, and while helping a resident he stole her credit card. Although he was able to purchase a few things, he quit using the card before it was terminated. It was so easy he stole a second and then a third card from other residents. He was arrested and charged with three counts of theft from a vulnerable population. One day he went to his storage unit and hanged himself. In his note he said, "I've been carrying a big ball of guilt, shame, embarrassment hopelessness and worthlessness in my gut."

Following interpersonal crimes and substance/addiction related crimes, the next largest category of criminal offenses involved money and property, including breaking and entering, theft and robbery (9%). Some of these crimes occurred in the context of other criminal activity or legal involvement. One man broke into his ex-wife's home, damaged property, and then stole her jewelry. Other common crimes included assault and homicide (7%), and rape, sexual assault, child molestation, or child pornography (4%). Conviction for any of these crimes would likely result in a long prison sentence.

Some individuals, like Norbert, expressed remorse for their crimes. Others were angry at their victims. In his note, one middle-aged man spoke of his love for his fiancée, children, and grandchildren, then quoted Bible verses extensively. Intermittently his note turned bitter and vengeful as he placed fault with the victim. He stated,

> I'm sorry I was just realy scared. I am not a child molester or Rapist. Chloe made her own decision to go with it. I know she was only 15 but girls do it all the time at 15 and they make that choice. I did not force Chloe into anything but I'm the one

that has to pay. I hope she can live with it cause I can't. I'm telling you the truth. She just didn't want to look bad to Ralph. She thought she wasn't a virgin for him. I'm not lying and I'm saying it to my grave! I love (my fiance) with all my heart and it not fare for her to go threw this. I'm sorry...I'm screwed. I even have lost my family because of a little bitch that is living. I have no where to go but Hell. Tell Chloe I'll see her there. She may lie to you all but not to God. We both did wrong and I may die but she has to live with it if she can.

A college student, charged with drunk and disorderly conduct and felonious assault on a police officer, blamed the female officer for his actions. He said,

> This whole felony... is the straw that broke the camels back. I wish you all the best and love you...but the pain is just to strong....Sgt. Roehm XSU police-your lucky I did this...this gun was meant for you! You have to be the dumbest bitch I know!! I did not have a drink that night with the headlight and you let a drunk girl park my car. STUPID MOTHERFUCKER! You need to be fired cuz your so fucking dumb!!!!!

Beyond remorse and blame, the notes were interesting in what they addressed and did not address. Most of the notes were organized, and many provided some justification for why the victims were choosing suicide. For example, one individual who committed rape left a note saying, "I'm sorry for my actions! I can't live with myself. Please forgive me. My insides are just full of guilt!" Like the overall set of note writers, most individuals expressed love for others (77%) and many offered an apology to a specific person (58%). One woman who was charged with prescription fraud wrote, "I love you very much but I just can't stay out of trouble and you deserve better." They frequently talked about God (42%) and many asked for forgiveness (39%). About one-fourth of the notes absolved someone from blame or, conversely, blamed someone. Approximately a third talked about their legal problems. Some talked about justice in general. For example, a 56-year-old man closely paraphrased the King James Bible, Philippians 4:8, changing the word "virtue" in the original to "justice" in the note, "And finally whatsoever things are just, whatsoever things are true, whatsoever things are pure, whatsoever things are lovely, whatsoever things are of good report, if there be any justice, if there be any praise, think on these things. Dont cry bean it's only trying to fix a whole in the ocean." The last sentence was a blended quotation from a movie, *El Camino de la Vida* (1956), about three boys awaiting sentencing in a juvenile court, and "Glass Onion" by the Beatles on *The White Album* (1969).

These notes had a very different tone from those found with individuals who were motivated by interpersonal issues. It was rare to see anyone speak about being sad, lonely, or lacking joy. Unlike those suffering from physical or mental illness, no one talked about being tired or tired of living. More often the decision to commit suicide referred to the "mess" they had made which was solely or partly related to their legal involvement.

Many left advice, "Don't let Bernie grow up to be like his dad and don't let him grow up not knowing his grandma and Grandpa Paulson. I've screwed up my life. I don't need to screw his up to…This is no ones fault but mine."

In short, most of these individuals did not seem to want to die but they simply saw no way out. For some, a chain of events resulted in a total collapse of their lives. Child support represents one of those situations.

Child Support

Jeff was 34 years old and had three children. His ex-wife, Jill, had divorced him over his substance abuse issues. He was $1600 in arrears, and if he could not pay it by the end of the month he was facing six months in jail. He had moved in with his parents and was about to have his beloved truck repossessed. Jeff had told friends that he had a terrible fear of being locked up. As the end of the month drew near, he selected a day, downed a bottle of ibuprofen with a pint of whisky, then slashed his wrists with a box cutter.

Child support begins as a civil issue in family court but can become a criminal issue when there is a failure to provide support. Jeff's story is representative of many of the child support cases we encountered. Clearly, finances were a problem in most cases. In addition, stable employment eluded most of them, often because of their substance abuse. Finally, many were living in a transient housing situation, such as a motel or with friends or relatives, due to their financial difficulties.

Most of the individuals in our sample owed tens of thousands of dollars in child support and were facing felony charges as a result. One note writer who had been unable to work as a result of the recession in the late 1990s indicated, "I have really work in a year and they still won't lower my support. I can't live not noing if I am not going to Jail for it agian and freeze just paid 10,000 and they still won't lower it." It was mid-January when he died. Later in the same note the victim wrote, "I do love all five kids with all my heart…I will always take care of you." In fact, it was common in these notes to find expressions of love for the children.

Inmates and Suicide

In our sample, 25 individuals committed suicide in jail and one in prison. The annual suicide rates are over three times higher in jails when compared to prisons (Cook, 2013). Hayes (2012) has suggested that two precipitating factors for suicide in jail are the environment itself and the fact that the individual is facing a crisis. The jail environment includes a "fear of the unknown, distrust of an authoritarian environment, perceived lack of control over the future, isolation from family and significant others, shame of incarceration, and perceived dehumanizing effects of incarceration" (p. 234). Furthermore, inmates facing a crisis may have numerous personal factors that predispose them to handle the situation poorly, such as a history of substance abuse or mental illness. In addition, they do not know the outcome of their trials as most will be appearing in court in the near future to learn their fates. Perhaps this is why the period before court appearances is a high-risk time for suicide. Suicide can occur any time during detainment, but a peak in suicide occurs following arrest (Cook, 2013), and a resurgence in the days prior to court appearances (Hayes, 2012). Once inmates are in prison, these factors change. This is not to suggest prison is less challenging than jail for inmates, but the environment and crises become more chronic and less acute. In some ways, the inmate may have greater perceived control and the challenge becomes more one of adaptation to the prison and loss of social support.

Consistent with a national sample, the jail inmates in our sample were an average age of 35 and male (93%), and they all hanged themselves in their cells (Hayes, 2012). At least one-third had a history of substance abuse and approximately one-fourth had a history of mental illness, including depression or multiple diagnoses. Additionally, 23% were known to have made previous suicide attempts.

When Joiner's (2005) model of interpersonal theory of suicide was applied to jail inmates in one sample, only thwarted belongingness was associated with past or predicted future suicidal behavior (Simlot, McFarland, & Lester, 2013). In our sample, only two inmates left notes that we could examine, but neither of them spoke of perceived burdensomeness. However, during this period, detainees have limited access to writing utensils or paper so it is difficult to leave a note. Coroners' reports indicated that at least 23% of our inmate sample had reported interpersonal problems and some were in jail on domestic violence charges (15%). These charges could have led to a perceived loss of social support and may have been the key factor for those who were in jail and considering their uncertain futures. The fact that they had not been bailed out of jail supports the notion that they had exhausted their social supports or thwarted their belongingness. Conversely, those who were out on bail spoke less of thwarted belongingness and more of causing trouble for others or creating a "mess." Since they had been bailed out they clearly still had social support, but they may have felt they were becoming a burden.

Comparing data from 1985 to 1986 to data from 2005 to 2006 shows that suicide rates have been declining in detention facilities (Hayes, 2012). This decline could be due to the fact that screening for suicide risk has increased, as have staff trainings. Also more protocols and policies are in place for how to handle at-risk individuals and what to do when someone harms himself. Nevertheless, trainings can be inadequate and infrequent, and screenings may not always be conducted (Hayes, 2012). Much more could be done, including enhancing the safety of cells and creating a death review process when inmates do commit suicide. A death review would involve an examination of the circumstances surrounding the suicide which could provide policy recommendations (Hayes, 2012).

In spite of the fact that proportionately more suicides occur in jails than in prisons, much more research exists on suicide committed in prisons, perhaps because it is the leading cause of violent death in prisons. When prisoners who had attempted suicide were interviewed about when they formed the initial intent to commit suicide, how they planned, prepared and carried out the act, and their reflections on it, they identified many of the risk factors already presented (Rivlin, Ferris, Marzano, Fazel, & Hawton, 2013). The reasons for their self-harm were grouped into three categories: "adverse life events; criminal justice or prison-related issues; and psychiatric or psychological factors" (p. 311). Adverse life events involved interpersonal relationship issues including bereavement. The most frequently cited psychiatric or psychological factor was drug or alcohol withdrawal. However, most prisoners indicated that they had multiple reasons for their suicide attempt. Moreover, they acted impulsively, with 40% indicating they did not think about the act for more than a few minutes and another 20% considered it for three hours or less. Approximately one-third left a note while another third had told someone, usually family or mental health personnel, of their wishes to die. Prisoners were interviewed within four weeks of their attempts and, in retrospect, commonly reported their actions were "stupid."

CONCLUSIONS RELATED TO CRIMINAL INVOLVEMENT AND SUICIDE

The patterns associated with criminal involvement are not like those of many other individuals who commit suicide. Frequently, their mental illnesses or addictions have created life circumstances that are spiraling out of control. The chaos is compounded by the perceived loss of support systems among people who may be tiring of helping them. Their addictions are most likely a symptom of underlying emotional or psychological issues. In a study of female prisoners, adverse childhood experiences increased the risk of attempted suicide and current drug use (Friestad, Ase-Bente, & Kjelsberg, 2012). However, the women had generally not begun to face these issues, as they were still in the throes of addiction. It may have been too overwhelming to consider dealing with the addiction, much less the underlying problems. Because of this predicament, the initial point of intervention should have been their first contact with the criminal justice system; interagency collaboration with addiction treatment facilities and mental health systems are key at that point.

During incarceration, mental health services need to be easily accessible. As prisons have become the "new asylums," a large percentage of prisoners are on the mental health caseload ("The New Asylums," 2005). According to one blogpost, approximately 20% of inmates have a serious mental illness and about 30% to 60% have substance-related problems (Aufderheide, 2014). Moreover, Aufderheide suggests that deinstitutionalization of the mentally ill in the 1960s simply resulted in "trans-institutionalization," as the mentally ill now go into jails and prisons. He states, "Across the nation, individuals with severe mental illness are three times more likely to be in a jail or prisons than in a mental health facility and 40% of individuals with a severe mental illness will have spent some time in their lives in either jail, prison or community corrections" (para. 5). He further concludes that "our jails and prisons have become America's major mental health facilities, a purpose for which they were never intended."

There are often only enough mental health providers for the most severe cases. Only half of the suicide attempters who were interviewed said they received any type of support after their attempt (Rivlin et al., 2013). Yet, they also indicated that simple measures would have prevented their attempts, such as being allowed to contact someone on the outside via a phone call or being placed in a double cell. The researchers concluded that because prison represents such a unique set of circumstances, traditional risk models and typologies for suicide may not apply and clinicians and researchers may need to reformulate their assessment of intent (Rivlin et al., 2013). Due to the importance of social support, they suggest prisons also examine their visitation policies.

Some researchers have suggested that even following incarceration the suicide rates still remain higher for those released into the community than in the general population, especially during the first two weeks of reentry (Mackenzie, Borrill, & Dewart, 2013). Prisoners are usually released into the community with very little money and a short supply of medications and information about a community mental health center where they can obtain refills. Their medications often run out before they can be seen by a health-care provider. Additionally, limited options exist for therapy or recovery services. For most exoffenders, the environment which led them to incarceration has remained unchanged. Without additional resources, and lacking understanding of the environmental risk factors, many recidivate, or worse, commit suicide.

CIVIL ISSUES

Ross was 74 years old and retired when all his investments went south during the recession. He was forced to file for bankruptcy. His house was foreclosed on and was sold at sheriff's auction. He and his wife had received an eviction notice. Ross was worried about where and how they would live, as their only future income would be Social Security. He told his wife that "life was not worth living." She told him they had to keep moving forward. He reluctantly agreed and she left the home to find boxes for packing. When she left he began looking at the credit card bills and eviction notice. Then he found his handgun and while staring at himself in the mirror, put the gun to his temple and pulled the trigger. When his wife returned home, she found his body amidst the bills which were strewn about the living room.

FINANCIAL ISSUES—FORECLOSURE, EVICTION, BANKRUPTCY

It is likely no coincidence that the most frequently occurring civil issue related to suicide, and one of the most frequently occurring criminal issues, involved finances. Nine people in our sample had filed for bankruptcy, seven were facing foreclosure or eviction, and many were having their wages garnished for a number of reasons, including failure to pay taxes. One person who failed to pay taxes said in his note:

> More good news. The government actually wants yet another piece of me, and wants to garnish my wages to get it. Going after rich criminals who have actually stolen huge sums, and could also afford to return what they stole is obviously too much trouble. It's much easier to go after bankrupt folks like me who didn't steal anything and can afford neither the debt nor a lawyer to fight it. Government of the rich; by the rich and for the rich. I wish I were rich. That would be cool. I'd rather burn everything I own and every dime I have than see these vultures get a cent.

Major financial crises are one of the most robust predictors of suicide attempts for people who are diagnosed with major depressive disorder. Wang et al. (2015) tracked a large United States sample of depressed individuals over a three-year period on stressful life events. These events were grouped into four aggregate categories: relationship, friendship, or interpersonal stress; financial stress; loss or victimization; and legal problems. The first two categories had the highest correlation to risk of a future suicide attempt. In addition, patients who were admitted to a hospital emergency room for attempted suicide were more likely to have experienced bankruptcy in the two years prior to admission than patients admitted for other reasons (Kidger, Gunnell, Jarvik, Overstreet, & Hollingworth, 2011).

Still, these were generally not the only stressors the individual was facing. The backdrop of substance use, abuse, and addictions also continues in civil cases. In fact, among Japanese pathological gamblers, a family history of addiction is the strongest independent predictor of bankruptcy and subsequent suicide (Komoto, 2014). We found that half of the victims in our sample killed themselves to escape multiple issues. A large percentage

(83%) were dealing with psychological issues, generally depression (75%). Many of these individuals were depressed over their financial situations. In addition, 33% had a history of substance abuse and the same percentage had been using substances just before they died. As one woman stated, "The bills are not the problem. It is my dependency on antidepressants & anti-anxiety medications." Two-thirds of the individuals had expressed suicidal threats or had suicidal ideation, but these were ignored by family and friends. The sister of one 69-year-old victim specifically asked him if he was considering suicide. When he said "yes," she told him to pray, but did nothing else. Another 50-year-old man contacted a friend three days before he committed suicide and told her in great detail how he intended to kill himself. The night he died he was drinking heavily and called her to tell her he would be killing himself soon. She did nothing at all.

Individuals who were dealing with a major financial crisis were older than those dealing with criminal issues. Although the age range was 33–72, 50% were over 50 years old, with an average age of 51. Reinventing oneself in middle age is overwhelming to some individuals, especially when financial, mental, and social resources are frequently unavailable. Often, close interpersonal relationships were also strained or broken by the financial situation.

Most people experience financial difficulties at some point in their lives, but bankruptcy, eviction, foreclosure, and garnishment of wages are beyond financial stress. They involve more than just tightening up a budget. They present a very real threat to basic needs such as food and shelter. The public humiliation of losing one's home may occur. When these are compounded by multiple failures, advancing age and depression, the tunnel vision present in suicidal thinking takes over, and it becomes impossible to muster the energy to even consider a new beginning. Unfortunately, expressions of suicidal ideation were not taken seriously for those in our sample, likely adding to the depression. To them, it was probably just more evidence of failure since no one cared enough to intervene.

IT'S ALL RELATIVE

In some cases the level of legal involvement was minimal (6%) yet it was the main factor in the victim's decision to take his life. The following cases involve only minor car accidents. One 91-year-old man hit an emergency vehicle and then fled the scene. He was ordered to appear in court and feared he might lose his license. Instead, he chose to shoot himself. A United States Department of Transportation study found that elderly people were extremely afraid of losing their driver's licenses. One dominant reason for the fear was "feeling old," which "negatively related to social and emotional well-being" (Carp, 1988, p. 9). The preceding case demonstrates that the impact of legal entanglement is relative. To a senior citizen, the loss of driver's privileges means the loss of freedom. This man was in good health and fiercely independent. Losing his license could result in cascading consequences. He may no longer have been able to live in his home or attend his community activities. Although he may not have lost his license, the fear of losing it, and the repercussions, were overwhelming to him.

At the other end of the spectrum, a 16-year-old, who had struggled with depression, was found at fault in a "fender bender." He was so distraught when he arrived home that he hanged himself in the garage. Boys are more likely than girls to experience car accidents (Sigfusdotti & Silver, 2008). Severity of depression has been found to be associated with increased levels of hostility and anger experience (Riley, Treiber, & Woods, 1989). The young man in this case was already depressed, and the stress of the accident, however minor, put him at increased risk of suicide. Similar to someone with a mental illness who may not be fully functioning, the chaos, disruption, and loss of control from a traffic accident can be devastating, especially for someone who is not old enough to have developed coping mechanisms to deal with unexpected events. If a teenager is involved in even something as small as a "fender bender", he or she may feel overwhelmed by feelings of shame, failure or disappointment that an adult might be able to dismiss.

Finally, a middle-aged trucker's rig was hit after a driver ran a red light. Although he was not at fault, he had to take a drug test and failed the test. He received no violation but lost his job. In the United States, England and Europe, the suicide rate for men aged 45–59 went up 40% in the decade that this man lost his job (Young, 2015). His job loss and use of substances put the trucker at risk, as did the stress of the accident. The trucker was not cited for the accident but the legal entanglement affected his current and future employment opportunities. The positive drug test would be revealed every time he would apply for a new job. As an independent trucker, it would also affect his insurance options and rates. Like Eric, at this point in his life he felt he was too old to train for another career and too young to retire.

In all suicide cases, but especially those that suggest legal involvement, it is important to consider the individual's life circumstances and how the person interprets the event. The premise of cognitive psychology is that the same event can have different meaning for different individuals because of how it is interpreted. Changing the life circumstances of the previously discussed cases changes their meaning to the individual. If the 91-year-old had been 40 years younger, he may not have feared losing his license. Accidents happen and rarely result in anything more than fines or points on a license. It is not likely that the youth, at 40, would have been considering suicide, assuming his employment was not related to driving like it was for the trucker.

CONCLUSIONS RELATED TO LEGAL INVOLVEMENT AND SUICIDE

Crimes and civil actions are shrouded in personal beliefs and values. For example, many victims expressed fear of prison and preferred to die instead. Those fears are rooted in beliefs that frequently involve a fear of losing control. Similarly, many civil actions involve a loss of control over personal issues such as finances and trigger thoughts of failure. One man who lost everything to his gambling addiction said, "I am sorry to have put you in a bind with the money I owe you, — everything went wrong and I couldn't get control back."

Although it is possible to identify risk factors and triggers for suicide, these need to be interpreted in context. It is critical to listen to the individual's identified concerns and consider the impact s/he perceives the event will have on his or her life. Those listening to the individual must not supplant their own judgment about the importance of the event for that of the individual whose experience it was. Thinking one has lost control can create tunnel vision, which in turn makes one feel helpless or hopeless, and there then appear to be no other alternatives but suicide. The following quotation demonstrates how thoughts turned into feelings which led to suicide.

> I did a bad thing. I will not go to jail over this. I couldn't take that either. Just the thought of it scares me....We are ruined, our marriage & our financial situation. To me everything is gone, so I'm done too. Yeah I took the cowards way out, so just say what you like. I'll be listening....

It is virtually impossible to avoid all contact with the legal system. Some of these encounters may be pleasant (obtaining a marriage license) and some may be mundane (jury duty), but they can be unpredictable. Anyone who has been called for jury duty knows it may be the night before the trial before a decision is made as to whether a trial will even be held. This can be inconvenient and frustrating even though it only involves minimal life disruption. When someone is not a bystander to the legal system (like a juror), but rather the center of the controversy (a plaintiff or defendant), the uncertainty and unpredictability of the legal system can be terrifying. Legal decisions have direct and disruptive life consequences. The anxiety and stress from the unknown is difficult to bear, even for those who have stable lives.

9

Protective Factors and Resilience

A *Peanuts* cartoon (2016) portrays Charlie Brown and Snoopy sitting together on a dock looking across a lake. Charlie Brown says to Snoopy, "Some day we will all die, Snoopy!" Snoopy replies, "True, but on all the other days, we will not." Although between 30,000 and 40,000 people kill themselves per year in the United States, many more people go on living. Books on suicide all examine motivations for suicide, but often do not examine the motivations for living. We may simply take them for granted, or we may assume there are too many. Authors also examine risk factors in suicide, but frequently do not look at protective factors in the same analytical way. While methods for intervention in and prevention of suicide exist, some of which we discuss in Chapter 10, Conclusions and Implications, methods for living also exist—not just stopping a suicide, but creating the conditions that eliminate it. If that sounds too difficult, dreamy, impossible, or unrealistic—too utopian—we beg to differ. It is in fact the mundane and ordinary aspects of life that sustain people, and an approach to combatting suicide that recognizes those positive factors builds on what already exists.

FACTORS THAT LEAD TO LONGEVITY

It may seem strange to talk about longevity in a book focusing on premature, self-inflicted death. However, if we examine the factors that lead to longevity we perhaps can see what was missing in some individuals' lives that may have led them to suicide. Dan Buettner (2015) assembled a team of health professionals and academics to determine what factors contribute to a longer and better quality of life in five "blue zones," areas around the world where people with the greatest longevity reside. Buettner (2015) identified nine common characteristics among the

Explaining Suicide.
DOI: http://dx.doi.org/10.1016/B978-0-12-809289-7.00009-9 **185**

communities, which can be grouped into four areas. He arranged these factors into a pyramid with belonging forming the foundation, followed by eating wisely, having the right outlook and moving naturally.

In terms of belonging, people in the blue zones had a tremendous amount of social support. First, they belonged to social circles that supported healthy behaviors. They saw friends or family nearly every day for a pleasant activity. Second, most of them were involved in faith-based communities; any denomination was beneficial. Third, they put their families first. As Buettner (2015) describes, "They keep aging parents and grandparents nearby or in the home, which also lowers disease and mortality rates of their children. They commit to a life partner (which can add up to three years of life expectancy), and they invest in their children with time and love, which makes the children more likely to be caretakers when the time comes" (pp. 21–22).

Social support serves a protective function at all ages. Middle-aged women were interviewed about their social relationships and the greater their social integration, the less likely they were to commit suicide (Tsai, Lucas, & Kawachi, 2015). In fact, women who were not socially well integrated had a three-fold higher risk for suicide than those who were well integrated. In Alaska, "for every 5-degree increase in northerly latitude, suicide rates increased 18 percent" (Rosen, 2013). As social isolation increased, so did rates of suicide. According to the Centers for Disease Control and Prevention (CDC) statistics for 2014, the three states with the highest suicide rates were (in order) Wyoming, Alaska, and Montana, states with small communities and vast rural areas (CDC, 2014). Theorists have identified "thwarted belongingness" as one of the causes for suicide (Joiner, 2005); it makes sense that communities which provide opportunities and conditions for belonging have fewer suicides than those without.

One of our note writers wrote over a dozen notes to friends and family. In addition, he asked his parents to let anyone read a long generic note he had written explaining his reasons for suicide. Towards the end of the note, he asked readers for a few "favors." His first favor read, "Please turn your T.V. set's off more, and talk to each other a little more. You'll like it I swear." Although this writer appears to have had a lot of social support, the number of notes may not have reflected the quality of his social support. In his final communications, he is asking readers to engage in more social support. Numerous note writers recognized the devastating effect of isolating themselves or longed for more or better social support. If there is one factor that might have mitigated most suicides, this would be it. In blue zones, almost all of the people who lived to be over 100 years old enjoyed conversation with others on a daily basis.

The second area identified was eating wisely, and although these factors are important to longevity, they may not seem as crucial for prevention of or intervention in suicidal behavior as enhancing social support. Still, many individuals in our sample were dealing with the effects of poor health habits, or substance use or abuse, which contributed to their decline. Moreover, dietary patterns can lead to chronic health problems and pain, and many people who kill themselves wish to escape pain. Frazao (1999) noted the cycle of stress and poor quality of life that often contributed to poor dietary habits, which in turn contributed to more stress and poor quality of life. With suicide in the top 10 causes of death in the United States, improving one's diet and the diet of one's family seems like a positive step for suicide prevention.

The third area focused on having the right outlook on life, including having a sense of purpose and finding a way to deal with stress. Most people in blue zones had routines to deal with stress, so that when stressful situations occurred they had a response in place, whether it was taking a nap, praying, or having a happy hour. In this way, stress was overcome with something natural to one's habits and environment. Lack of purpose presents a deep problem in modern society, and in blue zones work alone was never enough. People found their purpose in their communities and among their loved ones. Among the suicide victims in our study, there were frequent references in the notes to life having no meaning.

One 32-year-old who hanged himself expressed his regret that he had no purpose. "I wish I could go back and change everything. We all know I cant so I am sorry to bring pain to everyone. My life has no meaning any more all I do is drag everyone around me down." A 60-year-old female left a note that said, "The life I have to look forward to had no meaning to me. I'd rather be dead." She asphyxiated herself with carbon monoxide. Others looked for meaning, but it eluded them. With a history of Crohn's disease, depression, anxiety, diabetes, and impotency, a 47-year-old man despaired of finding any purpose. "I've studied and read, but maybe I'm just a nihilist, existentialist at heart. Maybe there is no meaning in the universe."

Viktor Frankl (1946) spoke of how having a sense of purpose kept him alive in a Nazi concentration camp. He believed finding meaning in one's life was central to having a reason to continue living. To find meaning, Frankl wrote, one needed a combination of work, love, and the ability to rise above oneself. One's reason to live may seem inconsequential to others, but if the individual believes that s/he has a purpose in life, a motivation to endure follows. This sense of purpose was lacking for many suicide victims.

A related concept is called future time perspective (FTP). Chin and Holden (2013) suggest FTP can be a protective factor that may mitigate suicide. FTP has three components: future thinking, optimism, and future connectedness—envisioning how one's present actions affect the future. They recruited college students who had symptoms of depression and suicidal ideation and found FTP "attenuated the relationships between hopelessness and suicide motivation, as well as depressive symptoms and suicide motivation" and moderated "the impact of depressive symptoms on suicide preparation" (pp. 401–402). They noted that it may not have been FTP alone that served the protective function, but FTP may have been aided by other characteristics, such as having a reason for living.

The last area in Buettner's blue zone study, moving naturally, focuses on exercising the body, not through extreme activities, but rather by taking advantage of opportunities to move. These include walking when doing errands, walking to a friend's house or gardening. It is movement the body craves and it can be beneficial without extreme measures. Not only do these activities promote physical health, they can lead to stress reduction, healthy coping, and social support. The positive effects of exercise on depression are documented for all age groups. Older people often develop poorly responsive depressive disorder, and one study found a 30% decline in it when people attended group exercise activities (Mather et al., 2002). A recent study found also that spending time in nature, just taking a simple hike, decreases obsessive, negative thoughts by a significant margin (Bratman, Hamilton, Hahn, Daily, & Gross, 2015). The exercise does not have to be rigorous or difficult to provide a benefit.

All four areas Buettner outlines are important, but two are critical for the prevention of suicide: helping an individual find purpose in life and enhancing social support. Some people in our sample felt they had lost their purpose and could not begin the process of finding a new one. Many of them suffered from depression and trying to find or re-create a purpose in life was too overwhelming. For others, like the school superintendent who had seemingly lost everything due to a DUI, it was impossible to believe life could ever have purpose again. Yet a sense of purpose can come from being responsible for a pet or providing volunteer services. Where the social support system is intertwined with the search for a purpose, people live longer. When at-risk adolescents were engaged in personally meaningful extracurricular activities, they were less likely to report suicidal ideation (Armstrong & Manion, 2013). Finding a sense of purpose can also lead to enhanced social support as the individual becomes linked with community systems.

In 2014, the World Health Organization (WHO) published a report titled *Preventing Suicide: A Global Imperative*. The report stemmed from the 2013 World Health Assembly which adopted the first-ever Mental Health Action Plan. A main focus of the plan was suicide prevention with a goal of reducing the suicide rate by 10% by 2020. Their findings underscore Buettner's conclusions regarding factors leading to health and longevity. Like Buettner they found that strong personal relationships, religious or spiritual beliefs, and positive coping strategies enhance resilience. Although they recognized that some religions have prohibitions against suicide and stigma attaches to it, involvement in a community is what provides a protective function. Positive coping included healthy lifestyle choices related to diet, sleep, exercise, and management of stress. Development of positive well-being also increases the chances that someone will ask for help when needed.

FACTORS THAT LEAD TO LIVES CUT SHORT

In United States football, the chances of scoring a touchdown are statistically higher in an area near the end zone known as the "red zone." The area is not marked on the field, but commentators and advertisers know where it is. Just as blue zones exist in which people have high longevity, red zones also exist where people have a statistically higher chance of dying young. They are not marked on a map, but experts know where they are. And once they are pointed out, it's easy to understand why.

Most blue zones are not wealthy areas, but neither are they areas with the poor social and economic conditions that embody the term "poverty." Premature death appears in areas with higher "poverty rates," i.e., lower incomes. Metro areas with the shortest life expectancy at birth also have poverty rates often higher than the national rate (Frohlich, Kent, Comen, & Stebbins, 2015). Behavior and biology also contribute to lower longevity. Cities with higher obesity and smoking and the fewest hours of exercise saw shortened lifespans for their residents. Gadsden, Alabama, which has low income and high rates of obesity, has the lowest life expectancy of any city in the United States, at just over 72 years (Frohlich et al., 2015).

Just as some communities have low life expectancy, some communities in the United States have higher rates of suicide than others. These are not typically cities with low life expectancy on the whole. Las Vegas is the city with the highest suicide rate, at 34.5 per 100,000 people. Las Vegas's particular allure for the suicidal seems predictable, but the other cities that appeared in the top 15 in 2011 had rates of suicide that varied widely from year to year and lacked any obvious characteristic associated with suicide. Tulsa, Phoenix, Fresno, Portland (OR), Pittsburgh, Wichita, Jacksonville, Denver, Miami, Tucson, Mesa (AZ), Albuquerque, Sacramento, and Colorado Springs were on the list. Many of these cities are thriving places, and at least 10 are often sunny and warm. While some of the cities had high crime (Pittsburgh) or high unemployment (Wichita, Jacksonville), these cities did not have the highest rates nationwide for those problems (Giang & Lubin, 2011). What makes a community suicide-prone?

One study of Brazilian and American cities found that, as cities grew, so did their mortality rates from car accidents and murders. Suicide rates, on the other hand, declined (Melo, Moreira, Battista, Makse, & Andrade, as cited in Khazan, 2014). Cities provide opportunity for social interaction. The researchers, citing Durkheim, opined that the decision to kill oneself, like the decision to commit murder, "instead of being purely a consequence of individual choices, might have strong correlations with the underlying complex social organization and interactions" (p. 2). It is possible that larger cities provide some of the things that blue zones do: more social interaction and greater productivity (and thus a sense of purpose), but more study is needed. Cities may also offer greater access to health care, education, and services that help people cope with stress. The 15 United States cities identified as having the highest rates of suicide were mostly midsized cities, some of them in states lately strained to provide medical services. Arizona, e.g., ranked 50th among the states in mental health care (Stuart, 2015). Florida ranked 17th among the states in suicide deaths, and had two cities in the top 15, but its small towns were the places where suicide was especially high. Miller and Klingener (2015) found that isolation, poverty, access to firearms, and a lack of mental health resources were the causes of the increased suicide rate in small towns.

As many communities struggle with dwindling state budgets, it may seem like a daunting task to create new measures to combat suicide. Yet implementing health literacy policies is one solution that need not be expensive. Health literacy is a new concept that involves educating people about their health in ways that are useful and understandable. If information is delivered but people are not able to turn it into practical application, it will have little effect. Health literacy programs seek to provide information that several components of a community then put to use. If a community wishes to improve eating habits, e.g., a collective effort between schools, health centers, workplaces, and retailers might focus on healthy eating activities so that the delivery of information coincides with a positive intervention in practices (Nutbeam, 2000). Applying this to suicide intervention is even more complex than applying it to dietary habits, but with strong civic leaders committed to suicide prevention, health literacy can become an important new tool.

Most states already have community health centers, and using these to their fullest capacity in suicide prevention is critical. Many states are reducing their spending on mental health care and on community health; some states are privatizing care and limiting the scope of their community health centers. Given the reduction of fiscal resources, it may not seem reasonable to expect community health centers to do more, but it requires strategy as well as collaborative will.

Community resilience is something we witness whenever natural disasters occur, for example. A town is destroyed by a tornado, and neighbors and strangers get together to rebuild. This same model of community resilience, researchers posit, might "serve as a sustainable paradigm for organizing public health and medical preparedness, response, and recovery" (Wulff, Donato, & Lurie, 2015, p. 361). Communities in disaster often receive help from outside, including money and materials. In normal times, however, subsistence is all stakeholders expect. That needs to change. Wulff et al. (2015) suggest that the first thing that needs to be done is to convince stakeholders that by "strengthening health systems, meeting the needs of vulnerable populations, and promoting organizational competence, social connectedness, and psychological health," (p. 361) everyone benefits. "Community resilience encourages actions that build preparedness, promote strong day-to-day systems, and address the underlying social determinants of health" (p. 361). Community resilience needs to become part of the normal routine of our communities. With respect to suicide that means implementing prevention objectives at all levels and treating all of the risk areas, from the individual to the communal. Access to counseling for individuals, couples, and families, as well as the creation of strong social bonds in the community as a whole, can prevent suicide.

In trying to create communities that by their very structure promote well-being and prevent the risk factors for suicide, we cannot ignore that death comes for everyone, and sometimes, for those with agonizing illnesses, it may not come soon enough. This has prompted four states to enact, and many others to consider enacting, legislation to allow for physician-assisted suicide. As the movement grows, it raises ethical and medical questions with which families and communities must grapple.

DEATH WITH DIGNITY

The vast majority of individuals in this project would have benefited from many of the protective factors discussed here, such as increased social support or finding a sense of purpose. Nevertheless, one group ostensibly would not have been affected by most of these protective factors—people who were suffering from a physical illness. They generally appeared to have a good social support system and were neither suffering from a mental illness nor searching for a purpose in life. They were simply unable to endure the illness and/or pain any longer. Their chronic pain affected their bodies, minds and spirits: "Mindy Sweetheart—My Nerves have snapped—Never thought would do this but I can't take any more of this punishment!! I see no help in getting well." "I know you'll miss me at first, but if it helps think of me up in heaven pain free." "I couldn't stand the pain any longer. Thanks for all you done for me." "I'm ready to be done here. I don't know what awaits me, if anything, but I've had all I can bear and I want the pain to stop."

Some of these individuals may have opted for a "death with dignity" option if they lived in a state that allowed it. Death with Dignity is a nonprofit organization that "expands the freedom of all qualified terminally ill Americans to make their own end-of-life decisions, including how they die" ("About Us–Death with Dignity," n.d.). The notion of dying with dignity has been referred to by numerous other terms such as assisted suicide or right to die. National debate about the topic gained momentum in 2014 when Brittany Maynard, a 29-year-old woman diagnosed with a stage-four glioblastoma, was told she had six months to live. Unlike other advocates for assisted suicide, Maynard was young and vivacious and gained national attention for the cause. Maynard lived in California, a state that did not provide for assisted suicide, so she moved to Oregon where they had enacted a Death with Dignity law in 1994. She also partnered with Compassion & Choices, establishing the Brittany Maynard fund to promote assisted suicide legislation in states where it is not legal (Compassion & Choices, 2016). Eventually, in 2015, Maynard's home state of California approved legislation for death with dignity. Washington State and Vermont are the other states that have laws allowing for it and Montana allows for assisted suicide by a Supreme Court ruling. It should be noted that since it was enacted in 1994, only about 50 people per year have taken advantage of the Oregon law.

Gleckman (2015) suggests that the Death with Dignity discussion should focus on how to allow people to live the best life they can. Often, when someone has a chronic illness they lose social support at the very time when they need it the most. He suggests, "This is not about death with dignity, as the physician-assisted movement describes itself. It is about life with dignity. And, as a society, we do far too little to preserve it." Although the laws provide a way for people to have a sense of control over their deaths, Gleckman suggests the focus should be on allowing them to live life. Even for these individuals, social support is key. Does that mean they will reach a point where they do not want to die? Maybe or maybe not. However, social support may prolong life satisfaction and even in death, social support eases the transition. Brittany Maynard died surrounded by those she loved.

Some institutions and groups oppose "right to die," "death with dignity," or euthanasia legislation. Twenty-six states and the Commonwealth of Puerto Rico have legislation prohibiting assisted suicide. Belgium, the Netherlands, and Luxembourg are examples of European countries that allow it; throughout the western world legislative bodies have debated it. The Roman Catholic Church remains opposed to all forms of assisted suicide or euthanasia for any reason, but not all Christians believe it to be wrong. Muslims, Hindus, and Jains accept it under certain circumstances. Political opposition exists as well, especially among people who associate it with the former Nazi regime in Germany. Disability activists such as Not Dead Yet object to laws which they say provide not just for terminally ill patients to kill themselves, but for patients with chronic, nonfatal illnesses (Not Dead Yet, 2016). The "death with dignity" movement challenges the idea that suicide is always something to be prevented, or the popular perception that only the mentally ill commit suicide. Many factors, from ethical concerns to the fact that suicide is still associated with sin and stigma, have prevented this type of legislation from becoming universal.

LIVING WITH THOUGHTS OF DEATH

On social media such as Facebook, one of the activities many users engage in is taking quizzes. These are often silly, with no real right or wrong answers. One popular quiz is "How Well Do You Know X?" and individuals post this on their "timelines" (home pages) to see if their friends really know them. The individual selects answers to several questions, and when his or her friends take the quiz, they see if they match. In this quiz, one of the questions, after asking whether money or chocolate is one's favorite, is "What kind of death does X fear most?" Then there are choices: suffocating, being burned alive, plane crash, drowning, and lastly, "X does not fear death" (Heroquizz, 2016). Although the question is asked in jest, it is exactly one of the things we need to know when we are assessing someone's risk of suicide.

Most human beings have a strong desire to live. In the abstract, we may say we do not "fear" death, but unless we are faced with imminent death, we often are not too sure of our feelings. When a person is diagnosed with a terminal illness, e.g., the news is received and processed in stages. Kubler-Ross (1969) was the first to articulate what she called the five stages of loss and grief in which a person who is terminally ill, or one who loses another to terminal illness, responds with denial and isolation, anger, bargaining, depression, and acceptance. While some debate about the stages is found among scholars, few deny that change over time occurs from the first instance the news is received to the end when the patient finally dies. At the end, acceptance often comes, but even with no acceptance, the patient will die.

With the suicidal person, the natural order of dying may appear to be overturned. This was a person who could have lived! Those who knew the individual may have been taken completely by surprise. Many suicides are impulsive, but even when they are planned, the plans are kept from family and friends. The time between the decision or impulse and the completion of the act is often not long, though occasionally people plan their suicides for years or months. In either case, no stages of death and dying seem to be present.

With suicides that are well planned, it seems probable the person might have been able to proceed through the stages, with the only difference between the terminally ill patient and the suicide being the inevitability of the act. Still, it is possible that in every suicide the stages of death and dying have been completed, even in the impulsive act. Instead of thinking of suicide as an abnormal act counter to human nature, perhaps instead we should think of it as a different way of dying, incorporated by the individuals into an "ordinary" process that moves through stages to the point of acceptance.

Kübler-Ross (1969) described the five stages in linear fashion but in later years emphasized that the stages are not in a particular order or on a particular timetable (Kübler-Ross & Kessler, 2014). The first stage, denial and isolation, is one in which the dying person goes numb, feels overwhelmed, and withdraws. The denial is not necessarily of death itself, but can be denial of one's feelings of pain and grief about one's impending death. The Yale Bereavement Study changed the name of this stage to disbelief to indicate the surprise and shock one feels (Maciejewski, Zhang, Block & Prigerson, 2007). Anger is a stage in which the person can direct wrath at himself, his friends, his family or anyone, even God. It may open up other emotions as well. Bargaining before death often involves "if I am spared, then I will do that" thinking. It is a period in which the individual tries to negotiate for his or her life or a reduction in pain. Depression sets in, with thoughts about whether it makes sense to go on. Acceptance is not a state of being "OK" with death, but a realization that it is coming. While some people may find peace in acceptance, it is also possible for people to have good days and bad days as they get used to the idea that they are going to die. Some scholars do not agree that the stages laid out by Kübler-Ross are "stages," but instead think of them as emotions in the dying or grieving process (Stillion & McDowell, 2015). Whether stages or emotions, none of these is outside the norm for persons who are suicidal, and they could certainly experience them. In the minds of those with suicidal intent, they are dying.

Suicide victims' notes show evidence both of thinking about death for a long time and of working through the stages of dying. One 60-year-old woman left a note telling her family that "[t]his was not a sudden decision. It was made years ago. Hope I haven't waited too long." Some notes ran through the stages in one sitting. Nick, discussed in Chapter 5, Grief and Failure, started to face the idea of dying while he was studying for a course in economics. His notes for the course stop and the notes to himself about dying take up. He works through his failures and discusses his isolation. He examines his lack of belonging rather dispassionately, but then becomes angry, finally letting out some of the anger he had toward his parents. He previously made some half-hearted attempts at suicide with Tylenol, a kind of bargaining. "I ASKED FOR A SIGN NOT TO DO THIS," he wrote, "THERE WAS NOTHING." Finally, his note indicates a resignation to his fate.

Some individuals bargained with God or the cosmos, but often they bargained with themselves. One young man, discussed in Chapter 2, Findings, wrote, "IF YOU DON'T DIE IN THE NEXT 48 HOURS YOU MUST..." and then listed items like "GET A JOB." If he could get a job, he did not have to die. But he could not get a job. His poems reflect all the other stages of grief at the inevitability of his death: isolation: "lately I'm so desperate for a reader, a listener"; anger: "Another fucking journal entry, poor-excuse-for-a-poem. I'm so angry"; bargaining: "I could just keep writing, I could write without ever stopping...you could be entertained, and I could be of some use..."; depression: "The storm passes, The lightning and thunder is gone though the rain might continue all night"; and acceptance: "This is the end, this is all there is."

Individuals often acknowledged their acceptance of death in their notes. "I don't know where I go from here, And I don't care," wrote Jasmina. "If I end up in a alley somewhere dead That is on me." When one elderly man scrawled, "I Relise I' Am Never Going To be The SAME," he accepted death. Another man wrote, "Time has come for me to leave." In order to come to acceptance, the victims probably went through stages that were not visible to others then, or at least were not identifiable as stages or emotions of death and dying.

When Kübler-Ross introduced her stages in 1969, the objective was to make death for the dying and the grieving more humane. Health professionals were taught how to recognize the stages and even prepare people for them. Health professionals who recognize these stages or emotions in cancer patients perhaps could be trained to recognize them in suicidal patients, as could family and friends, if it could be supported that suicide victims did pass through such a process. When people give their possessions away, could that not be seen as fitting into these stages?

Much more research would need to be done to see if in fact distinguishable signs exist that a person is in the "stages" of suicide that echo the stages of grief identified by Kübler-Ross. The stages were devised for two groups, the dying and grieving. For the grieving group especially, the stages were supposed to be healing. For the dying, they were supposed to be therapeutic. For people who have embarked on a path toward suicide, the stages are not healing. The stages allow suicidal individuals to come to terms with their deaths, but if suicide is to be prevented, the stages need to be interrupted.

Stillion and McDowell (2015) have identified what they call "a trajectory of suicide" quite distinct from a Kübler-Ross model of stages of dying. They identified essential points on a path toward killing oneself. At some point in a person's life a foundation of risk factors arises: biological, psychological, cognitive, and environmental. A person needs only one but may have more. Upon that foundation is laid suicidal ideation. Once the idea is formed that death might be desirable and possible, it needs to be followed by triggering events which are mirrored by warning signs, usually verbal or action clues to suicidality. Ultimately, in completed suicides, this is followed by the suicidal behavior that ends one's life.

Whatever path or stages one follows toward suicide, if no interruptions of the trajectory, no stages of recovery, or no protective factors happen to counter risk factors, then suicide may occur.

PROTECTIVE FACTORS

Psychologists and sociologists have identified protective factors for those with mental illness and for suicidal ideation. These are hope, goals, pathways, agency, religiosity, and resilience. Many of the studies we consulted were conducted on special populations such as racial or sexual minorities, but the protective factors they identified are arguably not unique to these populations.

Davidson, Wingate, Slish, & Rasmus, (2010) compared African Americans and Caucasians to determine if African Americans, who have a low incidence of suicide, had more protective factors than Caucasians, who are at higher risk for suicide. They were testing Joiner's interpersonal theory. The researchers turned to positive psychology, the study of human strengths. They first looked at hope theory.

Hope is a cognitive motivational construct, like escape, but it is also part of goal-setting. Davidson et al. (2010) examined studies from the 1990s and 2000s that showed hope predicted lower levels of thwarted belongingness and perceived burdensomeness, but that it also predicted a greater capability for suicide. The finding surprised them. If hope was a protective factor, it was strange to see that it might also contribute to suicide. The researchers posited that because hope increased goal-setting and allowed people to take up challenges, individuals might have put themselves in situations at greater risk for both emotional and physical pain. They tested this hypothesis and found evidence that African Americans had higher levels of hope than whites. These protective factors may have buffered them from suicidal ideation, suicide attempts and completions, but in some individuals hope was not entirely protective. Other studies have found that hope is the major protective factor among African Americans. They attribute the power of hope in the black community to the unique history of oppression African Americans have endured (Hollingsworth, Wingate, Tuker, O'Keefe, & Cole, 2016).

Researchers have also examined hope as a protective factor against suicide in gay men diagnosed with HIV (Siegel & Meyer, 1999). Newly diagnosed HIV-positive men were at higher risk for suicide than non-HIV-positive men. Siegel and Meyer (1999) found that among gay men who attempted or contemplated suicide, the experience of the attempt or the serious contemplation of suicide "provoked a process of coping" among the men (p. 53). They posited that having frank discussions about suicide after the diagnosis and suicidal attempts or contemplations may have allowed the men to "move toward acceptance and commitment to life" (p. 53) and gave them a sense of control.

Davidson et al. (2010) also examined religiosity as a protective factor against suicide. African Americans reported a higher intrinsic religiosity than whites. Higher religiosity has been shown to have a higher protective value against suicide in African Americans, but the researchers called for more study, as the evidence is not unequivocal, and gender could also be a variable. Women may have gained more protection than men from religiosity. They did find that intrinsic religiosity may have been an even larger protective factor than extrinsic religiosity or social support, though both offered some protection.

Social support was also found to be a protective factor for transgender individuals who were suicidal, as were gender identity–related factors (such as coming out), transition-related factors, individual difference factors, and reasons for living. Among the individual difference factors were resilience, coping and problem solving, life evaluations, and optimism. Religiosity or spirituality was a protective factor for trans adults (Moody, Fuks, Peláez, & Smith, 2015).

Holm and Severinsson (2011) examined factors that helped women with borderline personality disorder (BPD) who were suicidal recover from their attempts. They found that the women benefited from assuming responsibility for themselves and others, giving them a reason to live, and from their search for strength, safety and their true selves.

The suicide rate among members of the US Army has increased significantly over the past several years and now exceeds that of the general population (Nock et al., 2013). Yet the period of highest risk was not during or after combat but just two months after starting military service. According to a study of more than 163,000 men and women in the Army, "61% of those who tried to take their own lives had not yet been deployed" (Fox, 2016). Nock et al. (2013) studied protective factors such as "resilience, stoicism, character strength, life satisfaction, positive moods, self-esteem, autonomy, hope (optimism), zest, gratitude, capacity to love (ability to form reciprocated relationships), and a sense of meaning and purpose" (p. 107). They identified coping skills, problem solving, and social support as key factors for soldiers' self-protection. Researchers who found that suicide attempts were highest in the first year think that the period of transition before deployment is the most difficult, because soldiers are still thinking of home and have not yet undertaken the responsibilities of the battlefield. More stress and even physical illness can occur in the first six months after joining the military (Fox, 2016). After that, soldiers' skills are more tested.

While more studies are needed on protective factors, those that exist highlight the same concepts. Coping skills and problem solving may combat feelings of being overwhelmed as well as prevent the development of constricted thinking. Hope or optimism may be hard to teach, but they are associated with goal seeking. The more goal-oriented a person becomes, the more protection he may receive. Having a reason for being was also important in every study. One of the factors that has received a lot of attention in the popular media today also featured largely in these studies: resilience. While the media is focused on resilience as a quality millennials (the generation that grew up in the 1980s and 1990s) allegedly do not have (Lipman, 2016), psychologists and social workers are seeking to understand how it protects against suicide (Gutierrez et al., 2012).

RESILIENCE

The American Psychological Association indicates that people who are resilient adapt well to tragedy, trauma, stress and other forms of adversity. Other researchers have defined resilience as "'a stable pattern of healthy adjustment' following an aversive event" (Nock et al., 2013, p. 108). Resilience was identified in almost all studies of protective factors against suicide, but how one acquired resilience was not described.

Researchers did try to measure it. Osman et al. (2004) developed the Suicide Resilience Inventory–25 (SRI-25). Analysis of the scale is complicated, but the questions are simple. Participants are asked if they like themselves, like things about themselves, can deal with rejection, can resist suicidal thoughts when humiliated, and so on. Rutter et al. (2008) found that the SRI-25 is a good predictor of suicide risk. Based on the questionnaire, resiliency appears to be the ability to resist suicide in the face of situations identified as risk factors and being able to find social support when feeling suicidal. In other words, being resilient was a combination of qualities one already possessed and the availability of others in a time of need.

What the scholarly literature that examined the protective factors described and cited here seemed to suggest is that when people confront their stresses, fears, and situations honestly and forthrightly, resilience is something that builds. In the studies in which interviewing the participants was part of the research, the participants' ability to spend time thinking constructively about their potentially bad situations and talk to other people helped build resilience.

CONCLUSIONS

If we want "life supporting" communities, we need to learn from blue zones, but we also need to learn from red zones. We need to construct communities that promote and foster social support systems, healthy lifestyles, and full use of people's skills and gifts. People need a reason to live, and that often comes from having responsibility—though not at such a level that it is overwhelming. We need to make sure our communities are not unhealthy places or places where health literacy is low. This will take resources, both financial and human, but if the results are that it lengthens life and raises productivity, the benefits will offset the costs.

We cannot assume people have good coping skills, problem-solving abilities, optimism, or sufficient social support and resiliency, and these need to be developed at home and at school, and fostered at places of employment. We also have to be aware of the failure of a person's coping abilities or cognition, or the development of pessimism and despair, or the loss of social supports. Many communities have resources in place, but those in need do not know where to look. Every university, for example, not only has wellness counselors, but tutors, time management educators, learning centers, and recreation facilities. Every town has community resources, though some have more than others. We cannot make people use resources, but we can encourage it in words and actions. Making life-supporting communities takes time, and people who need help if they are suicidal need it immediately. In Chapter 10, Conclusions and Implications, we examine the idea of a national agenda and spell out proposals to create national responses to the problem of suicide, but we will also look at how people implement intervention and prevention programs at the local level.

10

Conclusions and Implications

One objective that we began with in undertaking this book on suicide was to see if a simpler way could be found to understand suicidal motivation, so that it would be easier for family, friends, and professionals to intervene. Furthermore, we wanted to explore the best means for preventing suicide. Those close to a suicidal person are best able to intervene, but prevention requires a much larger, multifaceted effort.

If we think about what makes up an individual suicide scenario, we can frame it in terms of an equation: (risk factors + motivation) + (mental state + intent to die − fear of death) = need for intervention. We can simplify this even further: *warning signs + death preparation = need for intervention*. Warning signs consist of circumstantial, behavioral and environmental risk factors and motivations, while death preparation consists of one's mental state (made up of cognitive risk factors), intent to die and fear of death.

Two questions need to be answered for any assessment. *Warning signs*: Has the person been experiencing problems that are beyond the coping skills of this individual in his or her present situation? *Death preparation*: Is the person at a point where he or she accepts death as a possible resolution to those problems? If the answer to the first question is yes, the only reason not to intervene is if the answer to the second question is clearly no. If it is maybe or yes, intervention is necessary. Once the answer to the first question is yes, it is incumbent upon the people in contact with the person to assess the situation to the best of their abilities, and that often may mean asking for professional help.

It can be hard to know with certainty if a person has been experiencing problems that are beyond his or her coping skills, but to some extent logic and reason ("common sense") can help us in such an assessment. For example, if a child comes home from school and is extremely upset about a "trivial" thing—he was chastised because his shirttails were untucked, for example—the question is not whether he ought to get over it, but rather is he capable of getting over this without help? Most children probably will be. In the case of a child with emotional problems or who has had this happen repeatedly, it might not be as likely. The help might be a parent taking time, like this mother did, to calm the child down and taking a walk with him to give a break to the painful thoughts, and perhaps even finding out more about the interpersonal situation that led to his shirt being untucked. If an adult is facing a marital breakup that is not of her own desire, is she capable of coping with that without help? It might be necessary as a friend or family member to be watchful about ongoing social support, mood changes, and risk factors like bankruptcy, loss of child custody, and so on. However, the intervention of family or friends may not be enough.

It can also be difficult to know if someone is preparing to accept death, but there are both verbal and behavioral clues that most people would recognize in any other situation where a person was dying, such as giving away significant belongings, writing a will, withdrawing from activities and organizations and even making funeral arrangements, or going through stages of anger, bargaining, and depression. All of these can be quite normal activities, of course, and independently might mean nothing. It is only when coupled with the warning signs that these activities should be cause for intervention. For a young person, giving away such belongings as a favorite pair of sneakers might be a clue, whereas for an older person it might be the family heirlooms. Statements that indicate a person doesn't "know how to go on living" or wants to die should be taken seriously. Preparation for death may not be as evident for those who will kill themselves impulsively, but in many of the coroners' reports, witnesses and survivors said that the person had made prior threats, and they did not believe them.

It is not easy for most people to ask for help, and it is doubly difficult, perhaps, to take action that brings external interference into the life of someone else. "What if I'm wrong?" is a common concern of calling for help for someone else. Yet in the coroners' reports that we viewed, many people had called for welfare checks on their loved ones. They knew or feared that the person had harmed or killed himself or herself. If the impulse to intervene had occurred at an earlier point, the suicide might have been interrupted and averted. We must learn to trust our guts and to get past our own fears when someone is in trouble and in need of help.

RESOURCES ALREADY AVAILABLE

The American Foundation for Suicide Prevention (AFSP), 2016 has links on its website to prevent those considering suicide from completing the act and to help people who fear for a loved one. At https:// afsp.org/find-support/ phone numbers and links to support services are provided. The National Suicide Prevention Lifeline has a lifeline help number 1-800-273-8255, as well as instructions for how to set up a safety plan for those who feel suicidal: http://www.suicideprevention-lifeline.org/learn/safety.aspx. Crisis Chat is an online service in which crisis centers across the United States have joined together to form one national chat network for emotional support, crisis intervention, and suicide prevention services. Those who are suicidal or who are dealing with someone who may be suicidal can go to http://www.crisischat.org and immediately chat with someone at a crisis center.

Veterans can seek out help at https://www.veteranscrisisline.net, with a phone number to call, 1-800-273-8255, as well as an online chat service and a text messaging function. This center is also able to support those who are deaf and hard of hearing. All of the crisis centers are available 24/7, every hour of every day.

Innovative intervention methods are also being introduced, and only time will tell how well they work. For instance, the father of a young man who was involved in the fatal shooting of a police officer and was subsequently killed by police has developed an app called #Strikeback. Ronald Hummons believes his son committed suicide by cop after battling with severe depression, and he devoted his time to figuring out how to have an instant intervention. The app allows an individual contemplating suicide to get immediate social support as well as a direct reminder of his or her reason for living. The app sends a text message to three or more people in three categories (spiritual, family, and friend) that the user sets up in a profile. After the user's support community receives the text explaining his or her suicidal ideation or depression, they will also get a GPS location so they can find the person. As the texts go out, an automatic slide show will appear on the phone displaying a picture of loved ones, family, or friends (Hummons, 2016). This app is not available as of the date of publication of this book, but it represents one of the possibilities of connecting technology's ability to quickly deliver messages and information with those who are able to intervene effectively to save lives.

These resources are excellent avenues of assistance. Nevertheless, hotlines, apps, and peer counseling should not substitute peers or family members for trained professionals. No layperson without experience in counseling suicidal people should try to help someone by themselves. In situations where there is no time—it is an emergency—or when someone wants to intervene but does not want to call 911 or a hospital, contacting hotlines, chats or apps can provide help that is both immediate and future-oriented. Sometimes, though, it is necessary to simply dial 911 and ask for an ambulance or the police. While hospitalization is not always the best alternative for a suicidal person, and police officers are not always the best equipped to interact with mentally ill or suicidal people, in an emergency situation sometimes no other choice exists.

Right now, no standard protocol for training police and no optimal plan for treating patients who are suicidal exists. We need to do more as a nation for those who are suicidal than provide crisis intervention. We must develop a long-term, national prevention plan. That plan must go beyond words. It will involve a substantial financial commitment from the governments—local, state, and federal—as well as high-impact practices that use the financial resources efficiently and innovatively.

A NATIONAL AGENDA

What we are missing in the United States is a national agenda or an action plan for suicide prevention. Since 2001 we have had a National Strategy for Suicide Prevention under the supervision of the US Surgeon General, but it has not provided successful leadership on the question of suicide. Moreover, in the decade between its formation and the second report on its progress issued in 2012, suicide rose by 29% (Hogan & Clymer, 2014). The World Health Organization (WHO) indicates that a national agenda is key. They suggest that in order to create social change, there must be strong leadership, public support, and a strategy. Unfortunately, in the United States we do not have strong leadership, or a top-down directive, maintaining a focus on suicide prevention. With other health crises, such as HIV/AIDS, an action plan comes from the President (National HIV/AIDS Strategy Federal Action Plan, 2015). There is no presidential commission on suicide prevention. Although there is a presidential proclamation of World Suicide Day each September, no single action plan is coordinated by the executive branch. Without such a plan it is difficult to have unified public support. Public support also continues to be undermined by the stigma of suicide and the lack of open dialogue.

Any suicide action plan would need to be comprehensive, integrated, and synergistic (WHO, 2014). It should include multiprofessional teams who work together. In 2010, former Health and Human Services Secretary Kathleen Sebelius and former Defense Secretary Robert Gates launched a Zero Suicide campaign to try to make suicide a national priority while they were in office. The National Action Alliance for Suicide Prevention maintains a website, http://zerosuicide.sprc.org. A report, "Zero Suicide: An International Declaration for Better Healthcare," was issued by the Crisis Services Task Force of the National Action Alliance for Suicide Prevention that explains the initiative to change assumptions about suicide (Zero Suicide, 2016).

While the Zero Suicide approach is a model for integrated and synergistic prevention, it has only been implemented in a few areas; in a following section we discuss one of those implementations in Detroit, Michigan. Zero Suicide has hosted an annual "academy" for health care organizations and national suicide prevention organizations. Sebelius and Gates claimed they wanted to save 20,000 lives in 5 years, but currently little information about progress toward that goal is available. Some researchers see hope for future studies that enable "prioritization of high-risk subgroups for targeted suicide prevention efforts, identification of effective interventions ready for deployment, estimation of the implementation impact of effective interventions in real-world settings, and assessment of time horizons for taking implementation to scale" (Pringle et al., 2013, p. 71). Although there is a National Strategy for Suicide Prevention and a Zero Suicide partnership between the US government and national community partners, no actual single national agenda exists, as the WHO recommends.

A strong coordinated national action plan could provide funding to expand such endeavors. Any endeavor would need to create objectives and generate data that could be used to evaluate the success of the plan, something the WHO deems essential. Until an action plan exists, we are left with numerous suicide prevention projects that are often funded for a short period of time and cannot be sustained. WHO (2014) submits that, "In the long-term, importantly, reducing risk will go only part of the way towards reducing suicide. Furtherance of protective factors will help build for the future—a future in which community organizations provide support and appropriate referrals to those in need of assistance, families and social circles enhance resilience and intervene effectively to help loved ones, and there is a social climate where help-seeking is no longer taboo and public dialogue is encouraged" (The Way Forward section, para. 4). Thus far the US "action plans" that do exist, like Zero Suicide, seem focused on identifying and reducing risk.

THE RELATIONSHIP BETWEEN RISK FACTORS AND MOTIVATIONS

In this book, we have focused almost entirely on motivations for suicide, but one cannot understand how suicide occurs or engage in its prevention by examining motivation alone. Risk factors are those attributes a person has, or circumstances in which a person finds himself or herself, that may make one more likely to commit suicide. Risk factors play an important role in assessment of the necessity for suicide intervention. Often social workers, therapists, and even family and friends are not privy to a person's mental state or mindset, or to the motivations that may exist, such as escape from pain or interpersonal relationship issues. Moreover, the precipitant that is hardest to deduce—an ability to overcome the fear of death coupled with a desire to die—is often a deliberately hidden state. Thus, the most identifiable markers for suicide are risk factors.

Yet risk factors are ubiquitous. In the United States, being white and male is the single biggest risk factor for suicide, but most white men will not commit suicide. The Harvard School of Public Health's "Means Matter" website (2016) hosts several studies that show both guns and rurality increase the risk of suicide. Risk factors do not cause suicide, and they are not perfect predictors, as they can be present in people who will never attempt, let alone commit, suicide. Risk factors may also be a poor way to allocate resources in suicide prevention. The crucial work for a national agenda is to target those risk factors that will be most efficacious.

The WHO identified eight individual risk factors for suicide including previous attempts, mental disorders, harmful use of substances, job or financial loss, hopelessness, chronic pain or illness, family history of suicide, and genetic or biological factors. These risk factors, such as previous suicide attempts and substance abuse, can be seen throughout our cases. In fact, some formed the basis of our categories. Those struggling with job or financial loss are represented in our cases, and it was the driving force behind suicides in the Escape–Financial category. Similarly, mental illness is prevalent in our sample; those who were trying to escape the pain from mental disorders can be found in the Escape–Psychological section of Chapter 4, Escape as a Motivation for Suicide, and severe mental illness is discussed in Chapter 7, Severe Mental Illness. Hopelessness is a common characteristic associated with suicide, but those individuals in the Failure category had a sense of doom, an inability to see a light at the end of the tunnel. Finally, the individuals who had chronic pain and illness are embodied in the Escape–Pain section of Chapter 4, Escape as a Motivation for Suicide.

In addition to individual risk factors, the WHO also presents a spectrum of other risk areas including relationships, society, community, and health systems. The impact of relationship factors, such as social isolation and conflict, have been previously discussed. Societal risk factors include stigma associated with mental illness or help-seeking and access to means. Community factors relate to the stress of acculturation, discrimination, and trauma or abuse. Finally, the risk factors related to health systems are primarily due to barriers to accessing health care and quality of care.

SOCIETAL RISK FACTORS: OPENING THE DIALOGUE REGARDING SUICIDE AND MENTAL ILLNESS

A disability rights activist once suggested that what makes disability such a difficult topic is that we all have the potential to become disabled. At any given point anyone could succumb to a disease or accident that would leave them physically or mentally impaired. Death and suicide are similar. We will all die, and we could all get to the point where we would consider suicide. These topics become even more anxiety arousing when we shut them out of our lives and conversations. This makes it difficult to talk about, or sometimes even to take it seriously, when others reveal they are contemplating suicide.

Doughty (2014) argues that we have a structural denial of death in our society and that we avoid thinking and talking about it. In her book she discusses how we have evolved from a society where death was a part of life and when individuals died they remained in the home in a natural state, to one where our loved ones are whisked away as soon as they die and kept at a facility until ready for burial or cremation. Distancing ourselves from death, she points out, creates anxiety and fear of death.

Suicide is a form of death and we distance ourselves from conversations about it, even after it occurs. In the obituary she wrote for her sister Eleni Pinnow wrote, "Aletha Meyer Pinnow, 31, of Duluth (formerly of Oswego and Chicago, Ill.) died from depression and suicide on February 20, 2016" (Pinnow, 2016). Because it was unusual to be so candid in an obituary, the editors of the *Washington Post* reached out to Pinnow to tell her sister's story. Pinnow states that she arrived at her sister's house to find a note on the door indicating she should not go into the basement but call emergency personnel. In the aftermath she told friends and family about the wonderful characteristics that her sister had, but she also told them about her depression. She wrote,

> I told them that her depression created an impenetrable fortress that blocked the light, preventing the love of her friends, her family, and any sense of comfort and confidence from reaching her ... My sister's depression fed on her desire to keep it secret and hidden from everyone. I could not save my sister. I could not reach my sister through her depression. Aletha slipped from my grasp, and I cannot bring her back. I can only urge others to distrust the voice of depression. I can plead for people to seek help and treatment. I can talk about depression and invite others to the conversation. I can tell everyone who will listen that depression lies. I can tell the truth. The lies of depression can only exist in isolation. Brought out into the open, lies are revealed for what they are ... I know only two things for sure: Depression lies. I will tell the truth. Join me.

Pinnow highlighted the deafening silence surrounding suicide and mental illness. The shame, stigma, and ignorance can be heard in our private conversations and public forums. When rhythm and blues performer Kehlani Parrish attempted suicide in March 2016, instead of being supportive, Chris Brown, a fellow performer, made comments on social media indicating there is no "attempting" suicide and suggesting that such "attempts" are for sympathy (Howard, 2016). Howard wrote that "his comments on suicide arguably could set back an important conversation that has been brewing in communities of color about the internal stigma regarding mental health." This stigma may very well stem from relating mental illness to weakness. Stigma stifles conversations and leads to denial of mental illness and suicide. Ultimately it is very difficult to battle or eliminate something that is invisible.

That said, endeavors to reduce the stigma of mental illness have been gaining momentum. When he was in college Brian Malmon began experiencing symptoms of depression and psychosis, but he concealed them. He was later diagnosed with schizoaffective disorder and committed suicide during his senior year. His sister Alison formed Active Minds, an organization that promotes open dialogue about mental health, specifically on college campuses (Active Minds, 2016). Alison formed the organization shortly after Brian's death in March 2000. Today, over 400 chapters are on college campuses. The goal of Active Minds is to change the culture on campuses through education and advocacy. Perciful and Meyer (2016) found that stigma toward those with mental illness can be relatively easily influenced. They examined the impact of films on college students' attitudes toward mental illness and found that exposure to a brief film clip with an inaccurate portrayal of mental illness enhanced stigma while exposure to an accurate portrayal reduced stigma. As Active Minds continues to enhance awareness of mental illness and available resources, the stigma toward college students with mental illness should be lessened and help-seeking from those in crisis increased.

These efforts are opening the dialogue and reducing some of the stigma related to mental illness, and it may be having an impact. In August 2015, Harris Poll conducted a Mental Health and Suicide Survey with 2020 individuals (Harris Poll, 2015). They found that 38% of adults believed seeing a mental health professional was a sign of strength. However, in terms of attitudes towards suicide, although about half of the respondents thought people committed suicide as a way to escape pain, many saw it as a selfish (39%) or cowardly (20%) act. The lack of empathy for those perceived to be in pain who then kill themselves suggests that we are not teaching the right information about why people commit suicide.

As previously discussed, when a spate of mass killings occurred during the fall of 2015, Speaker of the US House of Representatives, Paul Ryan, said, "People with mental illness are getting guns and committing these mass shootings." Although no evidence supports that people with mental illness are violent (The Editorial Board, 2015), as Perciful and Meyer (2016) found, it is fairly easy to influence the public's perception of a stigma positively or negatively. Paul Ryan's misinformation, which negatively stigmatizes those with mental illnesses, is being heard in national settings. Almost half of the respondents to a recent survey indicated that they believed people with mental illness were more dangerous than the general population (Barry, McGinty, Vernick, & Webster, 2013). This inaccurate information supports the views of many in the general public who have distanced themselves from mental illness and suicide. Like death, such distancing just increases fear and anxiety related to those with mental illness. It makes people afraid to talk and those who listen are often at a loss as to how to respond or what to do. We have many examples of mental illness in our popular culture but very few examples of how to respond to it effectively.

In terms of other societal interventions, the WHO also suggests that impeding access to suicidal means would also decrease risk. In his note, one of the people in our study told the story of how he acquired a gun. He went to a gun shop, but there was a waiting period, so he looked in a local newspaper and had one right away. He said, "So the weird part is, all I do is go get a trading post, make one phone call & 15 minutes later, with no paperwork I'm holding a weapon that can kill people. What a fucked up country we live in."

THE MEANS MATTER

It is beyond the scope of this book to enter into a discussion about the rights of citizens to own guns. Acknowledging a right to own guns and supporting measures to remove firearms in life-threatening situations are not mutually exclusive positions. In many cases, the victim had threatened suicide or was currently threatening suicide, and despite the fact that someone knew a gun was in the house, s/he did not remove it. Their excuses for not removing it were varied: "I did not think he could get to it," "I did not think it worked," or, sadly, "I did not think he really meant to do it." A few actually handed the victims the gun and dared them to kill themselves. If one restricts access to guns, people may still choose to kill themselves by another means, but when one has to consider other means, s/he loses the impulsivity that is characteristic of so many suicides. While some people plan their suicides for days, weeks, months or years, the vast majority contemplate the act for less than a day and almost a fourth for less than five minutes. In general, having to find a substitute for the gun creates a delay and will almost always result in the choice of a less lethal means for the suicide attempt and a greater chance for survival.

Since the primary means of suicide in the United States is firearms, reducing access to guns is a preventative measure for suicide. The Harvard School of Public Health has collected data on the use of firearms in suicide. Their website "Means Matter" has a page for firearms dealers and range owners. In 2009, "Means Matter" took the unusual approach of reaching out to gun shop owners in New Hampshire (NH) on the role that they can play in suicide prevention. The NH Firearm Safety Coalition, a group of mental health and public health practitioners, worked with firearm retailers and firearm rights advocates to develop materials that other owners could use to help prevent suicide. Nearly 50% of gun shop owners in NH had disseminated the materials by 2012. By 2015, the program had spread to other states. While it is too soon to say what effect these programs have had, many owners realize the important role they have to play.

The Suicide Prevention Resource Center (SPRC) sponsors talks between individuals which focus on suicide prevention, innovation and action. In one of these talks between Cathy Barber, the director of the "Means Matter" project, and Ralph Demicco, a gun shop owner, they discussed reducing access to lethal means ("SPARK Talks," 2016). Demicco was "deeply impacted" after he found out that he had sold guns to three individuals who, within the span of a week, committed suicide. He said, "Let's not get on the antigun, let's not get on the progun bandwagon, but let's get on the antisuicide bandwagon." Demicco is part of the Firearm Safety Coalition in NH. Their "Gun Shop Project" has two prongs for intervention, family and friends and gun dealers. The responsibility of family and friends is to overcome prohibitions and stigma and ask family members who seem to be struggling how they are doing. The Harris Poll (2015) found the majority of adults (74%) indicated that "most people who die by suicide usually show some signs beforehand." Family and friends then have to be prepared to have the difficult conversation that may follow if the person is suicidal. Demicco frames it well when he says, "Uncle Harry, look, you're having a rough time. We're here to help. Can we hold onto your guns until you feel better?" The results of the Harris Poll indicated that most adults said they would intervene if someone close to them was thinking of suicide, but some said they might not help because the person may feel worse (24%) or they would not know what to do or say (23%).

The second prong is to heighten gun dealer awareness. Demicco says this can be accomplished quite simply by putting posters in shops, encouraging clerks to ask more questions and scrutinizing sales. In Washington State, legislators proposed a bill setting up a task force to create suicide prevention training for gun dealers, owners of shooting ranges and pharmacists (Kramer, 2016). Like Demicco's project, the bill is a collaborative effort and has the support of the National Rifle Association. The training may take the form of an online course and would be required for pharmacists to be accredited. As for gun shop owners, Alan Gottlieb, executive director of the Second Amendment Foundation said, "I have not spoken to any gun retailer in Washington State that doesn't want to be a part of this … It's in their interest to do it and they want to do it. People are very hungry for this" (Bach, 2016). The WHO also advocates for "gatekeeper" training where a "gatekeeper" is anyone who is in a position to identify those who may be contemplating suicide. In Colorado a Gun Shop Project began in 2014 that was modeled after Demicco's project. It was started in rural communities where the rate of suicide by firearm is higher than the national average.

Many people who buy guns do so for protection. Having a gun in the home, however, increases the risk of a violent death in the home (Dahlberg, Ikeda, & Kresnow, 2004). In addition, the risk of suicide was higher for males in homes with guns than those without guns, regardless of storage practice, type of gun, or number of firearms in the home. In a country where warning labels are on virtually everything, a simple warning label on guns might create the delay needed to allow someone to rethink their plans for suicide. More importantly, it may make friends and relatives, who are buying guns for their loved ones, consider the stability of the individual before they do so. This would not infringe on the rights of gun owners and may help gun shop owners, like Demicco, to enhance the antisuicide message. Currently, California requires child safety warnings on guns, and New York requires a label about locking devices. No state has a suicide warning label on guns at this time.

In 1988, Britain changed the packaging for an over-the-counter medication, similar to acetaminophen, to blister packs (Emanuel, 2013). Although results of studies were mixed, there is some support that it was related to a reduction in suicides. The packaging also makes it more difficult for accidental overdoses to occur. However, it is more expensive to produce blister packs than to package pills in bottles, and companies may be reluctant to take on such a burden. Creating barriers, even if they are only small barriers, may have a tremendous impact on impulsive suicides (Seupel, 2015).

While engaged in research on mothers who kill their children, the author, Cheryl Meyer, was approached by a woman in her sixties wanting to tell her story. When she was younger, she had quit her profession to take care of her two children who were under 5 years old. One day her husband, a successful attorney, came home to tell her he had begun another relationship and was leaving her. He had removed all money from their bank accounts and he was suing her for full custody. She had no money to fight the custody challenge and no job. Her children were her life, and she believed no one could ever care for them the way she did. She made a decision to kill herself and felt she had to take her kids with her, because they were an extension of her. As she explained it, you could not die without killing your arm and the children were like an appendage. She mixed some potent narcotics with ice cream and went to take her children their final snack. On the way, the phone rang and it was her pastor. As she talked, the ice cream melted and she lost her desire to die and instead chose to fight. Years later, she recalls this experience with sadness but also a sense of pride—she and her children lived. She retained custody, regained her profession, and remarried. At the time we met, she was happily approaching retirement and looking forward to being able to spend more time with her grandchildren. The point is, it only takes a minute, or even a small act or reminder to interrupt a suicide attempt.

One final societal risk factor that WHO discusses is inappropriate media reporting. There are extensive guidelines available for media reporting of suicides (Samaritans, n.d.). In general, suicides, especially high-profile suicides such as Robin Williams, can lead to imitative behavior. Therefore, responsible reporting by the media and social media can have an impact on suicide rates. The tone of reporting, detailing of methods and extent of coverage can all influence people who may be contemplating suicide. Ohio unveiled a comprehensive suicide prevention initiative in 2016, and one facet of this initiative involves sponsoring training for schools of journalism and communication to promote the use of these guidelines when reporting on suicides (Wandersleben, 2016). The suicide prevention initiative will receive two million dollars in funding and will focus on prevention measures such as reducing stigma, improving treatment with evidence-based practices and postvention measures such as responsible media reporting and support for survivors.

HEALTH AND FIRST-RESPONDER SYSTEMS RISK FACTORS

In July 2013, police were called to the home of Paul Schenck in the small village of Yellow Springs, Ohio, for a domestic disturbance (Bachman, 2014). The first responders knew Paul, who had grown up in the village, and they knew that he suffered from mental illness and was heavily armed. A standoff began with the police which ended in an exchange of gunfire. Paul was killed, and local residents decided to use this opportunity to form a local affiliate of the National Alliance on Mental Illness (NAMI). They now have monthly family support meetings and, working in conjunction with the village human relations commission, were able to raise enough money to cover the costs of a mental health first-aid training. This training teaches first responders, family members, and friends how to respond to someone having a mental health crisis. NAMI has also been raising awareness by using an educational bus to travel to events and communities. Schenck's death highlights the importance of support and education for first responders, professionals, and families.

Many professionals were involved in the lives of the individuals we studied. These ranged from therapists to clergy to medical doctors. Although many professionals were exemplary in their care of these individuals, others fell short. This could be related to the stigma surrounding mental illness and suicide. Approximately eight percent of emergency department admissions are for attempting or contemplating suicide (Preidt, 2016). Yet when Betz et al. (2013) examined the attitudes of emergency room health-care professionals, specifically nurses and physicians, toward suicidal behavior, they found that less than half of the respondents believed "most" or "all" suicides were preventable. Even when the risk of suicide was identified, despite the fact that national guidelines urge physicians to assess whether the patient has access to firearms or other lethal means, only about half of the physicians did so. Betz et al. found that "Many E[mergency] D[epartment] providers are skeptical about the preventability of suicide and the effectiveness of means restriction, and most do not assess suicidal patients' firearm access except when a patient has a firearm suicide plan. These findings suggest the need for targeted staff education concerning means restriction for suicide prevention (p. 1013)." If they asked patients about suicidal ideation and found they were contemplating it, they could work with the family to reduce access to means, such as firearms and poisons, in the home.

In the Harris Poll (2015), among those who knew someone who had attempted or completed suicide or had suicidal ideation, their top response for reducing the number of people who die by suicide was not psychotherapy or medication but rather better training for health-care providers. They found that most adults (89%) felt that mental and physical health were equally important to their overall health, but over half thought that in our current health-care system physical health was treated as more important. The WHO (2014) also points to better assessment and management of suicidal behavior and mental illness as key to prevention. Some physicians may be reluctant to ask questions about mental health when it is not the presenting problem, but if it were simply part of a standardized assessment then it would become routine. WHO also recommends that once patients are identified as at risk, regardless of whether they are hospitalized or not, there should be some protocol for follow-up. Ideally, some form of psychotherapy care should be available to all patients in the emergency room.

When an individual has identified that s/he is at risk for suicide, there is a standardized protocol available for health professionals. The Substance Abuse and Mental Health Services Administration (SAMHSA) provides a publication outlining a five-step evaluation and triage plan (SAMHSA, 2009). These include identifying risk and protective factors, conducting a suicide inquiry, determining risk level/intervention, and documenting the suicidal ideation. However, assessment for suicide should be included in routine emergency room admissions. Although emergency room procedures require screening for a number of health-related illnesses, there is no routine screening for suicide. This would be especially relevant to assess for high utilizers of the emergency room. Betz et al. (2013) report, "In the year before their death, 40% of suicide victims visit an ED at least once and they are more likely to have multiple ED visits than those who die by other causes" (p. 1014).

When a universal screening for suicide risk was implemented in emergency rooms, the detection rate almost doubled (University of

Massachusetts, 2016). Nurses at eight hospitals administered a screening tool that focused on three suicidal risk factors: symptoms of depression, previous suicide attempts, and active suicidal ideation. These patients were then further evaluated and either admitted or sent home with resources including a safety plan or information about community services.

There have been similar recommendations to routinely screen all adults over 18 years old for depression. In 2016, the United States Preventative Services Task Force (Siu et al., 2016) suggested that the benefits of such screenings outweigh the potential risks. Screenings could be administered by general practitioners as part of yearly physical exams. The physician is then tasked with determining what to do if a patient is depressed. The process would resemble the same one a physician would use if s/he found any physical anomaly—make a referral to an expert. If the patient-centered medical home (PCMH) approach continues to gain momentum, this process would be even more streamlined. In the patient-centered model, comprehensive care is provided by a team of experts ("Defining the PCMH," n. d.). Care is coordinated between professionals and the focus is on the patient as a whole person, not aspects of his/her health. If routine screenings were conducted, a record could also be established to determine changes in depression levels over time. When other yearly tests are conducted, such as blood work, the results are compared to previous and subsequent years to determine patterns. The same could be done with assessments of depression.

At the Henry Ford Health System in Detroit, Michigan, they have implemented a successful patient-centered program with the goal of "Zero Suicides" mentioned previously. Primary care physicians screen for mental health problems at every visit. If a patient exhibits signs of suicide, mental health professionals begin treatment, help him create safety plans, involve family and schedule immediate follow-up appointments. "Zero Suicide" is based on the premise that suicide deaths under health care are preventable and that many individuals "fall through the cracks" using a fragmented approach. The SPRC provides training on the process, including strategies and tools. They identify seven essential elements of suicide care. These include leadership that is committed to reducing suicide, a well-trained work force, systematically identifying at-risk people, engaging the person in a pathway to care, treating with evidence-based practices, transitioning the person into the community with support systems in place, and using data to improve patient outcomes. The WHO also emphasizes data collection and evaluation as integral parts of suicide prevention.

Not all individuals who are suicidal have a chronic course. As previously discussed, a large percentage of suicide attempts are impulsive and such screenings would not benefit these individuals. The WHO (2014) suggests that interventions can be universal, selective, or indicated. Universal preventions are designed to reach an entire population. Selective preventions target vulnerable groups within a population. Indicated prevention strategies target individuals at risk. Using a "Zero Suicide" approach is indicated or individualistic. As we showed in Chapter 6, The Complexity of Suicide Motivation, not all people considering suicide are alike in terms of the stability or chaos in their lives, or in how much they truly want to die, so tailored interventions and prevention strategies are necessary. However, universal approaches can solve universal problems. Creating obstacles to means is a universal approach. In other words, overall prevention must involve a multifaceted course.

LOCALIZING THE NATIONAL AGENDA

For any national agenda to take shape, it will need to be implemented on a local level. One danger of having a national agenda is that it will not be fully funded, and localities will find it hard to institute programs. The days of large federal programs such as those initiated during the New Deal in the 1930s are long past. Today, a national agenda will undoubtedly involve a coalition of federal, state, and local government entities as well as private for-profit and private nonprofit organizations implementing the model of "Zero Suicide."

Two very different states, California and Ohio, have made suicide prevention a priority. These states both have large numbers of liberals and conservatives. Their governorships frequently go from Republican to Democrat and back again. At this writing, California has a Democratic governor, Jerry Brown, and Ohio has a Republican governor, John Kasich. Their plans reflect bipartisan approaches to prevention.

The California Strategic Plan on Suicide Prevention (California Department of Mental Health, 2008) begins with a premise that "every Californian is part of the solution." It has a set of frameworks from which have evolved best practices that are assessed and published. The state provides opportunities for training using its own resources as well as those from national agencies. It provides toolkits for working with special populations, from LGBT Youth to Elderly Living Communities. Its strategic plan (California Mental Health Services Authority, n.d.) has four prongs to reach across the lifespan, beginning from youth to old age: Statewide Suicide Prevention Network; Regional and Local Suicide Prevention Capacity Building Program; Social Marketing; and Training and Workforce Enhancement. The plan is to create information that can be used at various government and corporate levels by people with different skill levels. It adheres closely to the WHO program.

In 2015, the California Mental Health Services Administration began two statewide suicide prevention and intervention strategies. The first strategy involves a mass media campaign to encourage people to "Know the Signs" related to suicide (Research and Development Corporation (RAND), 2015). This information and an educational website are widely advertised in many places including television and online. The mass media effort is designed to make people more confident in their abilities to handle a person who is suicidal. The second strategy involves providing intensive training to first responders and other gatekeepers about risk factors, how to intervene and how to link those at risk to resources. These efforts are intended to reduce stigma and discrimination, prevent suicides and improve the mental health of residents of California, especially students. Although it is estimated that these efforts will be successful, it is yet to be determined whether this program will be effective and whether it will be too costly. Without hard data, it will be difficult to sustain.

Ohio's pathway to a strategic plan to eliminate suicide is different from California's, but its strategies are similar. Ohio's 2016–17 strategic plan is ambitious and focuses on "access." Access to crisis centers, mental health services, multimedia application, and development of a student communication plan are all central. The plan involves data surveillance and LossTeams as part of its capacity-building program. These teams consist of trained survivor and mental health professionals acting as volunteers to bring immediate support to survivors of suicide, and the idea is to have teams in every community. Ohio will have a yearly conference on suicide prevention to train people in evidence-based practices to in order to enhance workforce capacity. Ohio's plan never mentions the WHO report or references its frameworks, though it has some features that the WHO highlighted as important.

Assessment data is important to see whether programs are working. At a park in Australia, which is known to be a "hotspot" for suicide, several measures were undertaken to prevent people from jumping off a cliff (Lockley et al., 2014). These included constructing a fence, installing phones that connect with no-wait crisis lines and installing closed circuit televisions so emergency personnel could arrive more quickly. These efforts were admirable but will not be able to be sustained without evidence of effectiveness to justify funding. It generally takes time to measure the impact of such measures. In 2012, the measures to prevent jumping from a cliff in Australia were completed and, although reported jumps and suicides have decreased, these trends are not yet statistically significant.

Similarly, Minnesota took action to see where in the state people were committing suicide. A bridge suspected of being a place where people went to die was confirmed as the place with the largest single number of suicide deaths in the state. The bridge was due for renovation, so a committee began working on ways to build suicide prevention into plans for roads, bridges, and highways. The state is also constructing a large database to identify patterns and is using the data to react more quickly to prevent a phenomenon known as "contagion," in which clusters of suicides occur in the same place or community (Serres, 2016). Both California and Ohio, as well as other states, can benefit from what Australia and Minnesota have learned from their initiatives.

The disparity between the California and Ohio programs is emblematic of the problem the United States faces. While suicide can indeed have regional aspects and prevention does need to be tailored to localities, the ability of localities to get access to funds, to follow the mandates of outcomes assessment, and to provide proper training to all of those involved in prevention, is not equal. Both Ohio and California have small, rural communities in addition to large cities, but California in 2004 passed a Mental Health Services Act that imposed an additional one percent tax on individuals. This act was unprecedented, and it made it possible for California to fund mental health programs that otherwise might be subject to cuts. It is consumer directed and consumer oriented, and it was passed by referendum. It focuses on developing preventive and innovative programs providing integrative wraparound services. The greatest obstacle facing the kind of national agenda program that the WHO recommends is funding. If states followed California's model, the United States could proceed with having both a local and a national agenda that implemented best practices based on WHO frameworks.

WORKING AT THE LOCAL LEVEL TO HELP FAMILIES AND SURVIVORS

A "Driver's Ed" Course for Suicide Prevention

When doctoral candidates in clinical psychology programs do hospital rotations as part of their education, they often spend three or four days focusing on important, lifesaving topics such as cardio-pulminary resusitation (CPR), severe persistent mental illness (SPMI), and other topics. Suicide is not generally a substantial part of that training and neither is learning how to interact or intervene with a person who is at risk for suicide. Likewise, many hospital staff are never trained to work with individuals who are at high risk for suicide. Sometimes, their interactions can make things worse. Families have even less education on the subject.

One example of creating such training could be modeled on "driver's ed," the course everyone needs to take to operate a motor vehicle. Everyone would learn how to identify warning signs of suicide, assess the situation, assist the person contemplating suicide to seek help, and combat one's own fears about suicide. Social workers, nurse practitioners, and healthcare administrators are among those who need training who may not receive it. Corrections officers and police officers need education with regard to individuals who are at high risk for suicide and how to intervene effectively (i.e., help them bridge the gap and seek professional help).

In addition, if family members are involved in treatment they need to have a separate, structured program for families to learn what to expect. Families need help to deal with individuals who are being discharged or transitioning back into the community, and they need help to learn how to navigate the health-care system, especially the areas in mental health with which they may be unfamiliar. Oftentimes, the families feel that after a person has visited the hospital he or she will be fine, but sometimes it requires consistent support and management while the patient transitions back home. Developing family-specific, formalized programs would enable teachers or professionals by providing a place to refer families for needed training.

Let's take the analogy of "driver's ed." If one looks at programs, they have courses for teens, adults, and mature individuals. A classroom part teaches the principles of driving and a traffic school part teaches the practical aspects. We would not want people with no actual driving experience to get out on the road. Education about suicide should be the same, designed for teen, adult and mature individuals. It should include classroom education based on current practices and research. A practical part is also needed, a chance to have frank and open discussions about suicide, perhaps with people who have survived it and are willing to share experiences.

A course on suicide should be available and mandatory for teens in middle or high schools; a course should be offered for adults in continuing education forums; another course should be offered for mature adults in senior centers and other venues accessible to them. For teens, the prevention focus should first aim to change certain structural threats to healthy relationships to combat interpersonal problems, and second provide problem-solving and coping skills. The WHO (2014) additionally recommends school-based interventions involving crisis management and self-esteem enhancement. For adults the course should focus on warning signs (risk factors + motivations) and on signs of death preparation, as well as resources for help. For mature adults the course should focus on managing pain and resources for help.

Caregivers

Caregivers may be professionals who care for patients or family and friends who care for their loved ones. In the United States, families generally bear the brunt of caregiving when it extends beyond a hospital stay. Not only do the family members need training, but they also need support and respite. They have a dual need for education and competence training on the one hand, but they also need to be able to identify their own compassion fatigue, their own physical fatigue, their fears, and their attitudes regarding suicide.

Many of these family members are already struggling with the fatigue that comes with being long-term caregivers for an adult with a mental illness. The National Alliance for Caregiving (NAC, 2016) found about half of the caregivers for adults with a serious-to-moderate mental or emotional health issue find it difficult to talk to others about their loved one's issues, often because of stigma. Additionally, they report feeling alone (47%) and do not have time for themselves. Caregivers who responded to their survey had been acting in this capacity for an average of 8.7 years and most (57%) said the person they cared for had a serious emotional or mental health problem (e.g., bipolar disorder, schizophrenia, depression). Among those, 74% also had a short- or long-term physical condition, and 28% had a substance abuse issue. Over two-thirds of caregivers (68%) were concerned their loved ones may hurt themselves or hurt someone else (35%). Nineteen percent were unable to leave their loved ones alone and 43% did not feel they had others they could rely on for help. Not surprisingly, almost three-fourths of the caregivers (74%) feel stress which can affect their physical health. Almost two-thirds indicate that caregiving has made their own health worse and demands on their time make it difficult to take care of their own issues.

Family Intervention

The NAC recommends that stakeholders work to reduce stigma related to mental illness by increasing public awareness, which could help alleviate isolation. In addition, they suggest that there needs to be greater resources for caregivers, including education and respite opportunities. The Family Intervention for Suicide Prevention (FISP) program may offer a model for intervention, education, and respite (Asarnow et al., 2011). It was developed initially for adolescents who had attempted suicide, using family systems theory and social learning theory, so that emergency personnel could effectively intervene in a suicide attempt within the context of the entire family.

The goals of this program were to help the family reconceptualize the suicide attempt as an incident of maladaptive coping or problem solving. This took the focus off of death and suicide. The next step was to teach strategies for healthy coping and problem solving, and to promote and improve family communication. FISP's focus is on providing the family with what it needs to build strength, not as a set of individuals but as a system (Asarnow et al., 2011). If the family feels empowered, suicide attempts and suicidal ideation may be reduced. As most suicide attempts are among those with mental health problems, the program encourages further treatment, and those who complete it do better than those who have no outpatient follow-up (Asarnow & Miranda, 2014). FISP is aimed at adolescents, but certain key responses would be helpful to anyone.

FISP is divided into three response sections. The first is the general intervention care that they receive in the hospital or emergency department. At this point, contact is made between the therapist and the patient to check in and to assure the patient that the therapist will be available when needed. The second is a therapy session with the family. (Separate therapists may be needed for the patient, and for the patient and family.) In this step, the patient creates an emergency kit of phone numbers of people she can contact, calming techniques, and reasons to live. During this stage, patients also create a response plan for emotional crises; family members all become familiar with the plan and are enabled to help the patient with executing the plan in an emergency. Family members are provided with a list of resources that they may contact for support or in an emergency. In addition to the plan family members are also given different strategies they can implement to improve family communication and interactions. The third stage is the follow-up stage, in which further psychological counseling is encouraged for the patient and/or further family counseling is recommended (Asarnow et al., 2011).

FISP works well for adolescents. Its steps, modified for age and circumstances, may help some adults. It may be appropriate for some elderly patients, as they too are sometimes dependent on their sons and daughters for caregiving. This model of intervention that is family-based may work best for certain kinds of people who are suicidal, namely those who are trying to escape psychological pain, those in bereavement, those who feel like failures, and those who want to escape physical pain. While it may also be part of the intervention plan for those escaping multiple problems, it is probably insufficient. It may be contraindicated for those in interpersonal abusive relationships, as the members of the family are often in violent conflict. It is necessary to think differently about intervention and prevention when the person contemplating suicide is violent, impulsive, depressed and angry, or when the person is facing legal and financial problems that traditional therapy alone cannot solve.

A Partners-in-Health Approach as a Model for Those Hard to Help

Men's suicide exceeds that of women in every country of the world except China (Bertolote & Fleischmann, 2002). In the United States those most at risk for suicide are white men. Much of what we have discussed previously, from the World Health Organization, to organizations involved in prevention, interventions in hospitals, and educational programs, is all aimed at those who attempt suicide as well as those who complete suicide, regardless of race, class, or gender, as it should be. Increasing high-risk suicide attempters' access to mental health treatment is crucial. Understanding the demographic characteristics of individuals who died by suicide can help identify higher risk attempters. Clinical assessments that take those factors into account can improve suicide prevention and intervention efforts (Han et al., 2016). It is also necessary to make sure prevention is aimed at the population most likely to complete the suicidal act, and that may include a population not among attempters at all. It may be especially difficult to use institutional means to reach the most difficult population: hegemonic masculine men, less well-educated men, and impoverished men, many of whom are in middle age, who do not use or rarely use the health-care system.

Partners in Health (PIH) is an organization founded by Dr. Paul Farmer, Ophelia Dahl, Dr. Jim Yong Kim, and Todd McCormack to bring medical care to those living in impoverished areas of the world. Many organizations had given up hope of trying to provide medical care in certain places as simply not a cost-effective use of resources, much like many health-care providers believe there is little point in trying to prevent suicide. PIH is successful because it uses both traditional institutions for providing care, such as hospitals, clinics, and health-care professionals, and nontraditional, trained, paid, and volunteer labor from the communities being served. Indeed, PIH assumes that most of the health care provided will not be in a traditional setting, but will be at home, and liaisons will be needed to help patients and health-care professionals connect. These liaisons are called *accompagnateurs*. A fundamental idea of PIH is that throughout life we all need to be accompanied by others (Farmer, 2013). Farmer describes accompaniment as "an elastic term … To accompany someone is to go somewhere with him or her, to break bread together, to be present on a journey with a beginning and an end … There's an element of mystery, of openness, of trust, in accompaniment" (p. xxv).

For those suffering from mental illness who may also have substance abuse disorders, who may be abusive to their family members, who may feel like failures, or who may have so many problems they are figuratively drowning in them—people whose poverty is not that of the developing world but of the developed world—hospitals, clinics, and primary care providers are not where they find their care. To the extent they find care at all, they find it in clubs, barrooms, sports venues, in their neighborhoods, and at work. Someone needs to accompany these men and women where they already are. Someone needs to be able to talk on the phone or come to the door late at night, when a man, out of work, is in a cheap motel with his rifle; or a judge is in his chambers after court is finished for the day, with a bottle and a rope; or a mother is waiting for her children to come home from school, pills by her side.

In the PIH system, accompagnateurs are paid employees of the hospitals or clinics, and they have training, but they are not professionals. Their job and their skill is talking to people, making sure that the person they have come to see or called on the phone is all right. They might drop in for a chat and take note of the fact that the person is out of medication, or they might convince the person to make an appointment with a doctor and then go with the person on the visit. They come from the community of the people whom they are helping and become trusted confidantes. They are not afraid to break bread with the individual in their care. They help the person on his or her journey. It is essential that the accompagnateurs be trained and have coping skills of her own.

PIH operates in the poorest countries of the world. Its accompaniment system does not cost much and many of the other features of its care system are inexpensive. In an era of funding cuts, using a model developed for countries without wealth may make sense for the United States. PIH works with American Indian partner organizations of the Navaho Nation and the Sicangu Lakota Nation. Farmer himself envisions the PIH accompaniment model being used elsewhere in the United States for what he calls "the great and chronic scourges in settings of poverty" (p. 238), like mental illness. PIH is also using its accompaniment model to help treat schizophrenia in rural Mexico. A huge emotional burden may be put on accompagnateurs who help people who have been suicidal. Yet witnessing large numbers of people dying from suicide may be more difficult still, not just for the witness but the entire society.

CONCLUSIONS AND RECOMMENDATIONS

Most people who kill themselves do so for interpersonal reasons or to escape pain. No suicide is inevitable. Suicides are both impulsive and planned, but in both cases limiting or delaying access to lethal means is a preventive public health measure. Manufacturers and sellers of not only guns but pills and other means can take steps to aid in suicide prevention. Education efforts must reach all levels in appropriate ways, and efforts between public and private entities in disseminating materials can make sure that education is universal. Funding must come from dedicated money at the state level with federal subsidies for additional prevention efforts and intervention among special populations.

Those at the forefront of education efforts should complete training offered by the National Center for Suicide Prevention, the CDC, or the SPRC or similar nonprofits, so that both volunteers and professionals become familiar with key concepts of primary prevention, the public health approach, and the social-ecological model, as well as youth prevention. Most of these trainings are free and online, and often several trainings are available.

Education efforts should focus on familiarizing people with warning signs and teaching them to recognize signs of constricted thinking or preparation for death. Yet education must go further, using practical demonstration techniques to show people how to have conversations about suicide. The NAMI, for example, has used such techniques to help caregivers of the mentally ill have hard conversations with their loved ones. If people do not know how to talk about suicide or how to raise the issue with those they fear might kill themselves, they cannot intervene effectively. People must also be taught when and how to seek professional help.

"Getting-the-word-out" efforts need to be seasonally targeted. While people can and do kill themselves at all times of the year, demonstrable seasonal peaks occur. It makes sense to target additional prevention messages at these times. Universities, e.g., often hold suicide awareness activities in the early fall. Autumn can be a peak time for suicide, but April and May are even more so. Additional awareness days should be instituted in the spring. At workplaces suicide awareness should also be addressed. Toolkits and media kits need to be produced for specific populations and not as one-size-fits-all.

Research needs to be funded. We have seen a spike in suicides between 1999 and 2014. Even though suicide has been around since time immemorial and has some unchanging, universal characteristics, it also has many changeable, culturally specific characteristics. Research on both risk factors and protective factors is necessary. If there are partners in research, such as university–faith-based-organization partnerships, they must be shown how to perform outcomes-based assessment so that meaningful data is generated. Studies must be funded for periods that have a chance of showing real results. Too often grants are for 3 to 5 years, but short of 10 years it can be difficult to obtain and assess data. Even though it is essential to have data assessment, it is also important to have a smooth flow of information between researchers and community partners, so bureaucracy should be kept to a minimum.

The President of the United States should appoint a commission on suicide prevention that is well funded, can work across federal agencies, and has the task of helping states to create strategic plans for suicide prevention. The commission should be available to assist states and to facilitate interstate communication. The commission needs strong leadership and should draw on the expertise of community activists and scholars across the natural sciences and social sciences.

Every effort should be made to create communities that support healthy lives. This too takes financial commitment. Some cities and towns have been able to invest in green spaces, bike lanes, and public improvement, but many have not. Innovative thinking and collaboration between workplaces and public groups can find ways to reduce stress and pull together for civic engagement. We know that to prevent suicide, people need both social support and a reason to live. Social support is something that can be given, but a reason to live has to come from within. Helping individuals build resiliency and other protective factors must be maintained in schools and after graduation, in workplaces and in communities.

 Suicide is a problem that affects all people in the United States and around the world. Despite the magnitude of the problem, it is possible to reduce suicide through simple but persistent efforts. That effort is not wasted. One August morning in 1985, Ken Baldwin told his wife he was going to be home late from work. He knew that was not true. He knew he was going to die that day. He drove to the Golden Gate Bridge and did a "cannonball" off the side of the bridge. It was a four-second drop to the water, and the second his hands left the bridge he knew he did not want to die, but it was too late. He hit the water. The Coast Guard arrived quickly and picked up his body. Miraculously, Baldwin was alive, bruised and battered, but breathing. It changed his life completely (Wheeler, 2016). Nearly eight million Americans have attempted suicide. Baldwin's jump should have placed his death among the statistics of completed suicides. Baldwin had convinced himself he was a loser and that his family would be better off without him. Baldwin said he survived in the aftermath of the jump, because he got help for his depression. Before the jump, Baldwin said, "I had no intervention." His tunnel vision increased and he thought his death was the best thing for everyone. After the jump he recovered and went on to teach school. He watched his daughter grow up. In the seconds that he was falling from the bridge, his present life flashed before his eyes, and he saw the faces of his family and his friends, and thought, "I can't leave all this."

POSTSCRIPT

To Those Who Have Lost Loved Ones to Suicide

One morning I was at my computer when I received an email from my friend Marlene that said, "I sent you a package. It's important. Make sure you pick up your mail at your PO Box today." I was running late for work, and I remember thinking that it would have to wait until tomorrow. As I was getting ready to leave the house, the phone rang, but by the time I picked it up, the person had hung up. It was 9:30 a.m. on a Monday, May 2, 2005. I had a long drive to work, so I had no time to check to see if it was Marlene. Although I owned a cellphone it did not occur to me to use it for a nonemergency. It was nagging at me that I missed the phone call and skipped the trip to my post office box, but by the time I got to my office a line of students was outside of my door, and I had to prepare for the courses to be taught that day. I'm a professor, and we were getting to the end of the semester, so things were hopping. About 4 p.m. my office phone rang.

The person on the other end of the line asked me if I knew Marlene. I felt a sinking feeling in my stomach and a pain in my heart. I knew. He hardly needed to tell me what came next. She shot herself that morning, around 10. She had killed her two dogs as well, her closest companions. She had not died instantly. It took two and half hours; she died as they airlifted her from the remote area where she lived to a hospital in a nearby city. I was Marlene's trustee and executor. The man on the phone, a federal ranger, faxed me the notes she had left with the names of people to contact and the notes that instructed her organs be donated (they were not, because too much time had elapsed and I had not been contacted in time to give the hospital permission). I didn't cry tears, but I must have cried out when I put down the phone. My colleague came over to see what was wrong. He sent me home. I wouldn't be back for the rest of the semester. I knew I couldn't make it to the post office before it closed. I'd have to wait until the morning.

We had been friends since grade school. She was the brainy science geek who was also athletic; I was a history nerd with no athletic ability at all. I loved Marlene like a sister. We knew one another's families, and now I would need to reconnect with her mother, sisters and brother. I made the phone calls. They wanted to know why. Why?

I knew why. Marlene had told me all the things that were going on at her job and in her personal life. She was 46 years old and it looked very much like she might not have a job, and since she lived where she worked, that meant no home; her boyfriend and she were not getting along; her friends were becoming alienated. In a way, it could have seemed rational, except that it was so crazy! She had so many people who loved her!

The next day I picked up my mail. The package contained her will, a map to her house in the remote area of California where she lived, keys to her house and car, and an eight-page note that explained her agony and gave instructions about what I was supposed to do with her body and her belongings. I took the package and went to the airport. My cellphone was now on. I called more people, including the funeral home, the human resources officer at her job, and her friends.

In her note, Marlene apologized to me for doing this at a time that was "inconvenient" for me. She said that her boss had made her life unbearable. I was aware that things were going badly. Back in February I had even asked her if she were suicidal. She told me no. I made her promise that if she ever were, she'd call me immediately. I thought we had a pact. Marlene was the most honest person I knew, so I felt like I could trust that promise. And of course, she might have tried to call. I had no idea who called that Monday when I was rushing out the door.

The next few days were a whirlwind of taking care of her immediate affairs. I met up with Marlene's sister and we visited her uncle. I went to the house. In it were packages marked for various individuals, each with an envelope. Little by little people arrived to collect what Marlene left them. Over the next month, I packed up the house. Sometimes I would go out and sit on the stoop in the hot California desert sun, drink a beer, and talk to Marlene's ghost. I could feel her loneliness and isolation. The beautiful scenery went on forever, but when you were alone, that beauty was almost painful.

After Marlene died, I was bereft. I did not feel guilty exactly. I lived in Connecticut and it's not like if I had picked up that package on Monday morning I could have saved her. She lived two hours from anywhere, and even the police could not have arrived there quickly. I told myself that her being unable to see a way out was in some way her rational mind being too rational. I didn't know then that this was called tunnel vision or constricted thinking. I read her note over and over. I was busy explaining why Marlene committed suicide, or at least trying to—that is what people wanted to know, including me. And I thought I had come to understand it. In a way. In a very unsatisfying way.

It was not until I began doing research for this book that I truly did come to understand Marlene's suicide. Many things that I had imagined were unique to her and her situation, as it turns out, were not. I thought a letter she got from her boss on the Friday before her death was the trigger for the suicide on Monday morning. In fact, if you were going to predict a peak time for a suicide, it might be a Monday morning in early May when the sun was shining and the flowers were out. As it turns out, most people have killed themselves on spring days just like that one for as long as we have recorded information about suicide.

Her suicide took me by surprise, despite my concerns for her well being. If you were going to look for signs, they were plentiful. In March she threw a party and offered some of her possessions to guests. I didn't find this out until much later. She told people she was moving, but she had not packed any boxes. One of the people who'd seen her a week before her death had thought that was strange, but he didn't say anything to anyone else. She made a will for her and her uncle, who was 80. That I knew, because she had asked me to be the trustee. It didn't seem strange. I had a will. I was sure she had not been planning suicide then. That was November, 2004. No one plans that far ahead, right? Well, that was not right. It is pretty clear now that she was planning it. She probably was not committed to it then, based on other actions. I think bargaining was going on—if this doesn't happen, then I won't have to kill myself.

In all of our conversations, I would say to her, "Why don't you..." and then make a suggestion. Why don't you move to Connecticut? It's great here and there are environmental jobs. You could live with me until you found something. Why don't you get a transfer to Washington, DC? Why don't you apply to a nonprofit? Every suggestion I made was met with "I can't, because..." The reasons were logical enough. She didn't want to be dependent on me, she hated DC and loved the desert, and if her boss wouldn't give her a recommendation, no nonprofit would hire her. I did not know this was called help-negation. I did that kind of thing myself sometimes. Help-negation is a trap.

I had assumed Marlene was not "at risk" for suicide. She was an Army veteran, but she hadn't been in or near combat. She had friends, though I didn't realize all of the alienation that was occurring for a variety of reasons, both because of Marlene's behavior and her stressful work situation.

She had a gun, which I had seen her purchase some 14 years before as she was about to move to Alaska. I had had guns, too, back then. I had not even asked her about her gun when I asked her about suicide. I did not realize that having a gun in the house was associated with a nearly fivefold risk of suicide (Dahlberg et al., 2004), or that a 45% increase in the suicide rate for women occurred between 1999 and 2014.

Marlene was diagnosed with severe recurrent depression. I didn't know that until I found an insurance letter in her personnel file with a diagnostic number. The numeric code had no description, so I looked up what the code meant. She had seen a psychiatrist and a therapist after she began having problems on the job, but her skepticism of psychology (not scientific enough) and reluctance to ask for help (stoicism from our German-Ohio heritage) meant that she had not established a very successful therapeutic relationship. She had been prescribed an antidepressant and clonazepam, an anti-anxiety drug also used for posttraumatic stress disorder, as well as trazodone for sleep, but she had not been taking them regularly.

I thought Marlene had lots of protective factors, like intelligence, and no risk factors, to use language I have only recently learned. But that was untrue. Intelligence is not a protective factor, and Marlene had all kinds of risk factors. Marlene had experienced abuse in a prior relationship. Victims of domestic violence have an eight-times greater risk of suicide compared with the general population (Catalano, 2007). Her work situation had become abusive. She had a gun. She was growing isolated and was seeking an escape, but was rejecting help to make that escape in any nonsuicidal or healthy way. She may also have been suicidal in the past.

If I had asked myself the questions posed in Chapter 10—"Has the person been experiencing problems that are beyond the coping skills of this individual in her current situation? And, is the person at a point where he or she accepts death as a possible resolution to those problems?"—I would have had to answer "yes" to the first and "maybe" to the second, just with what I knew at the time. If I am being honest with myself, though, I am not sure I would have had the courage of my convictions to call on outside help for Marlene. I doubt I would have known whom to call. Today, I would probably call the hotline for those seeking support on the American Foundation for the Prevention of Suicide website and ask for advice. I didn't know the AFPS existed in 2005.

In writing this postscript, I am not trying to write a scenario in which I, or anyone else, claim we could have seen with X-ray vision clarity what was coming. People who are determined to die, as Marlene came to be by May 2005, do try to hide what they are planning, even if they were dropping hints in their more ambivalent moments. Since Marlene's death, I have been concerned that other people I knew were going to commit suicide, and in those situations I did not always act with perfect calm, reason, and analytical acumen. We are all human beings with our own emotions and our own complex lives. When someone commits suicide, others in their lives are not responsible for that action. We do not hold the power of life and death in our hands. What we can do is inform ourselves and then use our knowledge and our compassion to try to assist the people we love in getting the help they need when we see them in distress.

I miss my friend Marlene. I can hear her laugh. It was a great, lilting, gorgeous laugh. I have happy memories of road trips up the California coast and around New Zealand. Marlene loved to argue about politics. We could do that for an hour and a day. There was so much richness to her life. After she died, I met other friends of hers that I hadn't known until then and we became friends. One of her close friends, Yan Fang, died recently of cancer. Yan was full of hope and determination to live. She was perhaps the most optimistic person I have ever known. She sought treatment for her cancer for nearly 5 years, so that she could spend as much time as possible with her husband and two children. Yan loved life.

Yan and Marlene may seem like polar opposites, one choosing to die, the other fighting to live. In fact, both of them struggled to live. Yan, whose personality was ebullient, might even have struggled less. Yan had resilience, and Marlene did not. A person who is suicidal is not the antithesis of a person fighting to overcome an illness. I know that now, but I didn't always.

All of the authors of this book have known people who have committed suicide. For me, it was a loss like no other has been. Although the information in this book was compiled by our scholar-selves, the labor in this book came from our heartfelt desire to help those who might consider suicide as a resolution to their problems, as well as the families and friends of those who have died.

Kathy

A

Detailed Methodology

This project was initiated at the request of the Montgomery County Coroner's Office who contacted Wright State University to see if there was any interest in carrying out a research project on suicide notes left by people determined by a coroner's investigation to have committed suicide. The coroner's office had been collecting these notes since 2000 but had never conducted any analysis of the contents. They were interested in having researchers examine the notes to determine if we could give them information that might prevent suicide. They approved the study and indicated their willingness to supply their data.

In addition to the notes, researchers had access to a spreadsheet containing demographic information such as name, age, gender, address of the decedent, and details of the suicide. A team of graduate students interested in the research was identified and met with faculty to review suicide note literature and to develop the system of analysis. A coding form was developed based on an extensive review of the literature concerning factors related to suicide and after a review of a subset of notes. There were five main categories: demographics; characteristics of the suicide (e.g., type of trauma); characteristics of the note (e.g., number of notes, whether it was dated, etc.); previous history (e.g., drug abuse); and the primary motivation suggested by the contents of the note. Also several areas were identified on the coding sheet where researchers could note any peculiarities of the suicide that were not coded for elsewhere.

After the initial coding sheet was developed, all researchers tested it by practicing with a small subset of three notes. This was done to determine if the coding sheet had face validity, produced interrater reliability, and was easy to use. To insure that all researchers were coding in a similar manner, definitions of each of the variables were generated by the group and available to all researchers.

The notes were randomly assigned to three teams, each consisting of three raters/coders. The coders independently analyzed each note and then met to review what had been individually coded and to seek consensus if raters disagreed on the presence or absence of a particular element. If the small group could not agree, the note was taken to the larger group for final determination. Some data on the coding sheet came from the note itself (e.g., statements about motivation) and other data from the coroner's reports (e.g., method of death and demographics). In analyzing the notes, the raters were blind to the coroner's data and later read and coded it only after the interrater consensus on the note had been reached. When all the note writer files had been completed, the researchers began the same process with the non-note writer files. The same coding sheet was used, with the section on characteristics of the notes deleted. When all of the data had been input into a statistical package, each file was cross-checked with the original database to insure all files were coded.

B

Coding Information

	Case # _____	
	Coder _____	
Demographics (Circle all that apply for each item)	*Source(D:Database, N-Note)*	

		D	N
Religion :	○ Y ○ N ○ UK		
Date of death :			
Age :	Zip Code :		
Gender :	○ Male ○ Female		
Race :	○ White ○ Black ○ Other		
Children :	○ Y ○ N ○ UK		
Pet(s):	○ Y ○ N ○ UK		
Occupation :	○ Student ○ Unemployed ○ Retired		
	○ Worker ○ Household duties ○ Other : _____		
Living	○ Alone ○ With Family/Parents ○ With Spouse/Partner		
Situation :	○ With Kids ○ UK		
Military	○ Y ○ N ○ UK		
Service			
Notes:			

D	N	*Previous History*		
			Did they seek help? ○ Y ○ N ○ UK	
		Legal Problems	○ Y ○ N ○ UK	Psychiatric Illness ○ Y ○ N ○ UK	
		Physical Illness	○ Y ○ N ○ UK	Homeless ○ Y ○ N ○ UK	
		Drug/Al Abuse	○ Y ○ N ○ UK	Financial Problems ○ Y ○ N ○ UK	
		Previous Suicide Attempt	○ Y ○ N ○ UK	Struggling with Minority Identity ○ Y ○ N ○ UK	
		School	○ Y ○ N ○ UK	Interpersonal ○ Y ○ N ○ UK	

Abuse :	O Sexual Assault O Verbal Abuse O Molestation O Rape		
	O Domestic Violence O Abuse as a child O Other : _____		

Notes:

Characteristic of Suicide

Date Note written	Time Note written	Season	Day		
_____	_____	_____	_____		
Location _____	Room Location_____				
When s/he write the Note? OSame Time OEarlier OUK					
Note was found? O With Body O Not with body O UK					
Type of Suicide O Single O Dual (Consensual or homicide) O UK					
Trauma Type O Asphyxia OToxic Substance OMultiple O Blunt Force O Thermal O Gunshot OSharp force					
Trauma Caused by O Carbon monoxide O Drowning O Fall ODrug Reaction O Handgun OLigature O Overdose O Poison O Rifle O Shotgun OSuffocation O Train O Vehicle OOther : _____					

Notes:

Characteristic of Notes

Number of Notes :_____ Word Count: O Under 50   O 51-199   O Over 200

Significant Loss : O Death O Relationship O Acquired Disability O None O Other _____

Who was addressed in the note?   OFriend   O Children   OPartner   O Sibling   OParent

OFamily   OUK   O None

Dated	O Y O N	Weight/Body Image Issue Mentioned O Y O N
Organized Thoughts	O Y O N	Guilt O Y O N
Addressee	O Y O N	Ambivalence O Y O N
Justification/ Rationalization	O Y O N	Illness- Psychological O Y O N
Burden	O Y O N	Dichotomous O Y O N
Apathy	O Y O N	Feeling- Sadness O Y O N
Advice	O Y O N	Feeling- Lonely O Y O N
Illness-Physical	O Y O N	Feeling-Joy O Y O N
Medication	O Y O N	Feeling-Angry O Y O N
Apology-General	O Y O N	Feeling-Tired O Y O N
Apology-Personal	O Y O N	Feeling-Hopeless O Y O N
Constriction/T. Vision	O Y O N	Feeling-Relief O Y O N
Quotations	O Y O N	Feeling-Worthless O Y O N
Blame	O Y O N	Feeling-Loved by others O Y O N
Shame	O Y O N	Feeling-Love for Others O Y O N
Life Not Worth Living	O Y O N	Feels Like Failure O Y O N
Precipitating Event	O Y O N	Signature O Y O N Unclear
Only Instructions?	O Y O N	Typed O Y O N

Afterlife :   O Positive   ONegative   O Neutral   O Unclear   O No Mention

Morality of suicide :   OMoral   OImmoral   O Neutral   O Unclear   O No Mention

Reunion   :   ODeceased   OLiving relative   O Watching over   O No Mention

Forgiveness :   OAsks for self   O Asks for others   O Gives to self

O Gives to others   O No Mention

If Instruction :   O No Foul Play   ODisposal-Body   O Disposal-Property

O Care of Family   ORepay Debt   OCustody

O Manage Affairs   O Other : Specify_____   O No Mention

Job/Financial   O Y   ON   OUK   O No Mention

Difficulties Mentioned: O Illness/Pain   OSchool   O Interpersonal Problems   ONone

O Financial   O Unknown   O Other _____

Notes :

Motivation (Choose Only One)				
Relationship	○ Family	○Children	○ Friend	○ Intimate Partner
Alienation	○ Family	○Children	○ Friend	○ Intimate Partner
Failure/Inadequacy	○ Children ○Parents ○Other Family ○ Friend ○ Intimate Partner ○Self			
Guilt	○ Specify_____			
Escape	○ Somatic ○ Legal ○ Financial ○Self ○Psychological			
Spiritual/Afterlife	○ Yes			
Revenge	○ Yes			
Altruism	○ Yes			
Abuse	○ Physical ○Emotional ○ Sexual ○ Unknown			
Oppression/ Discrimination	○ Yes			
Death	○ Yes			
Unclear	○ Cannot be Determined			
Notes:				
Y:Yes,N-No, UK- Unknown				

Motivation (Choose One Based on Information from the Entire File)			
Relationship	○ Family ○Children ○ Friend ○ Intimate Partner/Ex-partner ○ Multiple		
Alienation	○ Family ○Children ○ Friend ○ Intimate Partner/Ex-partner ○ Multiple		
Failure/ Inadequacy	○ Children ○Parents ○Other Family ○ Friend ○ Intimate Partner/Ex-partner ○Self ○Multiple		
Guilt	○ Specify_____		
Escape	○ Somatic ○ Legal ○ Financial ○Self ○Psychological ○ Multiple		
Spiritual/Afterlife	○ Yes		
Revenge	○ Yes		
Altruism	○ Yes		
Abuse	○ Physical ○Emotional ○ Sexual ○ Unknown		
Oppression/ Discrimination	○ Specify_____		
Death	○ Yes		
Unclear	○ Cannot be Determined		
Notes:			
Y:Yes,N-No, UK- Unknown			

For more information on the coding sheet, contact Taronish and Irani: H.

References

Abbott, C. H., Prigerson, H. G., & Maciejewski, P. K. (2014). The influence of patients' quality of life at the end of life on bereaved caregivers' suicidal ideation. *Journal of Pain and Symptom Management, 48*(3), 459–464. http://dx.doi.org/10.1016/j.jpainsymman.2013.09.011.

About Us – Death With Dignity. (n.d.). Retrieved June 21, 2016, from <https://www.deathwithdignity.org/about>.

Active Minds. (2016). Retrieved May 22, 2016, from <http://www.activeminds.org/>.

Acts and laws, passed by the great & general court or assembly of His Majesties province of the Massachusetts Bay in New England: Begun and held at Boston on Wednesday the twenty-ninth of May, 1700 [electronic resource]. Boston: s.n.

African American Suicide Fact Sheet. (No Date). American Association of Suicidology. Retrieved from http://211bigbend.net/PDFs/AfricanAmericanFactSheet.pdf.

Ajdacic-Gross, V., Weiss, M. G., Ring, M., Hepp, U., Bopp, M., Gutzwiller, F., & Rössler, W. (2008). Methods of suicide: International suicide patterns derived from the WHO mortality database. *Bulletin of the World Health Organization, 86*(9), 726–732. http://dx.doi.org/10.2471/BLT.07.043489.

Alzheimer's Association, (2013). 2013 Alzheimer's disease facts and figures. *Alzheimer's & Dementia, 9*(2), 208–245.

American Association of Suicidology. (No Date). African American Suicide Fact Sheet. Retrieved from http://211bigbend.net/PDFs/AfricanAmericanFactSheet.pdf.

American Association of Suicidology. (2014). *2014 facts and statistics*. Retrieved June 1, 2016. <http://www.suicidology.org/resources/facts-statistics>.

American Foundation for Suicide Prevention. (2016). *Executive summary: A survey about mental health and suicide in the United States*. Retrieved from <http://afsp.org/executive-summary-survey-mental-health-suicide-united-states/>.

American Psychiatric Association. (2013). *Diagnostic and statistical manual of mental disorders (DSM-5®)*. American Psychiatric Pub.

Anderson, M. A., Gillig, P. M., Sitaker, M., McCloskey, K., Malloy, K., & Grigsby, N. (2003). "Why doesn't she just leave?": A descriptive study of victim reported impediments to her safety. *Journal of Family Violence, 18*(3), 151–155.

Anestis, M. D., Soberay, K. A., Gutierrez, P. M., Hernández, T. D., & Joiner, T. E. (2014). Reconsidering the link between impulsivity and suicidal behavior. *Personality and Social Psychology Review, 18*(4), 366–386. 1–21. doi:1088868314535988.

Appleby, L., Shaw, J., Amos, T., McDonnell, R., Harris, C., McCann, K., … Parsons, R. (1999). Suicide within 12 months of contact with mental health services: National clinical survey. *British Medical Journal, 318*(7193), 1235–1239. <http://www.jstor.org/stable/25184564>.

Armstrong, L. L., & Manion, I. G. (2013). Meaningful youth engagement as a protective factor for youth suicidal ideation. *Journal of Research on Adolescence, 25*(1), 20–27. http://dx.doi.org/10.1111/jora.12098.

Arkoff, S. (Producer), & Fuest, R. (Director) (1970). *Wuthering heights*. Los Angeles, CA: MGM.

Asarnow, J. R., Baraff, L. J., Berk, M., Grob, C. S., Devich-Navarro, M., et al. (2011). *Psychiatric Services, 62*(11), 1303–1309.

Asarnow, J. R., & Miranda, J. (2014). Improving care for depression and suicide risk in adolescents: Innovative strategies for bringing treatments to community settings. *Annual Review of Clinical Psychology, 10*, 275–303.

Associated Press. (2011, May 8). Together, Phoebe Prince and Tyler Clementi alerted us to a crisis. *MLive* http://www.mlive.com/news/us-world/index.ssf/2011/05/together_phoebe_prince_and_tyl.html.

Auchter, B. (2010). Men who murder their families: What the research tells us. *NIJ Journal, 266*, 10–12.

Aufderheide, D. (2014, April 1). Mental illness in America's jails and prisons: Toward a public safety/public health model. *Health Affairs Blog*. www.healthaffairs.org/blog.

Axtell, J. (1981). *The Indian peoples of eastern America: A documentary history of the sexes*. New York: Oxford University Press.

Bach, D. (2016, March 31). *UW, gun-rights groups come together in new law to prevent suicide*. Retrieved from <http://www.washington.edu/news/2016/03/31/uw-gun-rights-groups-come-together-in-new-law-to-prevent-suicide/>.

Bachman, M. (2014, July 24). Spotlight on mental health. *Yellow Springs News*. Retrieved from <http://ysnews.com/news/2014/07/spotlight-on-mental-health>.

Baker, P.(Producer), & Boden, A. and Fleck, R.(Director). (2010). *It's kind of a funny story*. [Motion Picture] United States: Focus Feature.

Bandura, A. (1986). *Social foundations of thought and action: A social cognitive theory*. New York: Prentice-Hall, Inc.

Barber, J. G., Blackman, E. K., Talbot, C., & Saebel, J. (2004). The themes expressed in suicide calls to a telephone help line. *Social Psychiatry & Psychiatric Epidemiology, 39*(2), 121–125.

Barry, C. L., McGinty, E. E., Vernick, J. S., & Webster, D. W. (2013). After Newtown—public opinion on gun policy and mental illness. *New England Journal of Medicine., 368*(12), 1077–1081. http://dx.doi.org/10.1056/NEJMp1300512.

Baumeister, R. F. (1990). Suicide as escape from self. *Psychological Review, 97*(1), 90–113. http://dx.doi.org/10.1037/0033-295X.97.1.90.

Baumeister, R. F., Wotman, S. R., & Stillwell, A. M. (1993). Unrequited love: On heartbreak, anger, guilt, scriptlessness, and humiliation. *Journal of Personality and Social Psychology, 64*(3), 377–394.

Beatles, The. (1968). *The White Album*. Apple Records.

Beck, A. T., & Lester, D. (1976). Components of suicidal intent in completed and attempted suicides. *Journal of Psychology, 92*(1), 35. Retrieved from http://search.ebscohost.com/login.aspx?direct=true&db=aph&AN=5189334&site=ehost-live&scope=site.

Beekman, A. T., Bremmer, M. A., Deeg, D. J., Van Balkom, A. J. L. M., Smit, J. H., De Beurs, E., ... & Van Tilburg, W. (1998). Anxiety disorders in later life: A report from the longitudinal aging study amsterdam. *International Journal of Geriatric Psychiatry, 13*(10), 717.

Beekman, A. T., de Beurs, E., van Balkom, A. J., Deeg, D. J., van Dyck, R., & van Tilburg, W. (2000). Anxiety and depression in later life: Co-occurrence and communality of risk factors. *American Journal of Psychiatry, 157*(1), 89–95.

Behavioral Health Trends in the United States: Results from the 2014 National Survey on Drug Use and Health. (2015). Retrieved May 23, 2016, from <http://www.samhsa.gov/data/sites/default/files/NSDUH-FRR1-2014/NSDUH-FRR1-2014.htm>.

Bell, R. (2012). Slave suicide, abolition and the problem of resistance. *Slavery & Abolition, 33*(4), 525–549.

Beres, L. (1999). Beauty and the beast: The romanticization of abuse in popular culture. *European Journal of Cultural Studies, 2*(2), 191–207.

Berezin, R. (2014, August). The idea that suicide is caused by a gene defect is absurd. *Psychology Today*. <https://www.psychologytoday.com/blog/the-theater-the-brain/201408/the-idea-suicide-is-caused-gene-defect-is-absurd>.

Bernstein, R. (Producer), & Arnold, A. (Director) (2012). *Wuthering heights*. London: Artificial Eye.

Bertolote, J. M., & Fleischmann, A. (2002). Suicide and psychiatric diagnosis: A worldwide perspective. *World Psychiatry, 1*(3), 181–185.

Betz, M. E., Miller, M., Barber, C., Miller, I., Sullivan, A. F., Camargo, C. A., & Bourdeaux, E. (2013). Lethal means restriction for suicide prevention: Beliefs and behaviors of emergency department providers. *Depression and Anxiety, 30*, 1013–1020.

Bharadwaj, P., Pai, M. M., & Suziedelyte, A. (2015). *Mental health stigma (No. w21240)*. National Bureau of Economic Research. http://dx.doi.org/10.3386/w21240.

Biddle, L., Donovan, J., Owen-Smith, A., Potokar, J., Longson, D., Hawton, K., & Gunnell, D. (2010). Factors influencing the decision to use hanging as a method of suicide: Qualitative study. *British Journal of Psychiatry, 197*(4), 320–325. http://dx.doi.org/10.1192/bjp. bp.109.076349.

Billings, D. B. (1986). Many excellent people: Power and privilege in North Carolina, 1850–1900. *Journal of American History, 73*(3), 758–759.

Black, D. W., Winokur, G., & Nasrallah, A. (1988). Effect of psychosis on suicide risk in 1,593 patients with unipolar and bipolar affective disorders. *American Journal of Psychiatry, 145*(7), 849–852.

Bolton, J. M., Belik, S., Enns, M. W., Cox, B. J., & Sareen, J. (2008). Exploring the correlates of suicide attempts among individuals with major depressive disorder: Findings from the national epidemiologic survey on alcohol and related conditions. *Journal of Clinical Psychiatry, 69*(7), 1139–1149. http://dx.doi.org/10.4088/JCP.v69n0714.

Bolton, J. M., Robinson, J., & Sareen, J. (2009). Self-medication of mood disorders with alcohol and drugs in the National Epidemiologic Survey on Alcohol and Related Conditions. *Journal of Affective Disorders, 115*(3), 367–375.

Bolton, J. M., Walld, R., Chateau, D., Finlayson, G., & Sareen, J. (2015). Risk of suicide and suicide attempts associated with physical disorders: A population-based, balancing score-matched analysis. *Psychological Medicine, 45*(3), 495–504. http://dx.doi.org/10.1017/ S0033291714001639.

Bosanquet, C. (Producer), & Kosminsky, P., (Director) (1992). *Wuthering heights (1992)*. Hollywood, CA: Paramount Home Entertainment.

Bossarte, R. M., Simon, T. R., & Barker, L. (2006). Characteristics of homicide followed by suicide incidents in multiple states, 2003–04. *Injury Prevention: Journal of the International Society for Child and Adolescent Injury Prevention, 12*(Suppl. 2), ii33–ii38. http://dx.doi. org/10.1136/ip.2006.012807.

Boston, (1750, Feb. 5). *New York Gazette*.

Bowlby, J. (1969). *Attachment and loss*. Basic Books.

Brådvik, L. (2002). The occurrence of suicide in severe depression related to the months of the year and the days of the week. *European Archives of Psychiatry & Clinical Neuroscience, 252*(1), 28.

Brådvik, L. (2007). Violent and nonviolent methods of suicide: Different patterns may be found in men and women with severe depression. *Archives of Suicide Research, 11*(3), 255–264.

Braswell, H., & Kushner, H. I. (2012). Suicide, social integration, and masculinity in the U.S. military. *Social Science & Medicine, 74*(4), 530–536. http://dx.doi.org/10.1016/ j.socscimed.2010.07.031.

Bratman, G. N., Hamilton, J. P., Hahn, K. S., Daily, G. C., & Gross, J. J. (2015). Nature experience reduces rumination and subgenual prefrontal cortex activation. *Proceedings of the National Academy of Sciences of the United States of America, 112*(28), 8567.http://dx.doi. org/10.1073/pnas.1510459112.

Bronisch, T., & Wittchen, H. U. (1994). Suicidal ideation and suicide attempts: Comorbidity with depression, anxiety disorders, and substance abuse disorder. *European Archives of Psychiatry and Clinical Neuroscience, 244*(2), 93–98.

Buettner, D. (2015). *The blue zones solution*. Washington, DC: National Geographic Society.

Burr, J. A., Hartman, J. T., & Matteson, D. W. (1999). Black suicide in U.S. metropolitan areas: An examination of the racial inequality and social integration-regulation hypotheses. *Social Forces, 77*(3), 1049–1081.

California Department of Mental Health. (2008). *California strategic plan for suicide prevention*. Retrieved from <http://calmhsa.org/wp-content/uploads/2011/11/FINAL_ CalSPSP_V9.pdf>.

California Mental Health Services Authority (n.d.) Suicide Prevention, Retrieved May 28, 2016 from http://calmhsa.org/programs/pei-statewide-projects/2011-2015-phase-i/suicide-prevention/.

Callanan, V. J., & Davis, M. S. (2009). A comparison of suicide note writers with suicides who did not leave notes. *Suicide & Life-Threatening Behavior*, 39(5), 558–568. http://dx.doi.org/10.1521/suli.2009.39.5.558.

Cameron, S. (2005). Economics of suicide. In S. W. Bowmaker (Ed.), *Economics uncut: A complete guide to life, death and misadventure.* Northampton, MA: Edward Elgar Publishing.

Campbell, J. C., Webster, D., Koziol-McLain, J., Block, C., Campbell, D., Curry, M. A., ... Laughon, K. (2003). Risk factors for femicide in abusive relationships: Results from a multisite case control study. *American Journal of Public Health*, 93(7), 1089–1097.

Canetto, S. S., & Lester, D. (1998). Gender, culture, and suicidal behavior. *Transcultural Psychiatry*, 35(2), 163–190.

Capstick, A. (1960). Recognition of emotional disturbance and the prevention of suicide. *British Medical Journal*, 1(5180), 1179–1182.

Carmassi, C., Shear, M. K., Socci, C., Corsi, M., Dell'osso, L., & First, M. B. (2013). Clinical case discussion: Complicated grief and manic comorbidity in the aftermath of the loss of a son. *Journal of Psychiatric Practice*, 19(5), 419–428. http://dx.doi.org/10.1097/01.pra.0000435042.13921.73.

Carp, F. M. (1988). Significance of mobility for the well-being of the elderly. *Transportation in an aging society: Improving mobility and safety of older persons*, 2, 1–20.

Catalano, S. (2007). *Intimate partner violence in the United States.* Washington, DC: Bureau of Justice Statistics.

Catechism of the Catholic Church. (1992). Vatican City: Libreria Editrice Vaticana.

CDC (2014) "Leading Causes of Death Among Women", *Women's Health*, Center for Disease Control and Prevention. <http://www.cdc.gov/women/lcod>.

CDC (2014). QuickStats: Age-adjusted suicide rates, by state – United States, 2012. Centers for Disease Control. Retrieved May 22, 2016, from <http://www.cdc.gov/mmwr/preview/mmwrhtml/mm6345a10.htm>.

Cerel, J., Moore, M., Brown, M. M., van de Venne, J., & Brown, S. L. (2015). Who leaves suicide notes? A six-year population-based study. *Suicide and Life-Threatening Behavior*, 45(3), 326–334.

Chin, J., & Holden, R. R. (2013). Multidimensional future time perspective as moderators of the relationships between suicide motivation, preparation, and its predictors. *Suicide and Life-Threatening Behavior*, 43(4), 395–405. http://dx.doi.org/10.1111/sltb.12025.

Christodoulou, C., Douzenis, A., Papadopoulos, F. C., Papadopoulou, A., Bouras, G., Gournellis, R., & Lykouras, L. (2012). Suicide and seasonality. *Acta Psychiatrica Scandinavica*, 125(2), 127–146. http://dx.doi.org/10.1111/j.1600-0447.2011.01750.x.

Christodoulou, C., Papadopoulos, I. N., Douzenis, A., Kanakaris, N., Leukidis, C., Gournellis, R., & Lykouras, L. (2009). Seasonality of violent suicides in the Athens greater area. *Suicide & Life-Threatening Behavior*, 39(3), 321–331.

Clark, R. E., Ricketts, S. K., & McHugo, G. J. (1999). Legal system involvement and costs for persons in treatment for severe mental illness and substance use disorders. *Psychiatric Services*, 50(5), 641–647. http://dx.doi.org/10.1176/ps.50.5.641.

Cobain, K. (1994). *Suicide note.* <http://kurtcobainssuicidenote.com/kurt_cobains_suicide_note.html>.

Cohen, S. L., & Fiedler, J. E. (1974). Content analysis of multiple messages in suicide notes. *Suicide and Life-Threatening Behavior*, 4(2), 75–95.

Compassion & Choices. (2016). Retrieved June 21, 2016, from <https://www.compassionandchoices.org/>.

Cook, T. B. (2013). Recent criminal offending and suicide attempts: A national sample. *Social Psychiatry and Psychiatric Epidemiology*, 48(5), 767–774.

Cosgrove, B., Paula W.(Producer), & Reiner, R. (Director). (2005, December 25). *Rumor has it*. [Motion Picture] Warner Bros. Pictures.

Coyle, N. (2004). In their own words: Seven advanced cancer patients describe their experience with pain and the use of opioid drugs. *Journal of Pain and Symptom Management, 27*, 300–309. http://dx.doi.org/10.1016/j.jpainsymman.2003.08.008.

Crosby, A., & Molock, S. D. (2006). Suicidal behaviors in the African American community. *Journal of Black Psychology, 32*(3), 1–9.

Curious Facts About Suicide, (1870). *Appletons' Journal of Literature, Science & Art, 3*(51), 319.

Curtin, S. C., Warner, M., & Hedegaard, H. (2016). Increase in suicide in the United States, 1999–2014. *NCHS Data Brief, 241*, 1–8. <http://www.cdc.gov/nchs/products/databriefs/db241.htm>.

Dahlberg, L., Ikeda, R. M., & Kresnow, M. (2004). Guns in the home and risk of a violent death in the home: Findings from a national study. *American Journal of Epidemiology, 160*(10), 929–936. http://dx.doi.org/10.1093/aje/kwh309.

Daniulaityte, R., Carlson, R. G., & Siegal, H. A. (2007). "Heavy users," "Controlled users," and "Quitters": Understanding patterns of crack use among women in a Midwestern city. *Substance Use & Misuse, 42*(1), 129–152. http://dx.doi.org/10.1080/10826080601174678.

Davidson, C. L., Wingate, L. R., Slish, M. L., & Rasmus, K. A. (2010). The great black hope: Hope and its relation to suicide risk among African Americans. *Suicide and Life-Threatening Behavior, 40*(2), 170–180.

Davidson, C. L., & Wingate, L. R. (2011). Racial disparities in risk and protective factors for suicide. *Journal of Black Psychology, 37*(4), 499–516. http://dx.doi.org/10.1177/0095798410397543.

Davis, M. S., Callanan, V. J., Lester, D., & Haines, J. (2009). An inquiry into relationship suicides and reciprocity. *Suicide and Life-Threatening Behavior, 39*(5), 482–498. http://dx.doi.org/10.1521/suli.2009.39.5.482.

Deane, F. P., Wilson, C. J., & Ciarrochi, J. (2001). Suicidal ideation and help-negation: Not just hopelessness or prior help. *Journal of Clinical Psychology, 57*(7), 901–914.

de C. Williams, A. C. (1998). Depression in chronic pain: Mistaken models, missed opportunities. *Behaviour Therapy, 27*(2), 61–80.

de Catanzaro, D. (1995). Reproductive status, family interactions, and suicidal ideation: Surveys of the general public and high-risk groups. *Ethology & Sociobiology, 16*(5), 385–394. http://dx.doi.org/10.1016/0162-3095(95)00055-0.

De la Fuente, A., & Blake, A. C. (1956). *El Camino de la Vida*. Mexico: Cinematografica Latino Americana S.A.

Defining the PCMH (n.d.). Retrieved May 22, 2016, from <https://pcmh.ahrq.gov/page/defining-pcmh>.

Depression. U.S. Department of Health and Human Services, National Institutes of Health, National Institute of Mental Health. (2015). (NIH Publication No. 15-3561). Bethesda, MD: U.S. Government Printing Office.

Dicke, W. (2009). Edwin Shneidman, authority on suicide, dies at 91. *New York Times*, <http://www.nytimes.com/2009/05/21/us/21shneidman.html?_r=0>.

Dobash, R. E., Dobash, R. P., Cavanagh, K., & Medina-Ariza, J. (2007). Lethal and nonlethal violence against an intimate female partner: Comparing male murderers to nonlethal abusers. *Violence Against Women: An International and Interdisciplinary Journal, 13*(4), 329–353.

Don't blame mental illness for gun violence. (2015, December 15). *New York Times (1923–Current File)*, pp. A34.

Dougall, N., Lambert, P., Maxwell, M., Dawson, A., Sinnott, R., McCafferty, S., & Springbett, A. (2014). Deaths by suicide and their relationship with general and psychiatric hospital discharge: 30-year record linkage study. *British Journal of Psychiatry, 204*(4), 267–273. http://dx.doi.org/10.1192/bjp.bp.112.122374.

Doughty, C. (2014). *Smoke gets in your eyes*. New York, NY: W.W. Norton and Company.

Dowd, E. T. (2004). Depression: Theory, assessment, and new directions in practice. *International Journal of Clinical and Health Psychology, 4*(2), 415.

Draper, B., MacCuspie-Moore, C., & Brodaty, H. (1998). Suicidal ideation and the 'wish to die' in dementia patients: The role of depression. *Age and Ageing, 27*(4), 503–507.

Draper, J., Murphy, G., Vega, E., Covington, D. W., & McKeon, R. (2015). Helping callers to the National Suicide Prevention Lifeline who are at imminent risk of suicide: The importance of active engagement, active rescue, and collaboration between crisis and emergency services. *Suicide and Life-Threatening Behavior, 45*(3), 261–270.

Dublin, April 15, (1740, July 10–17). *Boston News-Letter.*

Durkheim, E. (1897, 2006). *Suicide: A study in sociology* (G. Simpson, Ed.; J. A. Spaulding & G. Simpson, Trans.). London: Routledge.

Early, K. E. (1992). *Religion and suicide in the African-American community (No. 158).* Westport, CT: Greenwood Publishing Group.

Eliason, S. (2009). Murder-suicide: A review of the recent literature. *Journal of the American Academy of Psychiatry & the Law, 37*(3), 371–376.

Ellis, T. E. (Ed.), (2006). *Cognition and suicide: Theory, research, and therapy.* Washington, DC: American Psychological Association.

Ellison, C. G. (1995). Race, religious involvement and depressive symptomatology in a southeastern US community. *Social Science & Medicine, 40*(11), 1561–1572.

Emanuel, E.J. (2013, June 2). A simple way to reduce suicides. *New York Times.* Retrieved April 20, 2016, from http://opinionator.blogs.nytimes.com/2013/06/02/a-simple-way-to-reduce-suicides/?_r=0.

Eranti, S. V., MacCabe, J. H., Bundy, H., & Murray, R. M. (2013). Gender difference in age at onset of schizophrenia: A meta-analysis. *Psychological Medicine, 43*(1), 155–167.

Escott, P. D. (1988). *Many excellent people: Power and privilege in North Carolina, 1850–1900.* Chapel Hill, NC: University of North Carolina Press.

Exline, J. J., & Zell, A. L. (2009). Empathy, self-affirmation, and forgiveness: The moderating roles of gender and entitlement. *Journal of Social and Clinical Psychology, 28*(9), 1071–1099.

Farmer, P. (2013). *To repair the world.* Berkeley, CA: University of California Press.

Farmer, R. F., Kosty, D. B., Seeley, J. R., Olino, T. M., & Lewinsohn, P. M. (2013). Aggregation of lifetime Axis I psychiatric disorders through age 30: Incidence, predictors, and associated psychosocial outcomes. *Journal of Abnormal Psychology, 122*(2), 573.

Fawcett, J., Scheftner, W. A., Fogg, L., Clark, D. C., Young, M. A., Hedeker, D., & Gibbons, R. (1990). Time-related predictors of suicide in major affective disorder. *American Journal of Psychiatry, 147*(9), 1189–1194.

Fenton, W. N. (1986). A further note on Iroquois suicide. *Ethnohistory, 33*(4), 448.

Fenton, W. S. (2000). Depression, suicide, and suicide prevention in schizophrenia. *Suicide and Life-Threatening Behavior, 30*(1), 34–49.

Ferguson, D. (2009). Dayton's Neighborhood School Centers. *New Directions for Youth Development, 2009*(122), 89.

Fischgrund, B. N., Halkitis, P. N., & Carroll, R. A. (2012). Conceptions of hypermasculinity and mental health states in gay and bisexual men. *Psychology of Men & Masculinity, 13*(2), 123.

Fisher, C. (2008). *Wishful drinking.* New York: Simon & Schuster.

Fisher, C. (2011). *Shockaholic.* New York: Simon & Schuster.

Fitzgerald, M. (2007). Suicide and Asperger's syndrome. *Crisis, 28*(1), 1–3.

Folse, K. A., & Peck, D. L. (1994). Toward a three-dimensional model of suicide. *Clinical Sociology Review, 12*(1), 135. 153.

Fond, G., Llorca, P. -M., Boucekine, M., Zendjidjian, X., Brunel, L., Lancon, C., … Boyer, L. (2016). Disparities in suicide mortality trends between United States of America and 25 European countries: Retrospective analysis of WHO mortality database. *Scientific Reports, 6* 20256. http://doi.org/10.1038/srep20256.

Foster, T. (2003). Suicide note themes and suicide prevention. *International Journal of Psychiatry in Medicine, 33*(4), 323–331. http://dx.doi.org/10.2190/T210-E2V5-A5M0-QLJU.

Fox, J. (1709). *The door of heaven opened and shut. Opened to the ready and prepared. Shut against the unready and unprepared. Or, a discourse concerning the absolute necessity of a timely preparation for a happy eternity. By John Fox, Minister of the Gospel, and author of the discourse concerning time, and the end of time [electronic resource]*. London: Printed for John Sprint, at the Blew-Bell in Little-Britain.

Fox, K. R., Millner, A. J., & Franklin, J. C. (2016). Classifying nonsuicidal overdoses: Nonsuicidal self-injury, suicide attempts, or neither? *Psychiatry Research, 244,* 235–242. http://dx.doi.org/10.1016/j.psychres.2016.07.052.

Fox, M. (2016, May 25). Military suicides: Most attempts come before soldiers ever see combat. *News Week.* http://www.nbcnews.com/health/health-news/military-suicides-most-attempts-come-soldiers-ever-see-combat-n580276.

Frankl, V. E. (1946). *Man's search for meaning.* Boston, MA: Beacon Press.

Frazao, E. (1999). High costs of poor eating patterns in the United States. *Heart Disease, 732,* 6. Retrieved June 21, 2016, from <http://www.ers.usda.gov/media/91018/aib750a_1_.pdf>.

Friestad, C., Åse-Bente, R., & Kjelsberg, E. (2012). Adverse childhood experiences among women prisoners: Relationships to suicide attempts and drug abuse. *International Journal of Social Psychiatry, 60*(1), 40–46. http://dx.doi.org/10.1177/0020764012461235.

Frohlich, T. C., Kent, A., Comen, E., Stebbins, S. (2015, December 21) Cities with the shortest life expectancy in every state. *24/7 Wall Street* <http://247wallst.com/special-report/2015/12/21/cities-with-the-shortest-life-expectancy-in-every-state/2/#ixzz49b4fz1jS>.

Frueh, B. C., & Smith, J. A. (2012). Suicide, alcoholism, and psychiatric illness among union forces during the U.S. civil war. *Journal of Anxiety Disorders, 26,* 769–775. http://dx.doi.org/10.1016/j.janxdis.2012.06.006.

Galisteo, M. D. C. G. (2007). But that I be not tedius: Women's role, representation, and lack of relevance in *Of Plymouth Plantation* by William Bradford. *Clepsydra: Revista de Estudios de Género y Teoría Feminista, 6,* 59–72.

Genovese, E. D. (1974). *Roll, Jordan, roll; the world the slaves made* (1st ed.). New York: Pantheon Books.

Gentry, D. S. (2006). *The art of dying: Suicide in the works of Kate Chopin and Sylvia Plath.* New York, NY: Peter Lang.

Giang, V. & Lubin, G. (2011, July 21). The 15 most suicidal cities in America. *Business Insider.* <http://www.businessinsider.com/most-suicidal-us-cities-2011-7>.

Gleckman, H. (2015, March 11). The death with dignity debate misses the point. Forbes. http://www.forbes.com/sites/howardgleckman/2015/03/11/the-death-with-dignity-debate-misses-the-point/#68205c5c3753.

Goethe, J. (2006). In: Hulse, M. (Ed.) *The sorrows of young Werther* (Vol. 10). UK: Penguin.

Goldwyn, S. (Producer), & Wyler, W. (Director). (1939). *Wuthering Heights.* [Motion picture].

Goldwyn, S. (Producer), & Wyler, W. (Director) (1939). *Wuthering heights.* Hollywood, CA: MGM.

Gorman, J. M. (1996). Comorbid depression and anxiety spectrum disorders. *Depression and Anxiety, 4*(4), 160–168.

Gould, M. S., Kleinman, M. H., Lake, A. M., Forman, J., & Midle, J. B. (2014). Newspaper coverage of suicide and initiation of suicide clusters in teenagers in the USA, 1988–96: A retrospective, population-based, case-control study. *Lancet Psychiatry, 1*(1), 34–43.

Granato, S. L., Smith, P. N., & Selwyn, C. N. (2015). Acquired capability and masculine gender norm adherence: Potential pathways to higher rates of male suicide. *Psychology of Men & Masculinity, 16*(3), 246.

Guintivano, J., Newcomer, T. B. A., Cox, M. J. O., Maher, B. S., Eaton, W. W., Payne, J. L., ... Kaminsky, Z. A. (2014). Identification and replication of a combined epigenetic and genetic biomarker predicting suicide and suicidal behaviors. *American Journal of Psychiatry Online, 171*(12), 1287–1296. <http://ajp.psychiatryonline.org/doi/full/10.1176/appi.ajp.2014.14010008>.

Gutierrez, P. M., Freedenthal, S., Wong, J. L., Osman, A., & Norizuki, T. (2012). Validation of the Suicide Resilience Inventory-25 (SRI-25) in adolescent psychiatric inpatient samples. *Journal of Personality Assessment, 94*(1), 53–61. http://dx.doi.org/10.1080/00223891.2011. 608755.

Haas, A. P., Eliason, M., Mays, V. M., Mathy, R. M., Cochran, S. D., D'Augelli, A. R., & Clayton, P. J. (2011). Suicide and suicide risk in lesbian, gay, bisexual, and transgender populations: Review and recommendations. *Journal of Homosexuality, 58*(1), 10–51.

Hacker, D. J., & Haines, M. R. (2005). American Indian mortality in the late nineteenth century: The impact of federal assimilation policies on a vulnerable population. *Annales De Demographie Historique, 2*, 17–45.

Hackney, S. (1969). Southern violence. *American Historical Review, 74*(3), 908–910.

Haines, J., Williams, C. L., & Lester, D. (2011). The characteristics of those who do and do not leave suicide notes: Is the method of residuals valid? *OMEGA-Journal of Death and Dying, 63*(1), 79–94.

Hall, R. C., Platt, D. E., & Hall, R. C. (1999). Suicide risk assessment: A review of risk factors for suicide in 100 patients who made severe suicide attempts: Evaluation of suicide risk in a time of managed care. *Psychosomatics, 40*(1), 18–27.

Handelman, L. D., & Lester, D. (2007). The content of suicide notes from attempters and completers. *Crisis, 28*(2), 102–104.

Han, B., Kott, P. S., Hughes, A., McKeon, R., Blanco, C., & Compton, W. M. (2016). Estimating the rates of deaths by suicide among adults who attempt suicide in the United States. *Journal of Psychiatric Research, 77*, 125–133.

Han, J., Batterham, P. J., Calear, A. L., Wu, Y., Shou, Y., & van Spijker, B. A. (2016). Translation and validation of the chinese versions of the suicidal ideation attributes scale, stigma of suicide scale, and literacy of suicide scale. *Death Studies, 0*(ja). Retrieved from http:// dx.doi.org/10.1080/07481187.2016.1214633.

Harkavy-Friedman, J. M. (2007). Risk factors for suicide in patient with schizophrenia. *Psychiatric Times, 24*(2)

Harwood, D. M. J., Hawton, K., Hope, T., Harriss, L., & Jacoby, R. (2006). Life problems and physical illness as risk factors for suicide in older people: A descriptive and case-control study. *Psychological Medicine, 36*(09), 1265–1274.

Hashimoto, S., & Ashizawa, T. (2012). Does participating in AA decrease the risk for suicide in alcohol dependence? *Nihon Arukoru Yakubutsu Igakkai zasshi= Japanese Journal of Alcohol Studies & Drug Dependence, 47*(6), 308–316.

Haw, C., Hawton, K., Houston, K., & Townsend, E. (2003). Correlates of relative lethality and suicidal intent among deliberate self-harm patients. *Suicide and Life-Threatening Behavior, 33*(4), 353–364.

Hawton, K., Sutton, L., Haw, C., Sinclair, J., & Deeks, J. J. (2005). Schizophrenia and suicide: Systematic review of risk factors. *British Journal of Psychiatry, 187*(1), 9–20.

Hayes, L. M. (2012). National study of jail suicide 20 years later. *Journal of Correctional Health Care, 18*(3), 233–245.

Hayes, L. M. (2013). Suicide prevention in correctional facilities: Reflections and next steps. *International Journal of Law and Psychiatry, 36*(3), 188–194.

Hempstead, K. A., & Phillips, J. A. (2015). Research article: Rising suicide among adults aged 40–64 years: The role of job and financial circumstances. *American Journal of Preventive Medicine, 48*, 491–500. http://dx.doi.org/10.1016/j.amepre.2014.11.006.

Hensley, N. (2016, April 25). Virginia firefighter victim of cyberbullying months before apparent suicide in Shenandoah National Park. *New York Daily News.* Retrieved from <http://www.nydailynews.com/news/national/body-thought-missing-firefighter-discovered-park-article-1.2610665>.

Heroquizz. (2016). Do your friends know you? Retrieved from http://en.heroquizz.com/t/ hpi9tmxp72.

Ho, A. O. (2014). Suicide: Rationality and responsibility for life. *Canadian Journal of Psychiatry, 59*(3), 141–147.

Hogan, M. F., & Clymer, J. M. (2014). Suicide in the health care neighborhood more can be done, now. *American Journal of Lifestyle Medicine* 1559827614554598. http://dx.doi.org/10.1177/1559827614554598.

Holm, A. L., & Severinsson, E. (2011). Struggling to recover by changing suicidal behaviour: Narratives from women with borderline personality disorder. *International Journal of Mental Health Nursing, 20*(3), 165–173. http://dx.doi.org/10.1111/j.1447-0349.2010.00713.x.

Hollingsworth, D. W., Wingate, L. R., Tucker, R. P., O'Keefe, V. M., & Cole, A. B. (2014, 2016). Hope as a moderator of the relationship between interpersonal predictors of suicide and suicidal thinking in African Americans. *Journal of Black Psychology, 42*(2), 175.http://dx.doi.org/10.1177/0095798414563748.

Hooks, B. (2004). *We real cool: Black men and masculinity.* New York: Routledge.

Hooper, C. (2012). *Manly states: Masculinities, international relations, and gender politics.* New York: Columbia University Press.

Houle, J. N., & Light, M. T. (2014). The home foreclosure crisis and rising suicide rates, 2005 to 2010. *American Journal of Public Health, 104*(6), 1073–1079. http://dx.doi.org/10.2105/AJPH.2013.301774.

Hourani, L. L., Davidson, L., Clinton-Sherrod, M., Patel, N., Marshall, M., & Crosby, A. E. (2006). Suicide prevention and community-level indictors. *Evaluation and Program Planning, 29*(4), 377–385.

Howard, A. (2016, March 30). Chris Brown suicide rant has consequences. *NBC News.* Retrieved from <http://www.nbcnews.com/news/nbcblk/chris-brown-suicide-rant-has-consequences-n548051>.

Huetteman, E., & Pérez-Peñadec, R. (2015, December 1). Paul Ryan pushes changes in mental health care after colorado shooting. *The New York Times.* Retrieved from <http://www.nytimes.com/2015/12/02/us/obama-repeats-call-for-stricter-gun-laws-after-colorado-shooting.html?_r=0>.

Hummons, R. (2016). Strikeback2gether. Retrieved May 22, 2016, from https://www.gofundme.com/strikeback2gether.

Impey, M., & Heun, R. (2012). Completed suicide, ideation and attempt in attention deficit hyperactivity disorder. *Acta Psychiatrica Scandinavica, 125*(2), 93–102. http://dx.doi.org/10.1111/j.1600-0447.2011.01798.x.

James, A., Lai, F. H., & Dahl, C. (2004). Attention deficit hyperactivity disorder and suicide: A review of possible associations. *Acta Psychiatrica Scandinavica, 110*(6), 408–415.

Jamieson, P., Jamieson, K. H., & Romer, D. (2003). The responsible reporting of suicide in print journalism. *American Behavioral Scientist, 46*(12), 1643–1660. http://dx.doi.org/10.1177/0002764203254620.

Jamison, K. R. (1999). *Night falls fast: Understanding suicide* (1st ed.). New York: Knopf.

Jobes, D. A., & Mann, R. E. (1999). Reasons for living versus reasons for dying: Examining the internal debate of suicide. *Suicide and Life-Threatening Behavior, 29*(2), 97–104.

Joiner, T., Jr. (2005). *Why people die by suicide.* Cambridge, MA: Harvard University Press.

Joiner, T., Jr. (2014). *The perversion of virtue: Understanding murder-suicide.* Oxford; New York: Oxford University Press.

Joiner, T. E., Jr., Walker, R. L., Rudd, M. D., & Jobes, D. A. (1999). Scientizing and routinizing the assessment of suicidality in outpatient practice. *Professional Psychology: Research and Practice, 30*(5), 447–453.

Jonas, J. B., Nangia, V., Rietschel, M., Paul, T., Behere, P., & Panda-Jonas, S. (2014). Prevalence of depression, suicidal ideation, alcohol intake and nicotine consumption in rural central india. the central india eye and medical study: E113550. *PLoS ONE, 9*(11). http://dx.doi.org/10.1371/journal.pone.0113550.

Kalish, R., & Kimmel, M. (2010). Suicide by mass murder: Masculinity, aggrieved entitlement, and rampage school shootings. *Health Sociology Review, 19*(4), 451–464.

Kang, H. K., & Bullman, T. A. (2008). Risk of suicide among US veterans after returning from the Iraq or Afghanistan war zones. *Journal of the American Medical Association, 300*(6), 652–653. http://dx.doi.org/10.1001/jama.300.6.652.

Karch, D. L., Dahlberg, L. L., Patel, N., Davis, T. W., Logan, J. E., Hill, H. A., & Ortega, L. (2009). Surveillance for violent deaths—National violent death reporting system, 16 States, 2006. *MMWR Surveillance Summaries, 58*(1), 1–44.

Kawa, I., Carter, J. D., Joyce, P. R., Doughty, C. J., Frampton, C. M., Elisabeth Wells, J., ... Olds, R. J. (2005). Gender differences in bipolar disorder: Age of onset, course, comorbidity, and symptom presentation. *Bipolar Disorders, 7*(2), 119–125.

Kelleher, I., Corcoran, P., Keeley, H., Wigman, J. T., Devlin, N., Ramsay, H., ... Wasserman, D. (2013). Psychotic symptoms and population risk for suicide attempt: A prospective cohort study. *JAMA Psychiatry, 70*(9), 940–948.

Kellerman, N. P. F. (2015). Epigenetic transgenerational transmission of holocaust trauma: A review. *Researchgate*, http://dx.doi.org/10.13140/RG.2.1.4960.7128.

Kessler, R. C., Borges, G., & Walters, E. E. (1999). Prevalence of and risk factors for lifetime suicide attempts in the National Comorbidity Survey. *Archives of General Psychiatry, 56*(7), 617–626.

Khazan, O. (2014, February 20). There's something about cities and suicide. *The Atlantic.* <http://www.theatlantic.com/health/archive/2014/02/theres-something-about-cities-and-suicide/283975/>.

Kheriaty, A. (2014, October 11). Suicide and depression: A Catholic perspective. *National Catholic Register.* <http://www.ncregister.com/site/article/depression-and-suicide-a-catholic-perspective/>.

Kidger, J., Gunnell, D., Jarvik, J. G., Overstreet, K. A., & Hollingworth, W. (2011). The association between bankruptcy and hospital-presenting attempted suicide: A record linkage study. *Suicide and Life-Threatening Behavior, 41*(6), 676–684.

Kimball, G. D. (2003). *American city, southern place: A cultural history of antebellum Richmond.* Athens, GA: University of Georgia Press.

King, C., Senior, J., Webb, R. T., Millar, T., Piper, M., Pearsall, A., ... Shaw, J. (2015). Suicide by people in a community justice pathway: Population-based nested case–control study. *British Journal of Psychiatry, 207*(2), 175–176. http://dx.doi.org/10.1192/bjp.bp.114.154831.

Kingsolver, B. (1988). *The bean trees.* New York: HarperTorch.

Komoto, Y. (2014). Factors associated with suicide and bankruptcy in Japanese pathological gamblers. *International Journal of Mental Health and Addiction, 12*(5), 600–606.

Kopacz, M. S., McCarten, J. M., Vance, C. G., & Connery, A. L. (2015). A preliminary study for exploring different sources of guilt in a sample of veterans who sought chaplaincy services. *Military Psychology, 27*(1), 1–8. http://dx.doi.org/10.1037/mil0000061.

Korff, J. (2016). Aboriginal suicide rates. Retrieved May 1, 2016, from http://www.creativespirits.info/aboriginalculture/people/aboriginal-suicide-rates#axzz46qZfZXCE.

Kowalski, R. M., Limber, S., & Agatston, P. W. (2012). *Cyberbullying: Bullying in the digital age.* Malden, MA: Wiley-Blackwell.

Kramer, B. (2016, March 13) NRA, prevention groups team up on bill to tackle suicide. *The Spokesman Review.* Retrieved from <http://www.heraldnet.com/article/20160313/NEWS03/160319605>.

Kross, E., Egner, T., Ochsner, K., Hirsch, J., & Downey, G. (2007). Neural dynamics of rejection sensitivity. *Journal of Cognitive Neuroscience, 19*(6), 945–956.

Kübler-Ross, E. (1969). *On death and dying.* New York: Macmillan.

Kübler-Ross, E., & Kessler, D. (2014). *Life lessons: Two experts on death and dying teach us about the mysteries of life and living.* New York: Simon and Schuster.

Kushner, H. I. (1984). Immigrant suicide in the United States: Toward a psycho-social history. *Journal of Social History, 18*(1), 3–24.

Kuwabara, H., Shioiri, T., Nishimura, A., Abe, R., Nushida, H., Ueno, Y., … Someya, T. (2006). Differences in characteristics between suicide victims who left notes or not. *Journal of Affective Disorders, 94*(1), 145–149.

Lane, R. (1979) *Violent death in the city: Suicide, accident, and murder in nineteenth-century Philadelphia.* Cambridge, MA: Harvard University Press.

Latham, A. E., & Prigerson, H. G. (2004). Suicidality and bereavement: Complicated grief as psychiatric disorder presenting greatest risk for suicidality. *Suicide and Life-Threatening Behavior, 34*(4), 350–362.

Law Center to Prevent Gun Violence (2016). *Mental Health Reporting.* Retrieved on May 22, 2016 from <http://smartgunlaws.org/gun-laws/policy-areas/background-checks/mental-health-reporting/>.

Lazar, A., (Producer), & Junger, G., (Director) (1999). *10 things I hate about you. [motion picture].* US: Touchstone Home Video.

Lerner, M. J., & Mikula, G. (Eds.), (2013). *Entitlement and the affectional bond: Justice in close relationships.* Springer Science & Business Media.

Lester, D., & Gunn, J. F. I., II (2012). Perceived burdensomeness and thwarted belonging: An investigation of the interpersonal theory of suicide. *Clinical Neuropsychiatry: Journal of Treatment Evaluation, 9*(6), 221–224.

Lichtenstein, R. L., Alcser, K. H., Corning, A. D., Bachman, J. G., & Doukas, D. J. (1997). Black/white differences in attitudes toward physician-assisted suicide. *Journal of the National Medical Association, 89*(2), 125–133.

Lieb, K., Zanarini, M. C., Schmahl, C., Linehan, M. M., & Bohus, M. (2004). Borderline personality disorder. *The Lancet, 364*, 453–461.

Lipman, V. (2016, January). 3 reasons resilience is an especially valuable quality for millennials. *Forbes.* <http://www.forbes.com/sites/victorlipman/2016/01/30/3-reasons-resilience-is-an-especially-valuable-quality-for-millennials/#6452bb3c3367>.

Lockley, A., Cheung, Y. T. D., Cox, G., Robinson, J., Williamson, M., Harris, M., & Pirkis, J. (2014). Preventing suicide at suicide hotspots: A case study from australia. *Suicide and Life-Threatening Behavior, 44*(4), 392–407.

Logue, L. M. (2015). Elephants and epistemology: Evidence of suicide in the gilded age. *Journal of Social History, 49*(2), 374–386.

London, April 6, (1751, July 1). *New York Gazette.*

London, October 13, (1784, February 24). Extract of a Letter from Paris, October 1, 1783, *Connecticut Courant.*

MacDonald, M., & Murphy, T. R. (1990). *Sleepless souls: Suicide in early modern England.* Oxford: Clarendon Press.

Maciejewski, P. K., Zhang, B., Block, S. D., & Prigerson, H. G. (2007). An empirical examination of the stage theory of grief. [Yale Bereavement Study]. *JAMA, 297*(7), 716–723.

Mackenzie, J. M., Borrill, J., & Dewart, H. (2013). Researching suicide, attempted suicide and near-lethal self-harm by offenders in community settings: Challenges for future research. *International Journal of Forensic Mental Health, 12*(1), 26–32.

Maes, M., Cosyns, P., Meltzer, H. Y., De Meyer, F., & Peeters, D. (1993). Seasonality in violent suicide but not in nonviolent suicide or homicide. *American Journal of Psychiatry, 150*(9), 1380–1385.

Maris, R. W. (1997). Social and familial risk factors in suicidal behavior. *Psychiatric Clinics of North America, 20*(3), 519–550.

Martin-Fumadó, C., & Hurtado-Ruíz, G. (2012). Clinical and epidemiological aspects of suicide in patients with schizophrenia. *Actas Españolas de Psiquiatría, 40*(6), 333–345.

Marzuk, P. M., Tardiff, K., & Hirsch, C. S. (1992). The epidemiology of murder-suicide. *Journal of the American Medical Association, 267*(23), 3179–3183.

Mastrofski, S. D., & Ritti, R. R. (1996). Police training and the effects of organization on drunk driving enforcement. *Justice Quarterly, 13*(2), 291–320.

Mather, A. S., Rodriguez, C., Guthrie, M. F., McHarg, A. M., Reid, I. C., & McMurdo, M. E. (2002). Effects of exercise on depressive symptoms in older adults with poorly responsive depressive disorder. *British Journal of Psychiatry, 180*(5), 411–415.

Matlock, S. (2012, December 8). Suicide shines light on workplace bullying. *The New Mexican.* <http://www.santafenewmexican.com/news/local_news/suicide-shines-light-on-workplace-bullying/article_112dc039-bfa6-54e9-88f0-9dead35101bd.html>.

Mauer, M. (2009). *The changing racial dynamics of the war on drugs.* Washington, DC: The Sentencing Project.

Mayo Clinic. (2016). *Depression in women: Understanding the gender gap.* <http://www.mayoclinic.org/diseases-conditions/depression/in-depth/depression/art-20047725>.

McDowell, C. P., Rothberg, J. M., & Koshes, R. J. (1994). Witnessed suicides. *Suicide and Life-Threatening Behavior, 24*(3), 213–223.

McLean, D. (1971). *Vincent: Starry, starry night [Vinyl recording].* United Artists Records.

ME Productions (Producer) & Salsi, M. (Director). (2006). *Love and suicide.* [Motion Picture] United States: Spiral Pictures.

Means matter: Harvard School of Public Health. (2016). Retrieved September 1, 2016, from https://www.hsph.harvard.edu/means-matter/.

Mee, S., Bunney, B. G., Reist, C., Potkin, S. G., & Bunney, W. E. (2006). Psychological pain: A review of evidence. *Journal of Psychiatric Research, 40*(8), 680–690.

Melo, H. P. M., Moreira, A. A., Batista, É., Makse, H. A., & Andrade, J. S. (2014). Statistical signs of social influence on suicides. *Scientific Reports, 4.* <http://www.nature.com/articles/srep06239>.

Mesoudi, A. (2009). The cultural dynamics of copycat suicide. *PLoS ONE, 4*(9), 1–9. http://dx.doi.org/10.1371/journal.pone.0007252.

Meyer, C. L., & Oberman, M. (2001). *Mothers who kill their children: Understanding the acts of moms from Susan Smith to the "prom mom."* New York: New York University Press.

Michael Phelps did not want to "be alive anymore" after DUI arrest. *The Guardian.* (2015, November 10). Retrieved from <http://theguardian.com>.

Miller, D., & Klingener, N. (2015, September 24). Isolation increases Florida's rural suicide rates. *Health News Florida,* <http://health.wusf.usf.edu/post/isolation-increases-floridas-rural-suicide-rates#stream/0>.

Miller, T. R., Furr-Holden, C., Lawrence, B. A., & Weiss, H. B. (2012). Suicide deaths and nonfatal hospital admissions for deliberate self-harm in the United States: Temporality by day of week and month of year. *Crisis, 33*(3), 169–177. http://dx.doi.org/10.1027/0227-5910/a000126.

Minois, G. (1999). *History of suicide: Voluntary death in western culture.* Baltimore: Johns Hopkins University Press.

Moghaddam, J. F., Yoon, G., Dickerson, D. L., Kim, S. W., & Westermeyer, J. (2015). Suicidal ideation and suicide attempts in five groups with different severities of gambling: Findings from the national epidemiologic survey on alcohol and related conditions. *American Journal on Addictions, 24*(4), 292–298.

Montgomery County Community Health Assessment. (2014). <http://www.phdmc.org/agency-publications/92-community-health-assessment-2014-complete-report/file>.

Montgomery County Metropolitan Data. (2010). *The Association of Religion Data Archives.* Retrieved May 31, 2016, from <http://www.thearda.com/rcms2010/r/m/19380/rcms2010_19380_metro_name_2000_ON.asp>.

Moody, C., Fuks, N., Peláez, S., & Smith, N. G. (2015). Without this, I would for sure already be dead': A qualitative inquiry regarding suicide protective factors among trans adults. *Psychology of Sexual Orientation and Gender Diversity, 2*(3), 266–280. http://dx.doi.org/10.1037/sgd0000130.

Morin, R. (2014). The demographics and politics of gun-owning households. *Pew Research Center, 7*(15), 14.

Namie, G., & Namie, R. (2009). *The bully at work: What you can do to stop the hurt and reclaim your dignity on the job* (2nd ed.). Naperville, IL: Sourcebooks.

Namie, G., & Namie, R. (2012). 2012 Survey: Workplace bullying health impact report. Retrieved from <http://www.workplacebullying.org/2012-d/>.

Naroll, R. (1970). What have we learned from cross-cultural surveys? *American Anthropologist, 72*(6), 1227–1288. Retrieved from <http://www.jstor.org/stable/672847>.

National Alliance on Caregiving. (2016). On pins and needles: Caregivers of adults with mental illness. www.caregiving.org.

National HIV/AIDS Strategy Federal Action Plan, *2016–2020.* (2015). Washington DC: U.S. Government.

Navasky, M., O'Connor, K. (Producer), Navasky, M., & O'Connor, K. (Director) (2005). *Frontline: The new asylums.* [Video/DVD] WGBH Educational Foundation.

NFO Research, Inc. (1999). *When a child dies. A survey of bereaved parents. Conducted by NFO Research, Inc. on Behalf of.* The Compassionate Friends, Inc. <https://www.compassion-atefriends.org/pdf/When_a_Child_Dies_-_1999_Survey.pdf>.

Nielsen, M. B., Einarsen, S., Notelaers, G., & Nielsen, G. H. (2016). Does exposure to bullying behaviors at the workplace contribute to later suicidal ideation? A three-wave longitudinal study. *Scandinavian Journal of Work, Environment and Health, 42*(3), 246–250.

Nock, M. K., Deming, C. A., Fullerton, C. S., Gilman, S. E., Goldenberg, M., Kessler, R. C., ... Ursano, R. J. (2013). Suicide among soldiers: A review of psychosocial risk and protective factors. *Psychiatry: Interpersonal and Biological Processes, 76*(2), 97–125. http://dx.doi.org/10.1521/psyc.2013.76.2.97.

Nolen-Hoeksema, S. (2001). Gender differences in depression. *Current Directions in Psychological Science, 10*(5), 173–176.

Not dead yet. (2016). Retrieved from <http://notdeadyet.org>.

Nutbeam, D. (2000). Health literacy as a public health goal: A challenge for contemporary health education and communication strategies into the 21st century. *Health Promotion International, 15*(3), 259–267.

O'Hagan, C. (2014, May 9). *How I learned to live after trying to kill myself.* New York, NY: CNN. <http://www.cnn.com/2014/05/09/health/suicide-attempt-irpt-christine-ohagan/>.

Oliffe, J. L., Han, C. S., Drummond, M., Maria, E. S., Bottorff, J. L., & Creighton, G. (2014). Men, masculinities, and murder-suicide. *American Journal of Men's Health, 9,* 473–485.

On Mental Health Concerns and the Heart of God, Southern Baptist Convention Resolutions. (2013). Retrieved from <http://www.sbc.net/resolutions/1232/on-mental-health-concerns-and-the-heart-of-god>.

Only a Lost Woman. (1879, August 9). *The National Police Gazette (1845–1906),* 3.

Osman, A., Gutierrez, P. M., Muehlenkamp, J. J., Dix-Richardson, F., Barrios, F. X., & Kopper, B. A. (2004). Suicide resilience inventory-25: Development and preliminary psychometric properties. *Psychological Reports, 94*(3 Pt 2), 1349–1360. http://dx.doi.org/10.2466/pr0.94.3c.1349-1360.

Ostacher, M. J., Frye, M. A., & Suppes, T. (2016). Bipolar disorders in DSM-5: Changes and implications for clinical research. In *Bipolar Disorders: Basic Mechanisms and Therapeutic Implications.* New York: Basic Books.

Parks, S. E., Johnson, L. L., McDaniel, D. D., Gladden, M., & Centers for Disease Control and Prevention (CDC), (2014). Surveillance for violent deaths—National violent death reporting system, 16 states, 2010. *MMWR Surveillance Summaries, 63*(1), 1–33.

Patel, N., Webb, K., White, D., Barker, L., Crosby, A., De-Berry, M., & Thomas, S. (2006). Homicides and suicides--national violent death reporting system, United States, 2003–2004. *Journal of the American Medical Association, 296*(5), 506.

Patterson, A. A., & Holden, R. R. (2012). Psychache and suicide ideation among men who are homeless: A test of Shneidman's model. *Suicide and Life-Threatening Behavior, 42,* 147–156. http://dx.doi.org/10.1111/j.1943-278X.2011.00078.x.

Paykel, E. S., Scott, J., Teasdale, J. D., Johnson, A. L., Garland, A., Moore, R., ... Pope, M. (1999). Prevention of relapse in residual depression by cognitive therapy: A controlled trial. *Archives of General Psychiatry, 56*(9), 829–835.

Peanuts. *Someday we will all die* [Cartoon]. Retrieved June 17, 2016, from <https://s-media-cache-ak0.pinimg.com/736x/aa/22/81/aa228173af1c0b50ae92446455e49704.jpg>.

Pelletier, G. (1980). The Micmac dilemma at the end of the seventeenth century. *Journal of the New Brunswick Museum*, 103–111.

Perciful, S., & Meyer, C. (2016). The impact of films on viewer attitudes towards people with schizophrenia. *Current Psychology*, April, 1–11. http://dx.doi.org/10.1007/s12144-016-9436-0.

Peters, S. (2014). Tempests and utopians. *Cultural Politics, 10*(1), 62–69. http://dx.doi.org/10.1215/17432197-2397236.

Pew Forum. (2016). Featured religion data. In *Religious Landscape Study*. Pew Research Center. <http://www.pewforum.org/data/>.

Pew Forum. (2016). Religious composition of adults in Ohio. In *Religious Landscape Study*. Pew Research Center, Religion and Public Life. <http://www.pewforum.org/religious-landscape-study/state/ohio/>.

Piersen, W. D. (1977). *White cannibals, black martyrs: Fear, depression, and religious faith as causes of suicide among new slaves. Journal of Negro History, 62*, 147–159.

Pinnow, E. (2016, March 24). Blunt obituary told the painful truth about Duluth sister's suicide: Sister was candid about what happened, hoping that others would choose life. *Washington Post*. Retrieved from <https://www.washingtonpost.com/news/inspired-life/wp/2016/03/23/i-told-the-truth-in-my-sisters-obituary-so-that-others-might-choose-to-live/>.

Poll, H. (2015). *Executive summary: Mental health and suicide survey*. ADAA, AFSP, and NAASP.

Pompili, M., Gonda, X., Serafini, G., Innamorati, M., Sher, L., Amore, M., ... Girardi, P. (2013). Epidemiology of suicide in bipolar disorders: A systematic review of the literature. *Bipolar Disorders, 15*(5), 457–490.

Poussaint, A. F., & Alexander, A. (2000). *Lay my burden down: Unraveling suicide and the mental health crisis among African-Americans*. Boston: Beacon Press.

Preidt, R. (2016, March 25) ER Docs only ask half of suicidal patients about guns, study shows. *HealthDay*. Retrieved from <http://health.usnews.com/health-news/articles/2016-03-25/er-docs-only-ask-half-of-suicidal-patients-about-guns-study-shows>.

Price, J. H., & Khubchandani, J. (2016). Firearm violence by the mentally ill: Mental health professionals' perceptions and practices. *Violence and Gender, 3*(2), 92–99.

Prigerson, H. G., Frank, E., Reynolds, C. F., George, C. J., & Kupfer, D. J. (1993). Protective psychosocial factors in depression among spousally bereaved elders. *The American Journal of Geriatric Psychiatry, 1*(4), 296–309.

Prigerson, H. G., Maciejewski, P. K., Reynolds, C. F. I., II, Bierhals, A. J., Newsom, J. T., Fasiczka, A., & Miller, M. (1995). Inventory of complicated grief: A scale to measure maladaptive symptoms of loss. *Psychiatry Research, 59*(1–2), 65–79. http://dx.doi.org/10.1016/0165-1781(95)02757-2.

Pringle, B., Colpe, L. J., Heinssen, R. K., Schoenbaum, M., Sherrill, J. T., Claassen, C. A., & Pearson, J. L. (2013). A strategic approach for prioritizing research and action to prevent suicide. *Psychiatric Services*.

Research and Development Corporation (RAND). (2015, May 18). *California suicide prevention program demonstrates promise, studies find*. Retrieved from <http://medicalxpress.com/news/2015-05-california-suicide.html>.

Reuters, (2015). Suicide rates rising among black kids. *Al Jazeera America*.

Richter, D. K. (1992). *The ordeal of the longhouse: The peoples of the Iroquois league in the era of European colonization*. Chapel Hill, NC: Published for the Institute of Early American History and Culture, Williamsburg, Virginia, by the University of North Carolina Press.

Riley, W. T., Treiber, F. A., & Woods, M. G. (1989). Anger and hostility in depression. *Journal of Nervous and Mental Disease, 177*(11), 668–674.

Rivlin, A., Fazel, S., Marzano, L., Hawton, K., Dejong, T. M., Overholser, J. C., & Stockmeier, C. A. (2010). *The suicidal process in male prisoners making near-lethal suicide attempts.* http://dx.doi.org/10.1080/1068316X.2011.631540.

Rivlin, A., Ferris, R., Marzano, L., Fazel, S., & Hawton, K. (2013). A typology of male prisoners making near-lethal suicide attempts. *Crisis, 34*(5), 335–347.

Roberts, S. E., Jaremin, B., & Lloyd, K. (2013). High-risk occupations for suicide. *Psychological Medicine, 43*(06), 1231–1240.

Rosen, Y. (2013, November 16). Study: Suicide rates increase as Alaska communities get smaller, farther north. *Alaska Dispatch News.* Retrieved June 17, 2016. <http://www.adn.com/rural-alaska/article/high-latitudes-small-populations-correlated-alaska-suicide-prevalance/2013/11/17/>.

Roshanaei-Moghaddam, B., & Katon, W. (2009). Premature mortality from general medical illnesses among persons with bipolar disorder: A review. *Psychiatric Services, 60*(2), 147–156.

Rubinstein, D. H. (1986). A stress-diathesis theory of suicide. *Suicide and Life-Threatening Behavior, 16*(2), 182–197.

Runyan, A. S., & Wenning, M. V. (2004). *Prospects for renewed feminist activism in the heartland: A study of Daytonian women's politics.* Indianapolis: Indiana University Press.

Rutter, P. A., Freedenthal, S., & Osman, A. (2008). Assessing protection from suicidal risk: Psychometric properties of the suicide resilience inventory. *Death Studies, 32*(2), 142–153. http://dx.doi.org/10.1080/07481180701801295.

Salib, E., Cawley, S., & Healy, R. (2002). The significance of suicide notes in the elderly. *Aging & Mental Health, 6*(2), 186–190.

Samaritans. (n.d.). *Media Guidelines for the reporting of suicide.* Retrieved from <http://www.samaritans.org/media-centre/media-guidelines-reporting-suicide>.

Sanchez, G. J. (1997). Face the nation: Race, immigration, and the rise of nativism in late twentieth-century America. *International Migration Review, 31*(4), 1009–1030.

Sandefur, G. D., Rindfuss, R. R., & Cohen, B. (1996). *Changing numbers, changing needs: American Indian demography and public health.* National Academies Press.

Sanger, S., & Veach, P. M. (2008). The interpersonal nature of suicide: A qualitative investigation of suicide notes. *Archives of Suicide Research, 12*(4), 352–365.

Sarchiapone, M., & D'Aulerio, M. (2014). Genetic risk factors for suicidal behavior. *Suicide: Phenomenology & Neurobiology, 125.*

Sareen, J., Isaak, C., Bolton, S. L., Enns, M. W., Elias, B., Deane, F., ... Katz, L. Y. (2013). Gatekeeper training for suicide prevention in First Nations community members: A randomized controlled trial. *Depression and Anxiety, 30*(10), 1021–1029.

Sartorius, N., Gaebel, W., Cleveland, H. R., Stuart, H., Akiyama, T., Arboleda-Flórez, J., ... Tasman, A. (2010). WPA guidance on how to combat stigmatization of psychiatry and psychiatrists. *World Psychiatry, 9*(3), 131–144.

Schneidman, E. S., & Farberow, N. L. (Eds.). (1957) *Clues to suicide.* New York: McGraw-Hill Companies.

Schneidman, E. S. (1993). Suicide as psychache. *Journal of Nervous and Mental Disorders, 181,* 145–147.

Schneidman, E. S. (1999). *Suicide as psychache: A clinical approach to self-destructive behavior* (2nd ed.). Northvale, NJ: Jason Aronson.

Schiff, L. B., Holland, K. M., Stone, D. M., Logan, J., Marshall, K. J., Martell, B., & Bartholow, B. (2015). Acute and chronic risk preceding suicidal crises among middle-aged men without known mental health and/or substance abuse problems. *Crisis, 36*(5), 304–315. http://dx.doi.org/10.1027/0227-5910/a000329.

Sederholm, C. (2012). *The trouble with grace: Reading Jonathan Edwards's 'faithful narrative.'.* The MIT Press.

Serres, C. (2016, May 1). Battling a surge in suicides, Minnesota investigators wield a new weapon: Data. *Minneapolis Star Tribune.* <http://www.startribune.com/battling-a-surge-in-suicides-minnesota-investigators-wield-a-new-weapon-data/377669031/>.

Seupel, C.W. (2015, March 9). Blocking the paths to suicide. *New York Times*. Retrieved from <http://www.nytimes.com/2015/03/10/health/blocking-the-paths-to-suicide.html>.

Seyfried, L. S., Kales, H. C., Ignacio, R. V., Conwell, Y., & Valenstein, M. (2011). Predictors of suicide in patients with dementia. *Alzheimer's & Dementia, 7*(6), 567–573.

Sher, L. (2015). Parental alienation and suicide in men. *Psychiatria Danubina, 27*(3), 288–289.

Shiratori, Y., Tachikawa, H., Nemoto, K., Endo, G., Aiba, M., Matsui, Y., & Asada, T. (2014). Network analysis for motives in suicide cases: A cross-sectional study. *Psychiatry & Clinical Neurosciences, 68*(4), 299–307. http://dx.doi.org/10.1111/pcn.12132.

Siegel, C., & Meyer, I. H. (1999). Hope and resilience in suicide ideation and behavior of gay and bisexual men following notification of HIV infection. *AIDS Education and Prevention, 11*(1), 53.

Sigfusdotti, I. D., & Silver, E. (2008). Emotional reactions to stress among adolescent boys and girls: An examination of the mediating mechanisms proposed by general strain theory. *Youth & Society, 40*, 578–585.

Silkenat, D. (2011). *Moments of despair: Suicide, divorce, & debt in civil war era North Carolina*. Chapel Hill: University of North Carolina Press.

Simlot, R., McFarland, K., & Lester, D. (2013). Testing Joiner's theory of suicide in jail inmates: An exploratory study. *Psychological Reports, 112*(1), 100–105.

Sinyor, M., Schaffer, A., Hull, I., Peisah, C., & Shulman, K. (2015). Last wills and testaments in a large sample of suicide notes: Implications for testamentary capacity. *British Journal of Psychiatry, 206*(1), 72–76.

Siu, A. L., Bibbins-Domingo, K., Grossman, D. C., Baumann, L. C., Davidson, K. W., Ebell, M., & Kemper, A. R. (2016). Screening for depression in adults: US preventive services task force recommendation statement. *JAMA, 315*(4), 380–387.

Snipp, C. M. (1997). The size and distribution of the American Indian population: Fertility, mortality, migration, and residence. *Population Research and Policy Review, 16*(1/2), 61–93. http://dx.doi.org/10.1023/A:1005784813513.

Snyder, R. L. (2013, July 22). A Raised Hand: Can a new approach curb domestic homicide. *The New Yorker*. Retrieved May 23, 2016, from <http://www.newyorker.com/magazine/2013/07/22/a-raised-hand>.

Snyder, T. L. (2010). Suicide, slavery, and memory in North America. *Journal of American History, 97*(1), 39–62.

Sommerville, D. M. (2014). 'Cumberer of the earth': Suffering and suicide among the faithful in the civil war south. In C. T. Friend & L. Glover (Eds.), *Death and the American South*. Cambridge University Press.

Southworth, P. M. (2016). Hegemonic masculinity and suicide: A review of the literature. *European Health Psychologist, 18*(1), 7–12.

SPARK Talks: Suicide Prevention Innovation and Action. (2016). Retrieved May 22, 2016, from <http://sparktalks.sprc.org/>.

Spicer, R. S., & Miller, T. R. (2000). Suicide acts in 8 states: Incidence and case fatality rates by demographics and method. *American Journal of Public Health, 90*(12), 1885–1891.

Spijker, J., de Graaf, R., ten Have, M., Nolen, W. A., & Speckens, A. (2010). Predictors of suicidality in depressive spectrum disorders in the general population: Results of the Netherlands mental health survey and incidence study. *Social Psychiatry & Psychiatric Epidemiology, 45*(5), 513–521. http://dx.doi.org/10.1007/s00127-009-0093-6.

Stack, S. (2003). *Media coverage as a risk factor in suicide*. BMJ Publishing Group.

Stack, S. (2004). Emile Durkheim and altruistic suicide. *Archives of Suicide Research, 8*(1), 9–22.

Stack, S., & Scourfield, J. (2015). Recency of divorce, depression, and suicide risk. *Journal of Family Issues, 36*(6), 695–715. http://dx.doi.org/10.1177/0192513X13494824.

Stallones, L., Doenges, T., Dik, B. J., & Valley, M. A. (2013). Occupation and suicide: Colorado, 2004–2006. *American Journal of Industrial Medicine, 56*(11), 1290–1295.

Stillion, J. M., & McDowell, E. E. (2015). *Suicide across the life span: Premature exits*. Taylor & Francis.

Stuart, E. (2015, December 23). Arizona ranked 50th for access to mental health care. *Phoenix New Times.* <http://www.phoenixnewtimes.com/news/arizona-ranked-50th-for-access-to-mental-healthcare-7917250>.

Substance Abuse and Mental Health Services Administration. (2009). *Suicide assessment five-step evaluation and triage (SAFE-T): Pocket card for clinicians.* Retrieved from <http://store.samhsa.gov/product/Suicide-Assessment-Five-Step-Evaluation-and-Triage-SAFE-T-Pocket-Card-for-Clinicians/SMA09-4432>.

Suicide assessment five-step evaluation and triage (SAFE-T): Pocket card for clinicians. (2009). (No. SMA09-4432). Washington, DC: Substance Abuse and Mental Health Services Administration.

Suicide Prevention Resource Center. (n.d.). Retrieved May 22, 2016, from <http://www.sprc.org/>.

"Suicide Statistics." (2014). *American Foundation for Suicide Prevention.* <https://www.afsp.org/understanding-suicide/facts-and-figures>.

Swanson, J. W., McGinty, E. E., Fazel, S., & Mays, V. M. (2015). Policy mini-symposium: Mental illness and reduction of gun violence and suicide: Bringing epidemiologic research to policy. *Annals of Epidemiology, 25,* 366–376. http://dx.doi.org/10.1016/j.annepidem.2014.03.004.

Szanto, K., Shear, K., Houck, P. R., Reynolds, C. F. I., II, Frank, E., Caroff, K., & Silowash, R. (2006). Indirect self-destructive behavior and overt suicidality in patients with complicated grief. *Journal of Clinical Psychiatry, 67*(2), 233–239. http://dx.doi.org/10.4088/JCP.v67n0209.

Taft, C. T., Bryant-Davis, T., Woodward, H. E., Tillman, S., & Torres, S. E. (2009). Intimate partner violence against African American women: An examination of the socio-cultural context. *Aggression and Violent Behavior, 14*(1), 50–58.

Tarrier, N., Khan, S., Cater, J., & Picken, A. (2007). The subjective consequences of suffering a first episode psychosis: Trauma and suicide behaviour. *Social Psychiatry & Psychiatric Epidemiology, 42*(1), 29–35. http://dx.doi.org/10.1007/s00127-006-0127-2.

Tavernise, S. (2016). Sweeping pain as suicides hit a 30-year high. *The New York Times,* A1.

Taylor, P. J., & Gunn, J. (1999). Homicides by people with mental illness: Myth and reality. *British Journal of Psychiatry, 174*(1), 9–14.

Teasdale, J. D., Segal, Z. V., Williams, J. M. G., Ridgeway, V. A., Soulsby, J. M., & Lau, M. A. (2000). Prevention of relapse/recurrence in major depression by mindfulness-based cognitive therapy. *Journal of Consulting and Clinical Psychology, 68*(4), 615.

Templer, D., Connelly, H. J., Lester, D., Arikawa, H., & Mancuso, L. (2007). Relationship of IQ to suicide and homicide rate: An international perspective. *Psychological Reports, 100*(1), 108–112.

The Continuation of Our Last, (1739, April 9). *New York Weekly Journal.*

The Editorial Board. (2015, December 15). Don't blame mental illness for gun violence. *New York Times.* Retrieved from <http://www.nytimes.com/2015/12/16/opinion/dont-blame-mental-illness-for-gun-violence.html?_r=0>.

Thwaites, R.G. (Ed.). (1898). Le Jeune, P. *The Jesuit relations and allied documents: Travels and explorations of the Jesuit missionaries in New France, 1610–1791; the original French, Latin, and Italian texts, with English translations and notes* (Vol. 13, ch. 1). Burrows Bros. Company.

Tondo, L., Isacsson, G., & Baldessarini, R. J. (2003). Suicidal behaviour in bipolar disorder. *CNS Drugs, 17*(7), 491–511.

Travis, J., Western, B., & Redburn, F. S. (2014). *The growth of incarceration in the United States: Exploring causes and consequences.* Washington, DC: The National Academies Press.

Troister, T., Davis, M. P., Lowndes, A., & Holden, R. R. (2013). A five-month longitudinal study of psychache and suicide ideation: Replication in general and high-risk university Students. *Suicide and Life-Threatening Behavior, 43,* 611–620. http://dx.doi.org/10.1111/sltb.12043.

Tsai, A. C., Lucas, M., & Kawachi, I. (2015). Association between social integration and suicide among women in the United States. *JAMA Psychiatry*, 72(10), 987–993. http://dx.doi.org/10.1001/jamapsychiatry.2015.1002.

Tyler-McGraw, M. (1994). *At the falls: Richmond, Virginia and its people*. Chapel Hill, NC: University of North Carolina Press Books.

Ulleberg, P. (2001). Personality subtypes of young drivers. Relationship to risk-taking preferences, accident involvement, and response to a traffic safety campaign. *Transportation Research Part F: Traffic Psychology and Behaviour*, 4(4), 279–297.

Unrequited love: Was it the cause of Jennie Benson's suicide? (1890, May 31). *The National Police Gazette (1845–1906)*, 7.

U.S. Census Bureau. (2000). *Profile of general demographic characteristics for Ohio: 2000.* Retrieved May 31, 2016, from <http://www.census.gov/census2000/states/oh.html>.

U.S. Census Bureau. (2010). *Montgomery County, Ohio, 2010 Census Quick Facts*. Retrieved May 31, 2016, from <http://www.census.gov/quickfacts/table/PST045215/39113>.

U.S. Preventative Services Task Force, (2016, January 26). Final recommendation statement. *Journal of the American Medical Association*, 315(4), 380–387. Retrieved from <http://www.uspreventiveservicestaskforce.org/Page/Document/RecommendationStatementFinal/depression-in-adults-screening1>.

University of Massachusetts Medical School, Worcester. (2016, April 5). Suicide risk can be intercepted in the emergency department. *Science Daily*. Retrieved from <www.sciencedaily.com/releases/2016/04/160405182355.htm>.

Van Orden, K. A., Witte, T. K., Cukrowicz, K. C., Braithwaite, S. R., Selby, E. A., & Joiner, T. E., Jr (2010). The interpersonal theory of suicide. *Psychological Review*, 117(2), 575.

Vincent, G. K., & Velkoff, V. A. (2010). *The next four decades: The older population in the United States: 2010 to 2050 (No. 1138)*. US Census Bureau: US Department of Commerce, Economics and Statistics Administration.

Voracek, M. (2005). National intelligence, suicide rate in the elderly, and a threshold intelligence for suicidality: An ecological study of 48 Eurasian countries. *Journal of Biosocial Science*, 37(06), 721–740.

Waern, M., Runeson, B. S., Allebeck, P., Beskow, J., Rubenowitz, E., Skoog, I., & Wilhelmsson, K. (2002). Mental disorder in elderly suicides: A case-control study. *American Journal of Psychiatry*, 159(3), 450–455.

Wandersleben, E. (2016). *Ohio unveils suicide prevention initiative*. Press Release.

Wang, Y., Sareen, J., Afifi, T. O., Bolton, S., Johnson, E. A., & Bolton, J. M. (2015). A population-based longitudinal study of recent stressful life events as risk factors for suicidal behavior in major depressive disorder. *Archives of Suicide Research*, 19(2), 202–217. http://dx.doi.org/10.1080/13811118.2014.957448.

Warren-Gordon, K., Byers, B. D., Brodt, S. J., Wartak, M., & Biskupski, B. (2010). Murder followed by suicide: A newspaper surveillance study using the New York Times index. *Journal of Forensic Sciences (Wiley-Blackwell)*, 55(6), 1592–1597. http://dx.doi.org/10.1111/j.1556-4029.2010.01473.x.

Web-based injury statistics query and reporting system. (2016). Retrieved from <https://www.cdc.gov/injury/wisqars/>.

Weinstein, L. (Producer), & Zucker, J. (Director) (1990). *Ghost*. US: Paramount Pictures.

Weissman, M. M. (2014). Treatment of depression: Men and women are different? *American Journal of Psychiatry*, 171(4), 384–387.

Wheeler, S. (2016). 4 Seconds Down on *After Life*. <http://www.radiolab.org/story/91680-after-life/>. Radiolab, National Public Radio.

Whitt, H. P. (2006). Where did the bodies go? The social construction of suicide data, New York City, 1976–1992. *Sociological Inquiry*, 76(2), 166–187. http://dx.doi.org/10.1111/j.1475682X.2006.00150.x.

Winston, C. A., Leshner, P., Kramer, J., & Allen, G. (2005). Overcoming barriers to access and utilization of hospice and palliative care services in African-American communities. *OMEGA-Journal of Death and Dying, 50*(2), 151–163.

Worden, J. W. (2008). *Grief counseling and grief therapy: A handbook for the mental health practitioner.* Springer Publishing Company.

World Health Organization. (2014). *Preventing suicide: A global imperative.* <http://www.who.int/mental_health/suicide-prevention/world_report_2014/en/>.

Wright, S. L., & Persad, C. (2007). Distinguishing between depression and dementia in older persons: Neuropsychological and neuropathological correlates. *Journal of Geriatric Psychiatry and Neurology, 20*(4), 189–198.

Wulff, K., Donato, D., & Lurie, N. (2015). What is health resilience and how can we build it? *Annual Review of Public Health, 36*(1), 361–374. http://dx.doi.org/10.1146/annurev-publhealth-031914-122829.

Yakunina, E. S., Rogers, J. R., Waehler, C. A., & Werth, J. L. (2010). College students' intentions to seek help for suicidal ideation: Accounting for the help-negation effect. *Suicide and Life-Threatening Behavior, 40*(5), 438–450.

Yamada, D. (2000). The phenomenon of 'workplace bullying' and the need for status-blind hostile work environment protection. *Georgetown Law Journal, 88,* 475–536.

Yamada, D. C. (2004). Crafting a legislative response to workplace bullying. *Employee Rights and Employment Policy Journal, 8*(2), 475–521.

Young, F. (2015, February 12). Why men are killing themselves. *Newsweek.* <http://www.newsweek.com/2015/02/20/suicide-men-305913.htm>.

Zai, C. C., de Luca, V., Strauss, J., Tong, R. P., Sakinofsky, I., & Kennedy, J. L. (2012). 11 Genetic factors and suicidal behavior. *The Neurobiological Basis of Suicide,* 213–235.

Zero suicide: An international declaration for better healthcare. (2016). http://www.slideshare.net/davidwcovington/zero-suicide-international-declaration-draft-01-september-2015.

Zetumer, S., Young, I., Shear, M. K., Skritskaya, N., Lebowitz, B., Simon, N., & Zisook, S. (2015). The impact of losing a child on the clinical presentation of complicated grief. *Journal of Affective Disorders, 170,* 15–21. http://dx.doi.org/10.1016/j.jad.2014.08.021.

Zisook, S., & Shear, K. (2009). Grief and bereavement: What psychiatrists need to know. *World Psychiatry, 8*(2), 67–74.

Index

Edwards Brothers Malloy
Ann Arbor MI. USA
March 8, 2017